ASCENT

CENTER FOR TECHNICAL KNOWLEDGE

Autodesk® InfraWorks® 360 2017.3 Fundamentals

Student Guide for the January 2017 Software Release
1st Edition

A AUTODESK.
Authorized Publisher

ASCENT - Center for Technical Knowledge®
Autodesk® InfraWorks® 360 2017.3
Fundamentals

1st Edition - January 2017 Software Release

Prepared and produced by:

ASCENT Center for Technical Knowledge
630 Peter Jefferson Parkway, Suite 175
Charlottesville, VA 22911

866-527-2368
www.ASCENTed.com

Lead Contributor: Michelle Rasmussen

ASCENT - Center for Technical Knowledge is a division of Rand Worldwide, Inc., providing custom developed knowledge products and services for leading engineering software applications. ASCENT is focused on specializing in the creation of education programs that incorporate the best of classroom learning and technology-based training offerings.

We welcome any comments you may have regarding this student guide, or any of our products. To contact us please email: feedback@ASCENTed.com.

The following are registered trademarks or trademarks of Autodesk, Inc., and/or its subsidiaries and/or affiliates in the USA and other countries: 123D, 3ds Max, Alias, ATC, AutoCAD LT, AutoCAD, Autodesk, the Autodesk logo, Autodesk 123D, Autodesk Homestyler, Autodesk Inventor, Autodesk MapGuide, Autodesk Streamline, AutoLISP, AutoSketch, AutoSnap, AutoTrack, Backburner, Backdraft, Beast, BIM 360, Burn, Buzzsaw, CADmep, CAiCE, CAMduct, Civil 3D, Combustion, Communication Specification, Configurator 360, Constructware, Content Explorer, Creative Bridge, Dancing Baby (image), DesignCenter, DesignKids, DesignStudio, Discreet, DWF, DWG, DWG (design/logo), DWG Extreme, DWG TrueConvert, DWG TrueView, DWGX, DXF, Ecotect, Ember, ESTmep, FABmep, Face Robot, FBX, Fempro, Fire, Flame, Flare, Flint, ForceEffect, FormIt 360, Freewheel, Fusion 360, Glue, Green Building Studio, Heidi, Homestyler, HumanIK, i-drop, ImageModeler, Incinerator, Inferno, InfraWorks, Instructables, Instructables (stylized robot design/logo), Inventor, Inventor HSM, Inventor LT, Lustre, Maya, Maya LT, MIMI, Mockup 360, Moldflow Plastics Advisers, Moldflow Plastics Insight, Moldflow, Moondust, MotionBuilder, Movimento, MPA (design/logo), MPA, MPI (design/logo), MPX (design/logo), MPX, Mudbox, Navisworks, ObjectARX, ObjectDBX, Opticore, P9, Pier 9, Pixlr, Pixlr-o-matic, Productstream, Publisher 360, RasterDWG, RealDWG, ReCap, ReCap 360, Remote, Revit LT, Revit, RiverCAD, Robot, Scaleform, Showcase, Showcase 360, SketchBook, Smoke, Socialcam, Softimage, Spark & Design, Spark Logo, Sparks, SteeringWheels, Stitcher, Stone, StormNET, TinkerBox, Tinkercad, Tinkerplay, ToolClip, Topobase, Toxik, TrustedDWG, T-Splines, ViewCube, Visual LISP, Visual, VRED, Wire, Wiretap, WiretapCentral, XSI.

NASTRAN is a registered trademark of the National Aeronautics Space Administration.

All other brand names, product names, or trademarks belong to their respective holders.

General Disclaimer:

Notwithstanding any language to the contrary, nothing contained herein constitutes nor is intended to constitute an offer, inducement, promise, or contract of any kind. The data contained herein is for informational purposes only and is not represented to be error free. ASCENT, its agents and employees, expressly disclaim any liability for any damages, losses or other expenses arising in connection with the use of its materials or in connection with any failure of performance, error, omission even if ASCENT, or its representatives, are advised of the possibility of such damages, losses or other expenses. No consequential damages can be sought against ASCENT or Rand Worldwide, Inc. for the use of these materials by any third parties or for any direct or indirect result of that use.

The information contained herein is intended to be of general interest to you and is provided "as is", and it does not address the circumstances of any particular individual or entity. Nothing herein constitutes professional advice, nor does it constitute a comprehensive or complete statement of the issues discussed thereto. ASCENT does not warrant that the document or information will be error free or will meet any particular criteria of performance or quality. In particular (but without limitation) information may be rendered inaccurate by changes made to the subject of the materials (i.e. applicable software). Rand Worldwide, Inc. specifically disclaims any warranty, either expressed or implied, including the warranty of fitness for a particular purpose.

Contents

Preface

Note: This guide is based on the January 2017 release of the Autodesk®
InfraWorks® 360 software. There might be slight differences between the software
used in this student guide and other versions of the software.

The *Autodesk® InfraWorks® 360 2017.3: Fundamentals* student guide is designed
for people using any of the following software packages:

- Autodesk® InfraWorks® 360 LT
- Autodesk® InfraWorks® 360

The training guide provides you with a fundamental knowledge of the accelerated
design process that uses data-rich 3D models with high-end visualizations. This
enables you to create, evaluate, and better communicate 3D site plan proposals
for faster approvals.

Topics Covered

- Navigate the Autodesk InfraWorks 360 user interface

- Create new models from scratch

- Incorporate existing data sources into the model

- Add essential design elements to the model

- Display features according to data behind the model

- Create new styles according to project requirements

- Analyze a model to ensure that project constraints are met

- Collaborate with other project team members

- Create high-impact visualizations of the project for better communication

- Generate videos by using storyboards

- Use the Roadway Design for InfraWorks 360 module to:
  - Create property boundaries for parcels, easements, and right-of-ways
  - Create and modify design roads with precise parameters
  - Design a road using component roads
  - Adjust roadside grading
  - Apply and review superrelevations in component roads
  - Modify how design roads intersect using a standard intersection or roundabout
  - Optimize the vertical design of a roadway
  - Create gradient maps based on selected feature sets to identify areas with low impact for site or corridor optimization (Preview)
  - Find an optimal horizontal design of the roadway which yields a cost effective and environmentally-friendly solution (Preview)
  - Run traffic simulation to analyze and animate design traffic (Preview)

- Use the Bridge Design for InfraWorks 360 Module to:
  - Add bridges to a design roadway
  - Work with bridge deck and girder cross sections
  - Perform analysis and design checks on all the pre-stressed girders of your bridge (Preview)

- Use the Drainage Design for InfraWorks 360 Module to:
  - Run a watershed analysis
  - Create or modify culverts
  - Create a pavement drainage network
  - Analyze the pavement drainage network

Note on Software Setup

This student guide assumes a standard installation of the software using the default preferences during installation. Lectures and practices use the standard software templates and default options for the Content Libraries.

Students and Educators can Access Free Autodesk Software and Resources

Autodesk challenges you to get started with free educational licenses for professional software and creativity apps used by millions of architects, engineers, designers, and hobbyists today. Bring Autodesk software into your classroom, studio, or workshop to learn, teach, and explore real-world design challenges the way professionals do.

Get started today - register at the Autodesk Education Community and download one of the many Autodesk software applications available.

Visit www.autodesk.com/joinedu/

Note: Free products are subject to the terms and conditions of the end-user license and services agreement that accompanies the software. The software is for personal use for education purposes and is not intended for classroom or lab use.

Lead Contributor: Michelle Rasmussen

Specializing in the civil engineering industry, Michelle authors training guides and provides instruction, support, and implementation on all Autodesk infrastructure solutions, in addition to general AutoCAD.

Michelle began her career in the Air Force working in the Civil Engineering unit as a surveyor, designer, and construction manager. She has also worked for municipalities and consulting engineering firms as an engineering/GIS technician. Michelle holds a Bachelor's of Science degree from the University of Utah along with a Master's of Business Administration from Kaplan University.

Michelle is an Autodesk Certified Instructor (ACI) as well as an Autodesk Certified Evaluator, teaching and evaluating other Autodesk Instructors for the ACI program. In addition, she holds the Autodesk Certified Professional certification for Civil 3D and is trained in Instructional Design.

As a skilled communicator, Michelle effectively leads classes, webcasts and consults with clients to achieve their business objectives.

Michelle Rasmussen has been the Lead Contributor for *Autodesk InfraWorks 360: Fundamentals* since its initial release in 2014.

In this Guide

The following images highlight some of the features that can be found in this Student Guide.

Practice Files

FTP link for practice files

Practice Files

The Practice Files page tells you how to download and install the practice files that are provided with this student guide.

Chapter 1

Getting Started

Learning Objectives for the chapter

Chapters

Each chapter begins with a brief introduction and a list of the chapter's Learning Objectives.

1.3 Working with Commands

Starting Commands

The main way to access commands in the AutoCAD software is to use the Ribbon. Several of the file commands are available in the Quick Access Toolbar or in the Application Menu. Some commands are available in the Status Bar or through shortcut menus. There are additional access methods, such as Tool Palettes. The names of all of the commands can also be typed in the Command Line. A table is included to help you to identify the various methods of accessing the commands.

When typing the name of a command in either the Command Line or Dynamic Input, the **AutoComplete** option automatically completes the entry when you pause as you type. It also supports mid-string search by displaying all of the commands that contain the word that you typed, as shown in Figure 1–12. You can then scroll through the list and select a command.

Figure 1–12

You can also click (Customize) to display the Input Settings for the AutoComplete feature.

To set specific options for the **AutoComplete** feature, right-click on the Command Line, expand Input Settings, and select from the various options, such as the ability to search for system variables or to set the delay response time, as shown in Figure 1–13.

Figure 1–13

If you need to stop a command, press <Esc> to cancel. You might need to press <Esc> more than once.

As you work in the AutoCAD software, the software prompts you for the information that is required to complete each command. These prompts are displayed in the drawing window near the cursor and in the Command Line. It is crucial that you read the command prompts as you work, as shown in Figure 1–14.

© 2015, ASCENT - Center for Technical Knowledge®   1–9

Instructional Content

Each chapter is split into a series of sections of instructional content on specific topics. These lectures include the descriptions, step-by-step procedures, figures, hints, and information you need to achieve the chapter's Learning Objectives.

Side notes

Side notes are hints or additional information for the current topic.

Practice 1c   **Saving a Drawing File**

Practice Objectives
- Open and save a drawing.
- Modify the **Automatic Saves** option

Estimated time for completion: under 5 minutes

In this practice you will open a drawing, save it, and modify the **Automatic saves** option, as shown in Figure 1–51.

Figure 1–51

1. Open **Building Valley-M.dwg** from your class files folder.

2. In the Quick Access Toolbar, click (Save). In the Command Line, _QSAVE displays indicating that the AutoCAD software has performed a quick save.

3. In the Application Menu, click Options to open the Options dialog box.

4. In the Open and Save tab, change the time for Automatic save to 15 minutes.

Practices

Practices enable you to use the software to perform a hands-on review of a topic.

Some practices require you to use prepared practice files, which can be downloaded from the link found on the Practice Files page.

Practice Objectives

Chapter Review Questions

1. How do you switch from the drawing window to the text window?
   a. Use the icons in the Status Bar.
   b. Press <Tab>.
   c. Press <F2>.
   d. Press the <Spacebar>.

2. How can you cancel a command using the keyboard?
   a. Press <F2>.
   b. Press <Esc>.
   c. Press <Ctrl>.
   d. Press <Delete>.

3. What is the quickest way to repeat a command?
   a. Press <Esc>.
   b. Press <F2>.
   c. Press <Enter>.
   d. Press <Ctrl>.

4. To display a specific Ribbon panel, you can right-click on the Ribbon and select the required panel in the shortcut menu.
   a. True
   b. False

5. How are points specified in the AutoCAD Cartesian workspace?
   a. X value x Y value

Chapter Review Questions

Chapter review questions, located at the end of each chapter, enable you to review the key concepts and learning objectives of the chapter.

Command Summary

The Command Summary is located at the end of each chapter. It contains a list of the software commands that are used throughout the chapter, and provides information on where the command is found in the software.

Autodesk Certification Exam Appendix

This appendix includes a list of the topics and objectives for the Autodesk Certification exams, and the chapter and section in which the relevant content can be found.

Icons in this Student Guide

The following icons are used to help you quickly and easily find helpful information.

New 💡	Indicates items that are new in the Autodesk InfraWorks 2017.3 software since the April 2016 version of the software.
Enhanced 🔍	Indicates items that have been enhanced in the Autodesk InfraWorks 2017.3 software since the April 2016 version of the software.

Practice Files

To download the practice files for this student guide, use the following steps:

1. Type the URL shown below into the address bar of your Internet browser. The URL must be typed **exactly as shown**. If you are using an ASCENT ebook, you can click on the link to download the file.

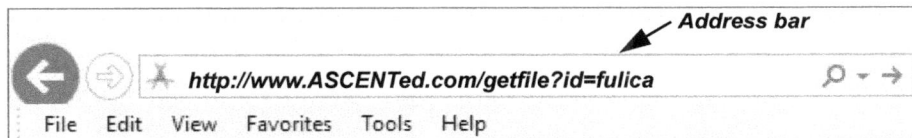

Address bar

http://www.ASCENTed.com/getfile?id=fulica

File   Edit   View   Favorites   Tools   Help

2. Press <Enter> to download the .ZIP file that contains the Practice Files.

3. Once the download is complete, unzip the file to a local folder. The unzipped file contains an .EXE file.

4. Double-click on the .EXE file and follow the instructions to automatically install the Practice Files on the C:\ drive of your computer.

   Do not change the location in which the Practice Files folder is installed. Doing so can cause errors when completing the practices in this student guide.

http://www.ASCENTed.com/getfile?id=fulica

Stay Informed!

Interested in receiving information about upcoming promotional offers, educational events, invitations to complimentary webcasts, and discounts? If so, please visit:

www.ASCENTed.com/updates/

Help us improve our product by completing the following survey:

www.ASCENTed.com/feedback

You can also contact us at: *feedback@ASCENTed.com*

Navigating the User Interface

In this chapter you learn about Building Information Modeling (BIM) and how it is used in the Autodesk® InfraWorks® software. This includes investigating the software interface and terminology, learning how to navigate and work with a model, and becoming familiar with the basic zoom controls, bookmarks, and other predefined views.

Learning Objectives in this Chapter

- Locate basic features and commands in the Autodesk InfraWorks 360 LT and Autodesk InfraWorks 360 software interface.
- Navigate a model using the mouse, ViewCube, and bookmarks.
- Create new proposals in a model to provide additional design options.

1.1 Building Information Modeling

The Autodesk InfraWorks 360 software is a powerful Building Information Modeling (BIM) program that streamlines site design and the design process for different types of infrastructure projects by using a 3D model. The BIM process supports the ability to coordinate, update, and share design data with team members throughout the design, construction, and management phases of a project's life cycle.

The Autodesk InfraWorks 360 software creates data-rich models using information about the existing environment. Using these models supports more informed decision-making and an accelerated site design process. You can create multiple design alternatives in one model, enabling you to quickly estimate the budget, scope, and schedule with an appropriate level of detail from the beginning of a project. The high-impact visuals that are automatically created during the design process better communicate the design intent to stakeholders.

The Autodesk InfraWorks 360 software coordinates with other software, such as the AutoCAD® Civil 3D® software and the Autodesk® Revit® software, to reduce rework and seamlessly enable coordination between project team members.

Launching the Software

The Autodesk InfraWorks 360 software can be launched by double-clicking on (Autodesk InfraWorks 360) on the desktop (as shown in Figure 1–1) or from the Start menu.

Figure 1–1

When you open the software for the first time, you must sign in to the Autodesk 360 (A360) service. The Autodesk Account Sign In screen displays automatically, as shown in Figure 1–2. Enter your username and password and then click **Sign In**.

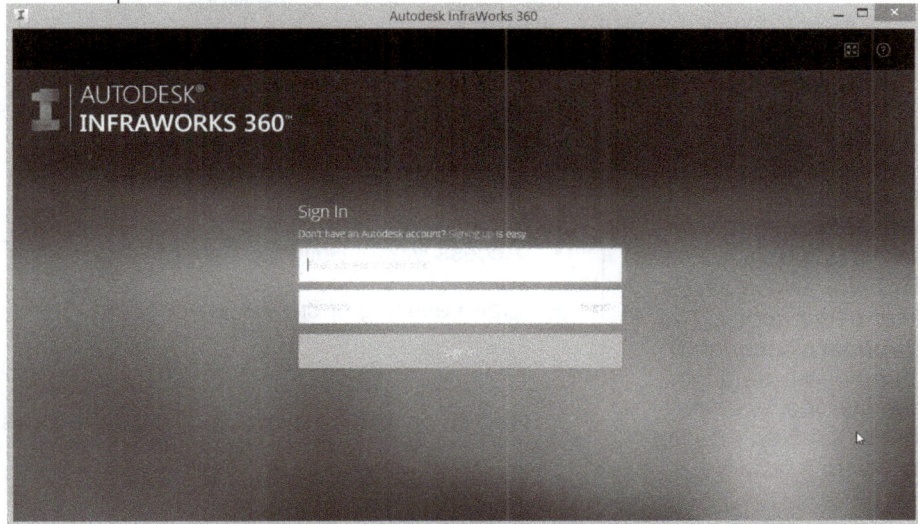

Figure 1–2

- Once you have signed in, your login credentials are stored for 14 days.

- Your sign in is connected to your subscription and determines what tools you can access in the software (e.g., Road Design, Drainage Design, etc.).

1.2 Overview of the Interface

The Autodesk InfraWorks 360 user interface is designed for intuitive and efficient access to commands and views. It includes the Home Screen and the Model View.

Home Screen

*A **Save** option is not available because the model is a database file (SQLite), which saves after every action. The **Duplicate** command, found under Settings and Utilities, enables you to save an existing model to a new file.*

When Autodesk InfraWorks 360 is initially launched, the Home Screen displays, as shown in Figure 1–3. This screen enables you to:

- Preview recent models.

- Access Model Builder.

- Open existing or create new models.

- Access the application's options.

- Toggle on and off available feature previews.

- Collaborate with others.

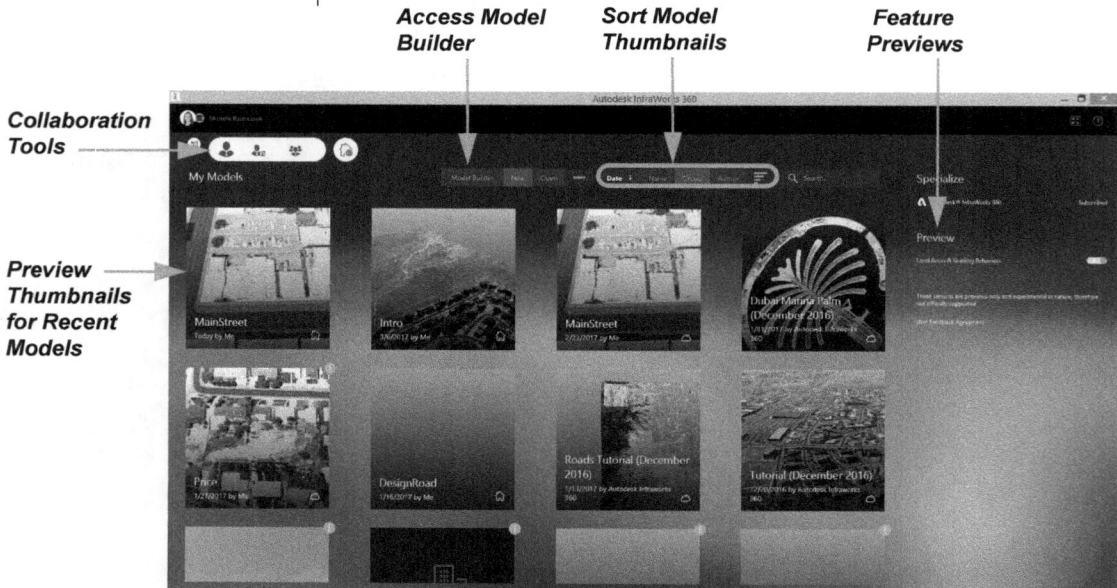

Figure 1–3

- The *Specialize* and *Cloud* areas of the Home Screen are only available to those users that are using the Autodesk InfraWorks 360 software.

  - Various icons display on each preview thumbnail, as shown in Figure 1–4.

Figure 1–4

How To: Open a Model

1. In the Home Screen, sort the models according to your needs by clicking the required button at the top.

   - Sort models by Date, Name, Group, or Author, as shown in Figure 1–5.

Figure 1–5

2. Click on the preview thumbnail for the model you wish to work in.

- If the model you need to open is not visible on the Home Screen, click the **Open** button at the top. Then browse for the file location and click **Open**.

- If the model you need to work with was saved in an older version of the software, you can either **Upgrade** the model or **Create a Copy**, as shown in Figure 1–6.

All team members should sync their changes before any cloud model is upgraded.

Figure 1–6

Model View

The Model View displays when a model is created or opened from the Home Screen. Figure 1–7 shows the components in the model view user interface.

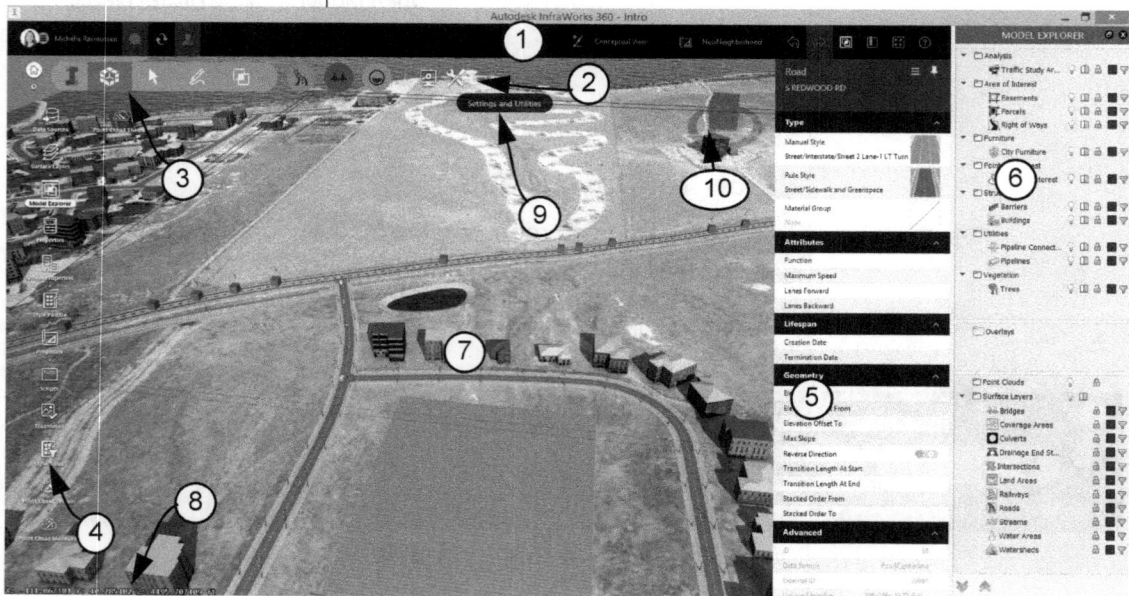

Figure 1–7

1. Utility Bar	5. Asset Card	9. Tooltips
2. In Canvas Tools	6. Model Explorer	10. ViewCube
3. Functional Tools	7. Model Window	
4. Expanded Tool Group	8. Model Coordinates	

1. Utility Bar

The Utility Bar (shown in Figure 1–8) provides a variety of frequently used tools.

- The Cloud Tools, shown on the left of the Utility Bar, provide options for discussing a design and sharing models with others over the Internet.

- The Common Tools, shown on the right of the Utility Bar, are included in both the LT and 360 versions of the Autodesk InfraWorks software. The Common Tools enable you to switch views and proposals, undo/redo commands, and select or edit model components.

Figure 1–8

2. In Canvas Tools

The In Canvas tools provide quick access to all of the commands used for creating and editing models. Figure 1–9 shows the In Canvas tools collapsed. In their collapsed state, the In Canvas tools maximize the view of the model, while remaining available for use.

Build, manage, and analyze your infrastructure model

Switch to Home

Settings and Utilities

Toolbar Options

Create and conduct infrastructure design presentations

Figure 1–9

Hint: Autodesk InfraWorks 360 Design Module Users

Depending on which modules you have purchased, you might see additional tools, as shown in Figure 1–10. Modules that you have purchased are enabled when you log in to your A360 account. Only the tools registered to your account are available.

Design, review, and engineer bridges

Design, review, and engineer roads

Design, review, and engineer drainage

Figure 1–10

3. Functional Tools

The In Canvas tools are grouped together by function. When an In Canvas Tool is clicked, it expands and enables access to additional tools according to the type of operation they perform, as shown in Figure 1–11.

Build, manage, and analyze your infrastructure model

Design, review, and engineer roads

Only available in Roadway Design for InfraWorks 360

Design, review, and engineer bridges

Only available in Bridge Design for InfraWorks 360

Design, review, and engineer drainage

Only available in Drainage Design for InfraWorks 360

Figure 1–11

Each command within the Functional Tools is described as follows:

Icon	Name	Description
	Create and manage your model	Tools for importing existing data and managing the display of model features.
	Select model features	Tools for selecting features in the model.
	Create design features	Tools that enable you to create conceptual design features or engineering design features.
	Analyze your model	Tools for analyzing a model.
	Review and modify (Specific) designs	Tools for reviewing and modifying specific design elements that are only found in Autodesk InfraWorks 360 modules.

4. Expanded Tool Group

When an In Canvas Tool or a Functional Tool is clicked, another set of tools are expanded down the left side of the model, as shown in Figure 1–12.

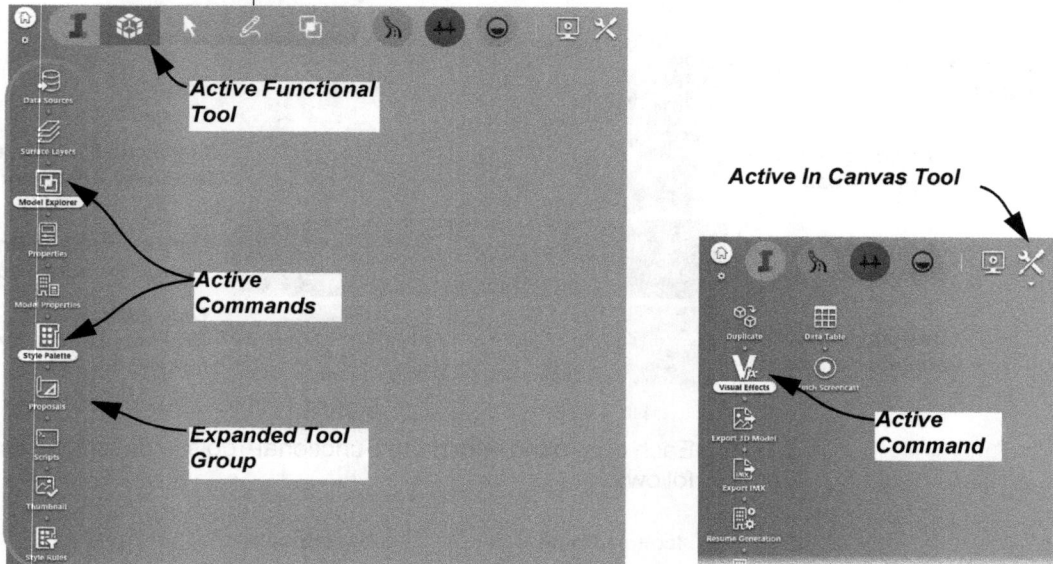

Figure 1–12

- When a Functional Tool is expanded, it changes color to indicate that it is active.

- Active commands are indicated by the highlighted label and icon, as shown in Figure 1–12.

- More than one expanded tool can be active at a time, as shown in Figure 1–12.

Toolbar Options

- Click ⚙ (Toolbar Options) in the In Canvas tools, as shown in Figure 1–13, to change their appearance.

- Expanded Tools can be displayed with or without labels, as shown in Figure 1–13.

- Expanded Tools can be hidden automatically by turning on Hide Tools, as shown in Figure 1–13.

- Toggling on *Shade Tools on Hover* causes a shadow to display behind the expanded tool group when you hover the cursor over the tools. When *Shade Tools on Hover* is toggled off, the shadow is constantly visible, as shown in Figure 1–13.

Figure 1–13

5. Asset Card

Asset Cards or Stacks are used to modify the model. They display when certain commands are active, or certain design features are selected in the model, as shown in Figure 1–14. Asset Cards offer relevant information for the currently selected feature. They enable you to do the following:

- View preview thumbnails for selected styles and colors.

- View and modify the properties of multiple features of the same type at the same time.

- Use the mini picker to change styles and colors of features.

- View warnings for attributes that violate specific parameters.

Command Asset Card
(View Settings Asset Card/
Visualization Stack)

Feature Asset Card
(Conceptual Road
Asset Card)

Figure 1–14

The contextual stacking of panels enables you to arrange and manage panels by doing the following:

- Maximize your model view by dragging panels to a second monitor.

- Show or hide specific attributes in a stack (customizable per asset type).

- Attach and detach individual panels to create stacks of information.

- Arrange panel sequences based on the information you need.

- Manage the display of information by collapsing and expanding individual panels.

- Hide or show panels using a menu on the top right of the stack.

- Reset the stack layout back to the default layout.

- Autohide the panels so that they only display when you are actively working with (hovering over) a stack area.

6. Model Explorer

The Model Explorer (shown in Figure 1–15) lists the layers that have been added to the model and enables you to hide or display individual model layers. Use any of the following methods to access the Model Explorer:

- In the In Canvas Tools, click ![icon] (Build, manage, and analyze your industry model) > ![icon] (Create and manage your model) > ![icon] (Model Explorer.

- In the Utility Bar, click ![icon] (Control visibility, display, and selectability of features).

- Press <Alt>+<3>.

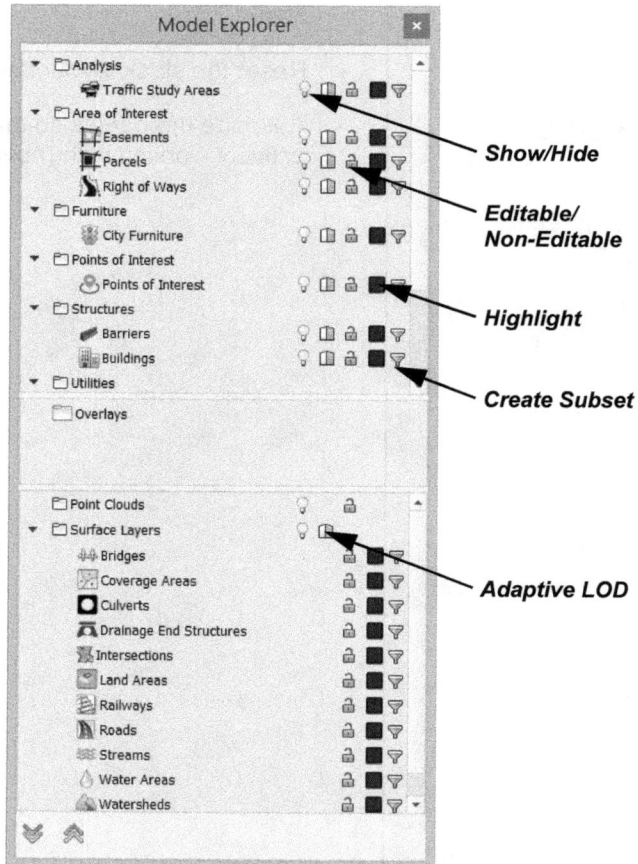

Figure 1–15

7. Model Window

The Model Window (shown in Figure 1–16) is the working area in which you create model elements.

Figure 1–16

New 💡

How elements display in the Model Window depends on the visual style selected in the Utility Bar. Different view settings can be set up to support different work flows, as shown in Figure 1–17. When working on design roads, you might want to display the surface and buildings in wireframe in order to view their triangular irregular network (TIN). In contrast, when you are communicating the design to stakeholders, you might want a more realistic appearance to communicate what the design should look like when the construction is complete.

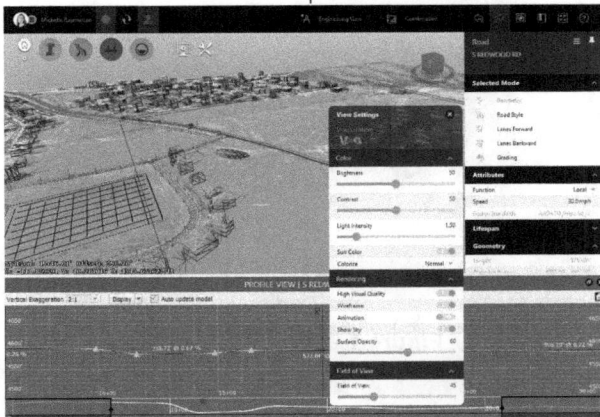

Engineering View Style Used for
Creating Design Elements

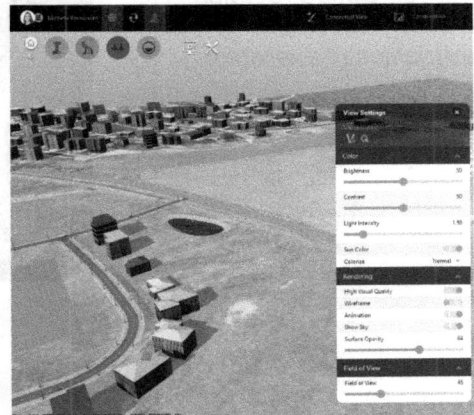

Conceptual View Style Used for
Communicating the Design

Figure 1–17

8. Model Coordinates

Each model is assigned a coordinate system that defines the project's location in the world. Once assigned, model coordinates display in the bottom left corner of the model window, as shown in Figure 1–18. The coordinates display the cursor's location in the model in the X, Y, and Z planes. They automatically update as the cursor moves around in the model.

Figure 1–18

9. Tooltips

Tooltips display when you hover the cursor over a command or feature in the model. These tooltips are labels and short descriptions that display to help ensure that you are selecting the correct items. Figure 1–19 shows an example of a feature tooltip on the left and a command tooltip on the right. If Tooltips do not display as you hover over an item, you need to enable them.

When a model is created using the Model Builder, OpenStreetMap feature names display as tooltips (if available).

Feature tooltip   **Command tooltip**

Figure 1–19

To toggle tooltips on or off, in the Utility Bar, expand the View Style drop-down and click ⚙ (Configure current view), as shown in Figure 1–20. In the View Settings asset card, click ⟳ (Change navigation and application feedback settings) to open the *Interaction* stack. Under *Feedback*, click the **Tooltips** slider to toggle them on or off, as shown in Figure 1–21.

	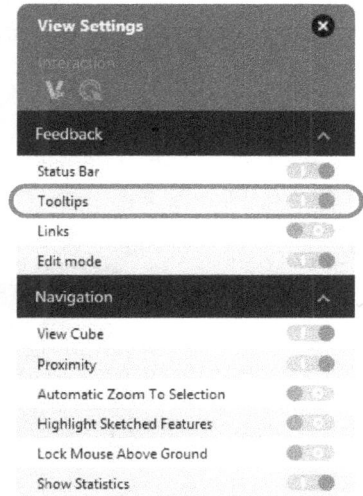
Figure 1–20	**Figure 1–21**

10. ViewCube

The ViewCube provides visual clues indicating the camera position in the model and the direction in which the camera is pointed. The ViewCube helps you to quickly move around the model by providing quick access to predefined views, as shown in Figure 1–22.

Figure 1–22

1.3 Navigating the Model

Navigation commands are critical for working efficiently in any drawing program. Sometimes you need to display the entire model, while other times you need to display more detail. When navigating the Autodesk InfraWorks 360 model, you can change the camera position to obtain a better view of the design.

Mouse

The mouse is the main model navigation tool. A three-button mouse can be used to pan around the model, zoom in/out, and orbit the model in 3D, as shown in Figure 1–23.

Unlike AutoCAD-based software, holding the mouse wheel to Pan does not work in the Autodesk InfraWorks 360 software.

Hold the mouse wheel to change the camera elevation.

Hold the right mouse button to Pan around.

Scroll the mouse wheel toward you to zoom out, and away from you to zoom in.

Hold the left mouse button to Orbit in 3D.

Figure 1–23

ViewCube

The ViewCube provides quick access to many different predefined views. As you move the cursor over it, each face or corner highlights. Once highlighted, you can click the face or corner to reorient the model to the highlighted predefined view, as shown in Figure 1–24. If you hover the cursor over the

ViewCube, ■ (Home) and ■ (Context Menu) both display, as shown in Figure 1–24.

Highlighted view

SE   TOP   SW

LEFT   FRONT   RIGHT   BACK

NE   BOTTOM   NW

Predefined views

Home

Context Menu

Figure 1–24

Home View

The default Home view is a top view that displays the entire model or a view specified which you define. To quickly go back to the Home view, hover the cursor over the ViewCube and click

 (Home). Alternatively, you can press <Home> or <F4>.

How To: Change the Home View

1. Move the camera to the view that you want to use as the new Home view.
2. Click (Context Menu) or right-click on the ViewCube and select **Set current view as home**.

ViewCube Properties

The ViewCube Properties dialog box (shown in Figure 1–25) controls the ViewCube location, size, opacity, and whether it displays in the model.

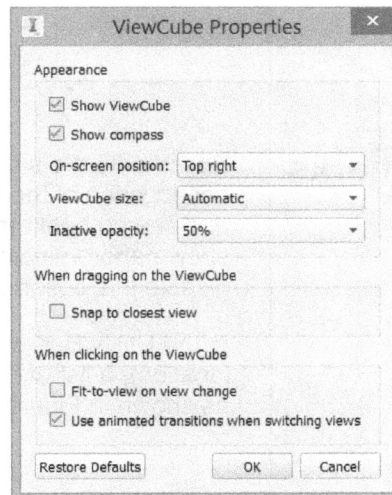

Figure 1–25

The ViewCube can display in any of the four corners of the model: top left, top right, bottom left, or bottom right. To open the ViewCube Properties dialog box, click (Context Menu) or right-click on the ViewCube and select **Properties**.

To toggle the ViewCube on or off, in the Utility Bar, expand the View Style drop-down and click ⚙ (Configure current view). In the View Settings asset card, click 🔍 (Change navigation and application feedback settings) to open the *Interaction* stack. Under *Navigation*, click the **ViewCube** slider to toggle it on or off, as shown in Figure 1–26.

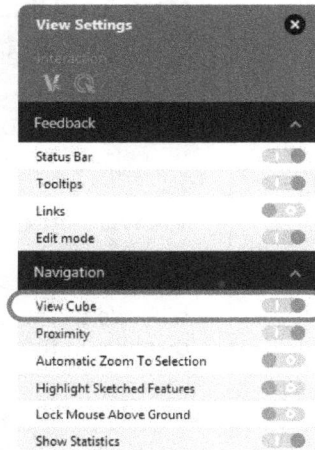

Figure 1–26

Bookmarks

Bookmarks are saved views that quickly reorient the view from one location of the model to another. You can create, preview, and search bookmarks. In addition, you can share bookmarks to show panoramic views on the web (however you can also disable this option for a specific view).

In the Utility Bar, when you click 🔖 (Bookmark your current location), a list of bookmarks with preview thumbnails displays, as shown in Figure 1–27.

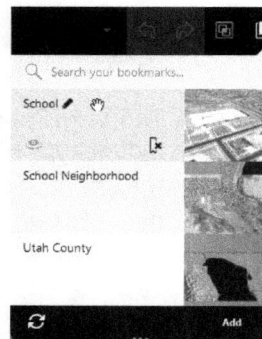

Figure 1–27

Hovering the cursor over a bookmark causes additional tools to display. The table below describes each tool available in the Bookmarks drop-down.

Icon	Description
	Enables you to rename a specific Bookmark.
	Disables the panorama view for the web for the specific Bookmark.
	Deletes the specific Bookmark.
	Refreshes the preview thumbnails for all the Bookmarks according to what is displayed in the current proposal.
Add	Adds a new Bookmark for the current model view.

Other Navigation Tools

Lock Above Terrain

Designers are usually more concerned with what is happening above ground than below ground. To lock the camera position above the terrain:

1. In the Utility Bar, expand the View Style drop-down and click ⚙ (Configure current view).

2. In the View Settings asset card, click 🔍 (Change navigation and application feedback settings) to open the *Interaction* stack.

3. Under *Navigation*, click the **Lock Mouse Above Ground** slider to toggle it on or off, as shown in Figure 1–28.

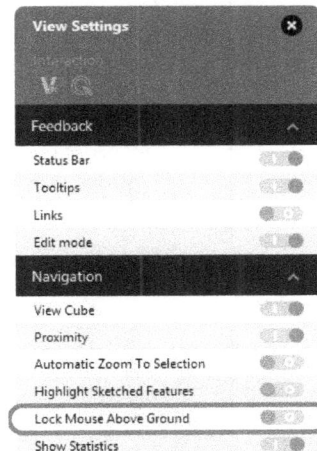

Figure 1–28

Elevate/Lower Camera

To move the camera position in the Z-direction, press <Q> or <1> to elevate the camera, or <E> or <0> (zero) to lower the camera elevation.

Using <1> or <0> to change the camera elevation only works on the numeric keypad of the keyboard.

Look Up/Down

The camera angle can be tilted up or down by pressing <S> to look up, or <W> to look down.

Zoom to Selected

 (Zoom to Selected) is used to zoom to a point of interest in the model.

How To: To zoom in on a selected feature

1. Click (Build, manage, and analyze your infrastructure model) > (Select model features).

   • Alternatively, in the Utility Bar, click (Select).

2. In the model, click on the feature to select it.

3. Click (Zoom selected), as shown in Figure 1–29.

Figure 1–29

• Alternatively, you can double-click in the model at the point of interest. Double-clicking inside the model to zoom in also rotates the view as it zooms.

1.4 Working with Proposals

A proposal is a design alternative in the model and should be created for each design alternative that you plan to explore or propose to the client. By default, every model has at least one proposal called the **Master**.

It is recommended that you only include base model information (existing conditions) in the master proposal. Then, create a new proposal for each new design alternative based on the master proposal. Everything in the current proposal is included in the new proposal.

For example, if you sketch new model elements in a proposal, any new proposals based on that proposal contain those model elements. By ensuring that the master proposal only contains the existing conditions, you can always create a clean proposal.

If you use pieces from multiple proposed designs, you can merge them to create one proposal that includes everything contained in the other proposals. You can then remove all but the required elements.

The Proposals list in the Utility Bar can be used to switch between proposals by expanding the ▨ (Switch Active Proposal) drop-down list and selecting the proposal that you want active, as shown in Figure 1–30.

Figure 1–30

Proposals Palette

The Proposals palette contains statistics about the proposals you have created, as shown in Figure 1–31. The statistics include the number of items added or removed per feature type. You can also quickly display measurements for added features, such as length, area, and volume. To display statistics for specific features, expand Details under the feature type, and then expand the specific feature ID to display its measurements.

Proposal Switching Tool/
Current Proposal

Feature Statistics

Feature Type categories

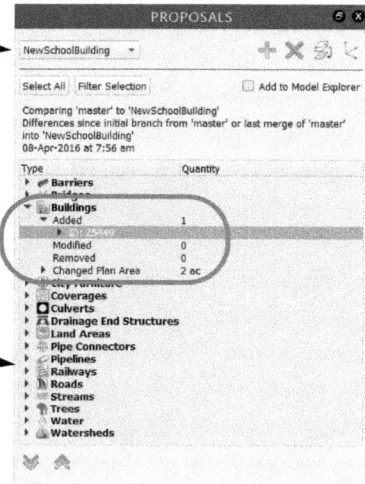

Figure 1–31

Proposal Tools

The following tools can help you manage the proposals in the current model. They are located at the top of the Proposals palette. These tools are described as follows:

Icon	Description
✛ (Add new proposal)	Creates a new proposal based on the current proposal. It includes everything in the current proposal.
✖ (Delete Proposal)	Removes the current proposal from the model.
⟳ (Merge Proposals)	Combines a selected proposal's edit history with the edit history in the current proposal.
⤡ / ⤓ (View 2D/3D)	Displays sketched features as 2D linework when in 2D mode or as a 3D model when in 3D mode, as shown in Figure 1–32.

3D model   *2D linework*

Figure 1–32

How To: Create a New Proposal

1. Create a base model in the master proposal by importing data from various sources.
2. In the In Canvas tools, click ![icon] (Build, manage, and analyze your industry model)> ![icon] (Create and manage your model)> ![icon] (Proposals) to display the Proposals palette.
3. In the Proposals palette, select the proposal that you want to use as the base, as shown in Figure 1–33.

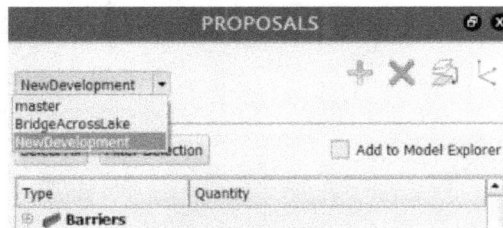

Figure 1–33

4. In the Proposals palette, click ![icon] (Add new proposal).
5. In the Add New Proposal dialog box, type a name for the proposal and click **OK**.

Alternatively, you can:

1. Select the proposal that you want to use as the base from the ![icon] (Switch Active Proposal) drop-down list to make it active.
2. Click remove **ADD NEW** from the ![icon] (Switch Active Proposal) drop-down list.
3. In the Add New Proposal dialog box, type a name for the proposal and click **OK**.

How To: Merge Proposals

1. In the In Canvas tools, click ![icon] (Build, manage, and analyze your industry model)>![icon] (Create and manage your model)>![icon] (Proposals) to display the Proposals palette.

2. Select the proposal into which you want to merge the features, as shown in Figure 1–34.

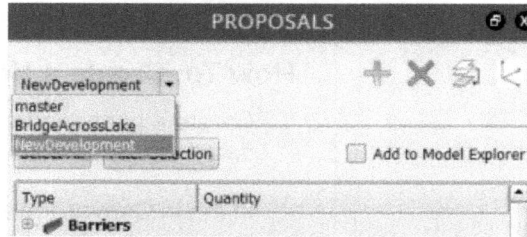

Figure 1–34

3. At the top of the Proposals palette, click ![icon] (Merge Proposals).

4. In the Merge Proposals dialog box, select the proposal that you want to merge into the current proposal, as shown in Figure 1–35. Click **OK**.

To easily browse added or modified features, the Merge panel provides a **Zoom to Selected** *option.*

Figure 1–35

Practice 1a

Estimated time for completion: 30 minutes

Navigating the User Interface

Practice Objectives

- Navigate around a 3D model using preset views, manual orbiting tools, and the ViewCube.
- Manage proposals by creating new proposals and merging existing proposals.

In this practice you will access preset views, orbit the drawing, and return to a previous view. Additionally, you will create a new proposal and merge it with another proposal.

Task 1 - Navigate the model.

1. In the Home Screen, click **Open**.

2. In the *C:\InfraWorks Fundamentals Practice Files\Introduction* folder, select **INTRO.sqlite**. Click **Open**.

3. In the Utility Bar, click 🖫 (Bookmark) and select **Bridge**.

4. In the Utility Bar, select **Bridge** from the 🖾 (Switch Active Proposal) drop-down list.

5. Scroll the middle mouse button toward you to zoom out.

6. Hold the left mouse button (Orbit) as you drag the mouse to orbit the model to display it as an elevation view with the camera south of the bridge, as shown in Figure 1–36.

Figure 1–36

7. Hold the right mouse button (Pan) as you drag the mouse to the left to pan the model to the intersection of the bridge road with Redwood Rd (the road that is running north and south), as shown in Figure 1–37.

Figure 1–37

8. In the Utility Bar, click ▣ (Bookmark) and select **New Neighborhood**.

9. In the Utility Bar, select **NewNeighborhood** from the ▨ (Active Proposal) drop-down list, as shown in Figure 1–38.

Figure 1–38

Task 2 - Create a new proposal.

---

1. In the In Canvas tools, click ▮ (Build, manage, and analyze your industry model)>▦ (Create and manage your model) > ▨ (Proposals).

2. In the Proposals palette, set the current proposal to the **master** proposal.

3. In the Proposals palette, click ✛ (Add new proposal).

4. In the Add New Proposal dialog box, for the proposal name type **Combination** and click **OK**. **Combination** is now the active proposal and includes everything that was in the master proposal.

Task 3 - Merge two proposals.

1. If you closed the Proposals palette, in the In Canvas tools, click ▣ (Build, manage, and analyze your industry model)> ▩ (Create and manage your model)>▣ (Proposals) to display the Proposals palette.

2. In the Utility Bar, click ▣ (Bookmark) and select **Railway**.

3. At the top of the Proposals palette, click ▱ (Merge Proposals).

4. In the Merge Proposals dialog box, select the **Bridge** proposal to merge it into the **Combination** proposal, as shown in Figure 1–39. Click **OK**.

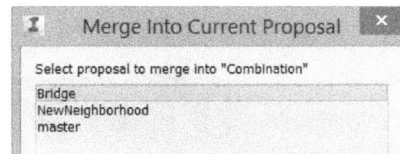

Figure 1–39

The bridge displays in the right side of the view.

5. At the top of the Proposals palette, click ▱ (Merge Proposals).

6. In the Merge Proposals dialog box, select the **NewNeighborhood** proposal to merge it into the Combination proposal, as shown in Figure 1–40. Click **OK**.

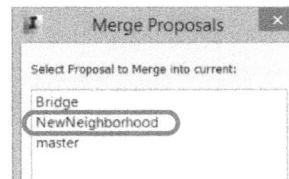

Figure 1–40

A new neighborhood with roads and buildings displays in the view.

7. Close the model.

Task 4 - Configure the view interaction settings.

1. In the Utility Bar, expand the View Style drop-down and click

   ⚙ (Configure current view), as shown in Figure 1–41.

2. In the View Settings asset card, click 🔍 (Change navigation and application feedback settings) to open the *Interaction* stack.

3. Under *Navigation*, click the **Lock Mouse Above Ground** slider to toggle it on, as shown in Figure 1–42. Ensure that **Tooltips** and **ViewCube** are also on.

Figure 1–41

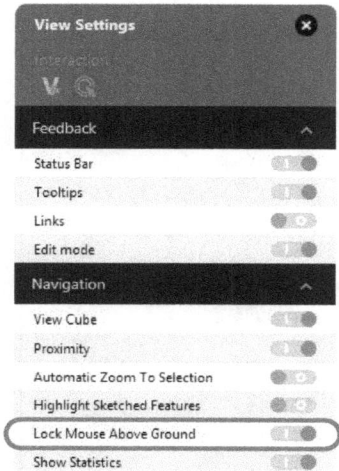

Figure 1–42

Chapter Review Questions

Use Figure 1–43 to answer Questions 1 and 2.

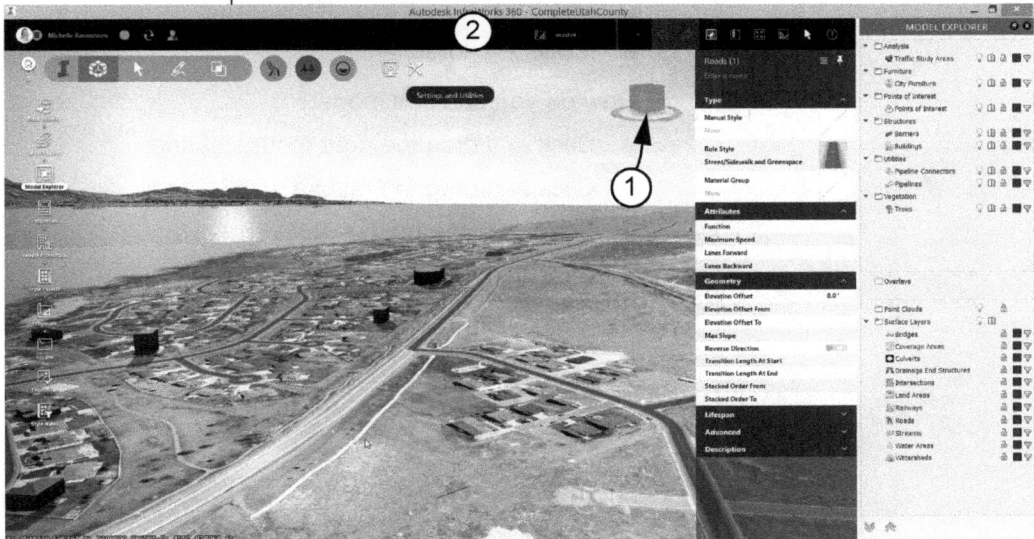

Figure 1–43

1. In Figure 1–43, which part of the user interface is indicated by number 1?

    a. In Canvas tools

    b. ViewCube

    c. Model Explorer

    d. Model Window

2. In Figure 1–43, what part of the user interface is indicated by number 2?

    a. ViewCube

    b. In Canvas tools

    c. Utility Bar

    d. Tooltips

3. Bookmarks are used to quickly change the view to a specific area of the model.

    a. True

    b. False

4. Which of the following should be used to display different design variations for the project?

    a. Bookmarks

    b. Proposals

    c. Coverages

    d. Model Explorer

5. How do you pan in a model?

    a. Click and drag the right mouse button.

    b. Click and drag the mouse scroll wheel.

    c. Scroll with the mouse scroll wheel.

    d. Click and drag the left mouse button.

Command Summary

Button	Command	Location
	Application Options	• **Home Screen** • **In Canvas Tools:** Settings and Utilities
	Bookmark	• **Utility Bar**
	Close Current Model	• **In Canvas Tools**
N/A	Elevate Camera Down	• **Mouse:** Hold scroll wheel • **Shortcut Key:** <E> or <0> (zero)
N/A	Elevate Camera Up	• **Mouse:** Hold scroll wheel • **Shortcut Key:** <Q> or <1>
/	Home	• **ViewCube** • **Keyboard:** <Home> or <F4>
N/A	Lock Above Terrain	• **View Settings>Interaction stack**
	Model Explorer	• **Utility Bar** • **In Canvas Tools:** Build, manage, and analyze your infrastructure model> Create and manage your model
N/A	Open	• **Home Screen**
N/A	Pitch Down	• **Shortcut Key:** <W>
N/A	Pitch Up	• **Shortcut Key:** <S>
	Proposals	• **Utility Bar** • **In Canvas Tools**: Build, manage, and analyze your industry model>Create and manage your model
N/A	Tooltips	• **View Settings>Interaction stack**
N/A	ViewCube	• **View Settings>Interaction stack**
N/A	Zoom In	• **Mouse:** Scroll Wheel • **Shortcut Key:** <+>
N/A	Zoom Out	• **Mouse:** Scroll Wheel • **Shortcut Key:** <->
	Zoom Selected	• **Shortcut Key:** <Alt>+<Z> • **In Canvas Tools:** Build, manage, and analyze your infrastructure model> Select model features • **In Model**: Double-click on point of interest

Connecting to Data Sources

Firms that use existing GIS data during the project planning or bid phases of a project can offer a more complete analysis of the project and better proposals to stakeholders. In this chapter, you learn how to create a new model and then how to connect additional existing data sources. Finally, you configure the data sources to display correctly in the model.

Learning Objectives in this Chapter

- Create a new model using the Model Builder.
- Create a new model from scratch.
- Set the model coordinate system, units, and extents.
- Connect to select data source types to display the existing conditions in a model.
- Configure the connected GIS data for correct display.

2.1 Geographic Information Systems Overview

All Autodesk® InfraWorks® models begin by importing existing data from various sources. These sources include building outlines, roads, utilities, terrain, images, etc. Typically, the data you start with comes from a Geographic Information System (GIS). A GIS enables organizations to better store, manage, and analyze geographical data.

In its most simple definition, a GIS is the creation of a smart map in which data is attached to geographical elements. It attempts to explain or predict spatial distribution or variation in human activity and its connection to physical features on the earth's surface.

Most GIS sources include multiple files. The most basic GIS data source often includes a raster or vector file and a database file containing information referenced by the raster/vector features. For example, an ESRI Shape File includes the vector file (.SHP), a database file (.DBF), a projection file (.PRJ), etc., as shown in Figure 2–1.

Name	Type
BuildingFootprint.dbf	DBF File
BuildingFootprint.idx	IDX File
BuildingFootprint.prj	PRJ File
BuildingFootprint.sbn	SBN File
BuildingFootprint.sbx	SBX File
BuildingFootprint	AutoCAD Shape Source
BuildingFootprint.shp	XML File
BuildingFootprint	AutoCAD Compiled Shape

Figure 2–1

Sample GIS Data

Many different agencies take advantage of the benefits of using GIS to analyze and manage their infrastructure and data. Uses of GIS data include:

- Cities store street centerline maps connected to pavement management system databases, ensuring the correct maintenance and repair of city roads.

- Utility companies store electronic maps indicating where pipes, manholes, and other utilities are buried to provide blue stake services to anyone needing a digging permit. If a utility is damaged due to a natural or man-made disaster, data connected to the utility maps can be used to quickly notify the affected residents about how long they are going to be without service.

- Retailers use GIS data to better analyze which customers buy certain goods. This enables them to send coupons and other marketing material directly to the customers that are most likely to buy their products. The data is also used to help them strategically locate merchandise within the store.

- GIS data is often created, managed, and stored by government agencies to help them track public infrastructure. During a project's planning phase, planners, developers, and civil engineers use GIS data to help select the best location for the proposed project. During this phase of the project, existing GIS data is collected from various agencies.

Model Builder

The easiest way to find GIS data, is to use the Model Builder. The Model Builder creates a new model and includes existing datasets from the following sources:

AUTODESK
INFRAWORKS 360

To use this feature, access to the Internet and Autodesk® InfraWorks® 360 are required.

Data Type	Source
Elevation	Terrain data for the United States and its territories uses 10 and 30 meter DEMs from the National Elevation Dataset (NED). The rest of the globe (between -60 degrees latitude) uses SRTM 90m DEM data processed by CIAT-CSI.
Imagery	Satellite imagery from Microsoft® Bing® Maps is draped over the model terrain.
Roads and Highways	OpenStreetMap's (OSM) Highway and Railway datasets are readily available. They are used to create roads and railway features in the model. If feature names are available from OSM, they appear as tooltips and provide a hyperlink to the source feature that opens in the default web browser.
Buildings	The building data is also from the OpenStreetMap dataset.

How To: Create a New Model Using Model Builder

Use the mouse to zoom and pan in the map.

1. In the Home Screen, click **Model Builder**.
2. In the Model Builder dialog box, type the project address in the *Search by Location* field or zoom in on the project area using the map in the right pane, as shown in Figure 2–2.

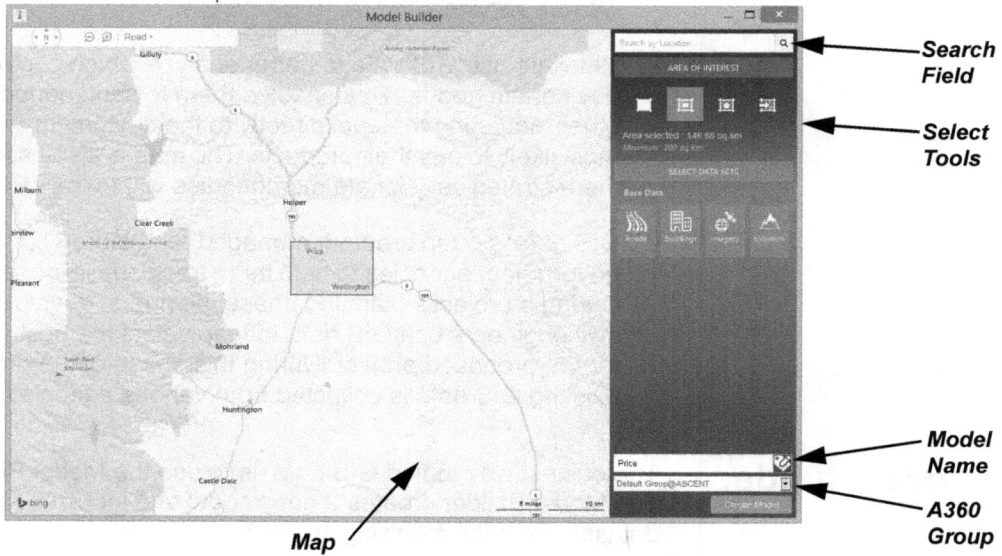

Figure 2–2

3. Use one of the Select tools to define the Area of Interest (AOI) to include in the model (Note: There is a 200 sq KM maximum area limit). You can chose between the following:
   - Select current map extents.
   - Draw a rectangle to select an AOI.
   - Draw a polygon to select an AOI.
   - Import a polygon to select an AOI.
4. Type a name for the model.
5. Select a group to share the model with through the Cloud.
6. Click **Create Model**. The model is created in the background and stored in A360. Click **Close** in the Model Builder message box.
7. Close the Model Builder.
8. In the Home screen, click on the newly created model to open it.
9. In the message box that displays, click **Download**.

You are notified by email when the model is ready.

Finding GIS Data

The second easiest way to find GIS data for your project site is to perform an Internet search for the city, state, and/or country where the project is located. Include the keywords **GIS data** in your search. Several agencies recognize the value that GIS data brings to a project and the importance of sharing it due to the exhausting cost of its collection.

The data for this course was downloaded from the AGRC (found at gis.utah.gov/) and the Utah County Government GIS site (www.utahcounty.gov/).

A large number of Internet sites provide free GIS data to the public, such as *www.GISDepot.com* and *www.USGS.gov*. There are also private and government organizations around the world that collect GIS data and act as a central resource for GIS data, which you can purchase or download for free. Ensure that when you download the data sources, you include all of the connected file types and download them to the same directory.

Geographic Coordinate Systems

When working with GIS data, note that it can be created in many different geographic coordinate systems. A geographical coordinate system is a mathematical equation that takes the earth's features (formed on a sphere) and projects them onto a flat sheet of paper. Cartographers first developed coordinate systems to help them map locations on Earth by assigning numbers or letters for ease in plotting them on a map. One or two numbers represent the horizontal position (*x, y* or *latitude* and *longitude*), and one number represents the vertical position (*z* or *elevation*).

Several coordinate systems have been developed over the centuries to assist in plotting elements on the Earth's surface. They include cylindrical, conical, and azimuthal, as shown in Figure 2–3. In each of the projection types, there are two ways to line up the projection plane.

- One is to make it tangent to the earth's surface so that there is only one line or point where the distances are 100% accurate.

- Another is to make it secant to the earth's surface. This provides two lines where distances are 100% accurate. The distances between the secant lines are within civil engineering error tolerances.

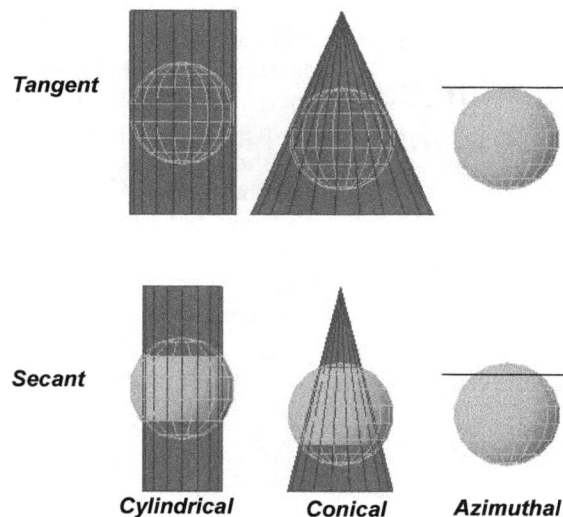

Figure 2–3

Setting Coordinate Systems and Model Extents in the Autodesk InfraWorks 360 software

When a model is created using the Model Builder, the coordinate system is automatically set to LL84 (WGS84 datum, Latitude-Longitude; Degrees).

When a new model is created using the Autodesk InfraWorks 360 software, the coordinate system and model extents can be set immediately. Setting the model extents focuses the model on the project area and reduces the size of the model file. The minimum and maximum X- and Y-values can be entered into the software.

Setting the coordinate system indicates which mathematical equation is going to be used for setting the coordinates of your project, and which values are displayed in the bottom left corner of the model area, as shown in Figure 2–4.

Model coordinates (X, Y, and Z) at the cursor location

X: 1529473.217353 Y: 7267597.802425 Z: 5270.229904 ft

Figure 2–4

When you import data from other sources, the Autodesk InfraWorks 360 software automatically transforms the data to your project's coordinate system and can trim the data at the project extents (minimum and maximum X,Y values). Over 6,000 coordinate systems are stored in the software.

When starting a new project, you might not know the coordinates for the model extents. In this situation or if you used Model Builder to create the model, you can set the model extents and/or coordinate system after you import the data. In the In Canvas Tools, click ![icon] (Settings and Utilities),> ![icon] (Model Properties).

You can import the model extents from any of the following formats: .ADF, .ASC, .BT, .DB, .DEM, .DOQ, .PNG, .SDF, .SQLITE, .SHP, .TIF, and .SID. This is helpful if you often work in the same geographical areas, or if you plan to set the model limits to the extents of an aerial image or .DEM file.

Design Standards

Design Standards are used to set the horizontal and vertical design control for creating design roads. It is important to set the design standard if you have purchased the Autodesk InfraWorks 360 Roadway Design module. Different design standards should be used depending on the location of the project and the units in which the project is being designed.

The Autodesk InfraWorks 360 Roadway Design module provides the opportunity to control curve radii, grades, and other parameters associated with road geometry. This is discussed in more depth in Chapter 9, Introduction to the Roadway Design for InfraWorks 360 Module.

How To: Start a New Model with the Correct Coordinate System

1. In the Home Screen, click **New**.
2. Type a filename in the *Name* field and a description in the *Description* field.
3. Set where to store the file:
   - If you select *Autodesk 360*, then you also need to select the group with which to share it.
   - If you select *My Computer*, then you also need to set the directory path.
4. Click **Model Extents**, as shown in Figure 2–5.

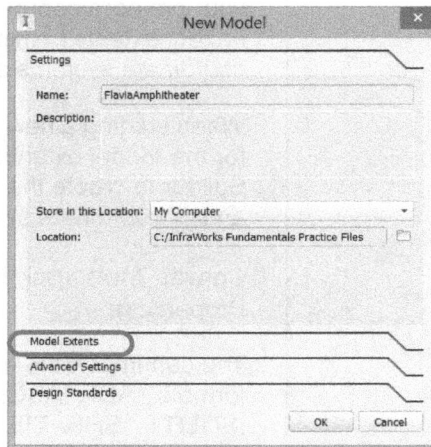

Figure 2–5

5. Select the **Define Model Extents** option to set the minimum and maximum X- and Y-values to set the model extents.
6. Click **Advanced Settings**.

7. In the *Coordinate Systems* area, click 🌐 (Choose coordinate system) in the *UCS* coordinate system field. Select a category in the left pane, and then double-click on the project coordinate system in the right pane, as shown in Figure 2–6.

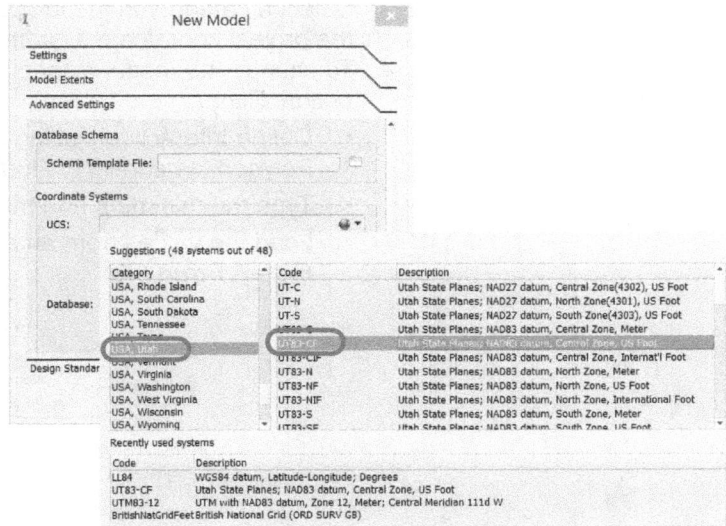

Figure 2–6

8. Repeat Step 7 for the *Database* coordinate system field.
9. If you have the Autodesk InfraWorks 360 Road Design module, it is important to also set the design standards. To do this, in the New Model dialog box, click **Design Standards**.
10. In the *Road Standards* drop-down list, select the appropriate standards for your project. Then, select which side of the road traffic travels on to indicate **Driving Direction**, as shown in Figure 2–7.

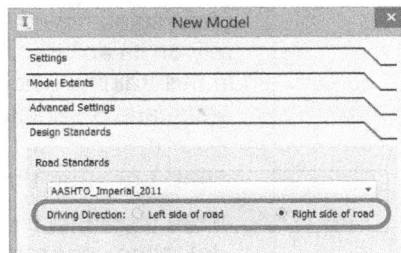

Figure 2–7

11. Click **OK** to create the model.

How To: Set the Coordinate System of an Existing Model

1. In the In Canvas tools, click ![icon] (Settings and Utilities)> ![icon] (Model Properties).
2. In the Model Settings dialog box, in the *Coordinate Systems* area, in the *UCS* field, click ![icon] (Choose coordinate system).

If Model Builder was used to create the model, the model extents are defined during the creation process.

3. Select a category in the left pane, and then double-click on the project coordinate system in the right pane.
4. To change the model extents, clear the **Use Entire Model** option. Either:
   - Define Interactively using a bounding box (BBox) or Polygon, as shown in Figure 2–8, or
   - Type the minimum and maximum X- and Y-values, or
   - Load the values from an external file by clicking **Load Extent From File**.

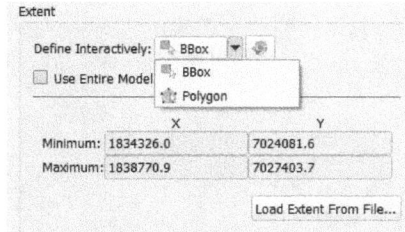

Figure 2–8

5. Click **Save**.

Metadata

Most GIS sources provide metadata in the form of an HTML or PDF file. This metadata file contains information on the contents of the file, coordinate system used in the file, limitations of the file, and the kind of data contained in each of the database fields.

Understanding how the GIS data was created helps you to understand how the data can be used, and how much you can rely on its accuracy. Metadata for all of the GIS source files used in this training guide is located in the class files folder under *Metadata*. A sample metadata file is also shown in Appendix A.

Hint: Locating the Information About the Database Fields

If the metadata file does not describe each of the fields in the database connected to the geographic features, you can use the AutoCAD® Map 3D software or the AutoCAD® Civil 3D® software to determine the information. Connect to the data using the **Planning** and **Analysis** tools and open the data table.

Units

The assigned coordinate system indicates which units are used for the model (feet or meters). However, those units do not display automatically. The default units that display in the model are meters. Once changed, the new units remain the display units for all the models opened in the Autodesk InfraWorks 360 software until it is changed.

> **Hint: Imperial Units - Feet verses US Survey Feet**
>
> If you are using imperial units, you can display them in feet or US Survey feet. The difference between the two measurements is only 2 parts per million. However, that difference is measured from the origin and results in a difference of two feet for every 189 miles from the origin point. Therefore, it is important to use the same units as the coordinate system.

How To: Set the Display Units for the Model

1. In the Home Screen, click ⚙ (Application Options).
   - Alternatively, if you already have a model open, in the In Canvas tools, click ✗ (Settings and Utilities)> ⚙ (Application Options).
2. In the Application Options dialog box, in the left pane, select **Unit Configuration**. On the right, select the required default units for the model, as shown in Figure 2–9.

Figure 2–9

3. Click **OK**.

Practice 2a

Create a New Model From Scratch

Estimated time for completion: 5 minutes

Practice Objectives

- Create a new model from scratch.
- Set the coordinate system and units for the model.

In this practice you will create a new model from scratch while simultaneously setting the coordinate system for the model.

Task 1 - Create a new model.

1. In the Home Screen, click **New**.

2. Set the following, as shown in Figure 2–10:

    - *Name*: **FlaviaAmphitheater**
    - *Location:* **C:\InfraWorks Fundamentals Practice Files**

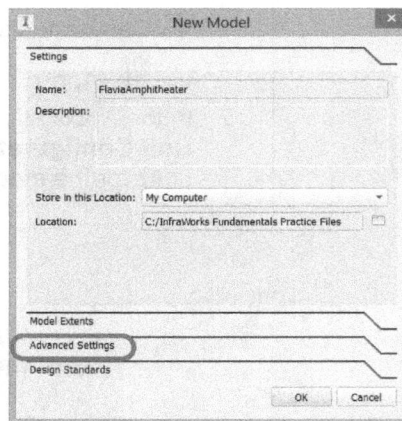

Figure 2–10

3. Click **Advanced Settings**.

4. Under Coordinate Systems, click 🌐 (Choose coordinate system). For the *Category*, select **USA, Utah**. Under code, double-click on the **UT83-CF** coordinate system, as shown in Figure 2–11.

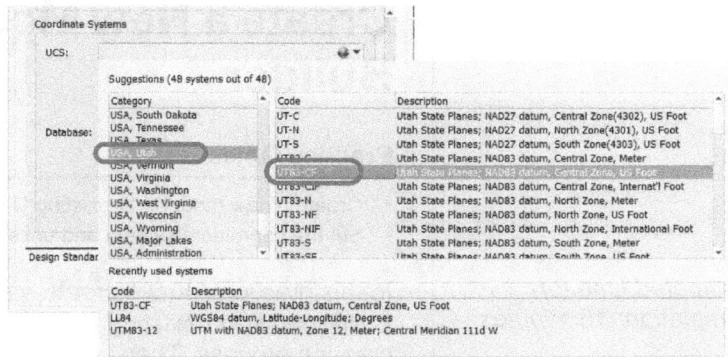

Figure 2–11

5. Repeat the previous step for the *Database* coordinate system field.

6. Click **OK** to create the model.

7. In the In Canvas tools, click ⚒ (Settings and Utilities)> ⚙ (Application Options).

8. In the Application Options dialog box, select **Unit Configuration**. Expand the *Default Units* drop-down list and select **Imperial,** as shown in Figure 2–12.

Figure 2–12

9. Click **OK**.

Practice 2b

Create a New Model Using Model Builder

Practice Objectives

- Create a new model with existing GIS data.
- Set the coordinate system and units for the model.

Estimated time for completion: 15 minutes

**AUTODESK®
INFRAWORKS™ 360**

To complete this practice, access to the Internet and Autodesk® InfraWorks® 360 are required.

In this practice you will create a new model using the Model Builder and add existing GIS data to it automatically during the creation process. Then you will change the coordinate system and units for display.

Task 1 - Create a new model.

1. In the Home Screen, click **Model Builder**.

2. In the Model Builder dialog box, under Area of Interest, click ▣ (Draw a rectangle to select an AOI). Zoom in on the state of Utah and select the area indicated in Figure 2–13.

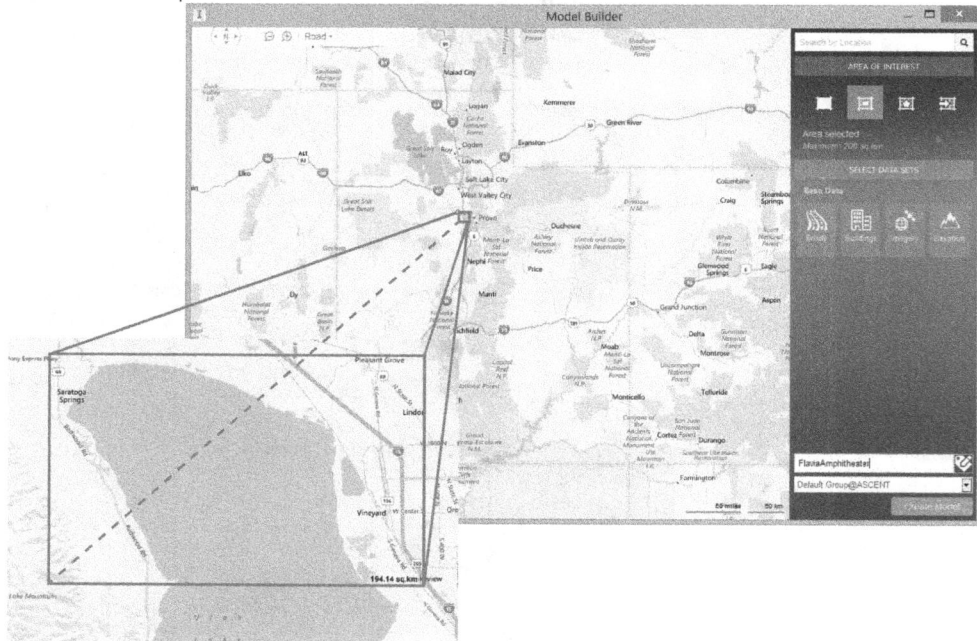

Figure 2–13

It might take a few minutes before the model displays on the Home screen.

3. In the *Name* field, type **FlaviaAmphitheater**. Click **Create Model**, as shown in Figure 2–13. Close the Model Builder dialog box.

4. In the Home Screen, select the **FlaviaAmphitheater.sqlite** model that was just created in the cloud.

5. In the In Canvas Tool, click ![icon] (Settings and Utilities)> ![icon] (Model Properties)

6. Under Coordinate Systems, click ![icon] (Choose coordinate system). For the *Category*, select **USA, Utah**. In the right pane, double-click on the UT83-CF coordinate system, as shown in Figure 2–14.

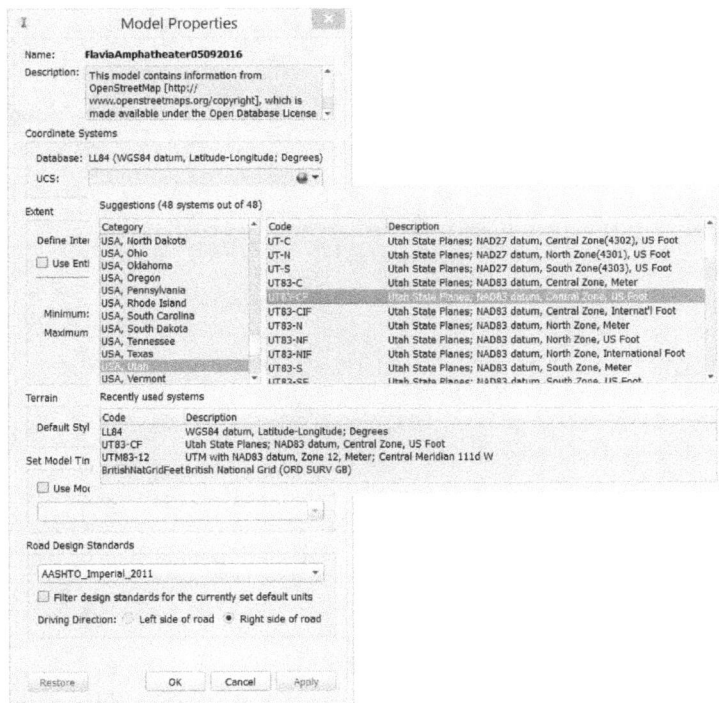

Figure 2–14

7. Click **OK** to update the model.

8. In the In Canvas tools, click ⚒ (Settings and Utilities)>
   ⚙ (Application Options).

9. In the Application Options dialog box, select **Unit
   Configuration**. Expand the Default Units drop-down list and
   select **Imperial,** as shown in Figure 2–15.

Figure 2–15

10. Click **OK**.

2.2 Connect to Data Sources

External GIS data is imported into the model as layers using the Model Builder or the Data Sources explorer, as shown in Figure 2–16. The Data Sources explorer opens when a new, empty model is created. If you close it before you have finished adding data, you can reopen it using the In Canvas tools.

In the Data Sources explorer, connected data is listed in the top area, while information about the data is listed in the bottom area. Two categories of data sources can be used in the model:

- ⬜▾ (File Data Source)

- 🗄 (Database Data Source)

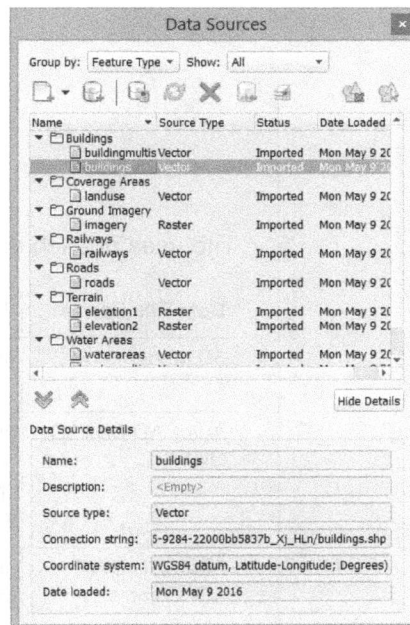

Figure 2–16

File Data Sources

A File Data Source can be a raster or a vector file. Several different file data sources can be imported into the Autodesk InfraWorks 360 model, as shown in Figure 2–17. For each file data source type, multiple file formats can be used. To add a file data source, click ⬜ ▾ (Add file data source) in the Data Sources explorer.

Figure 2–17

The uses of each data file format are described as follows:

Data File Format	Use and Accepted File Extensions
3D Model	Importing local 3D models (.3DS, .DAE, .DXF, .FBX, or .OBJ).
AutoCAD Civil 3D DWG	Importing AutoCAD Civil 3D objects which include corridors, surfaces, pipes, and pipe networks.
	To use this file format, you must have the AutoCAD Civil 3D 2017 software installed.
AutoCAD DWG (3D Objects)	Importing local or cloud-based 3D objects, including 3D solids, surfaces, and meshes.
	To use this file format, you must have the Autodesk Navisworks (Manage 2017 or Simulate 2017) software installed.
AutoCAD DWG as 2D Overlay	Importing local or cloud-based 2D line data from AutoCAD files (.DWG, .DXF).
	To use this file format, a connection to the Internet and an A360 account are required.
Autodesk IMX	Importing local AutoCAD Civil 3D design elements, such as surfaces, pipes, alignments, profiles, and corridor shapes (.IMX).

Autodesk Revit	Importing Autodesk Revit files (.RVT, .RFA).
	To use this file format, you must have the Autodesk Navisworks (Manage 2017 or Simulate 2017) software installed.
CityGML	Importing cloud-based virtual 3D city models (.CITYGML, .GML, or .XML).
	To use this file format, a connection to the Internet and an A360 account are required.
DGN 3D Model	Importing cloud-based or local 2D and 3D line work from Bentley v7 or v8 software (.DGN).
	To use this file format, you must have the Autodesk Navisworks (Manage 2017 or Simulate 2017) software installed.
IFC	Importing cloud-based or local Industry Foundation Classes (IFC) models.
	To use this file format, you must have the Autodesk Navisworks (Manage 2017 or Simulate 2017) software installed.
LandXML	Importing local terrain or surface models (.XML or .LANDXML).
Point Cloud	Importing local 3D laser scans (.RCS or .RCP).
	Note: Point clouds must be imported into Recap first to be configured. If you do not do this step, the point cloud does not render.
Raster	Importing local terrain or surface data from raster or vector-based data as well as imagery (.ADF, .ASC, .BT, .DDF, .DEM, .DT0, .DT1, .DT2, .GRD, .HGT, .DOG, .ECW, .IMG, .JP2, .JPG, .JPEG, .PNG, .SID, .TIF, .TIFF, .WMS, .XML, .VRT, .ZIP, or .GZ).
SDF	Importing local Autodesk Spatial Data Files 3.0 (.SDF).
SHP	Importing local ESRI Shape Files (.SHP).
	Note: It is important to ensure that you have all of the files that are associated with a shape file that is stored in the same location as the shape file (.PRJ, .SHX, .SBN, .DBF, .IDX, .SBX, etc.).
SketchUp Files	Importing cloud-based or local SketchUp (up to 2016) files (.SKP).
	To use this file format, you must have the Autodesk Navisworks (Manage 2017 or Simulate 2017) software installed.
SQLite	Importing SQLite 3.6 files (.SDX, .SQLITE, or .DB).

How To: Connect to File Data Sources

1. Open the Data Sources explorer using the In Canvas tools by clicking ▉ (Build, manage, and analyze your industry model)> 📦 (Create and manage your model)> 🗄 (Data Sources).

2. In the Data Sources panel, expand 🗂 ▾ (Add file data source) and select the file format, as shown in Figure 2–18.

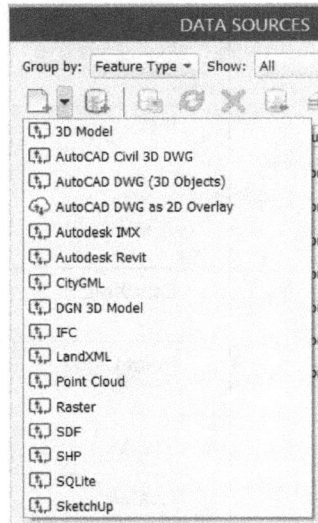

Figure 2–18

Hold <Shift> or <Ctrl> to select multiple files from the directory.

3. Browse to the directory in which the file is located. Select the required file(s) and click **Open**.

Hint: Cloud Vs Local Import

When importing files, the Autodesk InfraWorks software converts the files into a usable format. This conversion is usually completed in the cloud. You can modify the application options to enable local processing of supported formats.

If you want to use the Autodesk Navisworks software (rather than the cloud) to process files, in the In Canvas tools, click

![Settings and Utilities icon] (Settings and Utilities)>![Application Options icon] (Application Options). On the Data Import page, select **Navisworks based Local Import** .

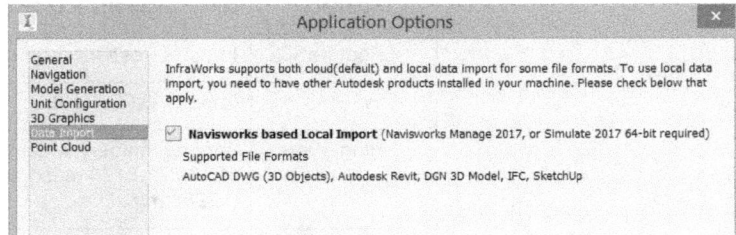

Figure 2–19

Database Data Sources

A Database Data Source can be a vector, ODBC, or OpenGIS raster file. Seven different database types can be added to the Autodesk InfraWorks 360 model. To connect to a database, click

![Add database data source icon] (Add database data source) in the Data Sources explorer. Select the database type in the expanded Connection type drop-down list (as shown in Figure 2–20) and fill in the required fields.

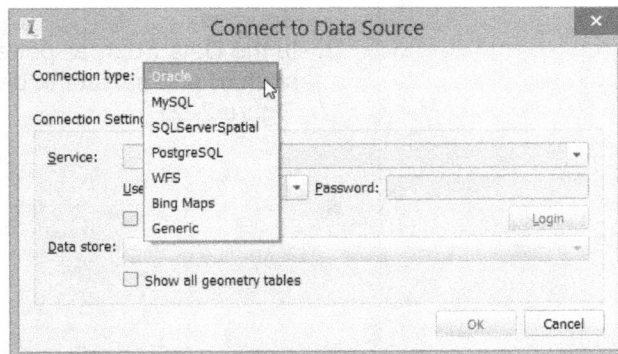

Figure 2–20

The types of database data source are described as follows:

Database	Use and Accepted File Extensions
Oracle	Imports Oracle Express, Standard, and Enterprise Editions (Oracle 10g, Release 2, or Oracle 11g, Release 2). Note: The Oracle Client or Instant Client must be installed and configured before the file can be connected.
MySQL	Imports MySQL 5.5. Note that to connect to your MySQL data source, you need to copy **libmySQL.dll** into the *\Autodesk\InfraWorks 2014* folder.
SQL Server Spatial	Imports Microsoft SQL Server 2008 R2, 2012, or 2014, which supports Express, Standard, and Enterprise Editions.
PostgreSQL	Imports PostGIS 1.50 and PostgreSQL 9.0
WFS	Imports WFS 1.1.0.
Bing Maps	Imports imagery which can be one tile at ground resolution of 78,271.5170 m/pxl, up to 19 tiles at ground resolution of 0.2986 m/pxl.
Generic	Imports a number of generic database types, such as ArcSDE 3.7, TIGER, DGN, UK.NTF, etc. Note: ArcSDE connections require a script that is unique to each instance.

How To: Connect to Database Data Sources

1. Open the Data Sources explorer using the In Canvas tools by clicking ![icon] (Build, manage, and analyze your industry model)> ![icon] (Create and manage your model)> ![icon] (Data Sources).
2. In the Data Sources panel, click ![icon] (Add database data source) and select the database type, as shown in Figure 2–21.

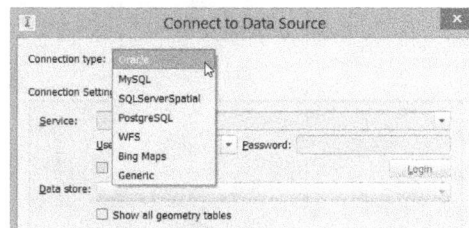

Figure 2–21

3. Fill in all of the required login information for the selected database and click **OK**.

Practice 2c

Import GIS Data

Practice Objective

- Connect to existing GIS data.

Estimated time for completion: 10 minutes

In this practice, you will connect additional data to the model that you obtained from the local government agencies. This data includes a more accurate DEM file, a higher resolution aerial image, and various shape files that contain roads, water bodies, buildings, etc. You can choose to add data to the blank canvas of the model created in Practice 2a, or you can add more accurate data to the model created using Model Builder in Practice 2b. However, the model created for this exercise includes predefined bookmarks to help you navigate the model more efficiently.

1. Open **CreateModel.sqlite** from the *...\ModelExplorer* folder.

2. Ensure that the **Master** proposal is active.

3. In the In Canvas tools, click ▓ (Build, manage, and analyze your infrastructure model) > ▓ (Create and manage your model> ▓ (Data Sources).

The data already in the model came from Model Builder.

4. In the Data Sources palette, take note of the data that is already connected to the model. Zoom in and view the data in the model a little closer.

5. In the Data Sources palette, double-click on any of the data sources. You should receive an error because you cannot modify data source connections that came from Model Builder. Click **OK**.

6. In the Data Sources panel, expand ▓ (Add file data source) and select **Raster**, as shown in Figure 2–22.

Figure 2–22

7. Browse to *C:\InfraWorks Fundamentals Practice Files\DEMs*. Press <Ctrl>+<A> to select all of the DEM files[1] in the list, and click **Open**.

8. In the Data Sources explorer, continue adding files using the following information. Figure 2–23 shows the Data Sources palette once all of the data has been added.

File Path	File Path	Files to Select
Raster	*C:\InfraWorks Fundamentals Practice Files\Images*[2]	All
SHP	*C:\InfraWorks Fundamentals Practice Files\ShapeFiles*[3]	All

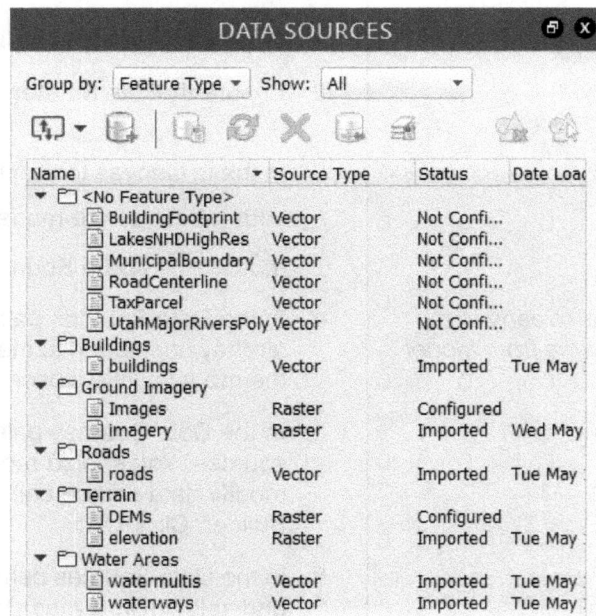

Figure 2–23

1.((AGRC), Utah Automated Geographic Reference Center, 2007)
2.((AGRC), Automated Geographic Reference Center, 2012)
3.(Department, GIS Division of the Utah County Information Systems, 2013)

2.3 Configure and Display Data Sources

Although the source data has been connected, it does not display in the model because the data must be configured first. Configuring the data is important because it enables you to:

- Set the coordinate system in which the source data is located.

- Map database fields located in the source data database file to the properties specified in the model template.

The more database fields you can map to your model, the more analysis can be done with the model. You can also add more accuracy to the model if database fields specify elevations, heights, and other numerical information about the raster or vector to which they pertain.

Data Source Configuration

Once a data source has been imported, it is configured in the Data Sources explorer by either double-clicking on the data source, or selecting the data source and clicking ⬛ (Configure Data), as shown in Figure 2–24.

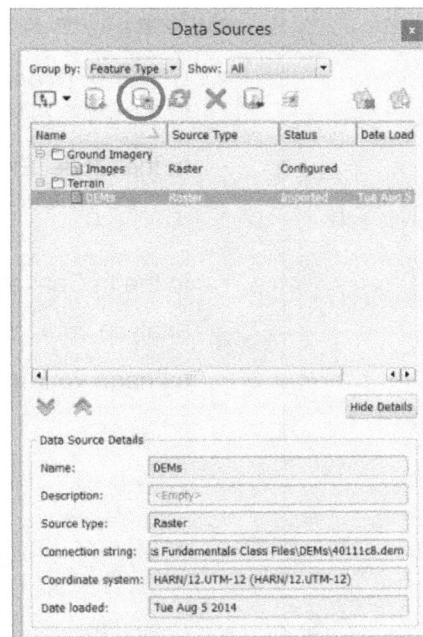

Figure 2–24

Hint: Terrain Data

It is essential that terrain data be added to the model first, since all other data sits on top of the terrain. Without a terrain surface, other data cannot be displayed. Additionally, only one terrain surface can display at any one time. If multiple terrain surfaces exist in a model, the visibility of the surfaces can be determined by setting the display order in the Surface Layers dialog box. Use the arrows at the top of the box to set the display priority, as shown in Figure 2–25.

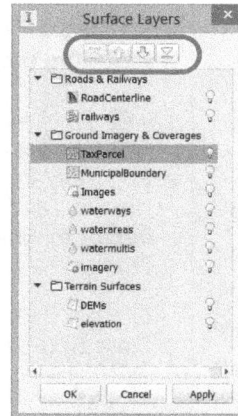

Figure 2–25

Surface Layers are available in multiple places:

- Click ![icon] (Manage the order and visibility of surface data) in the Data Sources palette.

- In the Model Explorer palette, right-click on *Surface Layers* and select **Surface Layers**.

- In the In Canvas tools, click ![icon] (Build, manage, and analyze your infrastructure model) > ![icon] (Create and manage your model> ![icon] (Surface Layers).

Data Source Details

When a data source is selected, in the Data Sources explorer, details about the source display in the Data Source Details panel. The Data Source Details include the name, description, source type, connection string (indicating where the source file is located), coordinate system, and date that the source was loaded into the model.

If a data source file is moved to a new location, the connection to the file is lost and errors might occur when working with features from that data source.Therefore, avoid moving files once you have connected them to an Autodesk InfraWorks 360 model unless doing so is absolutely necessary.

If the data source files must be moved, you must re-associate them from the new location.

How To: Reassociate Moved Data Sources

1. Select the data source in the Data Sources explorer, and click

   ▣ (Manage paths of file data sources).
2. In the File Data Source Reconnection dialog box, click

   [...] (Browse) under the New column, as shown in Figure 2–26. Locate and select the file.

Figure 2–26

- This must be done for every proposal in which the data source is located.
- If more than one file is listed under the source data and both are located in the same directory, the paths for the additional files in the File Data Source Reconnection dialog box should automatically be populated.

General Information

In the *General* area at the top of the Data Source Configuration dialog box, every layer includes a *Name*, *Description*, *Source*, and *Type* field, as shown in Figure 2–27. The *Description* and the *Type* are usually the only two fields required to input information in the *General* area.

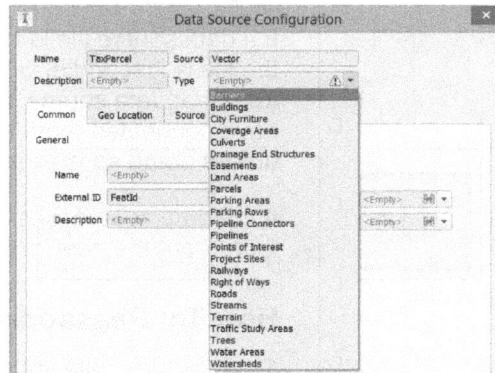

Figure 2–27

The *Type* field is the most important field in the *General* area. It determines the table and other settings that become available for the data source. Once the type has been configured in a model, it cannot be changed. The available configuration types are as follows:

• Barriers	• Pipelines
• Building	• Points of Interest
• City Furniture	• Project Sites
• Coverage Areas	• Railways
• Culverts	• Right of Ways
• Drainage End Structures	• Roads
• Easements	• Streams
• Land Areas (Only available with A360)	• Terrain
• Parcels	• Traffic Study Areas
• Parking Areas	• Trees
• Parking Rows	• Water Areas
• Pipeline Connectors	• Watersheds

Common Tab

The *Common* tab (shown in Figure 2–28) maps database fields to specific model properties and sets the styles to display the data source features.

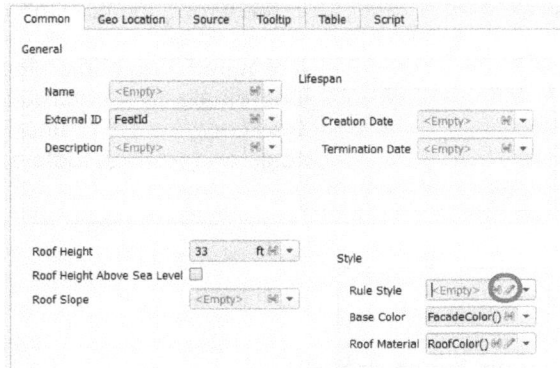

Figure 2–28

How To: Select a Style for Data Source Features

1. In the *Style* field, click ✎ (Style Chooser), as shown in Figure 2–28. Select the required style in the Select Style dialog box, as shown in Figure 2–29.

Figure 2–29

2. Click **OK**.

Geo Location Tab

The *Geo Location* tab (shown in Figure 2–30) sets the source data's original geographic coordinate system. It is important to ensure that the *Coordinate System* field is correct because it is used to project the source data to the model coordinate system. If the wrong coordinate system is selected, the features display in the wrong location in the model.

If required, you can change the coordinate system using the Coordinate System drop-down list. Additional commands in the *Geo Location* tab enable you to manually set the insertion point, scale and rotation factors, or interactively place the data source.

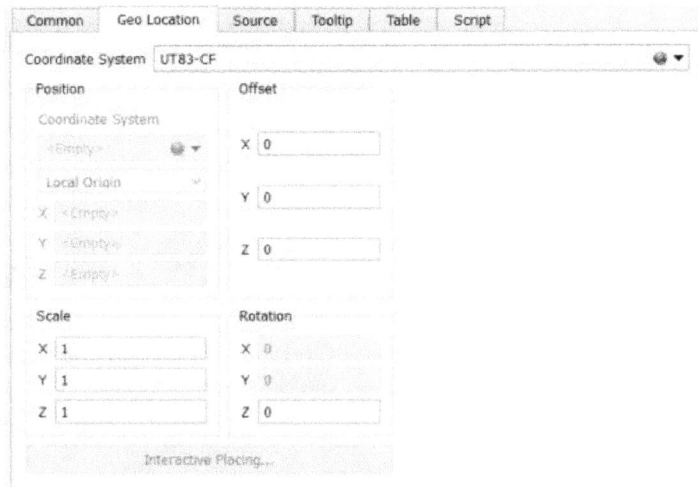

Figure 2–30

Source Tab

Clipping to the model extents helps keep the file size down.

The *Source* tab, imports a subset of the original data by creating a source filter. The source filter can be a property filter or location filter. If the option to **Clip to model extent** is selected, the source data is automatically trimmed to the model extents.

The *Source* tab also enables you to control whether features are placed at a set elevation according to a property, or draped on the terrain surface. The following three options are available for the elevation.

Option	Description
Don't drape	Features are not assigned an elevation. Instead they are imported at the elevation at which they were originally created.
Drape	Feature elevations are automatically taken from the terrain surface elevations.
Set Elevation	Enables you to select a field in the data table to be used to set the elevation.

If you are importing a source file that consists of polylines, you can select the option to **Convert closed polylines to polygons**, as shown in Figure 2–31.

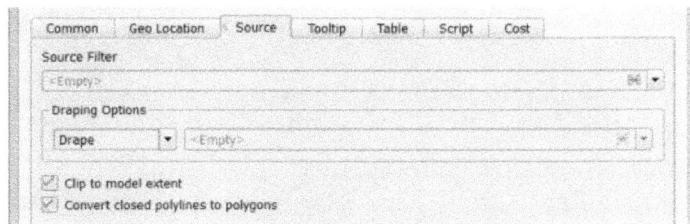

Figure 2–31

Tooltip Tab

The *Tooltip* tab temporarily labels a model element by displaying a selected property when the cursor hovers over a feature. Figure 2–32 shows the name of a city when the cursor hovers over any part of the city. Additionally, hyperlinks can be added to link features to a specific web page or other files.

Tooltips are automatically added to data obtained from Model Builder.

Figure 2–32

How To: Add a Tooltip to a Data Source

1. In the *Tooltip* tab, select the *Html* tab, and click 🏷️ (Insert Property).
2. In the Select Property dialog box, select the property that you want to display, as shown in Figure 2–33.

Figure 2–33

3. Click **OK**.

Table Tab

The *Table* tab maps (connects) fields from the original GIS data source database to the list of properties for the current data type. You must map any key fields that you plan to use later for stylizing and analyzing the model. In the example shown in Figure 2–34, the current market value (**MKT CNTVAL**) is mapped to the *User Data* property for a parcel coverage. This data can be used to display the coverage, with various fill patterns or colors, according to the property value.

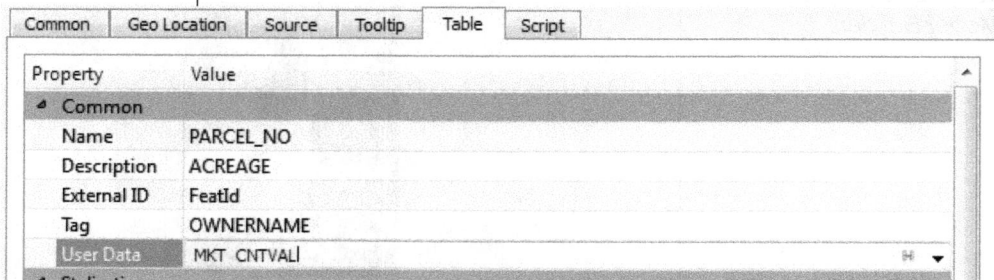

Figure 2–34

Script Tab

The *Script* tab specifies advanced import settings using JavaScript. The example script (shown in Figure 2–35) varies the style for streets based on their values for the *Elevation* property.

```
 1  function Process() {
 2      ROADS.ELEV_FROM = SOURCE.ElevStart;
 3      ROADS.ELEV_TO = SOURCE.ElevEnd;
 4      ROADS.LANES_BACKWARD = SOURCE.LanesTo;
 5      ROADS.LANES_FORWARD = SOURCE.LanesFrom;
 6      ROADS.NAME = SOURCE.Name;
 7      if ((ROADS.ELEV_FROM > 0) || (ROADS.ELEV_TO > 0)){
 8          ROADS.RULE_STYLE = "DefaultStreetStyles:Bridge0";
 9      if ((ROADS.ELEV_FROM > 0) || (ROADS.ELEV_TO > 0)){
10          ROADS.RULE_STYLE = "DefaultStreetStyles:Tunnel0";
11      } else {
12          ROADS.RULE_STYLE = "DefaultStreetStyles:Street0";
13      }
14  }
```

Figure 2–35

Converter Tab

The *Converter* tab (shown in Figure 2–36) is only available for terrain data source types. You can convert vector data, such as contours, into raster data by converting it to a grid and setting the grid size. The grid sizes must be between 0.5 and 500 meters. If the grid is too small, the model generation slows down. If the grid is too large there is a loss of detail in the terrain layer.

Geo Location	Source	Converter

☑ Convert to grid

Grid values

Grid size: 10

Please note:

The value of the grid size must be between 0.5 and 500 meters.
Choosing a **too small** grid size (under 2 m) can considerably slow down the model generation.
Choosing a **too big** grid size might lead to loss of terrain detail.

Figure 2–36

Expressions

Expressions are required when mapping a database field that does not directly match a property in the model. For example, the source data might list the number of floors or stories in a building, but not the actual roof height. To display the building with an accurate roof height, you need to create an expression in the *Roof Height* field that multiplies the number of floors by an average floor height.

How To: Create an Expression

1. In the Data Source Configuration dialog box, select the tab containing the field that you want to calculate (e.g., *Common*, *Table*, etc.).
2. In the field next to the property that you want to calculate, click ⊞ (Expression Editor), as shown in Figure 2–37.

Note: If ⊞ (Expression Editor) is not displayed, select the field to make it display.

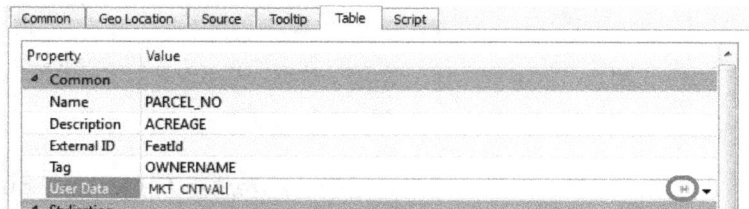

Figure 2–37

3. In the Expression Editor, create a simple numeric expression, as shown in Figure 2–38:

- Select a property in the expanded Property list.
- Select an operation in the expanded Operator list.
- Enter the value by which to modify the property.

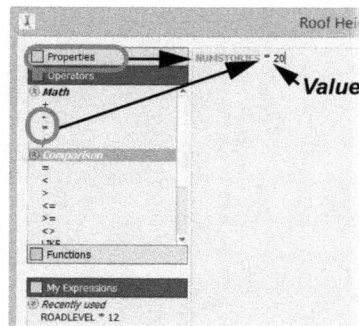

Figure 2–38

4. Click **OK**.

Model Explorer

Using the Model Explorer, you can hide/display, lock/unlock, and highlight layers that have been added to the model, such as shape files, raster images, and DEM files. You can also filter the data that is displayed to focus on a specific attribute, or to only display data in a specific area. To display the Model Explorer, in the In Canvas tools, click ▢ (Build, manage, and analyze your industry model)> ▣ (Create and manage your model)> ▢ (Model Explorer) or in the Utility Bar, click ▢ (Control visibility, display, and selectability of features).

In the Model Explorer, layers are listed on the left with icons on the right identifying their display and select-ability status, as shown in Figure 2–39.

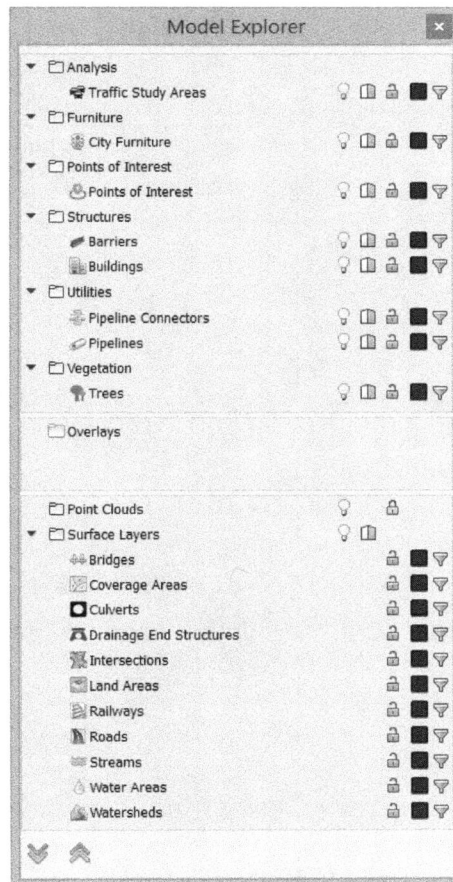

Figure 2–39

The icons in the Model Explorer are described as follows.

Icon	Purpose
(Display/Hide Layers)	Indicates whether the layer is displayed in the model. Yellow indicates that the layer is displayed in the model, while gray indicates that the layer is hidden.
(Level of Detail)	Specifies the level of detail displayed for various layers according to the zoom distance. Higher levels display more detail while lower levels display less detail. By default, *Level of Detail* is set to **Adaptive**, which displays objects that are closer with more detail and objects that are further away with less detail.
(Selectable/ Unselectable)	Makes items in the layer selectable when the lock is in the open position. When the lock is in the closed position, the layer cannot be selected.
(Highlight)	Highlights the layer features in the model. Note: The highlight is only used for identification. Highlighting a layer does not mean it has been selected for editing.
(Create Subset)	Filters the layer to only display the number of features that you specify.

Practice 2d

Configure Source Data for Display

Practice Objectives

Estimated time for completion: 45 minutes

- Display connected GIS data in the model.
- Set the model extents for the new model.

In the previous practice, you imported multiple data sources. In the Data Sources palette, the data is separated into three categories: *No Feature Type*, *Ground Imagery*, and *Terrain*. All of the DEM files are under the **Terrain** layer and can be configured at the same time. All of the Aerial Images are under **Ground Imagery** and can also be configured at the same time. However, all of the shape files are listed in the *No Feature Type* category and must be configured individually.

Task 1 - Configure terrain source data.

In this task you will configure the new DEM files for display.

1. Continue working in the same model as the last practice or open **CreateModel.sqlite** from the practice files *.../ModelExplorer* folder. Switch to the **D_Task1** proposal.

2. If the Data Sources explorer is not displayed, in the In Canvas tools, click ![icon] (Build, manage, and analyze your infrastructure model) > ![icon] (Create and manage your model)> ![icon] (Data Sources).

3. In the Data Sources explorer under *Terrain*, double-click on the **DEMs**[1] layer to configure all of the DEMs at the same time.

---

1. ((AGRC), Utah Automated Geographic Reference Center, 2007)

4. Note that *Type* is set to **Terrain** automatically. In the *Geo Location* tab, ensure that the *Coordinate System* is set to **Harn/12.UTM-12**, as shown in Figure 2–40.

The Coordinate System was set automatically because a projection file was included with the DEM file.

Figure 2–40

5. On the *Raster* tab, select the **Clip to Model Extent** option, as shown in Figure 2–41.

Figure 2–41

You might not notice a difference unless you started from the blank model created in Practice 2a.

6. Click **Close & Refresh** to display the terrain in the model.

Task 2 - Configure image source data.

In this task, you will configure a higher quality image for display in the project area.

1. Continue working in the same model as the last task. Switch to the **D_Task2** proposal.

2. On the Utility Bar, click ▣ (Bookmark your current location) and select **Image Quality**.

3. In the Data Sources explorer under *Ground Imagery*, double-click on the **Images** layer to open the Data Source Configuration dialog box.

4. Ensure that *Type* is set to **Ground Imagery**[1]. In the *Geo Location* tab, ensure that the *Coordinate System* is set to **UTM83-12**, as shown in Figure 2–42.

The coordinate systems often vary for different data sources, depending on who created them and when.

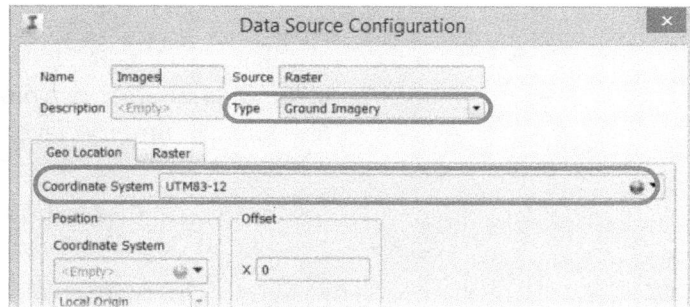

Figure 2–42

5. On the *Raster* tab, ensure that the option is selected to **Clip to Model Extents.**

6. Click **Close & Refresh** to display the images in the model. The quality of the new image is much better than the one inserted by the Model Builder, as shown in Figure 2–43.

*Since nothing changed in the Data Source Configuration dialog box, you could have also selected **Images** and clicked (Refresh data source).*

Figure 2–43

---

1. ((AGRC), Automated Geographic Reference Center, 2012)

Task 3 - Add tags to data sources.

In this task, you will take advantage of tags as you configure data sources for display.

1. Continue working in the same model as the last task. Switch to the **D_Task3** proposal.

2. On the ViewCube, click 🏠 (Home) to view the entire model.

3. In the Data Sources explorer, double-click on the **MunicipalBoundary**[1] layer to open the Data Source Configuration dialog box.

4. Set the *Type* to **Coverage Areas**. In the *Geo Location* tab, ensure that *Coordinate System* is set to **UT83-CF**.

5. In the *Source* tab, set the *Draping Options* to **Drape** and select the **Clip to model extent** option, as shown in Figure 2–44.

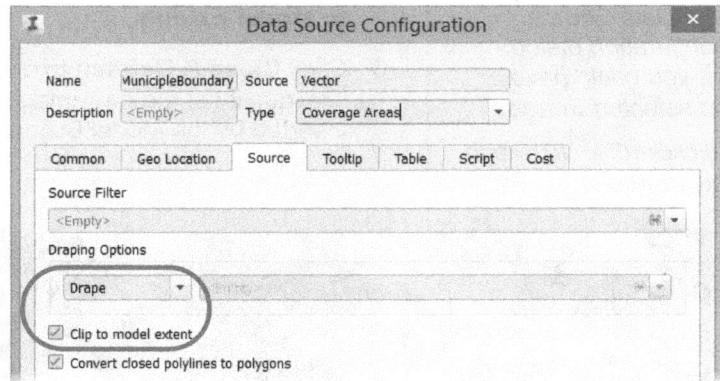

Figure 2–44

6. In the *Common* tab, in the *Rule Style* field, click ✎ (Style Chooser)

*The Boundary style was created for these practices. Therefore, it does not exist outside of the **CreateModel.sqlite** model.*

7. In the Select Style / Color window, in the *Coverage* tab, select **Boundary** for the style, as shown in Figure 2–45. Click **OK**.

---

1. (Department, GIS Division of the Utah County Information Systems, 2013)

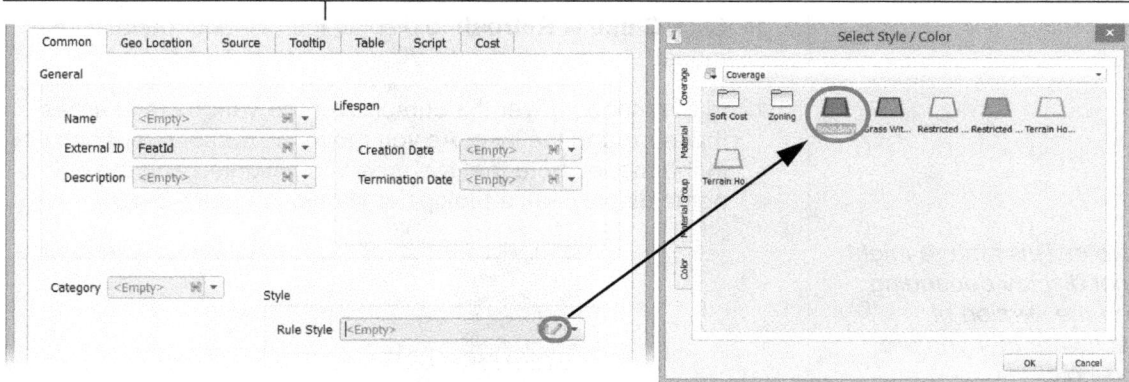

Figure 2–45

8. In the *Table* tab, set the following parameters, as shown in Figure 2–46:

   - *Name:* **NAME**
   - *Description:* **TYPE**

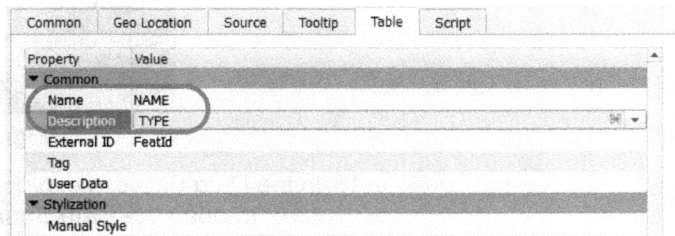

Figure 2–46

9. In the *Tooltip* tab, select the *Html* tab and click in the content area. Click [image] (Insert Property).

10. In the Select Property dialog box, expand the drop-down box and select **Name**, as shown in Figure 2–47. Click **OK**.

If green text does not display in the Tooltip script area (as shown below), the Tooltips will not work.

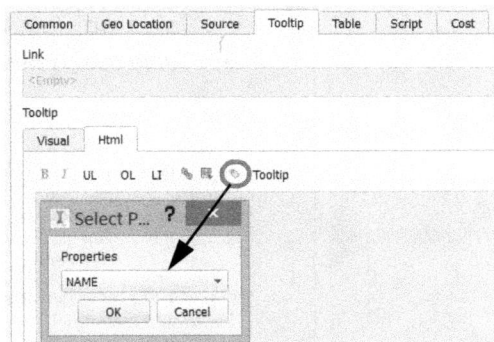

Figure 2–47

11. Click **Close & Refresh** to display the city boundaries in the model.

12. In the model, hover the cursor over the various land areas that surround the lake. As you move the cursor over each city in the model, note that the area is highlighted and the city name displays as a tooltip, as shown in Figure 2–48.

Note: This feature might not display depending on the version of software that you are using.

Figure 2–48

13. In the Data Sources explorer, double-click on the **TaxParcel**[1] layer to open the Data Source Configuration dialog box. Set the following parameters, as shown in Figure 2–49:

- *Type:* **Coverage Areas**
- *Geo Location* tab, *Coordinate System:* **UT83-CF**
- *Source* tab, *Draping Options:* **Drape**
- *Source* tab: **Clip to model extent**
- *Table* tab, *Name:* **PARCEL_NO**
- *Table* tab, *Description:* **ACREAGE**
- *Table* tab, *Tag:* **OWNERNAME**
- *Table* tab, *User Data:* **MKT_CNTVAL**

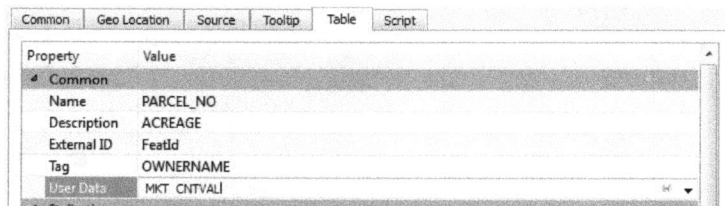

Figure 2–49

1. (Department, GIS Division of the Utah County Information Systems, 2013)

14. In the *Tooltip* tab, select the *Html* tab. Click 🏷 (Insert Property).

15. In the Select Property dialog box, expand the drop-down box and select **TAG**, as shown in Figure 2–50. Click **OK**.

Figure 2–50

16. Click **Close & Refresh** to display the parcel boundaries in the model. Note: Because a style was not set, it will display as though nothing has changed in the model. However, when you move the cursor over the terrain, the parcels of land highlight as shown in Figure 2–51.

Figure 2–51

Task 4 - Display data sources using expressions.

In this task, you will take advantage of expressions as you configure data sources for display.

1. Continue working in the same model as the last task. Switch to the **D_Task4** proposal.

2. On the ViewCube, click ⬒ (Home) to view the entire model.

3. In the Data Sources explorer, double-click on the **RoadCenterline**[1] layer to open the Data Source Configuration dialog box. Set the following parameters:
   - *Type:* **Roads**
   - *Geo Location* tab, *Coordinate System*: **UT83-CF**
   - *Source* tab, *Draping Options*: **Drape**
   - *Source* tab: **Clip to model extent**

4. In the *Common* tab, in the *Elevation Offset* field, click
   ⬚ (Expression Editor).

5. In the Expression Editor, expand Properties>*Numeric* and double-click **ROADLEVEL**, as shown in Figure 2–52.

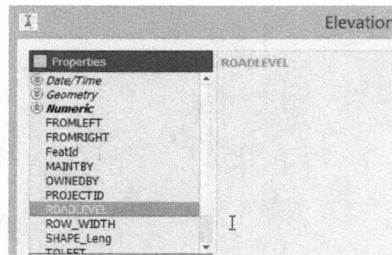

Figure 2–52

---

1. (Department, GIS Division of the Utah County Information Systems, 2013)

The ROADLEVEL field has three values: -1, 0, and 1. Multiplying it by 12 sets the elevation to 12 feet above or below ground level (used for overpasses or underpasses), or drapes on the terrain for zero values.

6. In the *Expression* area, after **ROADLEVEL**, type ***12,** as shown in Figure 2–53.

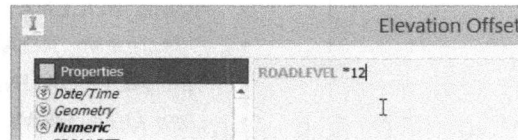

Figure 2–53

7. Click **OK**.

8. In the *Common* tab, in the *Rule Style* field, click ✎ (Style Chooser).

9. In the Select Style window, in the *Road* tab, for the style select **Sidewalk and Greenspace**, as shown in Figure 2–54. Click **OK**.

Figure 2–54

In the next step, you will map the data fields in the connected data base file to the fields created by the Autodesk InfraWorks 360 data scheme. This step is important if you plan to use the database information to label or analyze the model. In this case, you will map the *Roadclass* database field to the *Description* field so that you can use that information to set Style Rules later.

10. On the *Table* tab, set the following parameters, as shown in Figure 2–55:

- *Name:* **FULLNAME**
- *Description:* **ROADCLASS**
- *Tag:* **ALTROADNAM**
- *User Data:* **ROW_WIDTH**

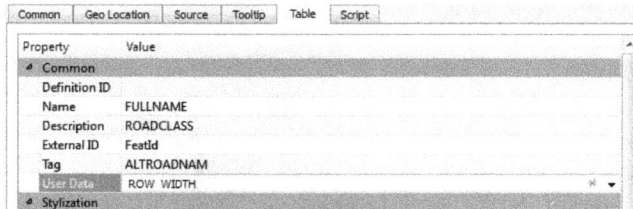

Figure 2–55

11. In the *Tooltip* tab, select the *Html* tab, and click ⬚ (Insert Property). In the Select Property dialog box, select **NAME** and click **OK**.

12. Click **Close & Refresh** to display the road centerlines in the model. If you started the model using Model Builder, it is likely that roads already existed in the model which causes confusion regarding which roads to display, as shown in Figure 2–56. In cases like this, it is best to remove one or the other sets of roads. Since we plan to use the information in the database to set road styles later, we need to remove the roads created in Model Builder.

Figure 2–56

These are the roads added by Model Builder.

13. In the Data Sources explorer under *Roads*, select **roads** and click ✖ (remove data source).

14. In the Data Sources explorer, double-click on the **BuildingFootprint**[1] layer to open the Data Source Configuration dialog box. Set the following parameters:
    - *Type:* **Buildings**
    - *Geo Location* tab, *Coordinate System:* **UT83-CF**
    - *Common* tab, *Roof Height:* **20**
    - *Source* tab, *Draping Options:* **Drape**
    - *Source* tab: **Clip to model extent**

15. Click **Close & Refresh** to display the buildings in the model, as shown in Figure 2–57. Use the mouse and/or ViewCube to view the model from different angles.

Figure 2–57

Task 5 - Set the model extents.

The model that you have configured includes several cities. The project you will create is a multi-use development on the west side of the lake. The development will connect to the east side of the lake using a bridge. To focus on the area of interest and trim the data to this area, you will set the model extents.

1. (Department, GIS Division of the Utah County Information Systems, 2013)

1. In the model, move the cursor around and note how the coordinates change in the bottom left corner of the model area, as shown in Figure 2–58. The minimum and maximum X,Y values required for the model determine the values you will set for the model extents.

Model coordinates (X, Y, and Z) at the cursor location

X: 1529473.217353 Y: 7267597.802425 Z: 5270.229904 ft

Figure 2–58

2. In the In Canvas tools, click ✖ (Settings)> ▦ (Model Properties).

3. In the Model Properties dialog box, clear the **Use Entire Model** option. Set the following parameters, as shown in Figure 2–59:

Field	X	Y
Minimum	1532500	7267000
Maximum	1543000	7274500

Alternatively, you could have chosen to define the extents using a bounding box or polyline.

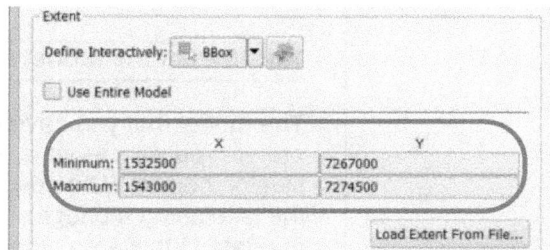

Figure 2–59

4. Click **Apply** and **OK**. The model will adjust to its new extents, as shown in Figure 2–60.

Note that the model does not need to be saved as it has been automatically saved while you were working.

Figure 2–60

Task 6 - Hide model elements.

In this task you will hide and lock a specific layer to help focus on the project area.

1. In the Utility Bar, click ▣ (Bookmark your current location). Select **Project Area** to return to the previously-saved view where the project will be focused. Note: When you hover the cursor over an area, a parcel is highlighted instead of the city outline.

2. In the Utility Bar, click ▣ (Control visibility, display, and selectability of features). Note: The Surface Layers are combined to make it easier to control all of them at the same time. This includes the DEM files, images, and other GIS data that was imported into the model.

3. In the Model Explorer panel, right-click on **Surface Layers** and select **Surface Layers** (as shown in Figure 2–61) to manage the surface layers separately.

Figure 2–61

---

4. In the Manage Surface Layers dialog box, click 💡 to the right of the **TaxParcels** layer to toggle it off, as shown in Figure 2–62.

Figure 2–62

5. Click **Apply** then **OK**.

6. Move the cursor over the model and note that the city is highlighted rather than the parcel.

Task 7 - Lock the existing GIS layers.

1. In the Utility Bar, click 🔲 (Bookmark your current location) and select **Buildings**.

2. In the Utility Bar, click 🔲 (Edit).

3. In the model, select one of the buildings. Note that the bottom of the building has gizmos that enable you to edit it, as shown in Figure 2–63. Press <Esc> to clear the selection of the building.

Figure 2–63

4. In the Model Explorer panel, click 🔓 to the right of the **Buildings** layer.

5. Try to select a building in the model. Note that the buildings can no longer be selected.

6. Close the model.

Chapter Review Questions

1. Why is the source data not displayed once it has been imported into the model?

   a. By default, it is toggled off in the Model Explorer.

   b. It needs to be configured before it can be displayed.

   c. The graphics card is not powerful enough to display the data.

   d. It might be hidden under another data source.

2. How can you determine whether the GIS data is usable for your project's needs? (Select all that apply)

   a. Communicate with the owner of the GIS data source.

   b. Download and read the metadata included with the GIS data source.

   c. Connect to the data in the AutoCAD Map 3D or AutoCAD Civil 3D software to preview the data and its data table before importing it into the Autodesk InfraWorks 360 model.

   d. There is no way of determining its usability.

3. Which of the following types is not available as an option when configuring data sources?

   a. Barriers

   b. Bridges

   c. Buildings

   d. Railways

4. Which configuration tab would you use to drape data on a terrain surface?

   a. *Common*

   b. *Geo Location*

   c. *Source*

   d. *Script*

5. Which configuration tab would you use to display feature attributes in the model as you hover the cursor over them?

a. *Common*

b. *Source*

c. *Table*

d. *Tooltip*

6. Why is it important to set both the model coordinate system and the data source coordinate system?

a. So that the software can automatically re-project the data sources for you and make everything line up with the correct insertion point, scale factor, and rotation value.

b. So that the correct units (feet or meters) display in the model.

c. So that the visual styles for the data sources all coordinate with the project.

d. You only have to set one or the other, not both.

Command Summary

Button	Command	Location
⚙	Application Options	• **Home Screen** • **In Canvas Tools:** Settings and Utilities
🗄	Data Sources	• **In Canvas Tools:** Build, manage, and analyze your infrastructure model> Create and manage your model
N/A	Deselect	• **Shortcut Key:** <Esc>
▨	Edit	• **Utility Bar**
🔒	Layer Lock/ Unlock	• **Palette:** Model Explorer
💡	Layer On/Off	• **Palette:** Model Explorer
▣	Model Explorer	• **Utility Bar** • **In Canvas Tools:** Build, manage, and analyze your infrastructure model> Create and manage your model
▤	Model Properties	• **In Canvas Tools:** Settings and Utilities
N/A	New Model	• **Home Screen**
N/A	Select All	• **Shortcut Key:** <Ctrl>+<A>
▨ / ▨	Surface Layers	• **Palette:** Data Sources and Model Explorer (Right-click Surface Layers) • **In Canvas Tools:** Build, manage, and analyze your infrastructure model> Create and manage your model

Stylize Data Sources

Model features are thought of as a single category. However, it might occasionally be necessary to display features in the same data source differently. For example, an interstate typically has more lanes than a local road. Additionally, a local road often has a sidewalk and lamp posts running along side, while an interstate does not have these design elements. In this chapter, you learn how to use scripts, expressions, and style rules to display data sources according to information connected to the model (i.e., in database fields). You also learn how to override style rules to manually change the display of specific features. If the required style is not available, it might be necessary to create a custom style to suit the project's needs. You learn how to create and share styles from one project to another.

Learning Objectives in this Chapter

- Display a data source according to specific data in the database that is connected to the feature.
- Change the style of selected features to override any style rules being used.
- Create/edit styles in catalogs.
- Share style catalogs with other users.

3.1 Using Multiple Styles to Display Features

You have learned how to select one style for an entire data source during the data configuration process. In the *Common* tab of the Data Configuration dialog box (shown in Figure 3–1), you used ✎ (Style Chooser) in the *Rule Style* field to select one style for the entire data source.

Figure 3–1

Alternatively, you can set the style for a data source subset by clicking ⊞ (Expression Editor) in the *Rule Style* field (shown in Figure 3–2).

Figure 3–2

Create Filter Expressions

To automatically stylize a feature based on the connected database data, you must create an expression. The Create Filter Expression dialog box enables you to create two types of filter expressions:

- Location Filters

- Property Filters

Location Filters

In the Create Filter Expression dialog box, click **Spatial**. The five types of location boundaries available are described as follows:

Disjoint	Selects all features that do not overlap the shape you draw.
Inside	Selects all features that do not overlap the shape you draw.
Intersects	Selects all features that intersect with the shape you draw.
Overlaps	Selects all features that overlap any part of the shape you draw.
Within	Selects all features within the shape you draw but are not touching the edges of the shape.

Property Filters

In the Create Filter Expression dialog box, click **Properties**, and select a property from the list. The available properties vary according to the database fields that are connected to the data source. After selecting a property, you need to set the values in the data field that you want to use to define the style. An operator is required to help filter the list of values. Some of the available comparison operators are shown in Figure 3–3.

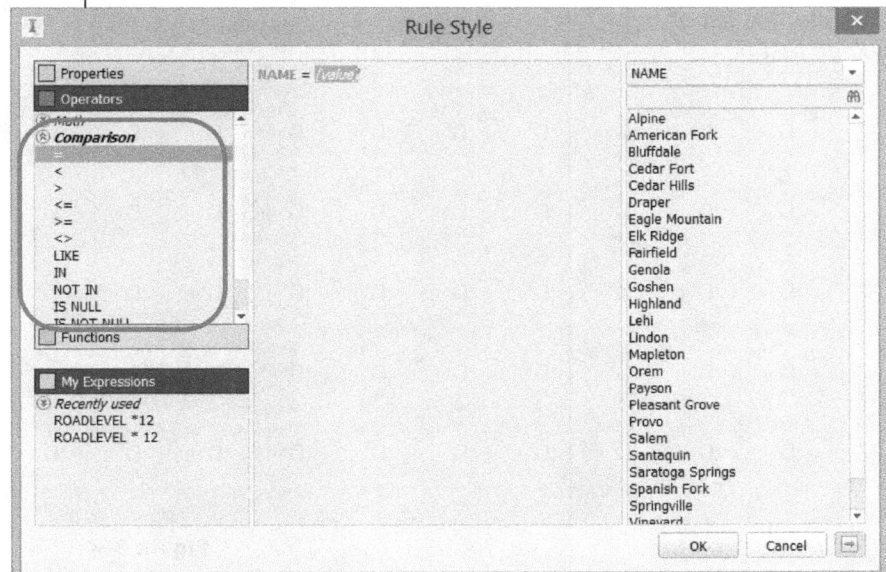

Figure 3–3

Find Available Values

It is important to determine which values are available in each property to determine which operator to use. You can determine the available values in a property by clicking ➡️ (Show/Hide the Values pane) in the Create Filter Expression dialog box. If you have selected a numeric property, you can use operators, such as **greater than**, **less than**, or **equal to**, to refine the selection. If a text property is selected, you must use a text operator, such as **Like**, **Not Like**, or **Null**. These and other operators are accessed by clicking **Operators** in the Create Filter Expression dialog box.

How To: Find Available Values

1. In the Create Filter Expression dialog box, click ➡️ (Show/Hide Values Pane) to display the Values pane.
2. In the Values pane, select a property to retrieve from the drop-down list, as shown in Figure 3–4. The list of available values displays.

If required, you can filter the list of values by entering keywords into the Filter the list of values text box.

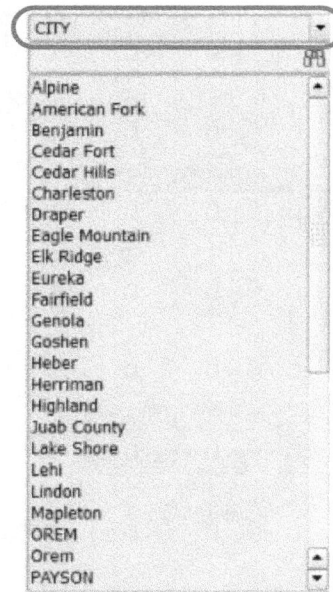

Figure 3–4

3. Select a value from the list and double-click on it to populate the value in the expression editor, as shown in Figure 3–5.

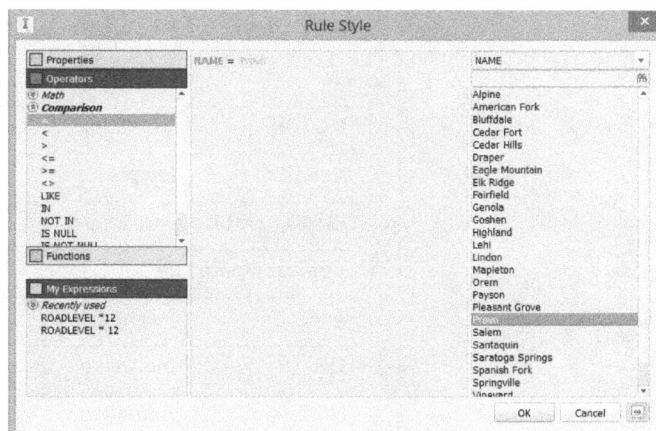

Figure 3–5

Operators

There are four groups of operators: **Math**, **Comparison**, **Logical**, and **Other**. The available operators are described as follows:

Math Operators

+	**Add**	Sums numerical properties.
-	**Subtract**	Subtracts numerical properties.
*	**Multiply**	Multiplies numerical properties.
/	**Divide**	Divides numerical properties.

Comparison Operators

=	**Equal To**	Text or numerical properties hold an exact value.
<	**Less Than**	Numerical properties are less than an exact value.
>	**Greater Than**	Numerical properties are greater than an exact value.
<=	**Less Than or Equal To**	Numerical properties are less than or equal to an exact value.
>=	**Greater Than or Equal To**	Numerical properties are greater than or equal to an exact value.
<>	**Not Equal To**	Does not equal a specific value.
LIKE	**Matching**	Text matches a pattern.

NOT LIKE	Not Matching	Text does not match a pattern.
IN	Equal To Any	Matches any value in a list.
NOT IN	Not Equal To Any	Does not match any value in a list.
IS NULL	Empty	Returns if property is empty.
IS NOT NULL	Not Empty	Returns if property has any value.

Logical Operators

AND	Exclusive	Must meet all conditions.
OR	Inclusive	Matches any one of the conditions.
NOT	Selective	Negates the expression.

Other

()	Group	Group the Selection in Parentheses.

How To: Create a Filter Expression

1. In the Create Filter Expression dialog box, expand Properties and select the property containing the appropriate values, as shown in Figure 3–6.

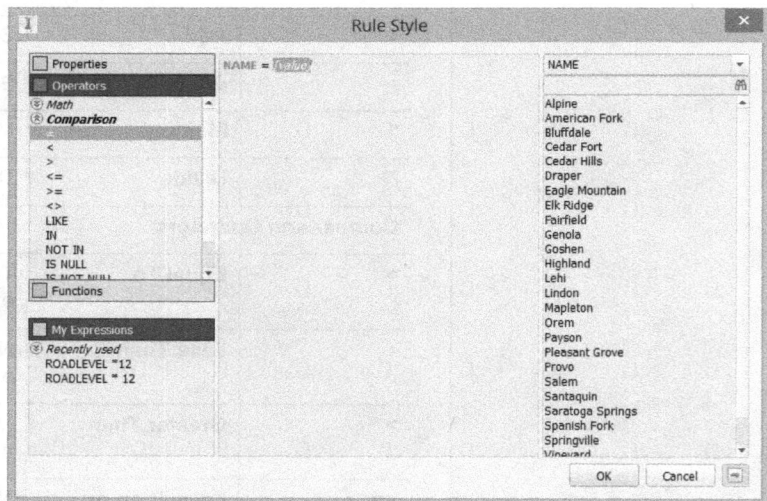

Figure 3–6

2. Select an appropriate operator, as shown in Figure 3–6.

3. In the Create Filter Expression dialog box, click

   ![] (Show/Hide Values Pane) to display the Values pane.

4. In the Values pane, in the drop-down list, select the required property, as shown in Figure 3–7.

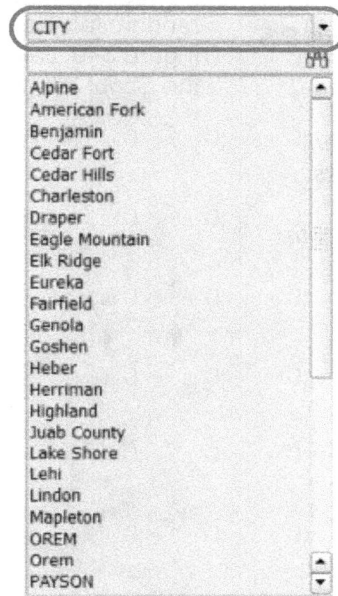

Figure 3–7

5. Select the value from the list and double-click on it to populate the value in the expression editor, as shown in Figure 3–8.

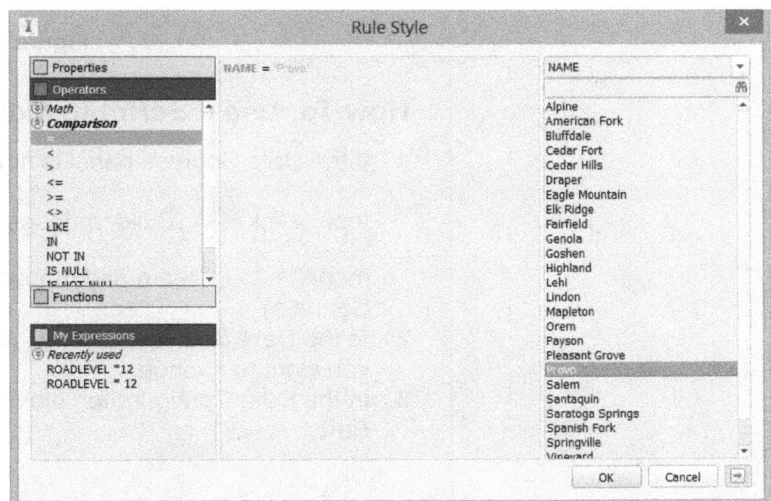

Figure 3–8

Using Scripts to Set Multiple Feature Styles

Custom scripts for an Autodesk InfraWorks 360 model can be created by anyone with a knowledge of JavaScript.

Scripts can be used to assign multiple styles simultaneously for one data source. For example, this can happen when you import a building's data source into the model. The buildings use random facade and roof colors from a default script, as shown in Figure 3–9. JavaScript® is used to create scripts that are used in the *Script* tab, in the Data Configuration dialog box.

Figure 3–9

How To: Use a Script to Modify Feature Styles

1. If the Data Sources panel is not displayed, in the In Canvas tools, click ▮ (Build, manage, and analyze your industry model)>▩ (Create and manage your model)>▤ (Data Sources).
2. In the Data Sources explorer, double-click on the layer that you want to change.
3. In the Data Configuration dialog box, in the *Script* tab, click **Edit**.

4. Using JavaScript, make the required changes. Figure 3–10 shows a script that varies the road styles based on the property value for *Elevation*.

```
1  function Process() {
2     ROADS.ELEV_FROM = SOURCE.ElevStart;
3     ROADS.ELEV_TO = SOURCE.ElevEnd;
4     ROADS.LANES_BACKWARD = SOURCE.LanesTo;
5     ROADS.LANES_FORWARD = SOURCE.LanesFrom;
6     ROADS.NAME = SOURCE.Name;
7     if ((ROADS.ELEV_FROM > 0) || (ROADS.ELEV_TO > 0)){
8        ROADS.RULE_STYLE = "DefaultStreetStyles:Bridge0".
9     if ((ROADS.ELEV_FROM > 0) || (ROADS.ELEV_TO > 0)){
10       ROADS.RULE_STYLE = "DefaultStreetStyles:Tunnel0".
11    } else {
12       ROADS.RULE_STYLE = "DefaultStreetStyles:Street0".
13    }
14 }
```

Figure 3–10

5. Click **Close & Refresh** to display the changes in the model.

Create Style Rules

You can also use style rules to modify how features display in the model according to data connected to each feature. Style rules override anything that was set during the data configuration process. Each feature class is stylized separately and has a tab in the Style Rules dialog box. In the example shown in Figure 3–11, the *Roads* class tab is active and six rules are listed.

Figure 3–11

Each class of features is stylized separately using expressions. Expressions can use values from source data fields or a location to stylize features. Once an expression has been created, a style is assigned to the rule.

How To: Create a New Style Rule

1. In the In Canvas tools, click ![icon] (Build, manage, and analyze your industry model)> ![icon] (Create and manage your model)> ![icon] (Style Rules). Select the required tab.

2. At the top of the Style Rules dialog box, click ✛ (Add a new Rule).

3. In the Add Rule Style dialog box, type a name, as shown in Figure 3–12. Click **OK**.

Figure 3–12

4. In the Style Rules dialog box, select the new rule and click ![icon] (Edit properties).

5. In the Rule Editor, in the *Expression* area, click ![icon] (Edit), as shown in Figure 3–13.

Figure 3–13

6. In the Create Filter Expression dialog box, define the required expression and click **OK**.

7. In the Rule Editor dialog box, in the *Styles* area, click ✛ (Add an existing style), as shown in Figure 3–14.

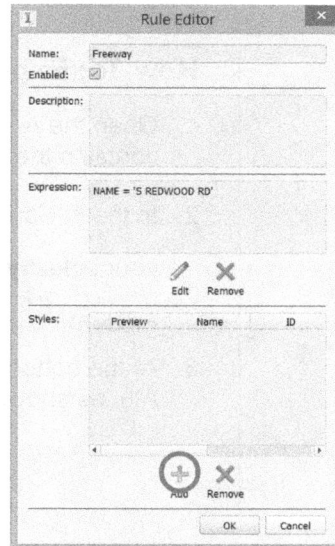

Figure 3–14

8. In the Select Style dialog box, in the *Road* tab, select a style, as shown in Figure 3–15. Click **OK**.

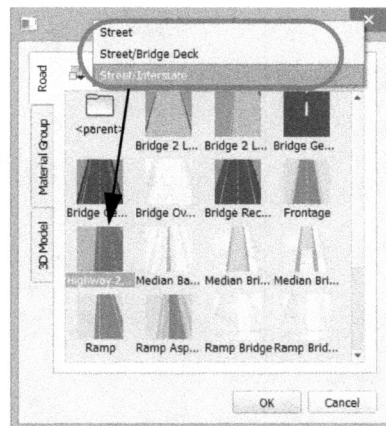

Figure 3–15

9. In the Rule Editor, click **OK** to return to the Style Rules dialog box.

10. In the Style Rules dialog box, click ▶ (Run Rules) to display the results of the style change.

Reuse/Share Style Rules

If the same rules are used repeatedly to stylize different models, it is possible to save the rules in an .XML file. The .XML file can be reused in other proposals in the same model, or imported into other models.

How To: Export Style Rules

1. Open the Autodesk® InfraWorks® model and proposal that contains the style rules that you want to reuse.

2. In the In Canvas tools, click ▨ (Build, manage, and analyze your industry model)>▨ (Create and manage your model)>▨ (Style Rules) and review the rules.

3. At the bottom of the Style Rules dialog box, click ▷ (Export All), as shown in Figure 3–16.

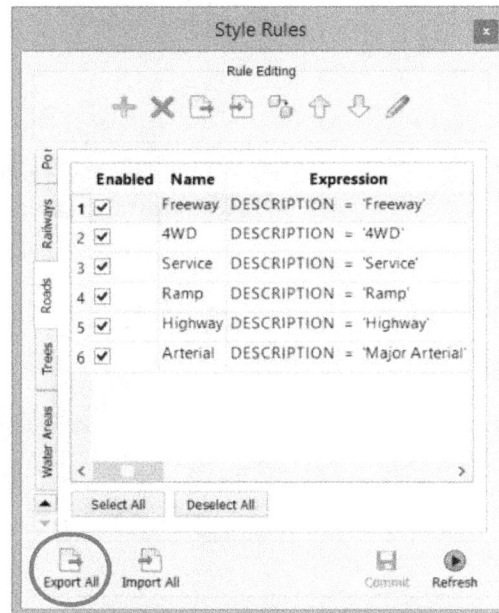

Figure 3–16

4. Select the path and enter a filename for the Style Rules (*.rules.json) file. Click **Save**.
5. Close the Style Rules dialog box.

How To: Import Style Rules

1. Open the Autodesk InfraWorks 360 model to which the style rules are to be imported.

2. In the In Canvas tools, click ![I] (Build, manage, and analyze your industry model)> ![icon] (Create and manage your model)> ![icon] (Style Rules). Review any existing rules.

3. At the bottom of the Style Rules dialog box, click ![icon] (Import All), as shown in Figure 3–17.

Rules in the saved file that have the same name as an existing rule in the model cannot be imported. Therefore, it is important to delete or change the names of any existing rules if you want to use the imported rules.

Figure 3–17

4. Select the path and filename for the Style Rules (*.rules.json) file that contains the required style rules. Click **Open**.
5. Close the Style Rules dialog box.

3.2 Overriding Style Rules

There always seems to be at least one exception to every rule. For example, it is common to stylize roads according to their road classification. However, if the road has a bridge on one of its sections, it might be necessary to override the road classification style given to that section with a bridge style, as shown in Figure 3–18.

Road style set by style rules

Road style overridden manually

Figure 3–18

How To: Change a Style Using the Style Palette

1. In the In Canvas tools, click ▣ (Build, manage, and analyze your industry model)> ▩ (Create and manage your model)> ▦ (Style Palette) and select the appropriate tab for the feature you are changing.
2. Select the style from the preview area and drag and drop it onto the feature to apply the style, as shown in Figure 3–19.

Figure 3–19

3. Close the Style Palette.

How To: Change a Style Using Feature Properties

1. In the model, select the model feature, right-click on the feature, and select **Properties**.
2. In the Properties palette, change the style in the *Manual Style* field, as shown in Figure 3–20.

You can remove a style override by deleting the Manual Style from the Properties palette and updating the model.

Figure 3–20

3. Click **Update** to display the change in the model.

How To: Change a Style Using a Feature's Asset Card

1. In the model, select the model feature.
2. In the feature asset card, click on the Manual Style thumbnail and select a frequently used style or click **More Styles** to select a style from the Select Style Dialog box, as shown in Figure 3–21.

Figure 3–21

3. Click **OK**.

Practice 3a

Estimated time for completion: 20 minutes

Stylize Data Sources

Practice Objective

- Change the visual style assigned to a model feature using scripts, style rules, and style overrides.

Task 1 - Use scripts to change the display of model features.

A default script is currently being used in the model to randomly set the color of the buildings. Additionally, all of the buildings in the model are currently the same height. A JavaScript expert has created a script for you that will randomize the building styles and heights throughout the model. In this task, you will use this script to automatically modify the building styles.

1. In the Home Screen click **Open**.

2. In the *C:\InfraWorks Fundamentals Practice Files\Styles* folder, select **Styles.sqlite** and click **Open**.

3. In the Utility Bar, click ▨ (Bookmark your current location) and select **Buildings**. Ensure that **A_Task1** is the current proposal.

4. If the Data Sources panel is not already displayed, in the In Canvas tools, click ▨ (Build, manage, and analyze your industry model)> ▨ (Create and manage your model)> ▨ (Data Sources).

5. In the Data Sources explorer, double-click on the **BuildingFootprint** layer.

6. In the **Start** menu on your computer, launch Notepad.

7. In the Notepad window, expand the **File** menu and select **Open**.

8. In the *C:\InfraWorks Fundamentals Practice Files\Styles* folder, select **BuildingScript.txt** and click **Open**.

9. Press <Ctrl>+<A> to select all of the contents of the file. Press <Ctrl>+<C> to copy the file contents.

10. Return to the Autodesk InfraWorks 360 software.

11. In the Data Configuration dialog box, in the *Script* tab, click **Edit**.

12. Place the cursor anywhere inside the script area and press <Ctrl>+<A> to select all of the content of the script.

13. Press <Delete> to remove the content of the script.

14. Press <Ctrl>+<V> to paste the contents from the text file into the script area.

*If the buildings do not change styles randomly according to the script, you might need to remove the **BuildingsFootprint** layer from the Data Sources explorer and re-import the buildings.*

15. Click **Close & Refresh** to display the changes in the model. Note that each building now has a different facade (including color and windows), a different height, and a different roof style.

16. Close the Data Sources panel.

Task 2 - Use style rules to change the display of the model features.

The roads in this model are currently only using one style. However, there are a number of different types of roads and many of them follow a similar pattern according to their road class. The **RoadCenterline.shp** file[1] lists each road's classification in a database field called *ROADCLASS*. When the layer was imported and configured, the *ROADCLASS* field was mapped to the *Road Description* property in the *Table* tab, in the Data Source Configuration dialog box. In this task you will use this property to set the styles for the road centerlines.

*If you did not complete the previous task, set the **A_Task2** proposal to current in the Utility Bar.*

1. In the Utility Bar, click ▣ (Bookmark your current location) and select **Road Styles**.

2. In the In Canvas tools, click ▣ (Build, manage, and analyze your industry model)> ▣ (Create and manage your model) > ▣ (Style Rules) and select the *Roads* tab.

You might have to scroll down in the Rule Editing tabs to locate the Road tab. There are several road rules already created.

3. At the top of the Style Rules dialog box, click ✛ (Add a new Rule).

1.(Department, GIS Division of the Utah County Information Systems, 2013)

4. In the Add Rule Style dialog box, type **Freeway**, as shown in Figure 3–22. Click **OK**.

Figure 3–22

5. In the Style Rules dialog box, double-click on **Freeway** to edit the rule.

6. In the Rule Editor, in the expression area, click ✎ (Edit) as shown in Figure 3–23.

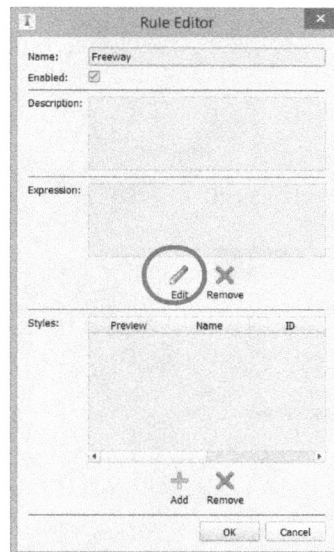

Figure 3–23

7. In the Create Filter Expression dialog box:
   - Expand **Properties**, and under **Common**, double-click on **DESCRIPTION**.
   - Expand **Operators**, and under **Comparison**, double-click on **=**.
   - Click [image] (Show/Hide Values Pane) to display a list of possible properties.
   - Expand the Properties drop-down list, and select **DESCRIPTION**.
   - In the expression area, select **[value]**.
   - In the Values pane, double-click on **Freeway**.
   - Click **OK**, as shown in Figure 3–24.

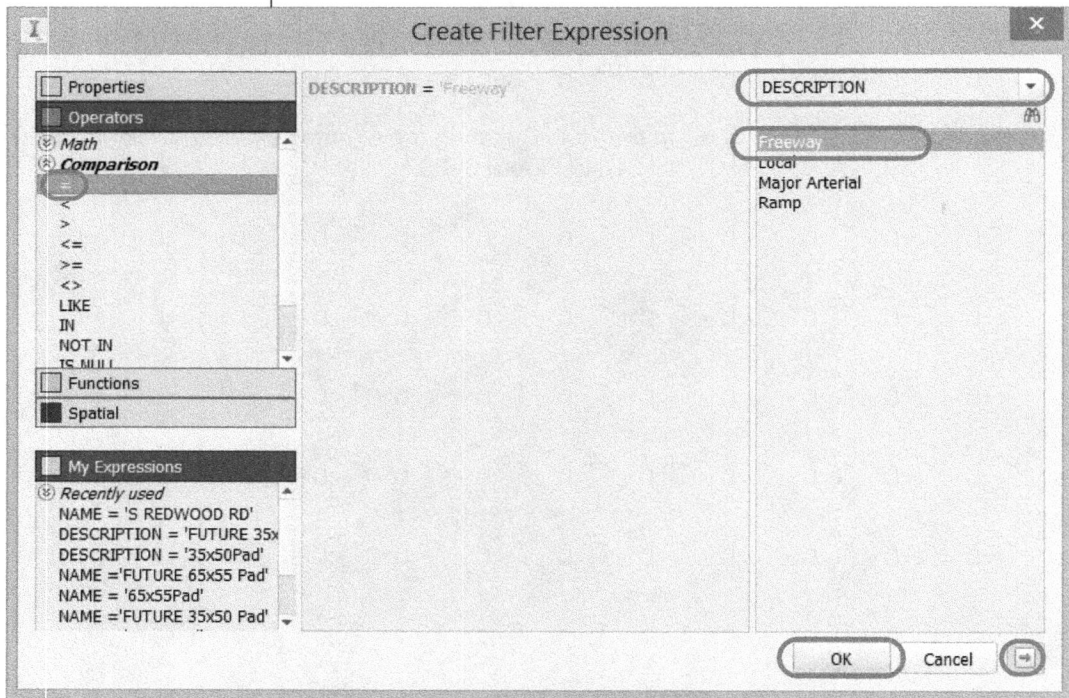

Figure 3–24

8. In the Rule Editor dialog box, in the *Styles* area, click ✛ (Add an existing style), as shown in Figure 3–25.

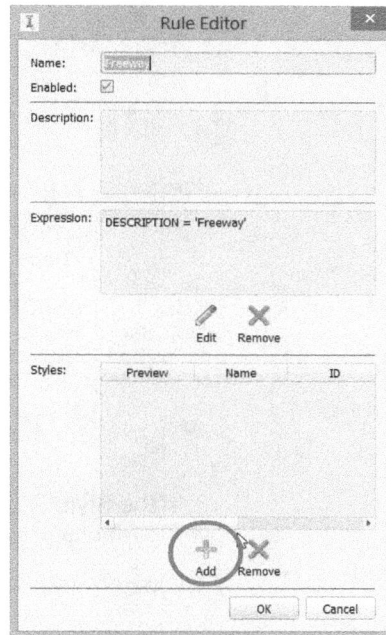

Figure 3–25

9. At the top of the Select Style dialog box, in the *Road* tab, expand the drop-down list and select **Street/Interstate**. In the *Preview* area, select **Highway 2 Lane Forward** and click **OK**, as shown in Figure 3–26.

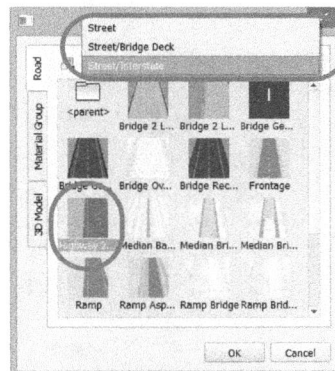

Figure 3–26

10. In the Rule Editor, click **OK** to return to the Style Rules dialog box.

11. In the Style Rules dialog box, click ⏯ (Run Rules) to display the results of the style change.

12. Repeat Steps 4 to 10 to add the following rules and styles.

Name	Expression	Style
Ramp	DESCRIPTION =Ramp	Street/Interstate/Ramp Asphalt
Major Arterial	DESCRIPTION =Major Arterial	Street/Interstate/Street 2 Lane-1 LT Turn
Local	DESCRIPTION =Local	Street/Old Paved Road, Grass Shoulder

13. In the Style Rules dialog box, click ⏯ (Run Rules) to display the results of the style changes.

14. Close the Style Rules dialog box.

Task 3 - Override the style rules.

Stylizing the road centerlines according to the road class helps create a more realistic model. In this model, part of the frontage road has been given the wrong styles and does not match what is actually there. In this task, you will override a style rule to give the road the correct style.

*If you did not complete the previous task, set the **A_Task3** proposal to current in the Utility Bar.*

1. In the Utility Bar, click 🔖 (Bookmark your current location) and select **Road Styles**.

2. In the In Canvas tools, click 🔧 (Build, manage, and analyze your industry model)> ⬦ (Create and manage your model)> 🔲 (Style Palette) and select the *Road* tab.

3. At the top of the Style Palette, expand the drop-down list and select **Street/Interstate**. Click and drag **Street 2 Lane-1 LT Turn** from the Style Palette to the model and drop it on the segment of frontage road that was styled incorrectly, as shown in Figure 3–27.

Figure 3–27

4. Close the Style Palette.

3.3 Create and Share Styles

Although many styles come with the Autodesk InfraWorks 360 software, you might need to create additional styles for your project. You can do so by creating a new catalog of styles or by adding a new style to an existing catalog.

Catalogs

A catalog is a collection of styles that are sorted by feature category. The catalog is listed in a drop-down list at the top of the Style Palette. You can manage style catalogs using the tools at the top of the Style Palette, as shown in Figure 3–28.

Figure 3–28

Catalog Editing Tools

The Catalog Editing tools at the top of the Style Palette only affect the style catalogs. The tools control how the styles are grouped together.

Icon	Description
✛ (Add New Style Catalog)	Creates a style catalog. It is added to the Style Palette and becomes the active catalog. The catalog is stored in an .XML file in a specified location.
✕ (Delete Selected Style Catalog)	Removes the current style catalog from the Style Palette. Note: Style catalogs can be re-imported if required. The catalogs are saved externally in an .XML file, which is not deleted when the catalog is removed from a model.

(Import Style Catalog From File)	Imports a style catalog from a specified file. The catalog is added to the Style Palette and becomes the active catalog.
(Export Selected Style Catalog)	Creates an external file of the current style catalog. The copy is stored in a specified location.
(Copy Selected Style Catalog)	Makes a copy of the current style catalog, which becomes the active catalog. The copy is stored in a specified location.
(Rename Selected Style Catalog)	Enables you to enter a new name for the current style catalog.

Styles

Styles are used to make a model look more realistic. Each style category contains unique settings that must be set to create a style.

The quickest way to create new styles is to create a new style based on an existing style. You can also create new styles from scratch or from 3D models. If you plan to make changes to an existing style, it is recommended that you copy the style first, and then make changes to the copy.

> **Hint: Creating Styles for a Model**
>
> The Autodesk InfraWorks 360 Online Help has additional information on creating specific styles. To open the Autodesk InfraWorks 360 Online Help, press <F1>.

Style Editing Tools

The Style Editing tools at the bottom of the Style Palette only affect the currently selected style. Using these tools enables you to copy and edit the available styles.

Icon	Description
(Add New Style)	Creates a style in the current catalog. A blank style entry displays in the preview area. Double-click on the style to specify the style components.
(Delete Selected Style)	Removes the selected style from the current style catalog.

⬚ (Copy Selected Style to Another Catalog)	Makes a copy of the selected style and moves the copy to another style catalog in the current feature category.
⬚ (Copy Selected Style Locally)	Makes a copy of the selected style in the current style catalog.
⬚ (Rename Selected Style)	Enables you to enter a new name for the selected style.
✎ (Edit Selected Style)	Opens the Style Editor, in which you can change the properties of the selected style.

Material Styles

Defining a material style enables you to create a fill pattern for any other style. Selecting a **Color** material style type enables you to use a color from the palette, or to create a custom color using HSV or RGB values. You can use a custom image by selecting the **Texture** material style type. If you use a custom image file to create the fill pattern, you can set the size of the image to control the size of the pattern in the model. The Define New Material dialog box is shown in Figure 3–29.

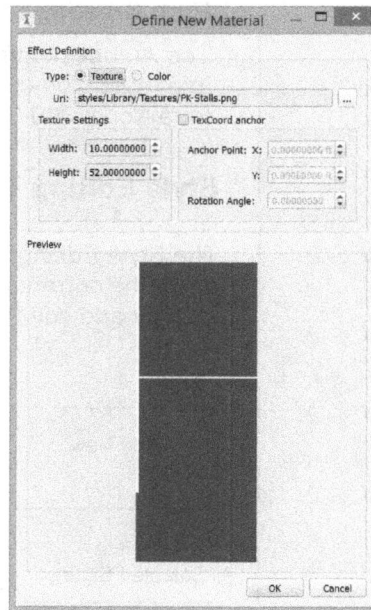

Figure 3–29

Barrier Styles

Barriers are often used to control traffic of various types, such as vehicular, bike, or pedestrian traffic. Defining a barrier style enables you to change the barrier segment length, the barrier height, the material for the barrier faces, and the spacing between each barrier. Changing the thickness changes the buffer along the polyline representing the barrier. The Configure Barrier dialog box is shown in Figure 3–30.

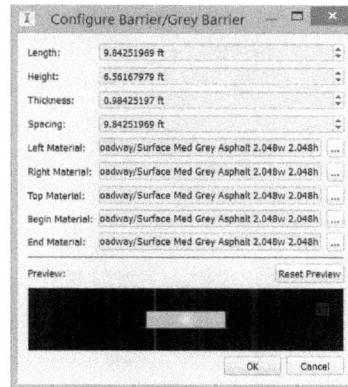

Figure 3–30

Coverage Styles

Coverages can represent parking areas, empty lots, parks, etc. Defining a coverage style enables you to select the material used to fill the interior area, and to select a material and width for the outline. The Configure Coverage dialog box is shown in Figure 3–31.

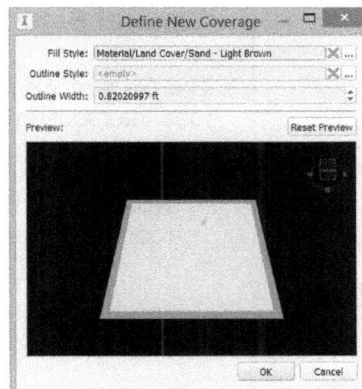

Figure 3–31

Road Styles

Road styles are more complex than most other styles. Defining a road style enables you to define the types of materials used by different parts of the road and the number of default travel lanes that are available. It also enables you to add barriers and other safety features to a road, such as lighting, park strips, and sidewalks. The Configure Street/Interstate dialog box has four settings areas, as shown in Figure 3–32.

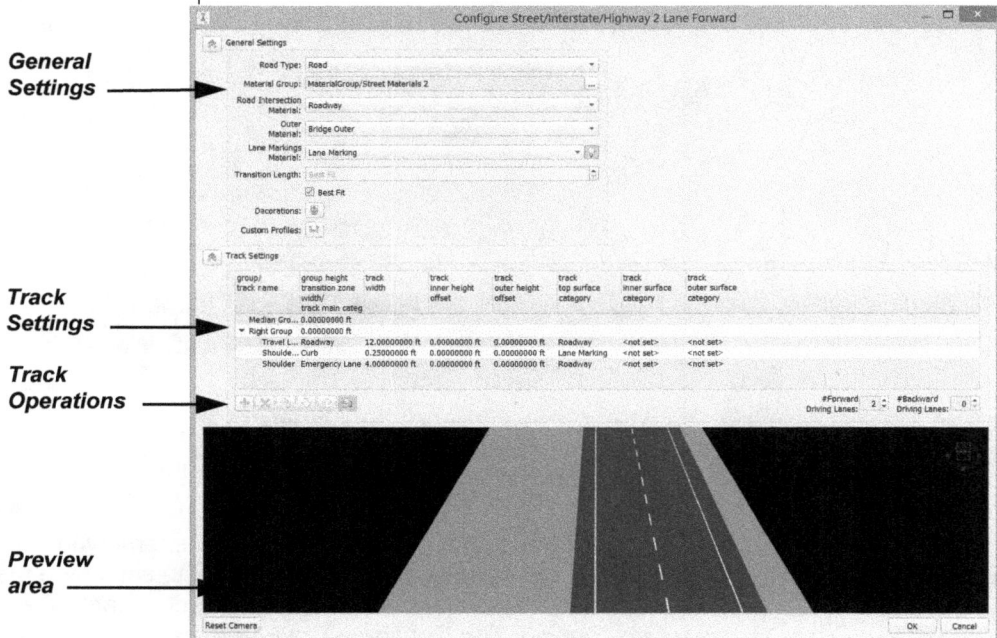

Figure 3–32

General Settings

The *General Settings* area enables you to specify the road type, road intersection material, lane marking material, and decorations.

- **Road Type:** Defines the road as a regular, above-ground road, a bridge, or a tunnel.

- **Material Group:** Maps the materials that are assigned to different parts of a road. Each component of the material groups can be defined separately in its catalog.

- **Road Intersection Material:** Specifies the category of material that is to be used for areas where road segments cross each other. If two roads with different styles share a crossing region, the road style of the road with the highest value in the *Importance* property is displayed. The *Importance* property is located in the Road Properties palette, as shown in Figure 3–33. You can access it by selecting the road, right-clicking and selecting **Properties**.

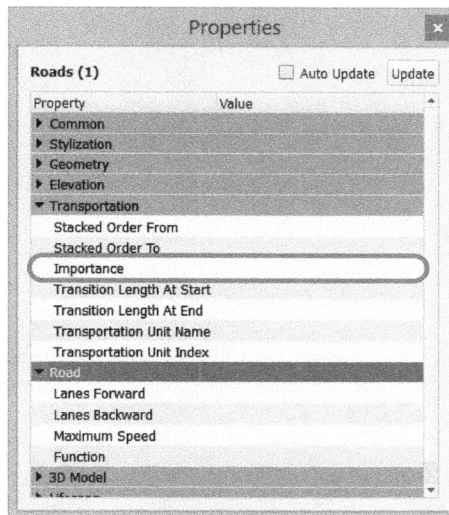

Figure 3–33

- **Outer Material:** Specifies the material applied to the terrain along the outer-most track.

- **Lane Markings Material:** Specifies the category of material to be used for lane markings. Lane markings can be toggled on or off using [icon] to the right of the *Lane Marking Material* field. By default, lane markings are not generated for intersecting regions.

- **Transition Length:** Specifies the default transition length for the style. Selecting the **Best Fit** option permits the software to set the transition length.

- **(Decorations):** Opens the Decoration Editor dialog box, as shown in Figure 3–34. It enables you to add 3D models to the roadway at specified intervals. The 3D models can include barriers, signs, light poles, and other city furniture. In the *Decoration Target* field, select the location that you want the 3D model to display. Click to select a 3D model in the Select Style dialog box. Finally, set the spacing and rotation for the 3D model in the *Decoration Settings* area in the Decoration Editor dialog box.

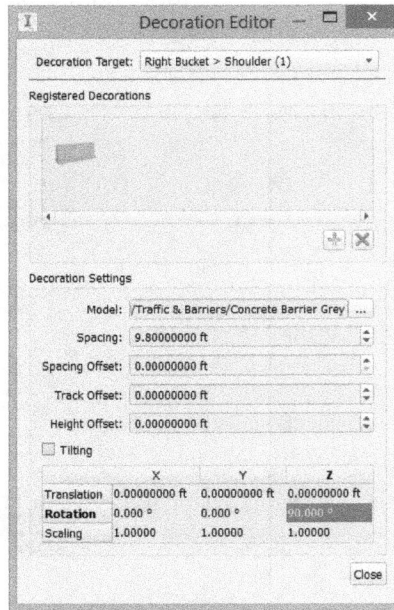

Figure 3–34

- **(Custom Profiles):** Specifies a 2D cross section (.SDF or SQLite file format) to create or display decorations that follow the path along curved roads. This is most useful for customizing the profile of medians, bike-ways, curbs, green space, sidewalks, etc.

Track Settings

The *Track Settings* area defines the road elements. Each row of the table sets the width, height, and surface categories for one element or track for the road. There is usually only one row dedicated for lane elements because the number of lanes is defined by the *#Forward/#Backward Driving Lanes* fields, as shown in Figure 3–35.

The order of the tracks in the Track Settings area determines the order in which they display in the model.

Figure 3–35

By default, only the right side of the road is displayed in the *Preview* area because the software mirrors the right side of the road to create the left side in the model. To create an asymmetric road and display the left side, click [icon] (Create Asymmetric Road) below the table. You can create additional rows/tracks by clicking [icon] (Add New Element) below the table. The columns in the *Track Settings* area are described as follows:

Column	Description
Group/Track Name	The track name identifies the track use. The group name identifies where the track falls: either in the median or on the left/right side of the road.
Group Height Transition Zone Width/Track Main Category	The *Track Main* category is the basic material type for the road element. Options in this column depend on the Material Group selected in the *General Settings* area. The *Group Height Transition Zone Width* category applies to the group.
Track Width	Sets the width for the corresponding road element.
Track Inner Height Offset	Sets the starting height of the corresponding road element relative to the previous track. Note: The initial height is based on the center line of the road.
Track Outer Height Offset	Sets the finishing height of the corresponding road element relative to the next track.
Track Top Surface Category	Sets the material to be used for the top surface of the road. Options in this column depend on the Material Group selected in the *General Settings* area.
Track Inner Surface Category	Sets the material to be used for the vertical geometry that is created if the inner offset height value is not equal to zero.
Track Outer Surface Category	Sets the material to be used for the vertical geometry that is created if the outer offset height value is not equal to zero.

Track Operations

The *Track Operations* area (shown in Figure 3–36) is where you set the number of lanes for the road, both forward and backward. It is also used to modify the Track Settings table.

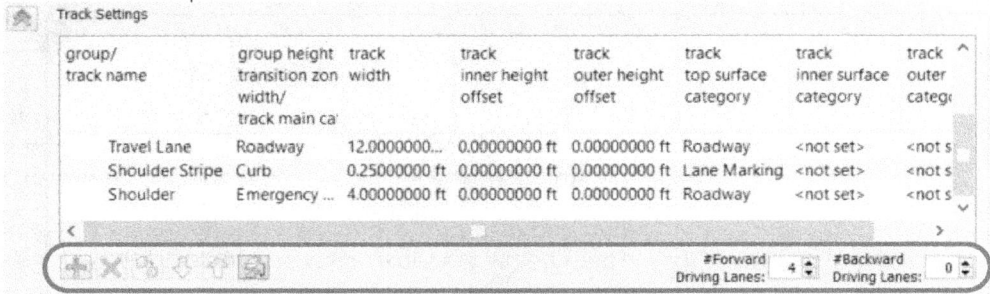

group/ track name	group height transition zon width/ track main ca	track width	track inner height offset	track outer height offset	track top surface category	track inner surface category	track outer categc
Travel Lane	Roadway	12.0000000...	0.00000000 ft	0.00000000 ft	Roadway	<not set>	<not s
Shoulder Stripe	Curb	0.25000000 ft	0.00000000 ft	0.00000000 ft	Lane Marking	<not set>	<not s
Shoulder	Emergency ...	4.00000000 ft	0.00000000 ft	0.00000000 ft	Roadway	<not set>	<not s

#Forward Driving Lanes: 4   #Backward Driving Lanes: 0

Figure 3–36

The available icons and their uses are described as follows:

Icon	Description
✛ (Add New Element)	Creates a new road element in the *Track Settings* area.
✕ (Delete Selected Element)	Removes the selected road element or group from the *Track Settings* area.
🗋 (Copy Selected Element)	Makes a copy of the selected road element in the *Track Settings* area.
⬆ (Move Element Up)	Moves the selected road element up in the track list and changes its location in the *Preview* area.
⬇ (Move Element Down)	Moves the selected road element up in the track list and changes its location in the *Preview* area.
⬓ (Create Asymmetric Road)	Adds a median group and a left group to the track list, which enables you to create an asymmetric road.

Preview Area

The *Preview* area displays an image of how the road is going to display when applied to road centerlines in the model. The camera position can be moved using the ViewCube in the *Preview* area, or by using the mouse, similar to working in the model.

Practice 3b

Estimated time for completion: 15 minutes

Create Styles

Practice Objective

- Create new visual style for model features.

In this practice you will create a coverage style for a parking lot and a road style.

Task 1 - Create and use a coverage style.

A new commuter parking lot is being built next to the freeway entrance. Coverages are a great way to grade parking lots and other grading sites. Using a custom coverage style, provides the opportunity to make the graded site look however you would like. In this task, you create a material style and a coverage style that looks like a parking lot. Then, you apply the style to a coverage in the model.

1. Continue working in the same model as the last practice. If you closed it, navigate to the *C:\InfraWorks Fundamentals Practice Files\Styles* folder, select **Styles.sqlite** and click **Open**.

2. In the Utility Bar, click (Bookmark your current location) and select **ParkingLot**. Also ensure that **B_Task1** is the current proposal.

3. In the In Canvas tools, click (Build, manage, and analyze your industry model)> (Create and manage your model)> (Style Palette), select the *Material* tab, and double-click on **Roadway** to display all of the available road materials.

4. In the *Style Editing* area at the bottom of the Style Palette, click (Add new style).

5. In the Define New Material dialog box:

- For the *Type*, select **Texture**.

- To the right of the *Uri* field, click ⋯ (Browse).

*Click **OK** in the Added Texture File to Model Resources dialog box.*

- In the *C:\InfraWorks Fundamentals Practice Files\Styles* folder, select **PK-Stalls.png** and click **Open**.

- In the *Texture Settings* area, for the *Width*, type **10** and for the *Height*, type **52**, as shown in Figure 3–37. Click **OK**.

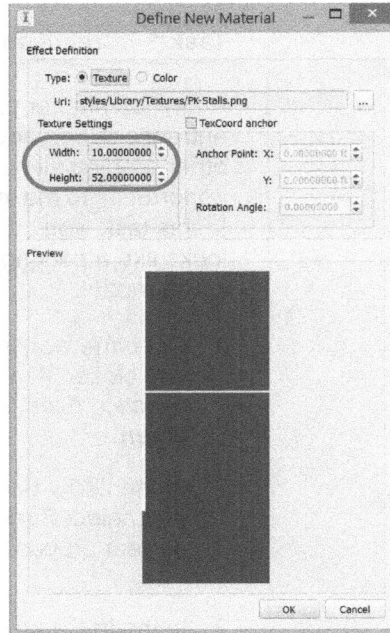

Figure 3–37

6. For the name of the new material, type **PK-Stalls**.

7. In the Style Palette, select the *Coverage* tab.

8. In the *Style Editing* area at the bottom of the Style Palette, click ✛ (Add new style).

9. In the Define New Coverage dialog box, to the right of the *Fill Style* field, click ⋯ (Browse).

10. In the Select Style/Color dialog box:
    - Select the *Material* tab.
    - Double-click on Roadway.
    - Select **PK-Stalls**, as shown in Figure 3–38. Click **OK**.

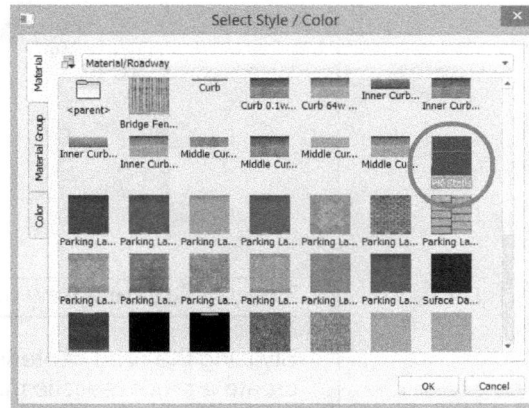

Figure 3–38

11. In the Define New Coverage dialog box, to the right of *Outline Style*, click ⋯ (Browse).

12. In the Select Style/Color dialog box:
    - Select the *Material* tab.
    - Double-click on Roadway.
    - Select **Curb 0.1w 2h** as shown in Figure 3–39. Click **OK**.

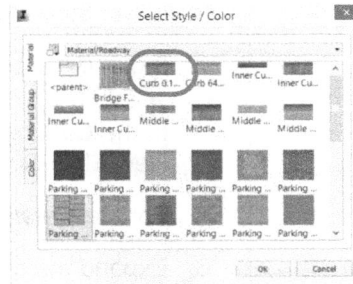

Figure 3–39

13. Leave the *Outline Width* set to **0.82** and click **OK**.

14. For the coverage style name, type **ParkingLot**.

15. Drag the new **ParkingLot** coverage style to the new commuter parking lot shown in Figure 3–40.

Figure 3–40

Task 2 - Create a new road style.

Stylizing the road centerlines according the road class helps create a more realistic model. However, the road style used to display the I-15 corridor does not have enough lanes and needs to have the correct barriers to protect drivers from running off the road or into oncoming traffic. In this task, you will create a new catalog and create a copy of the style that is currently used for I-15. You will make the required modifications to the style and apply it to the style rules.

*If you did not complete the previous task, set the **B_Task2** proposal to current in the Utility Bar.*

1. In the Utility Bar, click ▣ (Bookmark your current location) and select **Road Styles**.

2. In the Style Palette, select the *Road* tab.

3. Expand the drop-down list and select **Street/Interstate**.

4. In the *Catalog Editing Tools* area at the top, click ✛ (Add New Style Catalog).

5. For the *Catalog Name*, type **Training** and press <Enter>.

6. Expand the drop-down list and select **Street/Interstate**.

7. In the *Style Preview* area, select the **Highway 2 Lane Forward** style.

8. In the *Style Editing* area at the bottom of the Style Palette, click ⬚ (Copy Selected Style to Another Catalog).

9. In the Copy Item dialog box, select the **Street/Interstate/ Training** option, as shown in Figure 3–41. Click **OK**.

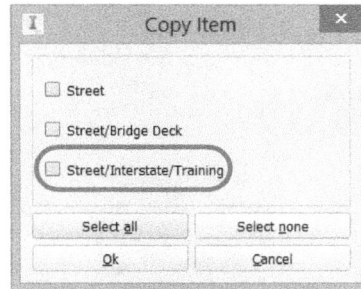

Figure 3–41

10. Expand the drop-down list and select **Street/Interstate/ Training**.

11. In the *Style Preview* area, select the **Highway 2 Lane Forward** style.

12. In the *Style Editing* area at the bottom of the Style Palette, click ⬚ (Rename Selected Style). Type **Highway 4 Lane Forward** and press <Enter>.

13. In the *Style Editing* area at the bottom of the Style Palette, click ✎ (Edit Selected Style).

14. In the Configure Style dialog box, do the following, as shown in Figure 3–42:

- Set the #*Forward Driving Lanes* to **4**.

- Click 🔲 (Create Asymmetric Road) to make the road asymmetrical.

- Click 🚦 (Decoration).

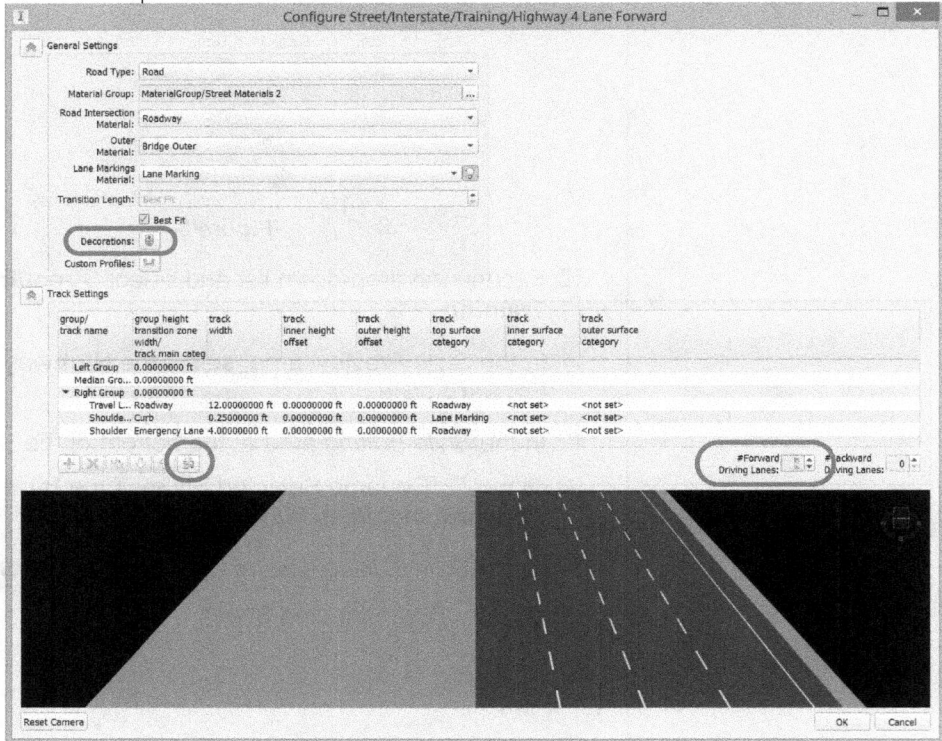

Figure 3–42

15. In the Decorations Editor dialog box:

- The Decoration Target drop-down list should be set to **Right Bucket>Travel Lane**.

16. In the Select 3D Model Style dialog box:

- Click ➕ (Add 3D Model) and double-click on **<parent>** then **Vehicles**.
- Select **BMW 7 Series**, as shown in Figure 3–43.

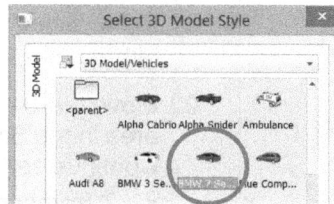

Figure 3–43

17. Click **OK**.

18. Move the Decoration Editor dialog box so that the *Preview* area in the Style Configuration dialog box is displayed. Continue setting the following, as shown in Figure 3–44:
    - *Track Offset* field: **6**
    - *Spacing* field: **50**.

    Note the change in the *Preview* area.

19. In the Select 3D Model Style dialog box, click ✛ (Add 3D Model) and then select **Blue Compact Car**. Continue setting the following, as shown in Figure 3–45:
    - *Track Offset* field: **30**
    - *Spacing* field: **55**

If you live in the United States (or another country that drives on the right side of the road), in the Z column, change the Rotation to 180.

Figure 3–44

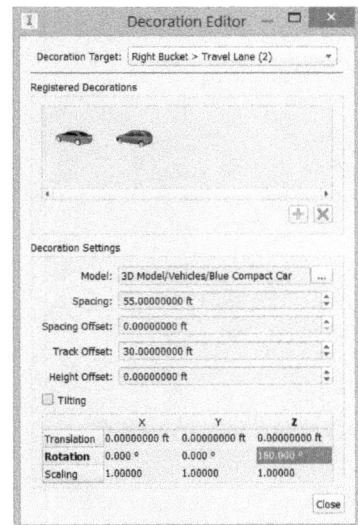

Figure 3–45

20. Expand the Decoration Target drop-down list and select **Right Bucket>Shoulder**.

21. In the Select 3D Model Style dialog box, click ✛ (Add 3D Model) and double-click on **Concrete Barrier Grey**.

22. Move the Decoration Editor dialog box so that the *Preview* area in the Style Configuration dialog box is displayed clearly. Continue setting the following, as shown in Figure 3–46:

    • *Z Rotation* field: **90**

    • *Track Offset* field: **-50**

    Note the change in the *Preview* area.

23. To the right of *Spacing*, click the down-arrow until the barriers abut each other in the *Preview* area in the Style Configuration dialog box (the *Spacing* should be close to 9.8'), as shown in Figure 3–46.

24. Click **Close**.

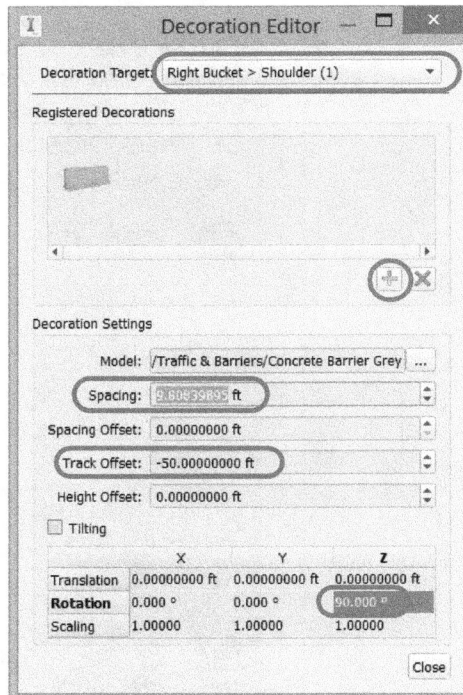

Figure 3–46

25. In the Style Configuration dialog box, click **OK** to accept the changes.

26. Open the Style Rules palette and change the **Freeway** style rule to make it use the **Highway 4 Lane Forward** style that you just created, as shown in Figure 3–47.

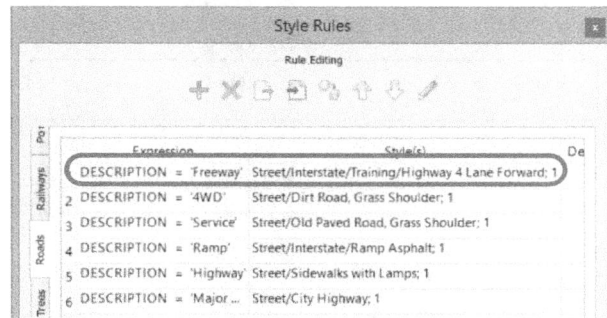

Figure 3–47

27. Click ▶ (Run Rules) to display the changes in the model.

28. Close the model.

Chapter Review Questions

1. Which programming language is used to change the appearance of data sources on import?

   a. HTML

   b. C++

   c. .Net

   d. JavaScript

2. When working with expressions, which of the following operators can be used for text fields?

   a. Like

   b. Not Like

   c. = (Equal To)

   d. All of the above.

3. When changing a model feature's style automatically, two filter types are available: Location and Property.

   a. True

   b. False

4. When creating new styles, which of the following cannot be set for a barrier style?

   a. Length

   b. 3D Model

   c. Height

   d. Spacing

5. When creating new styles, in which of the following areas would you set the number of lanes for a road style?

   a. *General Settings area*

   b. *Track Settings area*

   c. *Track Operations area*

   d. *Preview area*

Command Summary

Button	Command	Location
	Style Palette	• **In Canvas Tools:** Build, manage, and analyze your industry model>Create and manage your model
	Style Rules	• **In Canvas Tools:** Build, manage, and analyze your industry model>Create and manage your model

Create Model Elements

Using conceptual design tools, you can add roads, railway lines, bodies of water, and coverage areas to a model. In this chapter you learn how to add many of these model elements and how to edit the elements once they have been created.

Learning Objectives in this Chapter

- Review the basic commands that are available to make changes to model elements.
- Create conceptual designs of roads, bridges, and tunnels.
- Create coverages and land areas to shape and stylize the terrain surface.
- Add pipelines and pipeline connectors to a model to indicate where utilities are to be located.
- Create railways in a model to indicate the locations of the mass transit lines or freight lines.
- Create water features in a model to represent lakes, ponds, rivers, or streams.

4.1 Basic Commands

To work with features in the model, you must be able to select them. The same selection tools are used to select features from imported source data and features that you have created. Knowing which selection tools are available and how to use them helps you to be more efficient.

Selecting Features

Before you can edit an item, you must be able to select it. By default, you can click on any entity in the model to select it. In the

In Canvas Tools, click ![icon] (Build, manage, and analyze your

industry model)> ![icon] (Select Model Features) to see additional options. The following selection options are available:

Icon	Description
![icon] (Zoom to Selected)	Zooms in and center on the selected feature(s).
![icon] (Clear Selected)	Clears the current selection. You can also use the keyboard shortcut by pressing <Esc>
![icon] (Window Select)	Enables you to select an area based on two opposite corners of a rectangle by dragging the cursor over a region of the model. Any features that are within or touching the edge of the window are selected.
![icon] (Rectangular Select)	Enables you to define a box with three points (*Min/Max* for *X*, *Y*, and *Z*). Any features that are completely inside the box are selected. Note: You must double-click on the last point to complete the command.
![icon] (Polygon Select)	Enables you to define any shape based on three or more points. Any feature(s) that are inside or touching the edge of the polygon are selected. Note: You must double-click on the last point to complete the command.
![icon] (Radius Select)	Enables you to define a circular region by selecting the center point. Any features that are completely inside the defined circle are selected. Note: You must double-click to set the distance from the center and complete the command.
![icon] (Filter Select)	Enables you to define an expression to select features according to specific attributes. When clicked, the Create an attribute filter dialog box opens, which enables you to create filter expressions to use with this selection option.

- Multiple selections can be made by holding down <Ctrl> when selecting features in the model.

- To select a feature, the feature class or layer must be unlocked in the Model Explorer, and *Edit mode* must be toggled on in the View Settings asset card.

How To: Toggle Edit Mode On/Off

1. In the Utility Bar, expand the View Style drop-down and click ⚙ (Configure current view).

2. In the View Settings asset card, click 🔍 (Change navigation and application feedback settings) to open the *Interaction* stack.

3. Under *Feedback*, click the **Edit mode** slider to toggle it on or off, as shown in Figure 4–1.

This only toggles the Edit mode for the current view style.

Figure 4–1

Shortcut Commands

Many Windows programs use common shortcut keys. Many of these keys can also be used in the Autodesk® InfraWorks® 360 software. Shortcut keys can be used in conjunction with the clipboard to share features between different proposals or models. Some of the shortcut keys are listed below

Command /Icon	Keyboard Shortcut	Description
Select All	<Ctrl>+<A>	Selects all of the contents (i.e., created features and data sources) in the current model.

Invert Selection	<Alt>+<I>	Inverts the currently selected contents. These are cleared, while previously unselected objects become selected.
Deselect	<Esc>	Clears the selection of any objects that were selected in the model.
Zoom Selected	<F>	Zooms in on the currently selected objects in the model.
Copy	<Ctrl>+<C>	Copies features to a clipboard for use later. You can copy an individual feature, an entire feature class, or multiple feature classes using the **Copy** command.
Duplicate	<Ctrl>+<D>	Copies features without copying to the clipboard. You can duplicate an individual feature, an entire feature class, or multiple feature classes using the **Duplicate** command. Note: You can press <Shift>+<Ctrl> while dragging selected features to duplicate them without using the clipboard.
Paste	<Ctrl>+<V>	Pastes items from the clipboard into the model. Hold <Ctrl>+<V> and double-click in the model where you want the copied feature to be placed.
Paste in Place	<Shift>+<Ctrl>+ <V>	Pastes items at their original locations.
Delete	<Delete>	Removes selected features from the model.
Cut	<Ctrl>+<X>	Removes selected features from the model and places them on the clipboard for use later. You can cut an individual feature, an entire feature class, or multiple feature classes using the **Cut** command.
⤺ (Undo)	<Ctrl>+<Z>	Undoes the last command used in the model. Repeating the **Undo** command undoes commands in the order in which they were executed. The Icon is found on the Utility Bar.

	<Ctrl>+<Y>	Reverses an **Undo** command, reissuing the last command that was undone in the model.
(Redo)		Repeating the **Redo** command reissues commands in the order in which they were undone. Note: **Redo** only reissues commands that were successive. For example, if you undo five commands, redo three of those commands, and then issue a new command, the **Redo** command is disabled when you execute the new command. The Icon is found on the Utility Bar.

Gizmos

Gizmos enable you to quickly modify model features, similar to the way grips are used in AutoCAD®-based programs. In the model, click the entity you wish to edit to cause gizmos to display when objects are selected. Different gizmos display depending on the type of feature that is selected when you access the Edit Features mode.

A few of the available gizmos are as follows.

Gizmos	Transformation	Description
	Elevation	Used with linear features (i.e., roads, railways, and coverages). In a 3D View, it stretches features vertically by changing the elevation of a linear feature vertex.
	Height	Only used with buildings, city furniture, and trees. Changes the height of a building while leaving the footprint unchanged. Changes the scale of trees and city furniture proportionally.
	Rotate	Rotates a feature around the Z-axis.
	Control Point	Displays at each corner, point of intersection, or base of features. Stretches linear features (i.e., roads, rails, coverages, and building outlines) by moving the selected vertex of the feature. Moves the location of point features (i.e., trees or city furniture). Note: Additional control points can be added by holding down <Alt> and selecting the new control point location.
	Move	Moves the selected feature or vertex.

The Move gizmo has four handle options for moving model elements. These handles can be selected to move features in specific planes. The available handles are as follows.

Handle	Transformation	Description
	Move in XY Plane	Select the square between the X- and Y-axes to move a feature to a new location in the XY plane.
	Move in X Axis	Select the red arrow to constrain the movement of a feature to a new location along the X-axis.
	Move in Y Axis	Select the green arrow to constrain the movement of a feature to a new location along the Y-axis.
	Move in Z Axis	Select the blue arrow to constrain the movement of a feature to a new location along the Z-axis.

4.2 Create Conceptual Roads in a Model

Every design project needs to be accessed in some way, and this is easily done by creating a new road or simple driveway into the site. Using the **Create Roads** command you can add roads, bridges, and tunnels to a model. Which of these three features you create depends on the style of road that you select in the Select Draw Style Asset Card when starting the **Roads** command, as shown in Figure 4–2. To find a required style faster, you can filter the available styles by typing in the filter field.

Figure 4–2

How To: Create a Road

1. In the In Canvas tools, click [Build, manage, and analyze your infrastructure model)> (Create conceptual design features)> (Roads).

Once you have selected the first road style in the model, that style becomes the active style. To change the active style, click

[icon] *(Roads) and select a different style from the Select Draw Style asset card.*

2. The Select Draw Style asset card opens, as shown in Figure 4–3. In the Select Draw Style asset card, select the required style.

Figure 4–3

3. Click in the model where you want to start the road, bridge, or tunnel.
4. Move the cursor in the direction the road needs to follow. Type a distance to the first point of intersection (PI). Click the model at the locations of each additional required point of intersection (PI).
5. If crossing existing roads, ensure that you place a PI at the intersection to ensure that the intersection is created correctly.
6. For the final PI, double-click on the location at which you want to end the road, bridge, or tunnel. Doing so ends the **Road** command.
7. Press <Esc> to clear the selection of the newly created road, bridge, or tunnel.

Edit Roads

Once a road, bridge, or tunnel has been created, you can change the design options. For example, you might need to add more curves to the road or change the elevation at specific locations. To edit a road, select the road and use the gizmos to make changes. You can also right-click on the road to access the following options.

Icon	Command	Description
![Add Vertex icon]	**Add Vertex**	Adds a point of intersection (PI) at the point at which you right-clicked.
![Remove Vertex icon]	**Remove Vertex**	Removes the PI on which you right-clicked.
![Split Feature icon]	**Split Feature**	Breaks the road, bridge, or tunnel into multiple features at the point at which you right-clicked.
![Drape Feature icon]	**Drape Feature**	Drapes the roadway on the surface terrain, reducing the need to add PVIs along the road.
N/A	**Convert to Design Road**	Converts a conceptual road to a design road allowing you to add more design parameters (curve radius, daylight slope, etc). **Note:** This command is only available if you have the Road Design for InfraWorks 360 module installed.
N/A	**Properties**	Opens the Properties palette in which you can change the style, number of lanes, elevation offset, etc.

When working with roads created using the conceptual **Roads** tool, you must add a vertex where you need to add a horizontal or vertical curve to the road. This helps reduce the amount of cut and fill required to build the road, as shown in Figure 4–4.

Excessive cut/fill quantities

Cut/fill quantities reduced by adding a PI and adjusting its elevation

Figure 4–4

If you only need to change the style of road for part of the roadway, use the **Split Feature** command. Then use the Road asset card or Properties to change the style for the segment of road that needs to be changed. In the Properties palette, select an option in the *Manual Style* field and click **Update**, as shown in Figure 4–5.

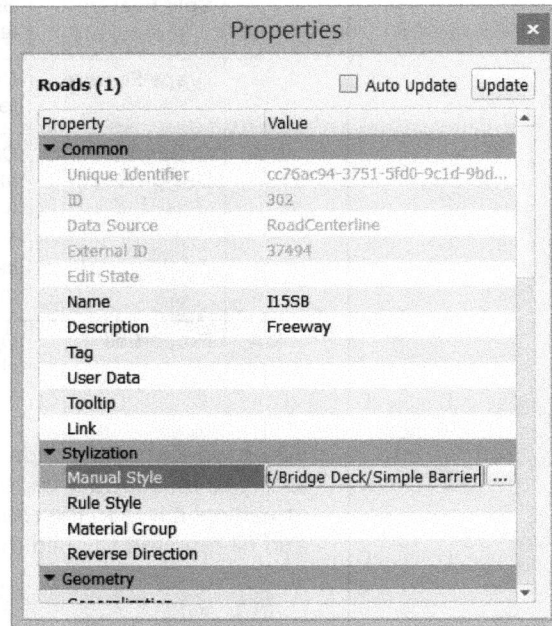

Figure 4–5

Practice 4a

Estimated time for completion: 25 minutes

Create Roads in the Model

Practice Objective

- Create multiple roads in the model to display the design concept.

In this practice you will create a road that ends at a pier. You will use a bridge style to create the pier. You will then create additional roads for a new subdivision that will connect to an existing subdivision.

Task 1 - Create roads.

1. In the Home Screen, click **Open**.

2. In the *C:\InfraWorks Fundamentals Practice Files\Create* folder, select **CreateFeatures.sqlite** and click **Open**.

3. In the Utility Bar, click ▣ (Bookmark your current location) and select **Bridge**.

4. In the Utility Bar, expand *Switch Active Proposal* and select **A_Task1**.

5. In the In Canvas tools, click ▣ (Build, manage, and analyze your infrastructure model)> ▨ (Create conceptual design features)> ▨ (Roads).

6. In the Select Draw Style asset card, type **Sidewalk** in the filter field, and then select **Street>Sidewalk with Lamps**, as shown in Figure 4–6.

Figure 4–6

7. To start the road in the model, click near the center line of Redwood Rd just south of the dirt road, as shown in Figure 4–7. Type **125**, press <Enter>, and then click north-east of that point to make the road perpendicular to Redwood Rd.

Note that going off the terrain created by the .DEM file can cause the model to crash.

8. Move the cursor due east and double-click to end the road inside the water, as shown in Figure 4–7.

First PI 125 ft perpendicular to Redwood Rd.

End the road here in the water.

Start the road here at Redwood Rd.

Figure 4–7

9. Press <Esc> twice to end the command and release the roadway selection.

Task 2 - Edit the roads.

1. Continue working in the same model. If you did not complete the last task, in the Utility Bar, expand *Switch Active Proposal and* select the **A_Task2** proposal.

2. In the model, select the new road. Right-click near the center of the road to the west of the barn in the fields and select **Split Feature**, as shown in Figure 4–8.

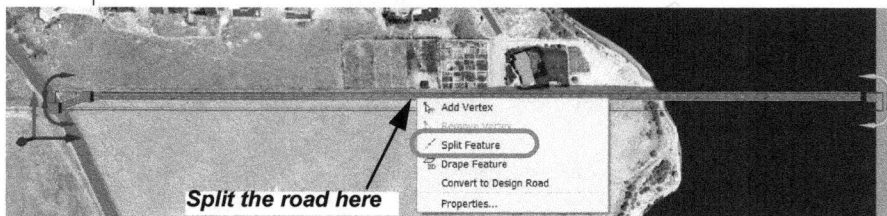

Split the road here

Add Vertex
Remove Vertex
Split Feature
Drape Feature
Convert to Design Road
Properties...

Figure 4–8

You might need to select close to the split point to select the correct portion of the road.

3. Select the segment of road to the right of the split. This section will become the new pier.

4. In the Road asset card, click the *Manual Style* thumbnail and select **More Styles**.

5. In the Select Style dialog box, select the **Street** catalog, then the **Bridge** style, as shown in Figure 4–9. Click **OK**.

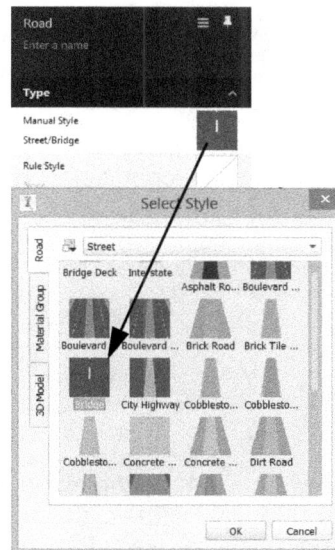

Figure 4–9

6. In the Utility Bar, click ▣ (Bookmark your current location) and select **Bridge Elevation**. The view displays as shown in Figure 4–10.

Figure 4–10

7. The bridge goes down into the water. Select the bridge and use ⬢ (Elevation Gizmo) to raise the right side of the bridge so that it is parallel with the water line, as shown in Figure 4–11.

Figure 4–11

Task 3 - Create subdivision roads.

1. Continue working in the same model. If you did not complete the last task, in the Utility Bar, expand *Switch Active Proposal* and select the **A_Task3** proposal.

2. In the Utility Bar, click ▣ (Bookmark your current location), and select **New Neighborhood**.

3. In the In Canvas tools, click ▣ (Build, manage, and analyze your infrastructure model)>✎ (Create conceptual design features)>▧ (Roads). The **Sidewalk with Lamps** road style is automatically selected because it was the last style that was used. Continue using this style.

Note that placing the west PIs causes the road to form one large curve. This is corrected in the next step.

4. In the model, create the road shown in Figure 4–12 by typing the distances and pressing <Enter> before clicking to place each PI. Double-click the last PI to end the command.

270 ft   2400 ft   2875 ft   335 ft

Figure 4–12

5. Press <Esc> to end the command and show the road's gizmos.

6. Orbit the model more than 45 degrees past the plan view orientation to display the vertical gizmos. Orient the view so that you are looking east, similar to the view shown in Figure 4–13.

This vertex reduces the curve radii of the horizontal curves at the north and south ends of the road.

7. Add a new vertex at the approximate mid-point of the north-south segment of the new road, as shown in Figure 4–13. To add a vertex, right-click where you want to place the vertex, and select **Add Vertex**. Adjust the elevation of the new vertex using 🔹 (Elevation Gizmo).

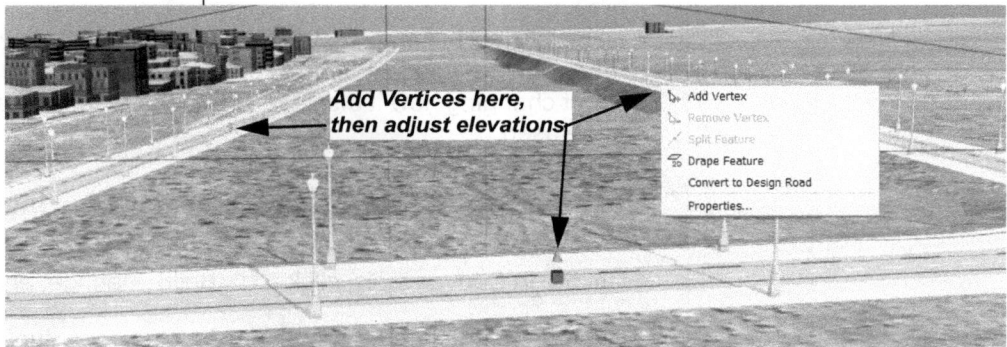

Figure 4–13

8. Add additional vertices as required to reduce the cut and fill volumes for the new road.

9. In the Utility Bar, click 🖼 (Bookmark your current location), and select **New Neighborhood**.

10. Add additional neighborhood roads, as shown in Figure 4–14. Place a point of intersection (PI) at locations where one road intersects another by clicking on the midpoint of the roads where they will intersect. Doing so results in clean intersections, rather than overpasses or underpasses.

Figure 4–14

11. Press <Esc> to clear the selection of all of the roads.

4.3 Create Coverages in a Model

Coverages are used to shape the terrain and change the way the ground displays. Coverages can be used to add ground cover in a landscape design, set the elevation of a building pad, or create a parking lot for a site design. Additionally, Terrain Hole material can be used on a coverage to create openings in a surface with a clean edge. This enables you to display what is going on underground. If you just need to reshape the terrain surface without changing how it displays, a transparent material style can be used.

How To: Shape and Style the Terrain Surface

1. In the In Canvas tools, click ⬛ (Build, manage, and analyze your infrastructure model)> ✎ (Create conceptual design features)> ▨ (Coverages).

2. Select the style for the surface you are creating from the Select Draw Style asset card that displays, as shown in Figure 4–15.

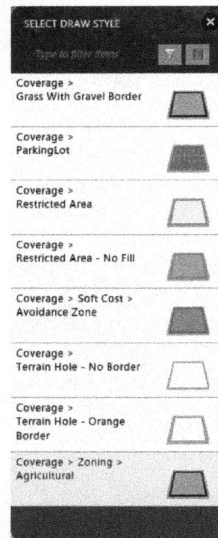

Figure 4–15

3. In the model, click to place the corners of the coverage footprint. After the first corner has been placed, move the cursor in the direction in which you want the next corner to be placed. Note the dimensions that display, as shown in Figure 4–16.

Area: 3751.07 sq.ft.

100

Figure 4–16

Locking a length means that even if you drag the cursor, the dimension value does not change.

4. Type the required length for that side of the coverage and press <Enter> to lock the length. Move the cursor as required to set the correct angle and click to place the vertex.
5. Continue clicking in the model until all but the last vertices have been set.
6. Double-click on the location at which you want to place the final vertex. Doing so ends the command.
7. Press <Esc> to clear the selection of the newly created coverage.

Edit Coverages

Once a coverage has been created, it can be re-shaped using

![icon] (Control Point Gizmo). The gizmos are displayed at each vertex when the coverage is selected in the model and Edit mode is toggled on in the View Settings Interaction stack. If you orbit the model more than 45 degrees, ![icon] (Elevation Gizmo) displays and can be used to adjust the elevation of each corner.

As you adjust the elevation of a coverage, the surrounding terrain updates to gradually slope toward the new elevation, as shown in Figure 4–17.

Figure 4–17

How gradual the slope is depends upon the *Smooth Radius* value for the coverage, as shown in Figure 4–18. This value is changed by selecting the coverage and changing the *Smooth Radius* value in the asset card or the Properties palette.

Figure 4–18

If a flat coverage is desired (i.e., with all vertices having the same elevation), right-click on the selected coverage and select **Shape Terrain**. Then use the ↑ (Elevation Gizmo) at the center of the coverage to adjust the elevation of all vertices at once, as shown in Figure 4–19.

Figure 4–19

Vertices can be added anywhere along a side to add additional control and elevation points. To add a vertex, select the coverage, right-click on the side at which you want to have additional control, and select **Add Vertex**, as shown in Figure 4–20.

Figure 4–20

Practice 4b

Create Coverages in the Model

Estimated time for completion: 25 minutes

Practice Objectives

- Change the look of the terrain surface using coverages to display parking lots and other surface materials.
- Shape the terrain surface using coverages to change the elevations.

In this practice you will create coverages to change the display settings and elevations associated with a terrain surface.

Task 1 - Create a parking lot.

1. In the Home Screen, click **Open**.

2. In the *C:\InfraWorks Fundamentals Practice Files\Create* folder, select **CreateFeatures.sqlite** and click **Open**.

3. In the Utility Bar, expand *Switch Active Proposal* and select **B_Task1**.

4. In the Utility Bar, click [] (Bookmark your current location) and select **Church**.

5. In the In Canvas tools, click [] (Build, manage, and analyze your infrastructure model)>[] (Create conceptual design features)>[] (Coverages).

6. In the Select Draw Style asset card, select the **ParkingLot** style that was created in an earlier practice, as shown in Figure 4–21.

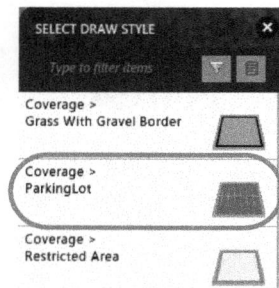

Figure 4–21

7. Click in the model to place the vertices of the parking lot similar to that shown in Figure 4–22. Ensure that you double-click on the last corner to place it and end the command.

A building will be added later which sits in the middle of the parking lot.

Figure 4–22

8. Press <Esc> twice to clear the selection of the newly created parking lot.

Task 2 - Shape the terrain using a coverage.

In this task you will shape the ground surface in preparation for a school. You will create another coverage and adjust its elevations.

1. In the Utility Bar, click ▣ (Bookmark your current location) and select **School**. Expand *Switch Active Proposal* and then select **B_Task2**.

2. In the In Canvas tools, click ▮ (Build, manage, and analyze your infrastructure model)> ✐ (Create conceptual design features)> ▨ (Coverages).

3. In the Select Draw Style asset card, select **Asphalt**.

4. In the model, click to place the corners of the asphalt slab in the field reserved for the school, as shown in Figure 4–23. Make the measurement **350' x 300'** with the long side running east to west. Double-click on the last corner to place it and end the command.

Figure 4–23

5. Press <Esc> to show the coverage's gizmos.

6. With the new asphalt coverage selected, orbit the view so that the elevation of the south side is displayed, as shown in Figure 4–24.

Figure 4–24

A box displays indicating orthogonal directions otherwise known as level lines. The level line in the view can help you to level the pad if you are shaping it manually.

7. Right-click and select **Shape Terrain**.

8. With the new asphalt coverage selected, click ↑ (Elevation Gizmo), type **4612** in the elevation field (as shown in Figure 4–25), and then press <Enter>.

Figure 4–25

The surrounding ground gradually slopes into the school pad based on the change in elevation and Smooth Radius value in the Coverage asset card.

9. With the coverage still selected, in the asset card, change the *Smooth Radius* value to **20**.

10. Change the *Smooth Radius* value to **100** and press <Enter>. Note the change in the surrounding grade.

11. Press <Esc> to clear the selection of the newly created school pad.

4.4 Create Pipe Networks in a Model

Utilities are a very important part of a project. They provide electricity, gas, water, etc., to a project site. They also provide a way to divert excess storm water.

Creating conceptual utilities in the Autodesk InfraWorks 360 software is a two step process, as both pipelines and pipeline connectors must be created separately. Once created, they can be imported into the AutoCAD® Civil 3D® software where they become a pipe network. Pipelines become AutoCAD Civil 3D pipes, while Pipeline Connectors become AutoCAD Civil 3D structures. If you enter a name for the Pipeline in the *Network Name* field in the Properties palette (as shown in Figure 4–26), the name can be used in the AutoCAD Civil 3D software to identify the pipe network.

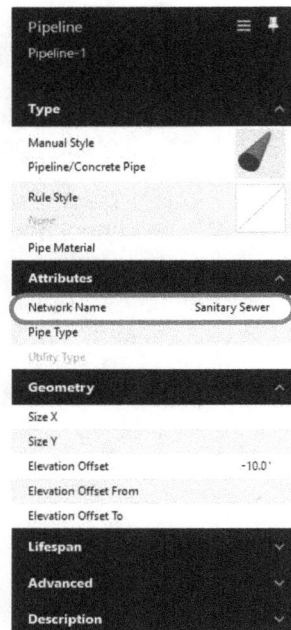

Figure 4–26

Hint: Order of Operations

It is easier to create the pipeline connectors first. Pipelines snap to existing pipeline connectors and stay connected. This enables you to control the location of any pipeline by moving the pipeline connectors to which it is connected.

Pipeline Connectors

Pipeline connectors are nodes that connect to pipe ends. They can represent pipeline structures (such as manholes and catch-basins) along a pipeline.

How To: Create Pipeline Connectors

1. In the In Canvas tools, click [icon] (Build, manage, and analyze your infrastructure model)> [icon] (Create conceptual design features)> [icon] (Pipeline Connectors). The Select Draw Style asset card displays.
2. In the Select Draw Style asset card, select a pipeline connector style, as shown in Figure 4–27.

Figure 4–27

3. Double-click in the model to place the Pipeline Connector. Each pipeline connector is added separately as required.

Create Pipelines

Pipelines represent various utility lines (e.g., gas, water, sanitary sewer, storm sewer, etc.). Pipelines can connect to pipeline connectors or other pipe ends.

How To: Create Pipelines

1. In the In Canvas tools, click ![icon] (Build, manage, and analyze your infrastructure model)> ![icon] (Create conceptual design features)> ![icon] (Pipelines).
2. In the Select Draw Style asset card, select the required pipeline style, as shown in Figure 4–28.

Figure 4–28

If you click in the model near a pipeline connector, the pipeline automatically snaps to the connector

3. Click in the model to place the first pipe end.
4. Move the cursor in the direction in which you want the pipeline to run. Type a distance for the pipe length and press <Enter> to set the distance. Click in the model to place a pipe bend.
5. Continue clicking in the model to place pipe bends until all of the lengths of pipe have been created for the Pipeline.
6. Double-click to place the last pipe segment and end the command.

Edit Pipelines

Pipelines are created as 2D features that drape on the terrain surface. However, in the real world, most pipes are buried below the ground. Therefore, once you lay out the horizontal location of pipelines, you must adjust the vertical layout by adding a negative value in the *Elevation Offset* field in the Pipeline asset card (as shown in Figure 4–29) or by using ▲● (Elevation Gizmo) in the model.

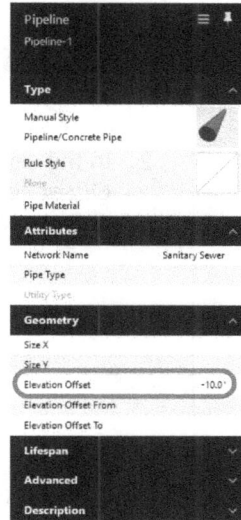

Figure 4–29

Note: After a pipeline elevation has been adjusted below a surface, the pipeline gizmos continue to drape on the terrain surface, as shown in Figure 4–30.

Figure 4–30

How To: Adjust the Pipeline Elevations

1. Select the Pipeline in the model and orbit the view to a side view. The pipes lie on the road surface, and a box displays indicating the orthogonal directions (also known as level lines), as shown in Figure 4–31.

Level
Line

Figure 4–31

2. In the asset card, type a negative value in the *Elevation Offset* field (as shown in Figure 4–32) to place the pipes below ground.

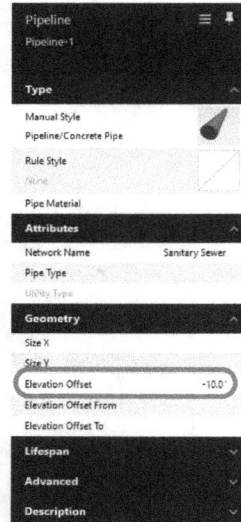

Figure 4–32

3. Use ⬢ (Elevation Gizmo) to make changes to individual pipe bend elevations.

Practice 4c

Estimated time for completion: 20 minutes

Create Utilities in the Model

Practice Objective

- Create a sanitary sewer in the model to illustrate the design concept.

In this practice you will create manholes and connect them with a pipeline that will act as a sanitary sewer for the project.

Task 1 - Create manholes.

1. In the Home Screen, click **Open**.

2. In the *C:\InfraWorks Fundamentals Practice Files\Create* folder, select **CreateFeatures.sqlite** and click **Open**.

3. In the Utility Bar, expand *Switch Active Proposal* and select **C_Task1**.

4. In the Utility Bar, click ▦ (Bookmark your current location) and select **Church**.

5. In the In Canvas tools, click ▮ (Build, manage, and analyze your infrastructure model)> ✎ (Create conceptual design features)> ▧ (Pipeline Connectors).

6. In the Select Draw Style asset card, select the **Manhole-Round** style, as shown in Figure 4–33.

Figure 4–33

7. Double-click near the centerline of the road in line with the edge of the parking lot (as shown in Figure 4–34) to place the first Pipeline Connector (Point 1).

Figure 4–34

8. Pan the model and double-click to place a pipeline connector at each intersection, as shown in Figure 4–35. You will place seven pipeline connectors in total.

Figure 4–35

Task 2 - Create the pipeline to connect the manholes.

1. In the Utility Bar, click ▯ (Bookmark your current location) and select **Church**. Expand *Switch Active Proposal* and then select **C_Task2**.

2. In the In Canvas tools, click (Build, manage, and analyze your infrastructure model)> (Create conceptual design features)> (Pipelines). The Select Draw Style asset card displays.

3. In the Select Draw Style asset card, select the **Concrete Pipe** pipeline style, as shown in Figure 4–36.

Figure 4–36

4. Click near the Point 1 Pipeline Connector to connect the Pipe.

5. Pan the model to the right and click in each intersection to connect the pipe to the pipeline connector located at each intersection, as shown in Figure 4–37. Double-click when you connect the pipeline to Point 7 to end the command.

Figure 4–37

6. Press <Esc> to show the pipe gizmos, and then orbit the view to a side view. The pipes lie on the road surface, and a box displays indicating the orthogonal directions (also known as level lines), as shown in Figure 4–38.

Level line

Figure 4–38

7. In the Pipeline asset card, for the *Network Name,* type **Storm**. In the *Elevation Offset* field, type **-10** (as shown in Figure 4–39) to place the pipes below ground.

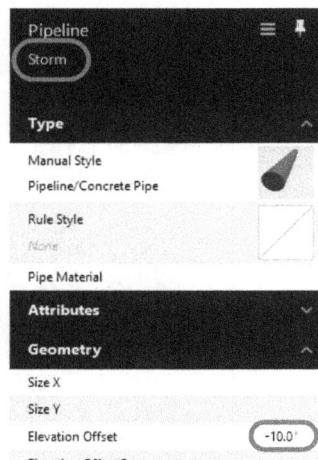

Figure 4–39

8. In the Utility Bar, expand the View Style drop-down and click ⚙ (Configure current view).

9. In the View Settings asset card, click 🔍 (Change navigation and application feedback settings) to open the *Interaction* stack.

10. Under *Navigation,* click the **Lock Mouse Above Ground** slider to the left to toggle it off.

11. Orbit the model to display the pipes below ground.

12. Press <Esc> to clear the selection of the Pipeline.

Although the pipes are below the ground, the gizmos remain draped on the terrain surface.

4.5 Create Railways in a Model

Many cities are searching for cost-effective, environmentally sensitive, and socially responsible ways to provide public transportation systems. At the same time, freight trains are still used for transporting goods from one location to another. Both freight and commuter rail projects can be modeled in the Autodesk InfraWorks 360 software.

Create Railways

It does not matter if you are creating a freight railway line or a commuter railway line. Both use the same command. The style for a railway determines how the railway tracks and the ground below and adjacent to the tracks display in the model. By default a dirt and grass look is provided, as shown in Figure 4–40. Additional styles can be created using the Railway material group provided with the software.

Figure 4–40

Regardless of the style that is used, the railway and road are automatically cleaned up where they intersect. This ensures that the rails display flush with the road surface, as they would in the real world. An example is shown in Figure 4–41.

Figure 4–41

How To: Create Railways

1. In the In Canvas tools, click (Build, manage, and analyze your infrastructure model)> (Create conceptual design features)> (Railways).
2. In the Select Draw Style asset card, select the railway style, as shown in Figure 4–42.

Figure 4–42

3. Click in the location at which you want the railway to start.
4. Move the cursor in the direction in which you want the railway to run. Type a distance for the length to the next point of intersection and press <Enter> to set the distance. Click in the model to place the point of intersection.

5. Continue clicking in the model to place points of intersection until all of the lengths of rail have been created for the railway.
6. Double-click to place the last railway point and end the command.

Edit Railways

Once a railway has been created, it can be re-shaped using

, which displays at each Point of Intersection (PI) when the railway is selected in the model. If you

orbit the model more than 45 degrees, displays and can be used to adjust the elevation of each PI.

Additional vertices can be added anywhere along the railway to add additional control and elevation points. To add a vertex, select the railway, right-click in the location to which you want the additional control, and select **Add Vertex**, as shown in Figure 4–43.

Figure 4–43

Similar to conceptual roads, conceptual railways must be split where bridges are required, and then the style must be changed where a section of the railway goes over a bridge. This can be accomplished by dragging the Railway>Bridge style from the Style palette, or by using the manual style field in the Railway asset card, as shown in Figure 4–44.

Figure 4–44

Practice 4d

Estimated time for completion: 15 minutes

Create a Passenger Railway in the Model

Practice Objective

- Create a passenger railway in the model.

In this practice you will create a light rail system for commuter passengers that provides transportation options for the new community.

Task 1 - Create a railway.

1. In the Home Screen, click ⬜ (Open).

2. In the *C:\InfraWorks Fundamentals Practice Files\Create* folder, select **CreateFeatures.sqlite** and click **Open**.

3. In the Utility Bar, expand the *Switch Active Proposal* and select **D_Task1**.

4. In the Utility Bar, click ⬜ (Bookmark your current location) and select **Railway**.

5. In the In Canvas tools, click ⬜ (Build, manage, and analyze your infrastructure model)> ⬜ (Create conceptual design features)> ⬜ (Railways).

6. In the Select Draw Style asset card, select the **Railway** style, as shown in Figure 4–45.

Figure 4–45

7. In the model, click points on the west side of Redwood Road to place the railway, similar to that shown in Figure 4–46.

Figure 4–46

8. Double-click north of the road that runs into the new neighborhood to place the last point and end the command.

9. In the Utility Bar, click ⬛ (Bookmark your current location) and select **RailCrossing**.

Note that the intersection at the road automatically adjusted where the railway crosses the road (the road elevation was modified).

4.6 Create Water Features in a Model

When designing a new community, water features are often required. Water features have a number of purposes. They can act as a water retention area that is used by local residents for drinking water, such as a reservoir. They can also be used to divert excess water away from homes and businesses to avoid flooding. This is often required when new hard surfaces prevent water from being absorbed into the ground, as it did before the land was developed. Finally, water areas can be used to provide recreation and make an area more visually appealing.

Water areas are a surface layer in the Model Explorer. You can create the following two types of water features:

- **Water Areas:** Enables you to create bodies of water, such as ponds, lakes, and wetlands. To create a body of water, you click points that act as a boundary for the water area. Figure 4–47 shows a small pond water area.

Figure 4–47

- **Rivers:** Enables you to create linear water features, such as canals, rivers, and streams. To create a river, you click points along a linear path. A buffer surrounds the water on either side. The buffer width is set in the Water asset card, as shown in Figure 4–48.

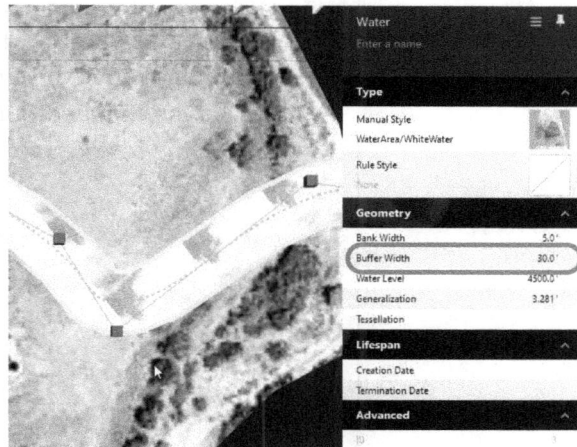

Figure 4–48

How To: Create Rivers or Streams

1. In the In Canvas tools, click ▮ (Build, manage, and analyze your infrastructure model)> ✏ (Create conceptual design features)> 🌊 (Rivers).
2. In the Select Draw Style asset card, select the required water style, as shown in Figure 4–49.

Figure 4–49

3. Click in the model to define the start location of the linear path for the water area.
4. Move the cursor in the direction in which you want the river or steam to run. Type a distance for the length to the next point of intersection (PI) and press <Enter> to set the distance. Click in the model to place the PI.
5. Continue clicking PIs until all of the lengths of the river or stream have been created for the water area.
6. Double-click to place the last point and end the command.

7. With the water area selected, in the Water asset card, do the following, as shown in Figure 4–50:
   - Set the required *Bank Width*.
   - Set the required *Buffer Width*.
   - Set the required *Water Level*.

Figure 4–50

How To: Create Lakes or Ponds

1. In the In Canvas tools, click (Build, manage, and analyze your infrastructure model)> (Create conceptual design features)> (Water Areas).

2. In the Select Draw Style asset card, select the required water style, as shown in Figure 4–51.

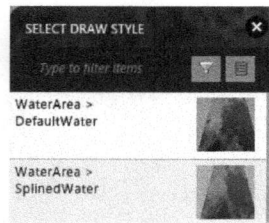

Figure 4–51

3. Click in the model to start the creation of the water boundary.
4. Move the cursor in the direction that you want the water boundary to follow. Type a distance for the length to the next point on the boundary and press <Enter> to set the distance. Click in the model to place the boundary point.
5. Continue clicking in the model until all of the boundary points have been created for the water area.
6. Double-click to place the last boundary point and end the command.

Practice 4e

Estimated time for completion: 20 minutes

Create Water Features in the Model

Practice Objective

- Create water features in the model to represent a retention pond.

In this practice you will create a water area that represents a water retention pond for the new subdivision and a new white water park.

Task 1 - Create water areas.

1. In the Home Screen, click **Open**.

2. In the *C:\InfraWorks Fundamentals Practice Files\Create* folder, select **CreateFeatures.sqlite** and click **Open**.

3. In the Utility Bar, expand *Switch Active Proposal* and select **E_Task1**.

4. In Utility Bar, click (Bookmark your current location) and select **Pond**.

5. In the In Canvas tools, click (Build, manage, and analyze your infrastructure model)> (Create conceptual design features)> (Water Areas).

6. In the Select Draw Style asset card, select **Splined Water**, as shown in Figure 4–52.

Figure 4–52

7. Click near the entrance to the new neighborhood to start the boundary, as shown in Figure 4–53. Ensure that you leave room for the new railway to be expanded in the future.

Figure 4–53

8. In the model, move the cursor to the west. Type **50** for the length to the next point on the boundary and press <Enter> to set the distance. Click in the model to place the boundary point.

9. Move the cursor to the south parallel to the road. Type **150** for the length to the next point on the boundary and press <Enter> to set the distance. Click in the model to place the boundary point.

10. Move the cursor to the east. Type **100** for the length to the next point on the boundary and press <Enter> to set the distance. Double-click to place the last boundary point and end the command, as shown in Figure 4–54.

Figure 4–54

11. Press <Esc> twice to clear the selection of the new water area.

Task 2 - Create a river.

The developer on the project is proposing that a white water park be created to attract active people to the community. For practice, you will create a new material style, and then add it to a new water style. You will then use the new water style to create a river to the east of Redwood Rd and south of the new bridge, as shown in Figure 4–55.

Figure 4–55

1. Continue working in the same model as the previous task.

2. In Utility Bar, click ▮▮ (Bookmark your current location) and select **River**. Expand *Switch Active Proposal* and then select **E_Task2**.

3. Open the Style palette and select the *Material* tab.

4. At the bottom of the *Material* tab, click ✛ (Add new style to current catalog above).

5. Use the following parameters to create the new material style, as shown in Figure 4–56:
   - Set the *Type* to **Texture**.
   - Browse for the **WhiteWater.png** (found in *C:\InfraWorks Fundamentals Practice Files\Create*) to use as the texture.
   - Set the sizes to be **100** ft by **100** ft.
   - Click **OK**.
   - Name it **WhiteWater**.

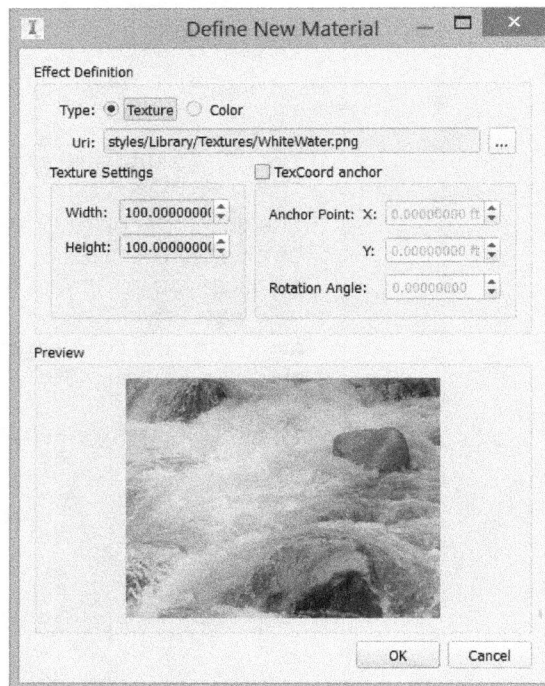

Figure 4–56

6. In the Style palette, select the *Water* tab.

7. Select the **SplinedWater** style, then at the bottom of the
   Water tab, click [icon] (Make a local copy of the selected style
   to the current catalog).

8. Name the copied style **WhiteWater**.

9. Double-click on the WhiteWater style. Modify the new style as
   follows so that it matches Figure 4–57:

   • Set the Bank width to **30 ft**.

   • Set the water level offset to **-5 ft**.

   • Set the Water surface material to **WhiteWater**.

   • Click **OK**.

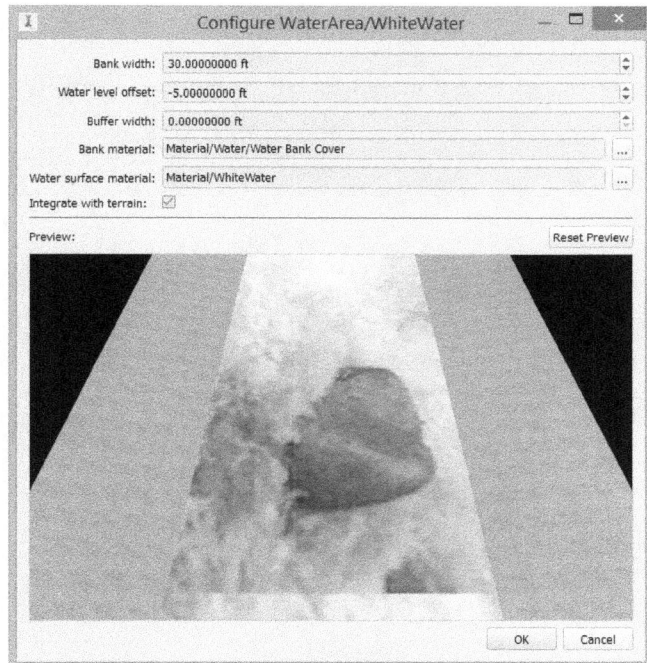

Figure 4–57

10. In the In Canvas tools, click [icon] (Build, manage, and analyze
    your infrastructure model)> [icon] (Create conceptual design
    features)> [icon] (Rivers).

11. In the Select Draw Style asset card, select **WhiteWater**.

12. Create a river similar to that shown in Figure 4–58.

Figure 4–58

13. Press <Esc> to show the river gizmos.

14. In the Water asset card, set the following:
    - *Bank Width* to **5 ft**
    - *Buffer Width* to **30 ft**
    - *Water Level* to **4500 ft**

15. Press <Esc> to release the river selection.

4.7 Create Land Areas (Preview)

Similar to coverages, land areas provide a way for you to grade areas and change how the terrain displays. There are two key differences that land areas provide over coverages:

AUTODESK®
INFRAWORKS™ 360

To use this feature, access to the Internet and Autodesk® InfraWorks® 360 are required.

- The top surface of a land area is automatically flattened, as shown in Figure 4–59. A coverage drapes on the surface until the terrain is manually shaped.

- Land areas enable you to control the display of cut and fill areas separately. Figure 4–59 shows a land area with a 3:1 grass material for the fill and a 1:1 stone wall material for the cut.

Figure 4–59

How To: Create a Land Area

1. In the In Canvas tools, click ▮ (Build, manage and analyze your infrastructure model) > ✎ (Create conceptual design features) > ▣ (Land Areas).

2. Select the material style for the top surface you are creating from the Select Draw Style asset card that displays, as shown in Figure 4–60.

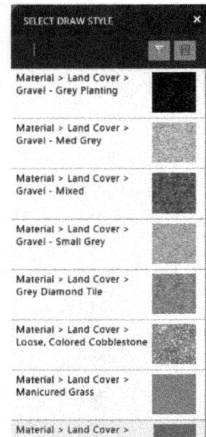

This style is used for the land area top surface only, not the cut and fill slopes. The cut and fill styles are set later.

Figure 4–60

3. In the model, click to place the vertices of the land area footprint. After the first vertex has been placed, move the cursor in the direction in which you want the next vertex to be placed.

Locking a length means that even if you move the cursor, the dimension value does not change.

4. Type the required length for the side of the land area and press <Enter> to lock the length. Move the cursor as required to set the correct angle and click to place the vertex.
5. Continue adding vertexes in the model until all but the last vertex has been set.
6. Double-click on the location at which you want to place the final vertex. Doing so ends the command.
7. Press <Esc> to clear the selection of the newly created land area.

Hint: Accessing the Land Areas Tool

If the (Land Areas) tool is not available in the In Canvas Tools, toggle on the **Land Areas & Grading Behaviors** option on the Home Screen, as shown in Figure 4–61.

Figure 4–61

Grading Styles

Grading styles control how the cut and fill slopes display. Several grading styles are provided in the Autodesk InfraWorks 360 software (as shown in Figure 4–62) and additional styles can be created as required. The thumbnails in the Style palette display a preview of the materials and slopes that are used in each style. If the cut and fill slopes use the same material, only one material is shown in the thumbnail. If the cut and fill slopes use different materials, both materials display in the thumbnail with their slope values, as shown in Figure 4–63.

Figure 4–62

Figure 4–63

How To: Create a New Grading Style

1. Open the Style palette and select the *Grading* tab.
2. In the *Style Editing* area at the bottom of the Style palette, click ✚ (Add new style to the current catalog above).
3. In the Define New Grading dialog box, set the *Grading Method to* either **Fixed Width** or **Fixed Slope**.

4. If **Fixed Slope** is selected, set the following options and then click **OK**, as shown in Figure 4–64. Otherwise, continue to the next step.

- Set the *Cut Slope* (Run:Rise)
- Set the *Fill Slope* (Run:Rise)
- If the Cut/Fill Materials use different styles, clear the **Cut and Fill Material use the same Style** checkbox.
- Select the appropriate Cut and Fill Material styles.
- Set the *Grading Limit*, if required. Otherwise, clear the **Set Limit for Grading** checkbox.

Figure 4–64

5. If **Fixed Width** is selected, set the following options, as shown in Figure 4–65.

- Set the *Grading Width*.
- Select a *Grading Material*.

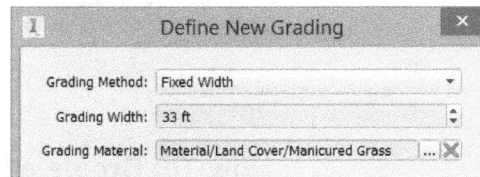

Figure 4–65

6. Click **OK**.

Edit Land Areas

Once a land area has been created, it can be re-shaped using

 (Control Point Gizmo). The gizmos are displayed at each vertex when the land area is selected in the model. By default, land area top surfaces are flat with all of the footprint vertices sharing the same elevation. If the model is orbited more than 45

degrees, (Elevation Gizmos) display and can be used to adjust the elevation of each vertex independently.

Vertices can be added anywhere along a side to add additional control and elevation points. To add a vertex, select the land area, right-click on the point at which you want to have additional control, and select **Add Vertex**, as shown in Figure 4–66.

Figure 4–66

Set Cut/Fill Slopes

The graduation of a slope that extends from a land area footprint depends upon the grading style selected for the land area. This value is changed by setting the *Rule Grading* value for the land area.

How To: Apply a Cut/Fill Slopes to a Land Area

1. Create a land area.

2. On the Utility Bar, click ▣ (Edit).

3. With the land area still selected, in the Land Areas asset card, change the *Rule Grading* style, as shown in Figure 4–67.

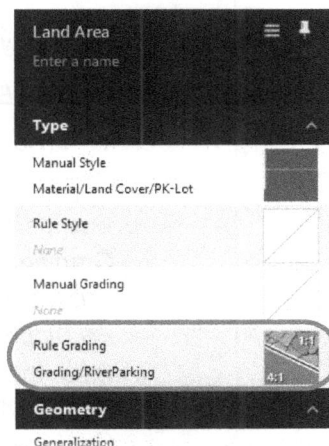

Figure 4–67

Practice 4f

Estimated time for completion: 20 minutes

Grade a Parking Lot Using a Land Area (Preview)

Practice Objective

- Create land areas in the model to represent a parking lot and surrounding grass.

In this practice you will use land areas to create a parking lot for the white water park, setting the cut and fill slope displays separately. You will then add another land area with a gradual slope covered in grass for the patrons to access the river.

Task 1 - Create a new grading style.

In this task, you will create a new grading style which uses river stone for the cut and grass for the fill of the proposed parking lot.

1. In the Home Screen, click **Open**.

2. In the *C:\InfraWorks Fundamentals Practice Files\Create* folder, select **CreateFeatures.sqlite** and then click **Open**.

3. In the Utility Bar, expand *Switch Active Proposal* and select **F_Task1**.

4. In Utility Bar, click ▦ (Bookmark your current location) and select **River**.

5. Open the Style palette and select the *Grading* tab.

6. In the *Style Editing* area at the bottom of the Style palette, click ✚ (Add new style to the current catalog above).

7. In the Define New Grading dialog box, set the following options, as shown in Figure 4–68:
   - *Grading Method:* **Fixed Slope**.
   - *Cut Slope*: **1:1**
   - *Fill Slope*: **4:1**
   - Clear the **Cut and Fill Material use the same Style** checkbox.
   - *Cut Material*: Select **Material>Land Cover>Riverstone**.
   - Fill Material: Select **Material>Land Cover>Manicured Grass**.
   - Clear the **Set Grading Limit** checkbox.
   - Click **OK**.

Figure 4–68

8. Type **RiverParking** for the name.

Task 2 - Create a parking lot and grass area for park patrons.

In this task, you will create a parking lot for the white water park patrons and a grass area which provides a more gradual slope to the river on the south side.

1. Continue working in the same model as the last task. If you did not complete the last task, in the Utility Bar, expand *Switch Active Proposal* and select **F_Task2**.

2. In the In Canvas tools, click ![icon] (Build, manage and analyze your infrastructure model) > ![icon] (Create conceptual design features) > ![icon] (Land Areas).

*If the Land Areas tool is unavailable, you might need to toggle on the Preview of **Land Areas & Grading Behaviors** in the Home Screen.*

3. In the Select Draw Style asset card that displays, type PK and select **PK-Lot**, as shown in Figure 4–69.

This style is used for the land area top surface only, not the cut and fill slopes. The cut and fill styles are set later.

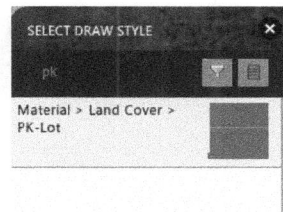

Figure 4–69

4. In the model, click to place the first vertex of the land area footprint, as shown in Figure 4–70.

Figure 4–70

5. Move the cursor in the Northwest direction, type **200**, and then press <Enter> to lock in the distance. Click to place the second vertex, as shown in Figure 4–70.

6. Move the cursor in the Northeast direction, type **100**, and then press <Enter> to lock in the distance. Click to place the third vertex, as shown in Figure 4–71.

7. Move the cursor in the Southeast direction, type **200**, and then press <Enter> to lock in the distance. Double-click to place the final vertex and end the command, as shown in Figure 4–71.

Figure 4–71

Ensure that you double-click the last point to end the command.

8. Restart the **Land Area** command.

9. Select **ManacuredGrass** for the style.

10. Set the points for the vertices, as shown in Figure 4–72.

Figure 4–72

11. Press <Esc> twice to end the command.

12. Select the Parking lot land area.

13. In the Land Area asset card, change the *Rule Grading* style to the new **RiverParking** grading style, as shown in Figure 4–73.

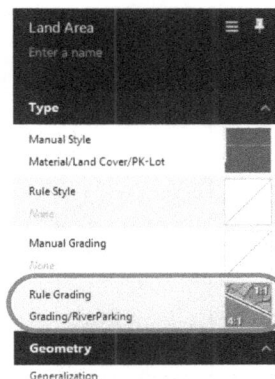

Figure 4–73

14. Press <Esc> to clear the selection of the parking lot land area.

15. Select the grass land area to the south of the parking lot.

16. In the Land Areas asset card, change the **Rule Grading** style to the **GrassCut, Fill** grading style.

17. Press <Esc> to clear the selection of the grass land area.

The results are shown in Figure 4–74.

Figure 4–74

Chapter Review Questions

1. Which selection tool would you use to select multiple model elements completely inside a specified area?

   a. ▢ (Window Select)

   b. ▢ (Rectangle Select)

   c. ▢ (Polygon Select)

2. Which of the following gizmos would not change the height or elevation of a model element?

   a. ▲ (Elevation Gizmo)

   b. ▯ (Height Gizmo)

   c. ▮ (Control Gizmo)

   d. ⤢ (Move Gizmo)

3. How do you change the elevation of a road at a point at which a point of intersection does not exist?

   a. Select the road, right-click and select **Add Vertex**. Use ▲ (Elevation Gizmo) to adjust the elevation.

   b. Select the road, right-click and select **Add Vertex**. Use ▮ (Control Gizmo) to adjust the elevation.

   c. Select the road, right-click and select **Split Feature**. Use ▲ (Elevation Gizmo) to adjust the elevation.

   d. You cannot adjust the elevation of roads.

4. How do you change the appearance or elevation of a terrain surface?

   a. Apply a different terrain style to it to change the appearance and right-click to add elevation points.

   b. Create a coverage or land area and adjust the elevations at each vertex along the boundary of the coverage.

   c. You cannot change the appearance or elevation of surfaces.

   d. Import a new surface from external data sources.

5. Where are pipeline gizmos located?

   a. At the end of each pipe length, draped on the terrain surface.

   b. At the end of each pipe length and at the elevation of the pipe ends.

   c. Only at the beginning and end of the entire pipe network, draped on the terrain surface.

   d. Only at the beginning and end of the entire pipe network and at the elevation of the pipe ends.

6. To make a railway flush with a road (as shown in Figure 4–75) you must split the railway into multiple segments and apply different styles at the road intersection.

Figure 4–75

   a. True

   b. False

7. How do you set the width of a river?

   a. Create a polyline area manually that sets where each bank ends.

   b. Select the river and change the buffer width in the Water Area asset card.

   c. After creating the centerline of the river, click a point to set the width.

   d. The width cannot be changed.

8. How are Land Areas different than Coverages? (Select all that apply.)

   a. Land Area top surfaces start out flat while coverages drape on the terrain surface.

   b. Land Areas are used to create piles of rock and dirt.

   c. Land Areas enable you to control the cut slope separate from the fill slope.

   d. There are no differences between land areas and coverages.

Command Summary

Button	Command	Location
N/A	Copy	• **Shortcut Key:** <Ctrl>+<C>
	Coverages	• **In Canvas Tools:** Build, manage, and analyze your industry model > Create conceptual design features
N/A	Cut	• **Shortcut Key:** <Ctrl>+<X>
N/A	De-select	• **Shortcut Key:** <Esc>
N/A	Delete	• **Shortcut Key:** <Delete>
N/A	Invert Selection	• **Shortcut Key**: <Alt>+<I>
	Land Areas	• **In Canvas Tools:** Build, manage, and analyze your industry model > Create conceptual design features
N/A	Paste	• **Shortcut Key:** <Ctrl>+<V>
N/A	Paste In Place	• **Shortcut Key:** <Shift>+<Ctrl>+<V>
	Pipeline Connectors	• **In Canvas Tools:** Build, manage, and analyze your industry model > Create conceptual design features
	Pipelines	• **In Canvas Tools:** Build, manage, and analyze your industry model > Create conceptual design features
	Railways	• **In Canvas Tools:** Build, manage, and analyze your industry model > Create conceptual design features
	Redo	• **Utility Bar** • **Shortcut Key:** <Ctrl>+<Y>
	Rivers	• **In Canvas Tools:** Build, manage, and analyze your industry model > Create conceptual design features
	Roads	• **In Canvas Tools:** Build, manage, and analyze your industry model > Create conceptual design features
N/A	Select All	• **Shortcut Key:** <Ctrl>+<A>
	Undo	• **Utility Bar** • **Shortcut Key:** <Ctrl>+<Z>
	Water Areas	• **In Canvas Tools:** Build, manage, and analyze your industry model > Create conceptual design features
N/A	Zoom Selected	• **Shortcut Key**: <Alt>+<Z>

Add Model Details

Using conceptual design tools, you can add additional details to a model, including buildings, landscaping, city furniture, and points of interest. In this chapter you learn how to add many of these model elements and how to edit the elements once they have been created.

Learning Objectives in this Chapter

- Create buildings in a model using the draw tools.
- Add predefined 3D buildings to a model.
- Create city furniture to add bike racks and other 3D models to a model.
- Add landscaping details to a model using trees and other vegetation.
- Create barriers to add fences and traffic control to a model.
- Draw attention to specific points in a model using points of interest markers.

5.1 Create Buildings in a Model

Custom buildings can be added to a model to add additional detail to the design. When creating a custom building, the look of the outside of the building is defined using a Facade style in the Select Draw Style asset card, as shown in Figure 5–1.

Figure 5–1

How To: Create Custom Buildings

1. In the In Canvas tools, click ![icon] (Build, manage, and analyze your infrastructure model)> ![icon] (Create conceptual design features)> ![icon] (Buildings).
2. The Select Draw Style asset card opens, as shown in Figure 5–2. Select the style for the exterior of the building.

Note that the asset card has the option to filter by building material types, such as bricks, marble, concrete, etc.

Figure 5–2

3. In the model, click to place the first corner of the building footprint.

4. After the first corner has been placed, move the cursor to where you want the next corner to be placed. The dimensions for that side of the building are displayed, as shown in Figure 5–3.

Figure 5–3

5. Type the required length for that side of the building and press <Enter> to lock the length. Move the cursor as required to set the correct angle and click to place the corner.
6. Repeat Steps 4 to 5 until all but the last corner have been set.
7. Double-click on the location at which you want to place the final corner to end the command.
8. Press <Esc> to clear the selection of the newly created building.

If you start drawing a building and enter a distance for the first side (for example 100') and then hold <Shift> you can snap to a right angle.

Edit Buildings

Once a building has been created, the height should be adjusted by using the Building asset card, or by using 🏠 (Height Gizmo) while the building is selected. Clicking and dragging 🟫 (Control Point Gizmo) enables you to reshape the building footprint.

Hint: Changing Building Attributes

The roof material, slope, height, and other attributes can be set in the Building asset card, as shown in Figure 5–4.

Figure 5–4

Practice 5a

Estimated time for completion: 15 minutes

Create Buildings in the Model

Practice Objective

- Create buildings in the model.

In this practice you will create buildings using exact measurements to populate the new subdivision.

Task 1 - Create a building using specific measurements.

1. In the Home Screen, click **Open**.

2. In the *C:\InfraWorks Fundamentals Practice Files\AddDetails* folder, select **CreateDetails.sqlite** and click **Open**.

3. Set the proposal to **A_Task1** in the Utility Bar.

4. In the Utility Bar, click 🖾 (Bookmark your current location) and select **AddHomes**.

5. In the In Canvas tools, click 🔳 (Build, manage, and analyze your infrastructure model)> 🖉 (Create conceptual design features)> 🖳 (Buildings)

6. In the Select Draw Style asset card, type **Brick** in the filter field. Then select **Servillius**.

7. In the model, click to place the first corner of the building footprint, as shown in Figure 5–5.

First point of building

Figure 5–5

8. After the first corner has been placed, move the cursor due east and type **40** for the length of the first side, as shown in Figure 5–6. Click to place the second corner.

Figure 5–6

9. In the model, move the cursor due south, type **40** for the length of the second side, and then press <Enter>. Hold <Shift> to snap to a right angle and click to place the third corner.

10. Move the cursor due west, type **30** for the length, and then press <Enter>. Hold <Shift> to snap to a right angle and click to place the fourth corner.

11. Move the cursor due north, type **15** for the length, and then press <Enter>. Hold <Shift> to snap to a right angle and click to place the fifth corner.

12. Move the cursor due west, type **10** for the length, and then press <Enter>. Hold <Shift> to snap to a right angle and double-click to place the sixth corner and end the command.

13. Press <Esc> twice to clear the selection of the newly created building. The last corner lines up with the first corner, as shown in Figure 5–7.

Figure 5–7

14. Create a similar building to the south of the one you just created. Use measurements that are close to those shown in Figure 5–8.

Figure 5–8

15. Press <Esc> to show the second building's gizmos. Hold <Ctrl> and click on the first build to select it as well.

16. In the Building asset card, set the *Roof Height* and *Roof Slope* to **30**, as shown in Figure 5–9. Both buildings should update.

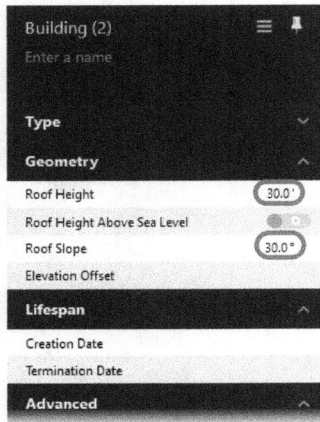

Figure 5–9

17. Press <Esc> to clear the selection.

5.2 Create City Furniture in a Model

If you need to create multiple predefined 3D buildings or other 3D models in your model, it is recommended that you use

![City Furniture icon] (City Furniture). This command enables you to create multiple 3D models spaced along a path or a single feature at the location specified. Any type of 3D model style can be selected as city furniture, including trees and railway models. However, these models display in the *Furniture* category in the Model Explorer and are furniture features in the database.

The following 3D models can be added as city furniture to a model:

*   **Bridge Components:** There several 3d models of various barriers and other components you would find on a bridge. Figure 5–10 shows a list of what is available in the software out of the box. Others can be added as required.

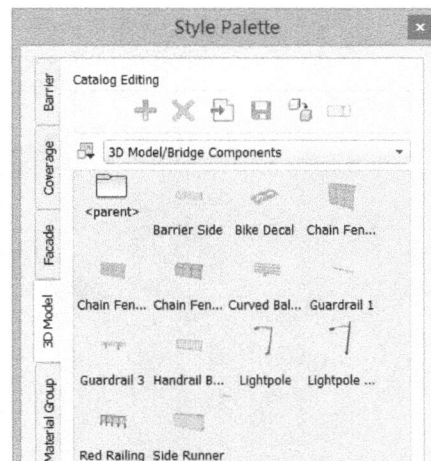

Figure 5–10

*   **Buildings:** There are a number of predefined 3D building models. They fall into three categories of from which you can select:
    *   **Furniture:** 3D models of roof-top items, such as solar panels and HVAC units.
    *   **Neighborhood:** A few common building types that are found in a typical city, such as gas stations, churches, and post offices.
    *   **Residential:** Multiple single-family home models.

These 3D model options are located in the *3D Model* tab of the Style Palette. The **Neighborhood** and **Residential** style options are shown in Figure 5–11.

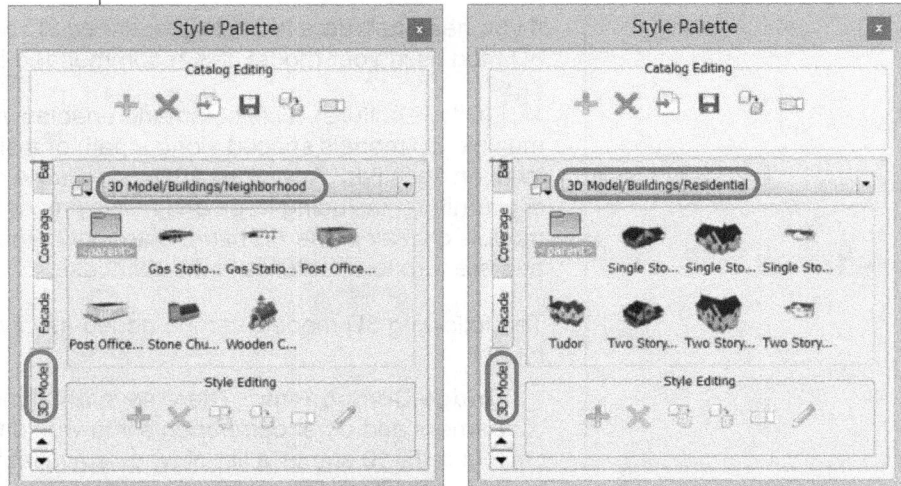

Figure 5–11

- **City Furniture:** Objects found in a city, including signs, fences, bike stands, parking meters, dumpsters, etc., as shown in Figure 5–12.

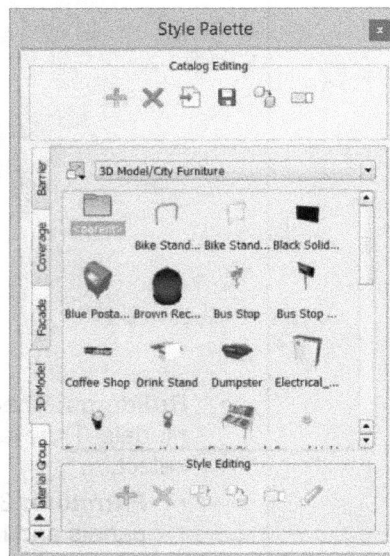

Figure 5–12

- **Construction:** Objects found on a construction site, including piles of dirt or sand, various pieces of equipment, Port-a-Potties, etc., as shown in Figure 5–13.

Figure 5–13

- **Energy:** Objects used to deliver energy to specific areas, including distribution pylons, solar panels, oil pumps, oil rigs, transmission poles, and wind turbines, as shown in Figure 5–14.

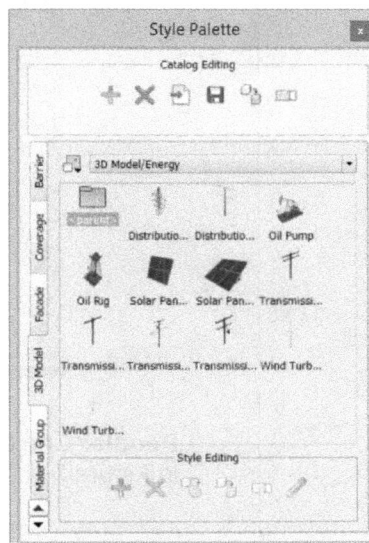

Figure 5–14

- **Highway:** Safety features used in road design, including guard rails and noise barriers, as shown in Figure 5–15.

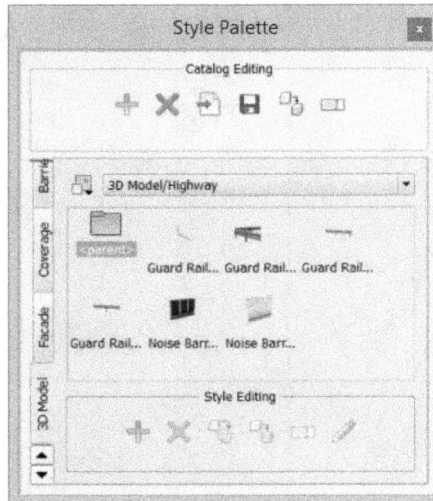

Figure 5–15

- **POI (Points of Interest):** Markers and flag pins used to draw attention to specific areas of the model, as shown in Figure 5–16.

Figure 5–16

- **People:** One or more people walking or standing, as shown in Figure 5–17.

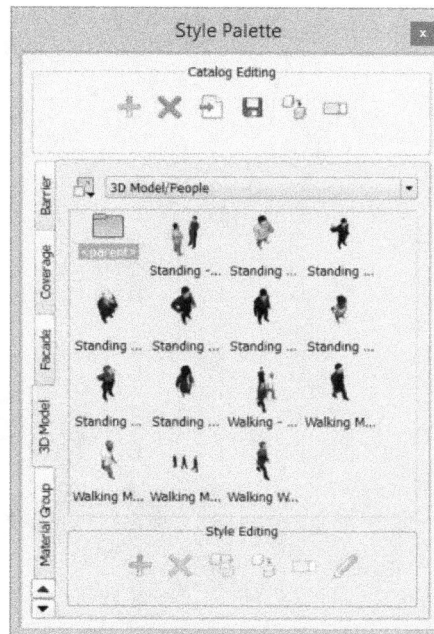

Figure 5–17

- **Planes & Ships:** Planes, helicopters, and water vessels, as shown in Figure 5–18.

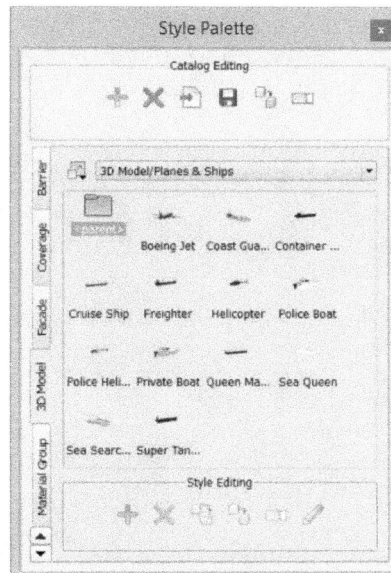

Figure 5–18

- **Railway:** Passenger cars, freight cars, and railway furniture, as shown in Figure 5–19.

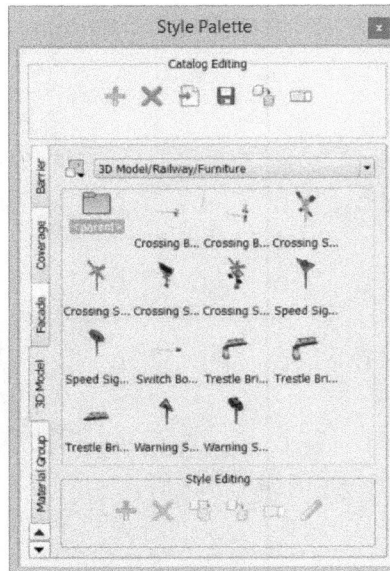

Figure 5–19

- **Shapes:** Shapes in multiple colors can be used to draw attention to specific areas of the model, as shown in Figure 5–20.

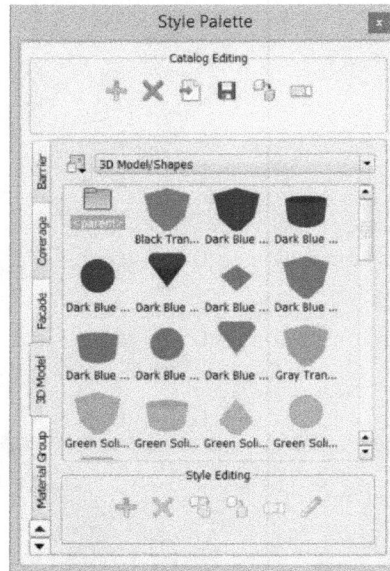

Figure 5–20

- **Traffic & Barriers:** Objects used to control traffic, including traffic lights, construction cones, metal fences, barriers, etc., as shown in Figure 5–21.

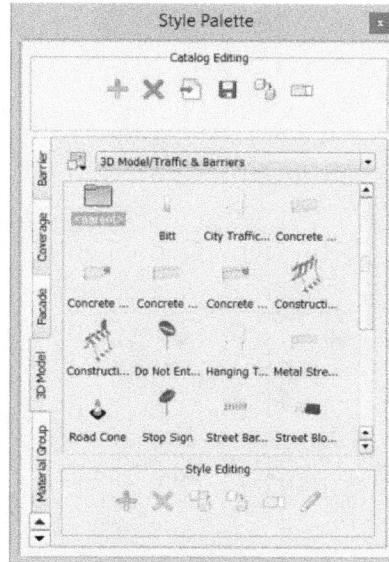

Figure 5–21

- **Vegetation:** Objects used in landscaping, including trees and bushes, as shown in Figure 5–22.

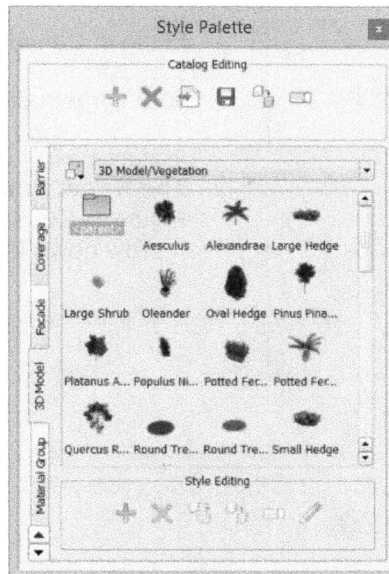

Figure 5–22

- **Vehicles:** Cars, trucks, vans, buses, and bicycles, as shown in Figure 5–23.

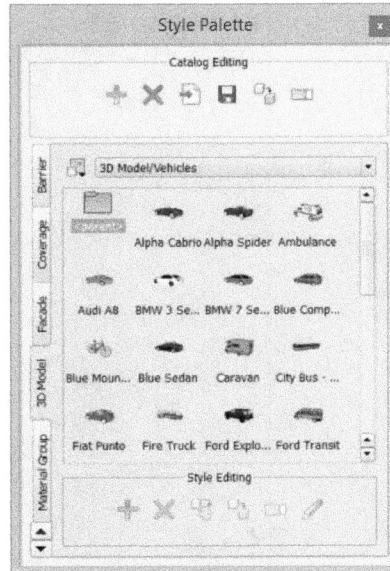

Figure 5–23

How To: Add One Predefined 3D Building or Another Single Piece of City Furniture

1. In the In Canvas tools, click ![icon] (Build, manage, and analyze your infrastructure model)> ![icon] (Create conceptual design features)> ![icon] (City Furniture).
2. The Select Draw Style asset card displays, as shown in Figure 5–24. Select the 3D Model or type in the filter area to narrow down the selection options.

Figure 5–24

3. In the model, double-click to place the model and end the command. The size is not important because the 3D Model size and shape are predetermined as part of the 3D model.

4. Press <Esc> to clear the selection of the newly created building.

Hint: Model Size/Shape

You cannot reshape or change the height of a building created from a 3D Model. The height and shape are predetermined by the model style. However, you can change the scale of the building using the 🗑 (Height Gizmo) or the Properties palette. Using the Height Gizmo causes the building to change scale while keeping the same ratio in the X,Y, and Z planes. However, changing the scale in the properties palette enables the model to be stretched in one or more directions, as shown in Figure 5–25.

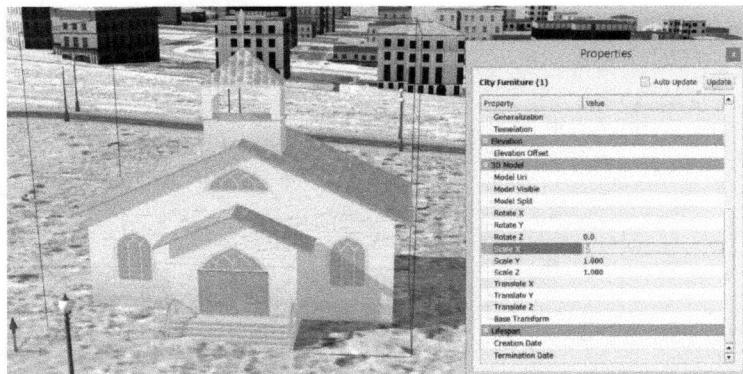

Figure 5–25

How To: Add Multiple Predefined 3D Buildings or Other City Furniture

1. In the In Canvas tools, click ▤ (Build, manage, and analyze your infrastructure model)>✏️ (Create conceptual design features)>▣ (City Furniture).
2. The Select Draw Style asset card displays, as shown in Figure 5–26. Select the 3D Model (or type in the filter area) to narrow down the selection options.

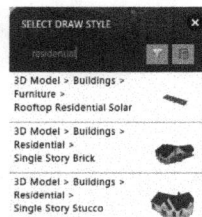

Figure 5–26

3. In the model, single-click to start the path to be followed by the 3D models.
4. In the model, move the cursor in the direction in which you want the 3D model path to follow. Type a distance for the length to the next point of intersection and press <Enter> to set the distance. Click in the model to place the point of intersection.
5. Continue clicking in the model until the full path has been created.
6. Double-click to place the last point and end the command.
7. To change the number of items that display along the path, slide the *Density* Slider (shown in Figure 5–27) until the model density is set as required.

Figure 5–27

8. Press <Esc> to clear the selection of the newly created 3D models.
9. Move and rotate each 3D model by selecting it and using

 (Rotate Gizmo), (Height Gizmo), and (Move Gizmo) as required. If you need to change which 3D model displays at specific locations, you can drag and drop another 3D model in its place from the Style Palette, as shown in Figure 5–28.

Figure 5–28

Practice 5b

Add Buildings and City Furniture to the Model

Estimated time for completion: 45 minutes

Practice Objective

- Add buildings and other 3D models to the model.

In this practice you will create buildings to populate the new subdivision. First, you will use a predefined 3D model to place a church and a row of houses. Next, you will create copies of existing buildings to make populating the subdivision more efficient. Finally, you will add vehicles and a traffic light to roads and a passenger car and a crossing barrier to the railway.

Task 1 - Add predefined buildings.

1. In the Home Screen, click **Open**.

2. In the *C:\InfraWorks Fundamentals Practice Files\AddDetails* folder, select **CreateDetails.sqlite**, and then click **Open**.

3. In the Utility Bar, expand *Switch Active Proposal* and select **B_Task1**.

4. In the Utility Bar, click ▣ (Bookmark your current location) and select **Church**.

5. In the In Canvas tools, click ▣ (Build, manage, and analyze your infrastructure model)> ✎ (Create conceptual design features)> ▣ (City Furniture).

6. In the Select Draw Style asset card that displays, type **church** in the search field. Select the **Wooden Church**, as shown in Figure 5–29.

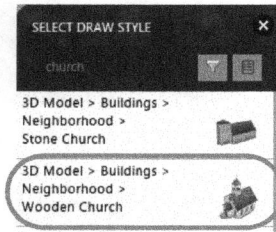

Figure 5–29

7. In the model, double-click in the open area at the center of the parking lot to place the church and end the command, as shown in Figure 5–30.

Figure 5–30

8. Press <Esc> to display the building gizmos.

9. With the church still selected, use ⌒ (Rotate Gizmo), 🔼 (Height Gizmo), and ✛ (Move Gizmo) as required to relocate it, as shown in Figure 5–31.

Figure 5–31

10. Press <Esc> to clear the selection of the church.

11. In the Utility Bar, click ▦ (Bookmark your current location) and select **New Neighborhood**.

12. In the In Canvas tools, click ▦ (Build, manage, and analyze your infrastructure model)> ▦ (Create conceptual design features)> ▦ (City Furniture).

13. In the Select Draw Style asset card, type **stucco** in the search field. Select the **Two Story Stucco**, as shown in Figure 5–32.

Figure 5–32

14. In the model, click to start a path, and then continue clicking PIs for the path the buildings should follow, as shown in Figure 5–33. Double-click to place the last point of the path and end the command.

Figure 5–33

15. Press <Esc> to display the gizmos and Feature Density slider.

16. Slide the Feature Density slider to the left to thin out the homes (set to approximately 40%), as shown in Figure 5–34.

Figure 5–34

17. With the homes still selected as a group, right-click and select **Properties.**

18. In the Properties palette, change *Scale X*, *Scale Y*, and *Scale Z* to **1.5**, as shown in Figure 5–35. Click **Update**.

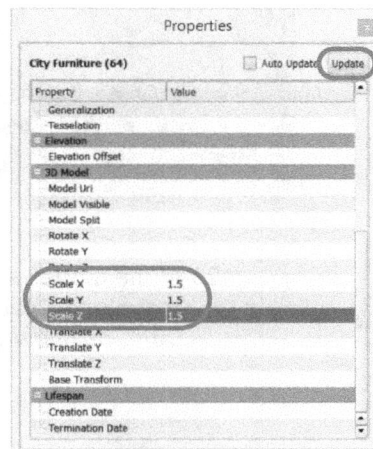

Figure 5–35

19. Press <Esc> to clear the selection. Close the Properties palette.

20. In the Utility Bar, click ⬛ (Bookmark your current location) and select **SingleStoryHome.**

21. In the In Canvas tools, click ⬛ (Build, manage, and analyze your infrastructure model)> ✏ (Create conceptual design features)> ⊞ (Style Palette).

22. In the Style palette, select the *3D Model* tab and double-click **Buildings>Residential**. Select the **Single Story Brick** style and drag it to the house closest to the church, as shown in Figure 5–36.

Figure 5–36

23. In the model, select the single story home and use gizmos to move and rotate it appropriately. then adjust the height to **30 ft**, as shown in Figure 5–37.

Figure 5–37

24. Press <Esc> to clear the selection.

Task 2 - Create copies of existing buildings.

1. Continue working in the same model. If you did not complete the last task, set the proposal to **B_Task2** in the Utility Bar.

2. In the Utility Bar, click 🔲 (Bookmark your current location) and select **New Neighborhood**. Pan the model to the north to display the yellow highlighted homes shown in Figure 5–38.

Figure 5–38

3. In the In Canvas tools, click ▮ (Build, manage, and analyze your industry model)> ◥ (Select model features)> ▣ (Rectangular Select).

4. In the model, create the selection rectangle as shown in Figure 5–39. Remember to double-click on the third point to end the selection.

Second point of rectangle

Third point of rectangle

First point of rectangle

Figure 5–39

5. Press <Ctrl>+<C> to copy the selected homes to the clipboard.

6. Press <Ctrl>+<V> and double-click in the model to place the homes as shown in Figure 5–40.

Figure 5–40

7. Continue to create or copy homes to fill in the new neighborhood using any of the tools discussed so far. Ensure that you leave an area open for the proposed commuter station, shown in white in Figure 5–41.

Figure 5–41

Task 3 - Create city furniture.

In this task, you will place a traffic light at the three-way intersection for the new neighborhood. You will then place cars on the roads to indicate how traffic should look as it enters the new neighborhood.

1. Continue working in the same model. If you did not complete the last task, set the proposal to **B_Task3** in the Utility Bar.

2. In the Utility Bar, click ▨ (Bookmark your current location) and select **Neighborhood Entrance**.

3. In the In Canvas tools, click ▨ (Build, manage, and analyze your infrastructure model)>✎ (Create conceptual design features)>▨ (City Furniture).

4. The Select Draw Style asset card displays. Type **Traffic** in the filter field and select the **City Traffic Light**, as shown in Figure 5–42.

Figure 5–42

5. Double-click in the model to place a traffic light on the east side of the intersection, as shown in Figure 5–43.

Figure 5–43

6. Press <Esc> to display the gizmos. Then move and rotate it using (Rotate Gizmo) and (Move Gizmo) as required to line it up as shown in Figure 5–44.

Figure 5–44

7. Press <Esc> to clear the selection of the traffic light.

8. In the Utility Bar, click (Bookmark your current location) and select **Pond**.

9. In the In Canvas tools, click (Build, manage, and analyze your infrastructure model)> (Create conceptual design features)> (City Furniture).

10. The Select Draw Style asset card displays. Type **Vehicle** in the filter field and select the **Alpha Spider**, as shown in Figure 5–45.

Figure 5–45

11. Create a path as shown in Figure 5–46. Remember to double-click to place the last point along the path.

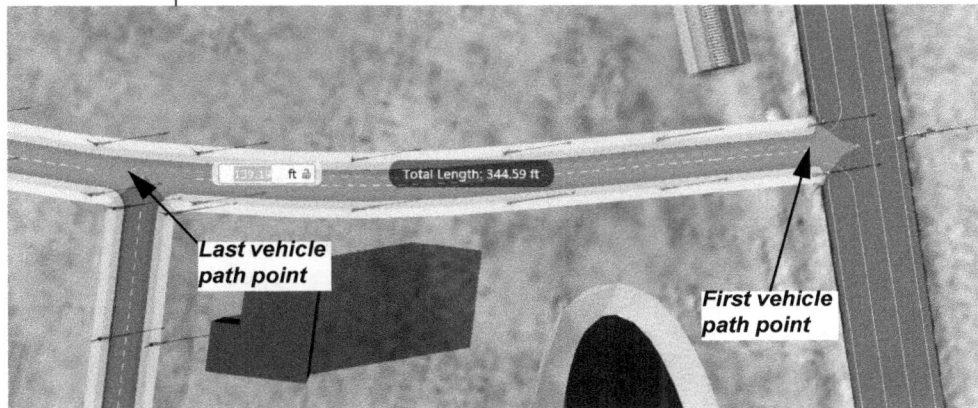

Figure 5–46

12. Press <Esc> to display the gizmos and the Density Slider. Slide the Density Slider (as shown in Figure 5–47) until the density is set close to **50%** so that there are 5 cars.

Figure 5–47

13. Press <Esc> to clear the selection of the newly created vehicles.

14. Move and rotate each vehicle using ⌒ (Rotate Gizmo) and ⬆ (Move Gizmos) as required to make them parallel to the road, as shown in Figure 5–48.

Figure 5–48

15. In the In Canvas tools, click 🔲 (Build, manage, and analyze your infrastructure model)> ✏ (Create conceptual design features)> 🔳 (Style palette).

16. In the Style palette, in the *3D Model* tab, double-click on Vehicles.

17. Drag and drop various vehicle styles or colors onto the existing vehicles in the model. Figure 5–49 shows that different vehicle styles have been applied.

Figure 5–49

18. Press <Esc> to clear the selection of all of the features.

Hint: Add City Furniture to Styles

Multiple styles can incorporate city furniture to make populating the model much easier. In chapter 3, we learned how to add vehicles to a road style to quickly populate the roadway. Other items that you might want to incorporate include fire hydrants, light poles, etc. Just keep in mind that adding 3D models to a style does cause the model size to increase. Therefore, it is recommended that you only add a few vehicles to the road styles that will be used for the proposed roads. Then add vehicles sparsely to an existing roadway only where required for visualization purposes.

Task 4 - Add railway 3D models.

1. Continue working in the same model. If you did not complete the previous task, set the proposal to **B_Task4** in the Utility Bar.

2. In the Utility Bar, click ![icon] (Bookmark your current location) and select **RailCrossing**.

3. In the In Canvas tools, click ![icon] (Build, manage, and analyze your infrastructure model)> ![icon] (Create conceptual design features)> ![icon] (City Furniture).

4. In the Select Draw Style asset card, type **Railway** and scroll down to select the **Crossing Barrier - US** style, as shown in Figure 5–50.

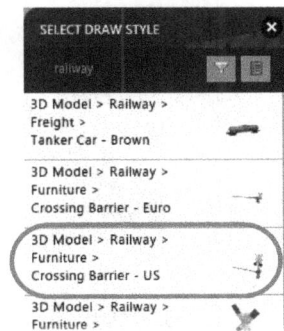

Figure 5–50

5. Double-click in the model to place the 3D model, as shown in Figure 5–51.

Figure 5–51

6. Press <Esc> to display the gizmos.

7. Use ⌒ (Rotate Gizmo) to rotate the crossing barrier arm to make it parallel to the tracks. Use ⬍ (Move Gizmo) to move the model to the park strip on the right side of the road, as shown in Figure 5–52.

Figure 5–52

8. With the Crossing Barrier still selected, press <Ctrl>+<C> to copy the model to the clipboard.

9. Press <Ctrl>+<V> to paste a second Crossing Barrier in the model. Double-click in the model to place it across the tracks from the first one.

10. With the second Crossing Barrier still selected, use

(Rotate Gizmo) and (Move Gizmo) to place and orient the 3D model similar to that shown in Figure 5–53.

Figure 5–53

11. Press <Esc> to clear the selection of the crossing barrier.

12. In the Utility Bar, click (Bookmark your current location) and select **RailCrossing**.

13. In the In Canvas tools, click (Build, manage, and analyze your infrastructure model)> (Create conceptual design features)> (City Furniture).

14. In the Select Draw Style asset card, type **Passenger** in the filter field. Select the **Light Rail - US Midwest** style, as shown in Figure 5–54.

Figure 5–54

15. Double-click to place the 3D model just north of the road crossing, as shown in Figure 5–55.

Figure 5–55

16. Press <Esc> and use ⌒ (Rotate Gizmo) to rotate the model and make it parallel to the tracks, as shown in Figure 5–56.

Make the car parallel to the tracks

Rotate gizmo

Figure 5–56

17. Press <Esc> to clear the selection of the railway car.

5.3 Add Vegetation to a Model

Adding vegetation can add privacy, shade, noise barriers, and landscape appeal to a project. Trees and other vegetation can also help stakeholders to better understand how the project could look when completed. You can add vegetation in three different ways:

- **Single Plant:** A single plant is placed in the model when you double-click on an insertion point, no matter which vegetation tool is used. Figure 5–57 shows a single tree.

Figure 5–57

- **Row of Trees:** A group of plants are placed in the model along a line, as shown in Figure 5–58.

Figure 5–58

- **Stand of Trees:** A group of randomly spaced plants are placed in the model inside a polygon, as shown in Figure 5–59.

Figure 5–59

If you create vegetation along a line or in a polygon, you can set the number of plants that display using the Density Slider, as shown in Figure 5–60. The higher the density (slider moved to the right), the more plants that display.

Figure 5–60

How To: Create Vegetation Within a Group

1. In the In Canvas tools, click ![icon] (Build, manage, and analyze your infrastructure model)> ![icon] (Create conceptual design features)> ![icon] (Stand of Trees).

2. In the Select Draw Style asset card, type select the type of plant required, as shown in Figure 5–61.

Figure 5–61

3. In the model, click the corners of a polygon for the vegetation group area, as shown in Figure 5–62. Remember to double-click on the final corner to finish the polygon.

Area: 28028.75 sq.ft.

Figure 5–62

4. Press <Esc> to make the Feature Density bar display. Slide the Density Slider (as shown in Figure 5–63) until the required number of plants display in the model.

Figure 5–63

5. Press <Esc> to clear the selection of the newly created trees.

How To: Create Vegetation Along a Line

1. In the In Canvas tools, click ▣ (Build, manage, and analyze your infrastructure model)> ✎ (Create conceptual design features)> 🐾 (Row of Trees).

2. In the Select Draw Style asset card, type vegetation in the filter field. Select the type of plant required, as shown in Figure 5–64.

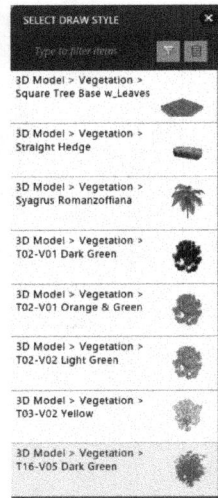

Figure 5–64

3. In the model, click the vertices of a polyline for the vegetation to follow, as shown in Figure 5–65. Remember to double-click on the final vertex to finish the polyline.

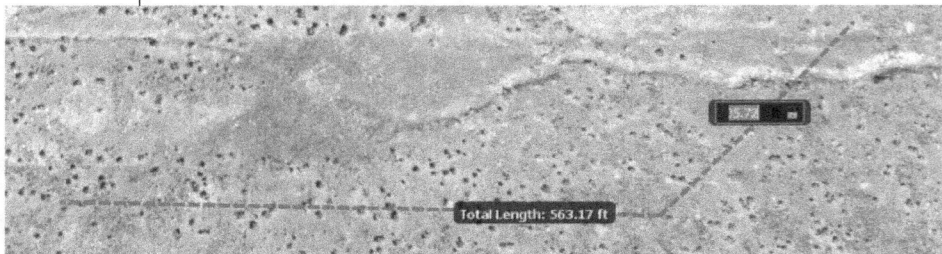

Figure 5–65

4. Press <Esc> to make the Feature Density bar display. Slide the Density Slider (shown in Figure 5–66) until the required number of plants display in the model.

Figure 5–66

5. Press <Esc> to clear the selection of the newly created trees.

Edit Vegetation

When you select vegetation, gizmos display to enable you to modify the plants. ● (Elevation Gizmo) enables you to adjust the height of the plants, while 🔺 (Height Gizmo) enables you to change the size and scale of the plants.

If you select a vegetation group (row or stand of trees), the Density Slider displays, enabling you to change the number of plants that display in the group. Move the slider left or right until the required number of plants display in the model. If the Density Slider is not displayed, orbit the view to a plan view to make it display, as shown in Figure 5–67.

Figure 5–67

Practice 5c

Add Trees to the Model

Practice Objective

- Add trees to the model to add landscaping details.

Estimated time for completion: 15 minutes

In this practice you will create vegetation that represents a small orchard to illustrate how the final design will look in a new development.

Task 1 - Create vegetation.

The church owns a piece of land next to the parking lot, which they want to turn into a small orchard to help with fundraising. In this task, you will create trees using the **Stand of Trees** command to create an orchard in the model.

1. In the Home Screen, click **Open**.

2. In the *C:\InfraWorks Fundamentals Practice Files\AddDetails* folder, select **CreateDetails.sqlite** and click **Open**.

3. In the Utility Bar, expand *Switch Active Proposal* and select **C_Task1**.

4. In the Utility Bar, click ⬛ (Bookmark your current location) and select **Church**.

5. In the In Canvas tools, click ⬛ (Build, manage, and analyze your infrastructure model)> ⬛ (Create conceptual design features)> ⬛ (Stand of Trees).

6. In the Select Draw Style asset card, type **vegetation** in the filter field, and select **T16-V05 Dark Green**, as shown in Figure 5–68.

Figure 5–68

7. Click the corners of a polygon for the orchard area, as shown in Figure 5–69. Note: Double-click on the final corner to finish the polygon.

Figure 5–69

8. Press <Esc> to display the Feature Density bar. Use the Density Slider to set the density close to **90%**, as shown in Figure 5–70.

Figure 5–70

9. Press <Esc> to clear the selection of the newly created trees.

5.4 Add Miscellaneous Details to a Model

You can enhance the overall visualization of the final design by indicating to stakeholders where sound barriers, signs, bike stands, etc. can be placed in the project.

Barriers

Barriers are useful items to add to any project. Sound barriers are placed along transportation corridors to muffle the sound of traffic experienced by neighboring residents. To control how traffic is to be handled during construction, barriers can be used to temporarily or permanently block off an area. You might need to create a construction proposal and indicate any barriers, alternative routes, and temporary roads that are to be used during the construction process. All of these uses and more can be added to an Autodesk InfraWorks 360 project to communicate design concepts.

Barriers can be linear features that are added using the Barrier command or 3D Models that are added using the City Furniture command. Multiple 3D Model style catalogs are available (as shown in Figure 5–71) and different barrier styles can be found in many of these catalogs.

Barriers can also be added to road or railway styles by adding Decorations.

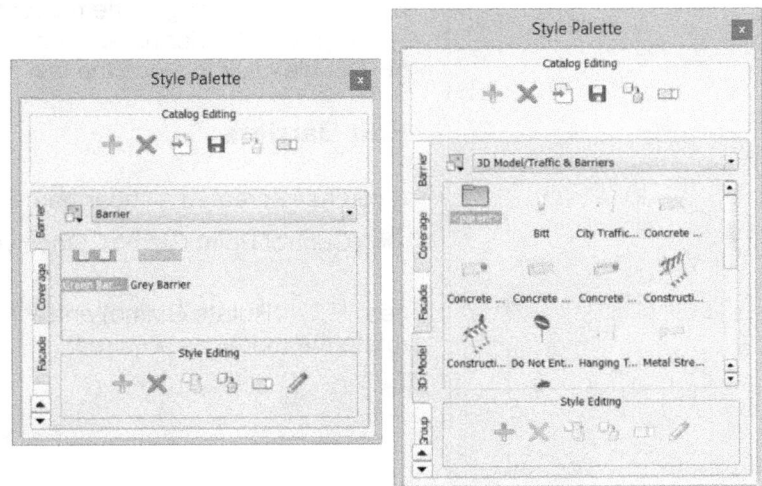

Figure 5–71

How To: Create Barriers

1. In the In Canvas tools, click ![icon] (Build, manage, and analyze your infrastructure model)> ![icon] (Create conceptual design features)> ![icon] (Barriers).
2. In the Select Draw Style asset card, in the *Barrier* tab, select the required barrier style, as shown in Figure 5–72.

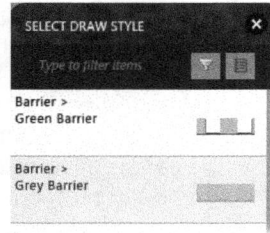

Figure 5–72

3. Click in the model to start the linear path for the barriers to follow.
4. Move the cursor in the direction in which you want the barrier to run. Type a distance for the length to the next point of intersection (PI) and press <Enter> to set the distance. Click in the model to place the next PI.
5. Continue clicking in the model to place PIs until all of the lengths of barrier have been created.
6. Double-click to place the last point and end the command.

Edit Barriers

If you have created a linear barrier, it can be modified using ![icon] (Control Point Gizmo). Once you have placed a 3D model, use ![icon] (Rotate Gizmo) and ![icon] (Move Gizmo) to move and rotate the model as required.

Points of Interest

You might need to draw attention to a specific area of your model. You can do so by adding Points of Interest (POI). In addition to drawing attention to an area, POI can be used to add text, HTML tooltips, or hyperlinks that automatically open a web page, image, or other file when you move the cursor to within a specified distance of the POI. This is done using the *Proximity Distance* field in the Point of Interest asset card, as shown in Figure 5–73.

Figure 5–73

How To: Create Points of Interest

1. In the In Canvas tools, click ▨ (Build, manage, and analyze your infrastructure model)> ✎ (Create conceptual design features)> ◉ (Points of Interest)
2. In the Select Draw Style asset card, select the required 3D model style, as shown in Figure 5–74.

You can select any 3D Model that is listed in the City Furniture section of this chapter.

Figure 5–74

3. Depending on the model, either double-click in the model to place a single POI, or single-click in the model to start the linear path that the POIs should follow.
4. Move the cursor in the direction that you want the POIs to run. Type a distance for the length to the next point of intersection and press <Enter> to set the distance. Click in the model to place the next point of intersection.
5. Continue clicking in the model as required until all of the lengths of POI path have been created.
6. Double-click to place the last point and end the command.

How To: Create Tooltips for Points of Interest

1. In the model, select the POI.

2. In the Point of Interest asset card, expand *Advanced* and select the *Tooltips* field, and click ⬚ (Edit Tooltip).

3. In the Edit Tooltip dialog box, either enter the text you want to display in the *Visual* tab (as shown in Figure 5–75) or use HTML code to create a link in the *Html* tab. Click **OK**.

Figure 5–75

4. In the Point of Interest asset card, type a value in the *Proximity Distance* field to specify how close the cursor needs to be to the POI to activate the Tooltip, as shown in Figure 5–76.

Figure 5–76

Edit Points of Interest

If you have placed a 3D model from any category other than POI,

you can select it and use ⬆ (Move Gizmo) and ⌒ (Rotate Gizmo) to move and rotate the model as required.

Practice 5d

Add Miscellaneous Details to the Model

Estimated time for completion: 25 minutes

Practice Objective

- Add miscellaneous details to the model to better communicate the design concept.

In this practice you will create a barrier around the pond to prevent children from playing in it. You will then add city furniture to the model to help communicate the final design to stakeholders.

Task 1 - Create a barrier.

In this task, you will create a barrier around the pond.

1. In the Home Screen, click **Open**.

2. In the *C:\InfraWorks Fundamentals Practice Files\AddDetails* folder, select **CreateDetails.sqlite** and click **Open**.

3. In the Quick Access Toolbar, expand *Switch Active Proposal* and select **D_Task1**.

4. In the Utility Bar, click ▣ (Bookmark your current location) and select **Pond**.

5. In the In Canvas tools, click 🔲 (Build, manage, and analyze your infrastructure model)> ✎ (Create conceptual design features)> 🔳 (Barriers).

6. In the Select Draw Style asset card, select the **Grey Barrier** style, as shown in Figure 5–77.

Figure 5–77

7. Click in the model to start the linear path that the barrier should follow, as shown in Figure 5–78.

Start barrier path here

Figure 5–78

8. Move the cursor to the west. Type **100** for the length to the next point on the boundary and press <Enter> to set the distance. Click in the model to place the barrier point parallel to the road.

9. Move the cursor south by approximately the same distance to the west of the pond as the PI placed in Step 8, as shown in Figure 5–79. Type **200** for the length to the next point on the barrier path and press <Enter> to set the distance. Click in the model to place the boundary point.

10. Move the cursor to the east. Type **150** for the length to the next point on the boundary and press <Enter> to set the distance. Click to place the barrier path point near the edge of the railway.

11. Move the cursor back to the first barrier point and double-click to place the last barrier path point and end the command. Figure 5–79 shows the complete barrier path.

Figure 5–79

12. Press <Esc> to clear the selection of the barrier.

Task 2 - Add bridge components.

In this task, you will add components to the pier so that it is only available to foot and bike traffic. **Note:** In order to challenge you to remember the steps and make them more automatic, not every step of the process is listed in this task.

1. Continue working in the same model. If you did not complete the previous task, set the proposal to **D_Task2** in the Utility Bar.

2. In the Utility Bar, click 🔲 (Bookmark your current location) and select **Pier**.

3. In the In Canvas tools, click 🔳 (Build, manage, and analyze your infrastructure model)> ✏️ (Create conceptual design features)> 🏙️ (City Furniture).

4. In the Select Draw Style asset card, type **bridge** and select the **Barrier Side** style, as shown in Figure 5–80.

Figure 5–80

5. Double-click in the model to place the barrier at the end of the pier. Add two more barriers.

6. Press <Esc> and use the ⬆ (Move gizmo) and ⌢ (Rotate gizmo) as required to correctly position the barriers side-by-side so that foot and bike traffic can not go off the end of the pier, as shown in Figure 5–81.

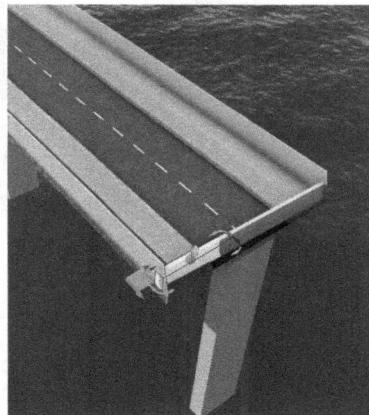

Figure 5–81

7. In the In Canvas tools, click ⬛ (Build, manage, and analyze your infrastructure model)> ✏ (Create conceptual design features)> 🏛 (City Furniture).

The barrier likely is placed on top of the water by default. You must move it vertically and horizontally, and then rotate it as required.

8. In the Select Draw Style asset card, type **bridge** and select the **Bike Decal** style, as shown in Figure 5–82.

Figure 5–82

The signs likely are placed on top of the water by default. You must move them vertically and horizontally, and then rotate as required.

9. Double-click in the model multiple times to place the sign on the pavement. Figure 5–83 shows suggested placements and rotations.

Figure 5–83.

10. Press <Esc> and use the ↑ (Move gizmo) and (Rotate gizmo) as required

11. Continue adding Bike Decals to communicate where bikes can travel and the direction of travel.

12. If time permits, add additional barriers at the beginning of the bridge to block vehicular traffic to protect bikers and pedestrians. Figure 5–83 shows the suggested placement and rotation.

Chapter Review Questions

1. Which of the following is not a category for a predefined 3D building model?

   a. *Furniture*

   b. *Residential*

   c. *Neighborhood*

   d. *Commercial*

2. Once placed, you can change the shape of a building that has been created from a 3D model.

   a. True

   b. False

3. Which **Create Tree** option would you use to create a grouping of multiple trees in a specified area?

   a. (Row of Trees)

   b. (Stand of Trees)

4. Which of the following commands should you use if you want to add tooltips that are activated within a specified distance from the location of the 3D model?

   a. (City Furniture)

   b. (Barriers)

   c. (Points of Interest)

Command Summary

Button	Command	Location
	Barriers	• **In Canvas Tools:** Build, manage, and analyze your industry model > Create conceptual design features
	Buildings	• **In Canvas Tools:** Build, manage, and analyze your industry model > Create conceptual design features
	City Furniture	• **In Canvas Tools:** Build, manage, and analyze your industry model > Create conceptual design features
	Points Of Interest	• **In Canvas Tools:** Build, manage, and analyze your industry model > Create conceptual design features
	Row of Trees	• **In Canvas Tools:** Build, manage, and analyze your industry model > Create conceptual design features
	Stand of Trees	• **In Canvas Tools:** Build, manage, and analyze your industry model > Create conceptual design features

Analyzing the Model

Before progressing too far into the design process, it is important to ensure that the project area meets the project needs. You should continually analyze what is happening in the project to address issues that arise along the way. In this chapter you learn how to analyze the model using spatial and numerical analysis tools to determine the feasibility of the project.

Learning Objectives in this Chapter

- Analyze features in a model using underlying data using themes.
- Select a subset of features in a layer.
- Graphically indicate avoidance zones in the model.
- Select features that are in the line of sight from a specified view point and angle.
- Measure a model to determine the length, area, or volume of specific features.
- Analyze a model to determine whether the project receives the appropriate amount of sunlight.

6.1 Theme a Data Source

The display of a feature class can be modified by creating a theme. Themes use underlying data found in the database to highlight sets of values using various colors. Figure 6–1 shows coverages themed by the current market value, which was pulled from a parcel database.

Figure 6–1

The Themes palette is used to create new themes, modify existing themes, delete themes, and change the display settings and priority of themes. Additionally, you can share themes with other models to ensure consistency across models that use similar data sources. The icons used in the Feature Themes palette (shown in Figure 6–2) are consistent for all theme types.

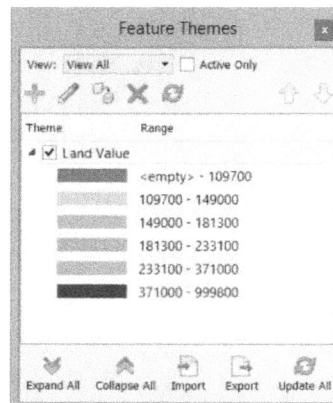

Figure 6–2

The icons in the Feature, Terrain, and Point Cloud Theme palettes are as follows.

Icon	Purpose
(Add a New Theme)	Adds a new theme for a feature class.
(Edit Selected Theme)	Enables you to edit the properties of a selected theme.
(Duplicate Selected Theme)	Enables you to copy a selected theme.
(Delete Selected Theme(s))	Deletes any selected themes.
(Refresh Selected Themes)	Refreshes the display of selected themes.
(Move Selected Theme Up/Down)	Changes the priority of the themes by moving the selected theme up or down in the list.
(Expand/Collapse All)	Shows/hides the details of the themes in the current model.
(Import Theme(s))	Used to import one or more theme properties from an external file created in another model.
(Export Theme(s))	Used to export one or more theme properties to an external file for use in other models.
(Update All)	Refreshes the display of all themes in the current model.

Feature Themes

Creating a feature theme helps visualize specific aspects of data sources. For example, if you want to display the location of various soil types in the model, you can display each category as a different color using the individual values that are associated with a soil data source. Additionally, you can display parcels according to their market value to ensure that the project location is appropriate, and fits in the project budget.

Nearly any data source can be themed and associated with features in the model, according to data found in the database. Using a variety of distribution methods, values are divided into ranges. The distribution methods available for Feature Themes include:

- **Equal:** The difference between the high and low values is the same for every range.

- **Standard Deviation:** Ranges are based on how much the value varies from the mean value. The mean value is calculated first, and then the standard deviation is added or subtracted from the mean to calculate the ranges.

- **Quantile:** An equal number of features are included in each range.

- **Jenks:** Ranges are based on natural groupings of the data values. This is the same as a natural breaks method, because features with similar values use the same display properties.

- **Individual Values:** Ranges look at values that are most often used when the values represent categories.

- **Logarithm:** Uses a logarithmic scale to distribute values after evaluating the highest and lowest values from the source.

The Feature Themes palette is shown in Figure 6–3.

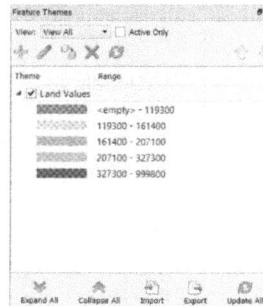

Figure 6–3

How To: Create a Feature Theme

1. In the In Canvas tools, click ![icon] (Build, manage, and analyze your infrastructure model)> ![icon] (Analyze your model)> ![icon] (Feature Themes).

2. In the Feature Themes palette, click ![icon] (Add a New Theme).

3. In the Theme Properties dialog box (shown in Figure 6–4), set the following properties and click **OK**:

   - **Name:** Enter a name for the theme.
   - **Feature Class:** Select the feature class to theme.
   - **Property:** Select the property in the database, which holds the values to be used for the theme.
   - **Distribution:** Select the distribution method to use.
   - **Number of Rules:** Set the number of rules.
   - **Color Range:** Select the color range and transparency.

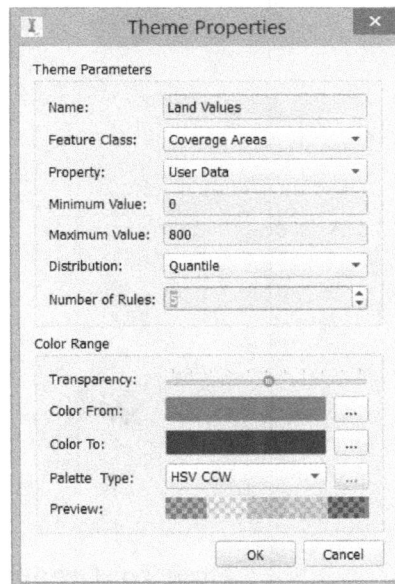

Figure 6–4

Terrain Themes

Terrain themes enable you to display surfaces according to their elevation, slope, or aspect. When creating a terrain theme, you can set the number of rules, colors, and transparency of the surface. Terrain themes only use the equal distribution method for creating ranges. There are a few predefined palettes that automatically set the number of rules and the color for each range according to the type of analysis being run. For example, the Land Cover palette sets up 13 ranges with colors starting with light cyan and ending with brown. The Slope palette sets up five ranges with colors starting with gray and ending with red, as shown in Figure 6–5.

Figure 6–5

How To: Create a Terrain Theme

1. In the In Canvas tools, click ▮ (Build, manage, and analyze your infrastructure model)> ▢ (Analyze your model)> ◮ (Terrain Themes).

2. In the Terrain Themes palette, click ✛ (Add a New Theme).

3. In the Theme Properties dialog box (shown in Figure 6–6) set the following parameters and click **OK**:

- **Name:** Type a name for the theme.
- **Analysis Type:** Select the analysis type.
- **Palette Type:** Select the palette type.
- **Number of Rules:** If the palette type was not set, set the number of rules.
- **Color Range:** Select the color range and transparency.

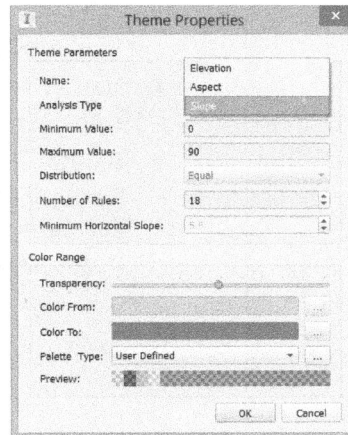

Figure 6–6

Point Cloud Themes

Normal usually refers to the direction in which a surface face is pointing. For points in a point cloud, normal is derived from other points that have a planar relationship with a specific point.

Theming a point cloud enables you to view its many points using different colors. The colors are based on one of the following analysis types:

- **Normal:** Identifies points that are aligned by displaying colors assigned to the X, Y, Z values associated with the direction of the normal for the point. Colors for this type of theme cannot be specified.

- **Elevation:** Similar to the terrain theme by elevation, it colors points according to their Z value or height. The minimum and maximum values are determined automatically, but can be adjusted as required.

- **Single Color:** All points become the same color and no further options are available.

- **Classification:** This option is only available if a point cloud is classified. Points are colored by their classification ID.

Point cloud themes only use the equal distribution method for creating ranges.

How To: Create a Point Cloud Theme

1. In the In Canvas tools, click ▣ (Build, manage, and analyze your infrastructure model)> ▣ (Analyze your model)> ▣ (Point Cloud Themes).

2. In the Point Cloud Themes palette, click ✛ (Add a New Theme).

3. In the Theme Properties dialog box, shown in Figure 6–7, define the following and click **OK**:

   • **Name:** Type a name for the theme.
   • **Analysis Type:** Select the Analysis Type.
   • **Palette Type:** Select the palette type.
   • **Number of Rules:** If the palette has not already been set, set the number of rules.
   • **Color Range:** Select the color range and transparency.

Figure 6–7

Practice 6a

Estimated time for completion: 10 minutes

Create Themes in the Model

Practice Objective

- Create themes that will be used to analyze data.

In this practice you will change the colors in the model according to underlying data to determine whether the project falls within parcels that fit the project budget. You will then perform a slope analysis to determine whether there are any unbuildable areas in the project.

Task 1 - Create a feature theme.

1. In the Home Screen, click **Open**.

2. In the *C:\InfraWorks Fundamentals Practice Files\Analyze* folder, select **Analyze.sqlite** and click **Open**.

3. In the Utility Bar, expand *Switch Active Proposal* and select **A_Task1**.

4. In the In Canvas tools, click ▮ (Build, manage, and analyze your infrastructure model)> ▢ (Analyze your model)> ▤ (Feature Themes).

5. In the Feature Themes palette, click ✛ (Add a New Theme).

6. In the Theme Properties dialog box (as shown in Figure 6–8) set the following parameters and click **OK**:

The current market value is already mapped to the User Data field.

- **Name:** Land Values
- **Feature Class:** Coverage Areas
- **Property:** User Data
- **Distribution Method:** Quantile
- **Number of Rules:** 5
- **Palette Type:** HSV CCW
- **Transparency:** 50%

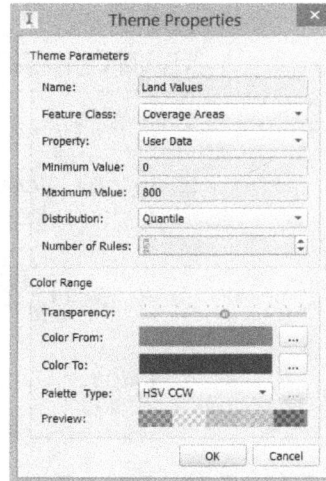

Figure 6–8

Your model should look similar to that shown in Figure 6–9.

Figure 6–9

*If all of the colors do not display, open the Data Sources panel and double-click on the **TaxParcel** layer. In the Table tab, ensure that **MKT_CNTVAL** is selected for the User Data property. Click **Close & Refresh**. The theme should automatically recognize the values and update the model display.*

7. In the Feature Themes palette, clear the checkmark next to *Land Values* to toggle off the display of the theme.

Task 2 - Create a terrain theme.

1. In the In Canvas tools, click ▮ (Build, manage, and analyze your infrastructure model)> ▣ (Analyze your model)> ▲ (Terrain Themes).

2. In the Terrain Themes palette, click ✛ (Add a New Theme).

3. In the Theme Properties dialog box (shown in Figure 6–10) set the following parameters and click **OK**:
   - **Name:** Slope
   - **Analysis Type:** Slope
   - **Palette Type:** Slope Palette
   - **Transparency:** 50%

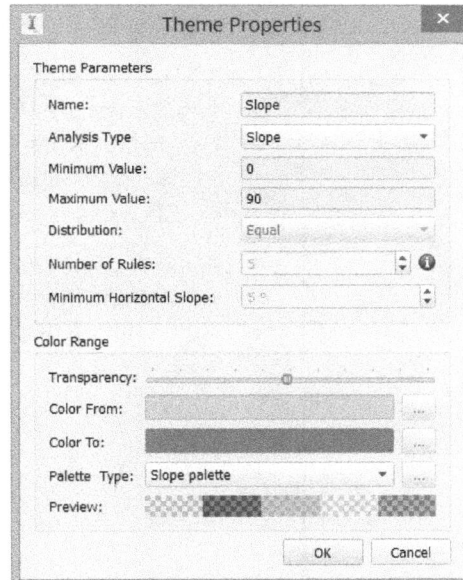

Figure 6–10

Your model should look similar to that shown in Figure 6–11. The client wants to see the slope of the site in 5% increments.

Figure 6–11

4. In the Terrain Themes palette, double-click on the *Slope* theme to open the Theme Properties dialog box. Position the box so that you can see the model as you make changes.

5. In the Theme Properties dialog box, do the following:
   - Change the Palette Type to **User Defined**.
   - Slowly click **Increase** to change the Number of Rules to **18**. Watch the model as you do so.
   - Click **OK**.

6. In the Terrain Themes palette, note that the ranges are now in 5% slope increments. Clear the checkmark next to *Slope* to toggle off the display of the theme.

6.2 Suitability Maps

Infrastructure projects can quickly become very expensive if the location or soil type are not suitable for the project. Suitability maps enable you to input your own data to help determine the most cost effective location for an infrastructure project. This data can come from a layer in the Model Explorer, or a subset of a layer in the Model Explorer, as shown in Figure 6–12. Layer settings enable you to set a gradient width or an offset around the feature.

AUTODESK®
INFRAWORKS™ 360

To use this feature, access to the Internet and Autodesk® InfraWorks® 360 are required.

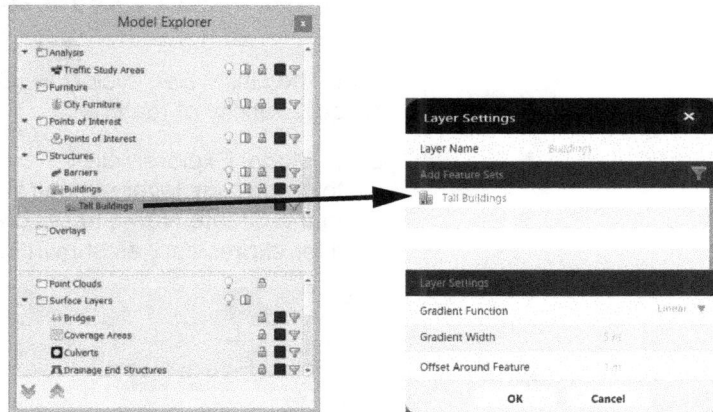

Figure 6–12

Multiple avoidance zone layers can be added to the suitability map. Weights can be adjusted to indicate that one avoidance zone has a higher or lower impact on the project cost over another, as shown in Figure 6–13.

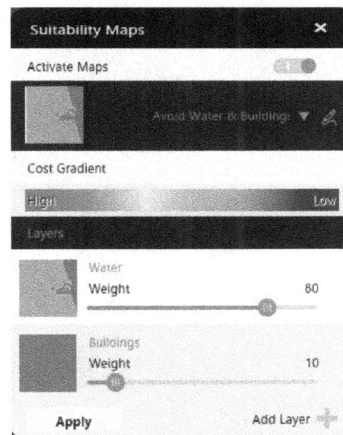

Figure 6–13

Layer Subsets

Many of the GIS layers that are used to create suitability maps require filtering to correctly create avoidance zones.

For example, it is not a good idea to place buildings or roads in liquefaction zones near fault lines. To address this, a soil map data source could be attached to the model. Then a layer subset could be created for specific soil types to indicate where liquefaction zones are expected. Finally, the layer subset(s) could be added to the suitability map with weights to indicate which soils to avoid building upon.

How To: Create a Layer Subset

1. In the Utility Bar, click [icon] (Control visibility, display, and selectability of features).
2. In Model Explorer, click [icon] (Create subset) next to the layer to create any layer subset(s) that might be required.
3. In the Create New Subset dialog box, create the necessary filter expression, as shown in Figure 6–14. Click **OK**.

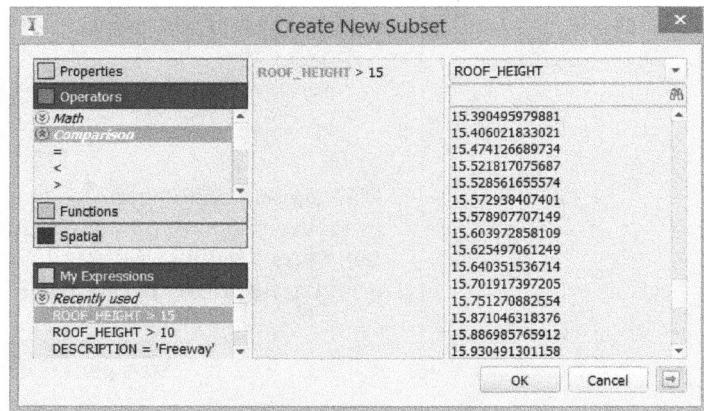

Figure 6–14

How To: Create a Suitability Map

1. In Model Explorer, create any layer subset(s) that might be required.

2. In the In Canvas tools, click ![icon] (Build, manage, and analyze your infrastructure model)> ![icon] (Analyze your model)> ![icon] (Suitability Maps).

3. In the Suitability Maps palette, toggle on the **Activate Maps** option. Then expand **Select item** and select **Create new map...**, as shown in Figure 6–15.

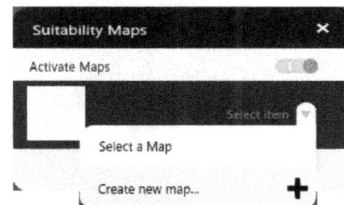

Figure 6–15

4. In the Suitability Maps palette, click ![icon] (Add new suitability map layer).

5. In the Layer Settings palette, click ![icon] (Select features through Model Explorer).

6. In the Feature Selection dialog box, select the layer(s) to apply a buffer to, as shown in Figure 6–16.

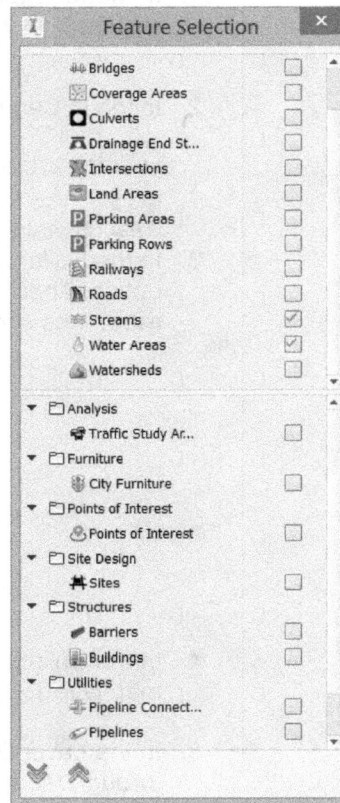

Figure 6–16

7. In the Layer Settings, type a value in the *Gradient Width* and/or *Offset Around Feature* field, as shown in Figure 6–17. Click **OK**.

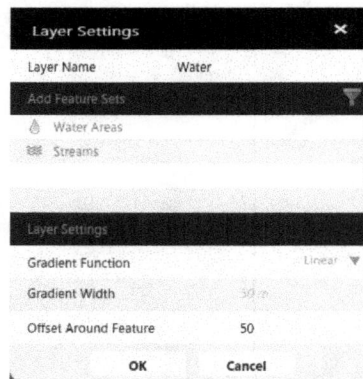

Figure 6–17

8. In the Suitability Maps palette, add any additional layers as required, and then set their weights using the sliders next to each layer, as shown in Figure 6–18.

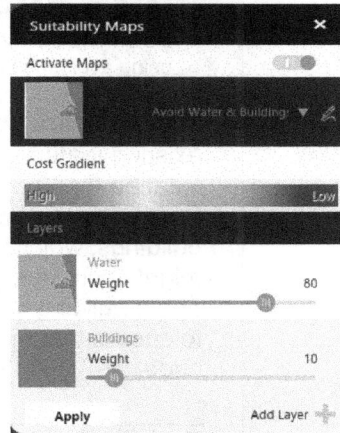

Figure 6–18

9. In the Suitability Maps palette, click **Apply** to display the results in the model.

Practice 6b

Create a Suitability Map

Practice Objective

Estimated time for completion: 15 minutes

- Determine the most cost effective location for an infrastructure project using avoidance zones.

In this practice you will create avoidance zones and analyze existing features to ensure that you have selected the best location for a new infrastructure project. First, you will create a layer subset to avoid building a road too close to the tallest buildings, which will help reduce the number of car accidents that might occur due to icy roads that are constantly in the shadows of the buildings. Next, you will use the water areas and streams to ensure that the road is not built within 50 meters of the water's edge.

Task 1 - Create a suitability map.

1. In the Home Screen, click **Open**.

2. In the *C:\InfraWorks Fundamentals Practice Files\Analyze* folder, select **Analyze.sqlite** and click **Open**.

3. In the Utility Bar, expand *Switch Active Proposal* and select **B_Task1**.

4. In the Utility Bar, click ▣ (Control visibility, display, and selectability of features).

5. In Model Explorer, next to the **Buildings** layer, click ▽ (Create subset).

6. In the Create New Subset dialog box, do the following, as shown in Figure 6–19:
   - Under *Properties*, expand *Building* and double-click on **ROOF_HEIGHT**.
   - Under *Operators*, expand *Comparison* and double-click on **>**.
   - Select the value in the *Expression* area and type **15**.
   - Click **OK**.
   - For the subset name, type **Tall Buildings**.

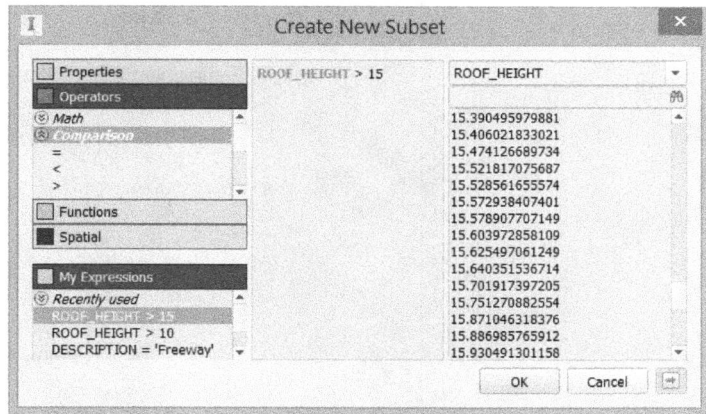

Figure 6–19

7. In the In Canvas tools, click ![icon] (Build, manage, and analyze your infrastructure model)> ![icon] (Analyze your model)> ![icon] (Suitability Maps).

8. In the Suitability Maps palette, toggle on the **Activate Maps** option. Expand **Select a Map** and select **Create new map...**, as shown in Figure 6–20.

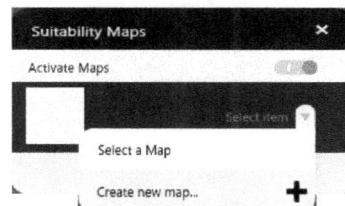

Figure 6–20

9. In the Suitability Maps palette, click ![icon] to rename the map. In the *Map Name* field, type **Avoid Water & Buildings**.

10. In the Suitability Maps palette, click ![icon] (Add a new suitability map layer).

11. In the Layer Settings palette, type **Water** for the name and then click ![icon] (Select features through Model Explorer).

12. In the Feature Selection dialog box, select the **Streams** and **Water Areas** layers, as shown in Figure 6–21. Close the Feature Selection dialog box.

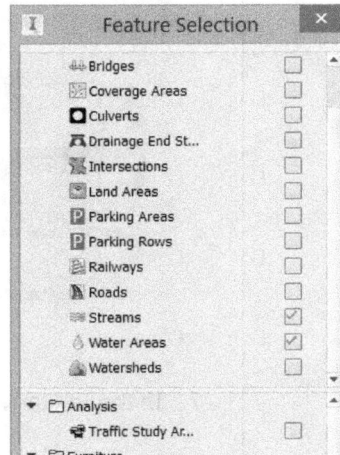

Figure 6–21

13. In the Layer Settings, in the *Gradient Width* and *Offset Around Feature* fields, type **50**, as shown in Figure 6–22. Click **OK**.

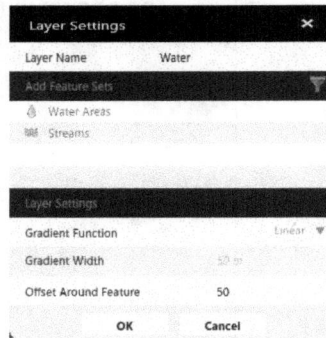

Figure 6–22

14. In the Suitability Maps palette, click **Apply** to see the results in the model.

15. In the Suitability Maps palette, click (Add new suitability map layer).

16. In the Layer Settings palette, type **Buildings** for the name and then click ▼ (Select features through Model Explorer).

17. In the Feature Selection dialog box, expand the *Buildings* layer and select the **Tall Buildings** subset. Close the Feature Selection dialog box.

18. In the Layer Settings, in the *Offset Around Feature* field, type **10**. Click **OK**.

19. In the Suitability Maps palette, click **Apply** to display the results in the model.

20. In the Suitability Maps palette, adjust the layer weights using the sliders next to each layer. Set the *Water* weight to **80** and the *Building* weight to **10**, as shown in Figure 6–23.

Figure 6–23

21. In the Suitability Maps palette, click **Apply** to display the results in the model.

6.3 Line of Sight Analysis

Stakeholders are often concerned about how a project is expected to look from a specific view. More importantly, they want to know what they can or cannot see from a specific point of view. Residents from the surrounding community might want to know that traffic cannot see into their backyards. Stakeholders might also want to know that views of the surrounding landscape are not going to be lost because of the proposed project. In these cases, a line of sight study can be conducted to better understand what can be seen from a specific location.

A Line of Sight analysis is conducted by orienting the view to the angle and direction to be analyzed. Anything in the line of sight becomes selected in the model when you run the analysis, as shown in Figure 6–24. These objects remain selected even when the view changes, enabling you to see what is selected after moving the camera.

Figure 6–24

How To: Conduct a Line of Sight Analysis

1. In the model, set the view point and angle using the standard navigation tools.

2. In the In Canvas tools, click ![icon] (Build, manage, and analyze your infrastructure model)> ![icon] (Analyze your model)> ![icon] (Select Visible).

3. Press <Esc> to clear all of the selected features.

6.4 Measure the Model

To meet project constraints, you must ensure that everything is being created with the correct measurements. It is best to continually check the model and ensure that features are the correct distance from each other, and have the correct area and volumes. These checks help you to avoid having to recreate and edit objects later. Measurement tools are found in the In Canvas tools, under ▮ (Build, manage, and analyze your infrastructure model)> ▢ (Analyze your model). The available tools are as follows.

Icon	Purpose
↔ (Point to Point Distance)	Measures length, width, and height from one point to another along a straight line. Distance displays in the model similar to a dimension.
◤ (2D Distance & Slope	Measures the slope between two points. Distance displays in the model similar to a triangle showing the 2D horizontal distance, vertical distance, and grade between two points.
⟩ (Path Distance)	Measures length, width, and height along a polyline path. Distance displays in the model similar to a series of dimensions with individual values displayed for each segment, as well as the total distance. It can be used to display measurements across a terrain.
⊕ (Range Finder)	Measures the distance of a target point from your current position. Distance displays in the model similar to a single point with a label indicating the distance, altitude, heading, and inclination from your position. You can set multiple target points in a session.
▨ (Terrain Statistics)	Measures the area and volume of a terrain by specifying the perimeter points.

How To: Measure Single Distances

1. In the In Canvas tools, click ▉ (Build, manage, and analyze your infrastructure model)>▉ (Analyze your model)> ▉ (Measure Point to Point).
2. Click the first point to start the measurement.
3. Click the second point where the measurement ends. The measured value displays similar to Figure 6–25.

Figure 6–25

4. Press <Esc> to remove the temporary dimension.

New

How To: Measure 2D Distance & Slope

1. In the In Canvas tools, click ▉ (Build, manage, and analyze your infrastructure model)>▉ (Analyze your model)> ▉ (2D Distance & Slope).
2. Click the first point to start the measurement.
3. Click the second point where the measurement ends. The measured value displays similar to Figure 6–26.

Figure 6–26

4. Press <Esc> to remove the temporary dimension.

How To: Measure a Series of Distances

1. In the In Canvas tools, click ![icon] (Build, manage, and analyze your infrastructure model)> ![icon] (Analyze your model)> ![icon] (Measure Path Distance).
2. Click the first point to start the measurement.
3. Click all of the subsequent points along the path as required. Double-click on where the measurement ends. The measured values display similar to those shown in Figure 6–27.

Figure 6–27

4. Press <Esc> to remove the temporary dimensions.

How To: Measure Ranges

1. In the In Canvas tools, click ![icon] (Build, manage, and analyze your infrastructure model)> ![icon] (Analyze your model)> ![icon] (Range Finder).
2. Click a point in the model. The range values display similar to those shown in Figure 6–28.

Figure 6–28

3. Press <Esc> to remove the temporary dimensions.

How To: Measure Terrain Statistics

1. In the In Canvas tools, click ![icon] (Build, manage, and analyze your infrastructure model)> ![icon] (Analyze your model)> ![icon] (Terrain Statistics).

2. Click the first point to start a boundary. The boundary defines the area to measure.

3. Click all of the subsequent points along the required boundary. Double-click on the point where the boundary should end. A boundary and its measure values display similar to that shown in Figure 6–29.

Figure 6–29

4. Press <Esc> to remove the temporary dimensions.

6.5 Analyze Shadows

Conducting a shadow study can help determine whether the project can expect to receive enough sunlight at specific times of day or throughout the year. During a shadow study, you can turn shadows on or off, and set various sun and sky settings.

Visual Effects

To adjust the lighting and appearance of your model, change the View Style settings in the Utility Bar. In the Utility Bar, expand the

View Style drop-down and click ⚙ (Configure current view). Then, change the settings on the Visualization stack of the View Settings asset card, as shown in Figure 6–30.

Figure 6–30

Turn Shadows On/Off

Studying how shadows are cast in a model helps you to determine whether solar panels can be used to power a building. It can also help you to determine whether horizontal and vertical curves need to be modified along a transportation corridor to reduce the effects of shadows. For instance, too much shade on a road that is prone to snow and ice can create dangerous conditions for commuters.

In the Visual Effects asset card, you can toggle on shadows by toggling the **High Visual Quality** setting to **On**, as shown in Figure 6–31. Changing this setting to **Off**, turns the shadows off.

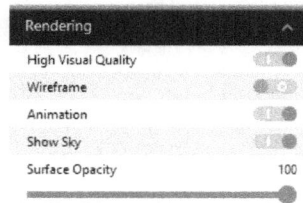

Figure 6–31

Brightness & Contrast

Both the brightness of the model and the contrast between light and dark can be controlled in the Visual Effects asset card, as shown in Figure 6–30. Additionally, you can change the color palette used by the model, selecting the normal, sepia, or grayscale palettes found in the Colorize drop-down list, as shown in Figure 6–32.

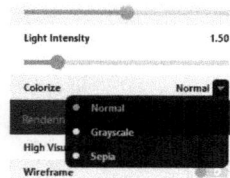

Figure 6–32

Field of View

The Field of View slider, found in the Visual Effects asset card, enables you to control how much of the model displays in the view as you zoom in and out.

Sun & Sky Settings

The time of year and time of day can both be set using the environment sliders in the Sun & Sky asset card, as shown in Figure 6–33. Additionally, you can set the amount of cloud coverage, wind speed/direction, and amount of cloud cover in the model. You can open the Sun & Sky asset card in the In

Canvas tools > [icon] (Build, Manage, and analyze your

infrastructure model)> [icon] (Analyze your model) > [icon] (Sun & Sky).

Figure 6–33

Practice 6c

Analyze the Model

Estimated time for completion: 10 minutes

Practice Objectives

- Analyze the model graphically by conducting a line of sight analysis and a shadow study.
- Analyze the model numerically by measuring the model.

In this practice you will conduct a line of sight analysis and measure the model to ensure that it meets the project requirements. You will then conduct a shadow study to ensure that the project receives enough sunlight and that shadows do not create any unforeseen issues.

Task 1 - Conduct a line of sight analysis.

In this task, you will conduct a line of sight analysis to determine whether certain homes can be seen from a specific point where you are considering putting a passenger loading station for the railway.

1. In the Home Screen, click ▇ (Open).

2. In the *C:\InfraWorks Fundamentals Practice Files\Analyze* folder, select **Analyze.sqlite** and click **Open**.

3. In the Quick Access Toolbar, expand *Switch Active Proposal* and select **C_Task1**.

4. In the Utility Bar, click ▇ (Bookmark you current location) and select **LOS**.

5. In the In Canvas tools, click ▇ (Build, manage, and analyze your infrastructure model)> ▇ (Analyze your model)> ▇ (Select Visible). All of the objects displayed in this line of sight are selected and highlighted in yellow to display them clearly.

6. In the Utility Bar, click ▇ (Bookmark your current location) and select **New Neighborhood**. Homes and roads will be selected, as shown in Figure 6–34. Note: After changing the view orientation, the selected objects remain selected and can be reviewed more easily.

Figure 6–34

7. Press <Esc> to clear the selection.

Task 2 - Measure the model.

In this task, you will measure the church building to ensure that it meets the project requirements for capacity. You will then measure the length of road to a specific cul-de-sac to ensure that it meets emergency evacuation codes.

1. In the In Canvas tools, click ▨ (Build, manage, and analyze your infrastructure model)> ▨ (Analyze your model)> ▨ (Measure Point to Point).

2. In the Utility Bar, click ▨ (Bookmark your current location) and select **Church**.

3. Measure the length and width of the main chapel of the church, as shown in Figure 6–35.

Figure 6–35

4. Press <Esc> to remove the temporary dimensions.

5. In the Utility Bar, click ▣ (Bookmark your current location) and select **Bridge Elevation**.

6. In the In Canvas tools, click ▣ (Build, manage, and analyze your infrastructure model)> ▣ (Analyze your model)> ◩ (2D Distance & Slope).

7. Click the first point to start the measurement near the start of the bridge, as shown in Figure 6–36.

8. Click the second point near the edge of the water. The measured value displays similar to Figure 6–36.

Figure 6–36

9. Press <Esc> to remove the temporary dimension.

10. In the Utility Bar, click ▣ (Bookmark your current location) and select **New Neighborhood**.

11. In the In Canvas tools, click ▣ (Build, manage, and analyze your infrastructure model)> ▣ (Analyze your model)> ◿ (Measure Path Distance).

12. Click the series of points shown in Figure 6–37 to measure the new roads from where they intersect Redwood Road, to where they end at the future cul-de-sac.

Figure 6–37

13. Press <Esc> to remove the temporary dimensions.

Task 3 - Conduct a shadow study.

In this task, you will conduct a shadow analysis to ensure that the new roads will not have increased numbers of accidents due to ice buildup on the roads that is caused by shadows.

1. In the Utility Bar, click ▣ (Bookmark your current location) and select **Church**.

2. In the Utility Bar, expand the View Style drop-down and click ⚙ (Configure current view).

3. In the View Style asset card, toggle on the **High Visual Quality**.

4. In the In Canvas tools, click ▮ (Build, manage, and analyze your infrastructure model)> ▢ (Analyze your model)> ☀ (Sun & Sky).

5. In the Sun & Sky asset card, set the *Date slider* to **January 1, 2017** and set the *Time slider* to **9:00 am**.

6. Continue moving the sliders to analyze the shadows over time.

7. Close the model.

Chapter Review Questions

1. Which of the following is not a theme that you can create in the model?

    a. Feature Theme

    b. Terrain Theme

    c. Point Cloud Theme

    d. Sky Theme

2. When conducting a Line of Sight analysis, the selected objects in the line of sight change when the view changes.

    a. True

    b. False

3. Which measurement tool would you use to determine the distance, altitude, or inclination of a point from the current camera viewpoint?

    a. (Measure Point to Point)

    b. (Measure Path Distance)

    c. (Range Finder)

    d. (Terrain Statistics)

4. Where can you find the measurement tools?

    a. (Create and manage your model)

    b. (Select model features)

    c. (Create conceptual design features)

    d. (Analyze your model)

5. How do you turn shadows on in the model?

    a. In the View Settings asset card.

    b. In the Sun & Sky asset card.

6. How do you filter a data source in preparation for adding it to a suitability map?

   a. Select the features in the model first.

   b. Create a Terrain Theme.

   c. Create a Feature Theme.

   d. Create a subset of the data source in the Model Explorer.

Command Summary

Button	Command	Location
	2D Distance & Slope	• **In Canvas Tools:** Build, manage, and analyze your industry model>Analyze your model
	Create Subset	• **Model Explorer**
	Feature Themes	• **In Canvas Tools:** Build, manage, and analyze your industry model>Analyze your model
	Path Distance	• **In Canvas Tools:** Build, manage, and analyze your industry model>Analyze your model
	Point Cloud Themes	• **In Canvas Tools:** Build, manage, and analyze your industry model>Analyze your model
	Point to Point Distance	• **In Canvas Tools:** Build, manage, and analyze your industry model>Analyze your model
	Range Finder	• **In Canvas Tools:** Build, manage, and analyze your industry model>Analyze your model
	Select Visible	• **In Canvas Tools:** Build, manage, and analyze your industry model>Analyze your model
	Sky & Sun	• **In Canvas Tools:** Build, manage, and analyze your industry model>Analyze your model
	Suitability Maps	• **In Canvas Tools:** Build, manage, and analyze your industry model>Analyze your model
	Terrain Statistics	• **In Canvas Tools:** Build, manage, and analyze your industry model>Analyze your model
	Terrain Themes	• **In Canvas Tools:** Build, manage, and analyze your industry model>Analyze your model
	Visual Effects	• **In Canvas Tools:** Build, manage, and analyze your industry model>Settings and Utilities

Chapter 7

Collaborating with Others

In most projects, multiple design professionals or departments work on different elements of the design. For the architectural elements, architects often use the Autodesk® Revit® software to model buildings, while civil engineers and surveyors work on the detailed design phase using the AutoCAD® Civil 3D® software. The Autodesk® InfraWorks® software can communicate with other Autodesk software types, which enables you to take advantage of models created by other departments. Additionally, if you have purchased the Autodesk InfraWorks 360 software, project files can be shared over the cloud to make accessing them much easier. In this chapter, you learn how to use the Autodesk InfraWorks 360 service to share files, import Autodesk Revit and AutoCAD Civil 3D files, and create scenarios for effective collaboration.

Learning Objectives in this Chapter

- Share design elements between Autodesk InfraWorks 360 and AutoCAD Civil 3D.
- Import an Autodesk Revit model.
- Create a scenario that includes storyboards to share on the Internet.

7.1 Share Design Elements with AutoCAD Civil 3D

Autodesk InfraWorks 360 models can be opened directly in the AutoCAD Civil 3D software. Therefore, you do not have to recreate these design elements for the detailed design phase of the modeling process. Additionally, AutoCAD Civil 3D drawing files can be imported into an Autodesk InfraWorks 360 model to help communicate the final design to stakeholders by taking advantage of the high definition graphics. When you add an AutoCAD Civil 3D DWG data source, the following AutoCAD Civil 3D data objects are imported:

This does not include pressure pipes at this time.

- Corridors

- Surfaces

- Pipes

- Pipe Networks

When importing AutoCAD Civil 3D DWG files into an Autodesk InfraWorks 360 model, you might want to start a new proposal and remove any roads that might end up duplicated before starting the import process. If you do not do this, your roads might display similar to that shown in Figure 7–1. The problem occurs when the software cannot determine which alignment to use, and tries to use both.

Figure 7–1

In order to import an AutoCAD Civil 3D DWG file directly, you must have the AutoCAD Civil 3D 2017 software installed on your computer.

How To: Import AutoCAD Civil 3D DWG Files

1. In the In Canvas tools, click ▊ (Build, manage, and analyze your infrastructure model) > ▦ (Create and manage your model> ▤ (Data Sources).
2. In the Data Sources palette, expand ⬚ ▾ (Add file data source) and select **AutoCAD Civil 3D DWG**.
3. In the Select Files dialog box, browse to the AutoCAD Civil 3D DWG file, select it and click **Open**.
   - Alternatively, you can drag and drop .DWG files into the Autodesk InfraWorks model from Windows Explorer. When you do, a DWG File Import dialog box displays that enables you to select what type of data source to use for the file, as shown in Figure 7–2. Select the **AutoCAD Civil 3D DWG** option and click **OK**.

Figure 7–2

4. In the Choose Data Sources dialog box, select all of the AEC objects you want in the Autodesk InfraWorks model, as shown in Figure 7–3. Click **OK**.

Figure 7–3

5. In the Data Sources palette, note that all of the imported AEC objects display under their appropriate source type and are selected, as shown in Figure 7–4. Click ♻ (Refresh data source).

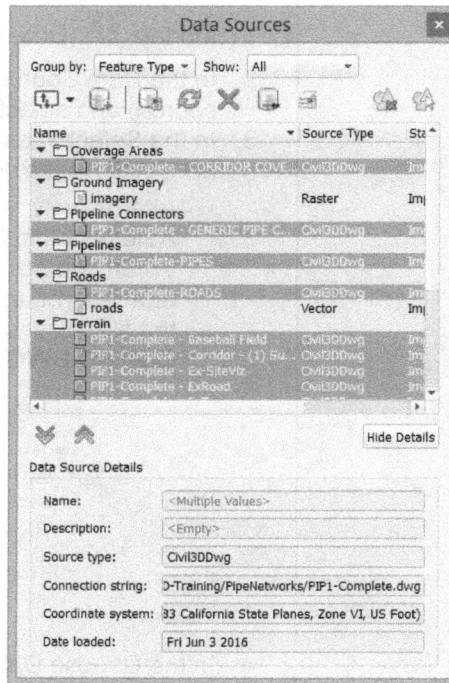

Figure 7–4

Drawing Overlays

When the AutoCAD Civil 3D DWG data source type is selected, only the AEC objects are imported into the Autodesk InfraWorks model. In order to import other linework (such as parcel lines and utilities other than pipe networks), you can use an *AutoCAD DWG as 2D Overlay* data source type. When working with terrain overlays, you can:

- Move

- Rotate

- Scale

- Control selectability

- Control transparency, as shown in Figure 7–5.

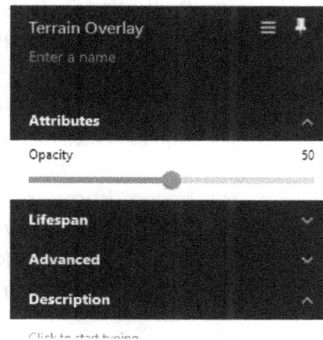

Figure 7–5

How To: Import AutoCAD Civil 3D DWG Files

AUTODESK®
INFRAWORKS™ 360

To use this feature, access to the Internet and Autodesk® InfraWorks® 360 are required.

1. In the In Canvas tools, click ▉ (Build, manage, and analyze your infrastructure model) > ▉ (Create and manage your model> ▉ (Data Sources).

2. In the Data Sources palette, expand ▉ ▾ (Add file data source) and select **AutoCAD DWG as 2D Overlay**.

3. In the Select Files dialog box, browse to the AutoCAD DWG file, select it and click **Open**.

   • Alternatively, you can drag and drop .DWG files into the Autodesk InfraWorks model from Windows Explorer. When you do, a DWG File Import dialog box displays that enables you to select what type of data source to use for the file, as shown in Figure 7–6. Select the **AutoCAD DWG as 2D Overlay** option and click **OK**.

Figure 7–6

4. In the Data Import dialog box, when the following warning displays, click **Send**:

   • *This feature requires an Internet connection and an Autodesk 360 account. By clicking "Send", you will be transmitting data to InfraWorks 360 cloud-based services.*

5. In the Data Source palette, under *Terrain Overlays*, double-click on the imported DWG data source.

6. In the Data Source Configuration dialog box, adjust the **Scale** and **Rotation** as necessary. Click **Interactive Placing...** and double-click on a point in the model where the drawing should be located, as shown in Figure 7–7.

   - Alternatively, you can set the coordinate system under *Position*. Then set the X and Y coordinate values if you know them. (These values can be found by hovering the cursor over the expected insertion point in the Autodesk InfraWorks model. Then take note of the coordinates in the bottom-left corner of the model window.)

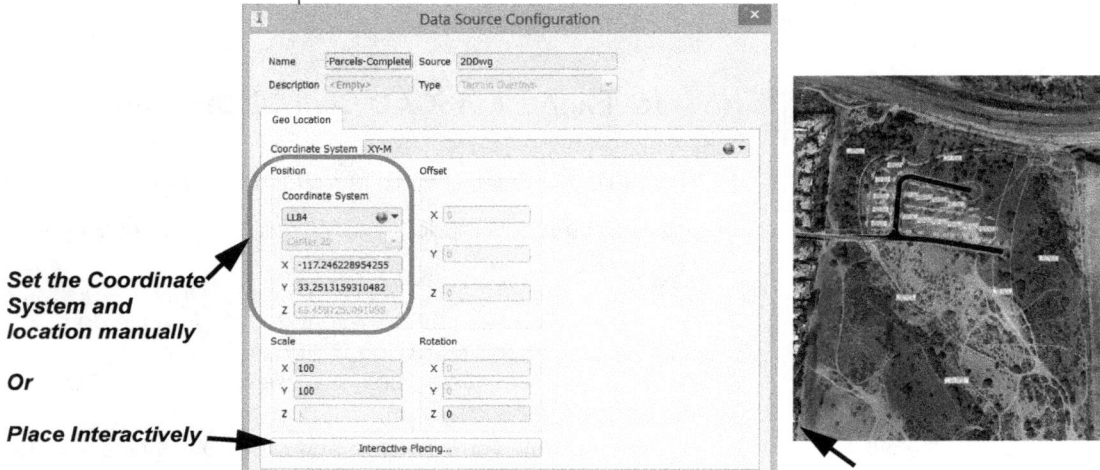

Set the Coordinate System and location manually

Or

Place Interactively

Figure 7–7

7. In the Data Source Configuration dialog box, click **Close & Refresh**.

8. In the model, select the overlay. Then use the gizmos to move, scale, or rotate the overlay as required.

Working with .IMX Files

The enhanced data exchange process makes it easy to import AutoCAD Civil 3D files directly. However, if any errors occur or if you do not have the AutoCAD Civil 3D software on your computer, files can also be transferred between the software packages using .IMX files. Alternatively, IMX files can be used to copy Autodesk InfraWorks features from one model to another.

Exporting .IMX Files

When exporting an .IMX file to be used in the AutoCAD Civil 3D software, you can export the entire Autodesk InfraWorks 360 model, or a portion of the model. When you export an .IMX file, everything becomes part of the .IMX, including the existing conditions of features that were imported from other data sources. To reduce the file size and duplication of model elements in the AutoCAD Civil 3D software, it is recommended that you only export a portion of the model by using a bounding box or polyline. In addition to setting how much of the model to include in the .IMX file, you can also set the target coordinate system.

How To: Create an .IMX file

1. In the In Canvas tools, click ![Settings and Utilities] (Settings and Utilities)> ![Export IMX] (Export IMX).
2. In the Export to IMX dialog box, set the model extents in the Defining Interactively drop-down list by selecting **BBox** or **Polygon** (as shown in Figure 7–8), or by selecting the **Use Entire Model** option.

Figure 7–8

3. In the Export to IMX dialog box, set the target coordinate system and the target's directory and filename.
4. Click **Export**.

Importing .IMX Files

When importing .IMX files into an Autodesk InfraWorks 360 model, you use the process that would be used to import any other data source. Importing files does not create a link to the file. Therefore, it is recommended that you create a new proposal before importing an .IMX file to ensure that you have a base model to revert to if anything changes. If the detailed design changes in the AutoCAD Civil 3D software, you have to create and import an updated .IMX file.

Only certain AutoCAD Civil 3D elements can be imported into the Autodesk InfraWorks 360 software. These elements include surfaces, alignments and profiles, corridor models, and pipe networks. Each element must be configured separately. When you import an .IMX file with multiple objects, you must select which type of data to include. The Choose Data Sources dialog box enables you to select the data to import, as shown in Figure 7–9.

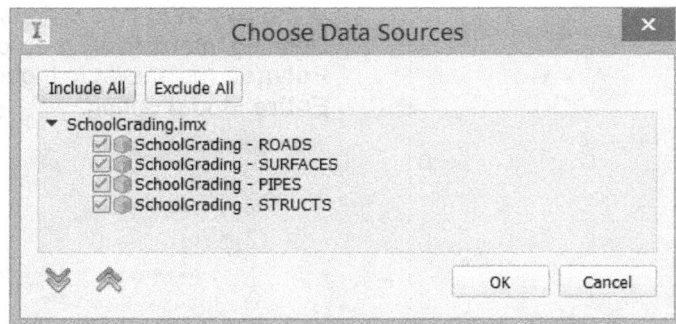

Figure 7–9

Once imported, each data type becomes its own data source in the Data Sources palette. Before they display in the model, the data source must be configured. The list below describes how each data source is handled and configured in the Autodesk InfraWorks 360 software.

- **Surfaces:** Both existing ground and finish ground surfaces can be imported, becoming terrain surfaces. If a grid surface is imported, it is converted into a TIN surface. Only one surface can be displayed in the model at a time, so you must select which surface to import in the *IMX* tab in the Data Source Configuration dialog box, as shown in Figure 7–10.

Figure 7–10

- **Alignments and Profiles:** Alignments and profiles are combined into one road feature. They are assigned a road style in the Data Source Configuration dialog box in the *Common* tab, in the *Style* area. Any alignments and profiles that are used to create a corridor model are imported separately. For any alignments that are not associated with a corridor model, you can set the style in the *Common* tab in the Data Source Configuration dialog box, as shown in Figure 7–11.

Figure 7–11

- **Corridors:** Alignments and profiles that have been assigned to a corridor model in the AutoCAD Civil 3D software can be imported into the model in a few different ways. You can use an Autodesk InfraWorks 360 road style, or you can use the AutoCAD Civil 3D corridor surface or regions to display the road design. If the Autodesk InfraWorks 360 styles are used to display the corridor model, only one centerline alignment associated with the corridor is used to stylize the road. All of the other alignments associated with the corridor are ignored. When using the corridor surface or regions to stylize the road, two options are available in the *IMX* tab in the Data Source Configuration Dialog Box, as shown in Figure 7–12.

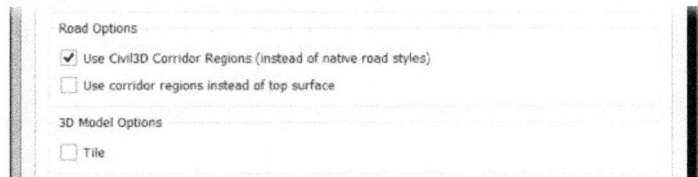

Road Options

☑ Use Civil3D Corridor Regions (instead of native road styles)

☐ Use corridor regions instead of top surface

3D Model Options

☐ Tile

Figure 7–12

The two **Road Options** are as follows.

- **Use Civil 3D Corridor Regions (instead of native road styles):** If the corridor surface is used to stylize the road, the surface becomes a coverage area rather than a road feature. The road in Figure 7–13 uses the native road styles, while the road in Figure 7–14 shows the same road using the Civil3D Corridor Regions setting.

Native road style

Figure 7–13

Civil3D corridor regions

Figure 7–14

- **Use corridor regions instead of top surface:** This option creates a more detailed display of the road surface. The detail is sharp enough to display curbs, medians and other raised or lowered areas more clearly. Figure 7–15 shows the changes that occur to the road used in Figure 7–14 when with both Road Options are selected.

Figure 7–15

This does not include pressure pipes at this time.

- **Pipe Networks:** Pipes from the AutoCAD Civil 3D software become Pipes in the Autodesk InfraWorks 360 software, while structures become Pipe Connectors. Pipes and Pipe Connectors display separately when a pipe network is imported from the AutoCAD Civil 3D software, as shown in Figure 7–16. When configuring the pipe networks, set the style in the *Common* tab in the Data Configuration dialog box.

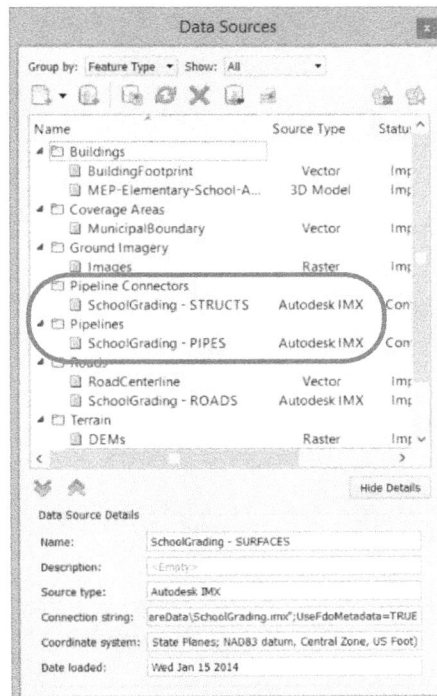

Figure 7–16

How To: Import an .IMX file

1. In the In Canvas tools, click [I] (Build, manage, and analyze your industry model)>[icon] (Create and manage your model)>[icon] (Data Sources).

2. In the Data Sources palette, expand [icon] (Add file data source) and select **Autodesk IMX**.

3. In the Select Files dialog box, browse to the location of the file, select it, and click **Open**.

4. In the Choose Data Source dialog box (shown in Figure 7–17) select the AutoCAD Civil 3D objects that you want to import. Click **OK**.

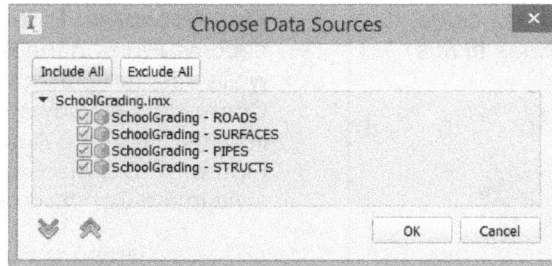

Figure 7–17

5. In the Data Sources palette, double-click on the .IMX files to configure them.

6. If it is a surface or corridor model, in the *IMX* tab, in the Data Source Configuration dialog box, select the required settings.

7. Click **Close & Refresh** to display the imported data in the model.

Practice 7a

Working with AutoCAD Civil 3D Users

Practice Objectives

- Import AutoCAD Civil 3D DWG files.
- Create .IMX files for sharing data with the AutoCAD Civil 3D software.
- Import .IMX files from the AutoCAD Civil 3D software to display the final design.

Estimated time for completion: 20 minutes

In this practice you will move data between the Autodesk InfraWorks 360 software and the AutoCAD Civil 3D software.

Task 1 - Remove potential duplicate roads.

In this task, you will remove roads that are being imported from AutoCAD Civil 3D to avoid duplicates..

1. In the Home Screen, click **Open**.

2. In the *C:\InfraWorks Fundamentals Practice Files\ShareData* folder, select **Sharing.sqlite** and click **Open**.

3. In the Quick Access Toolbar, expand *Switch Active Proposal* and select **A_Task1**.

4. In the Utility Bar, click ▥ (Bookmark your current location) and select **New Neighborhood**.

5. In the model, select the roads and coverage shown in Figure 7–18.

Figure 7–18

6. Press <Delete>.

Task 2 - Import a drawing overlay.

In this task, you will import a drawing overlay in order to display the linework for a parking lot.

1. Continue working in the same model as the last task. If you did not complete the last task, in the Quick Access Toolbar, expand *Switch Active Proposal* and select **A_Task2**.

2. In the Utility Bar, click ▊ (Bookmark your current location) and select **New Neighborhood**.

3. In the In Canvas tools, click ▊ (Build, manage, and analyze your infrastructure model) > ▊ (Create and manage your model> ▊ (Data Sources).

4. In the Data Sources palette, expand ▊ ▾ (Add file data source) and select **AutoCAD DWG as 2D Overlay**.

5. In the Select Files dialog box, browse to *C:\InfraWorks Fundamentals Practice Files\ShareData\Civil Files* folder, select **Site Layout - Base.dwg** and click **Open**.

6. In the Data Import dialog box, click **Send**.

7. Once you notice that the Status is no longer showing *Processing,* in the Data Source palette, under *Terrain Overlays*, double-click on the **Site Layout - Base** data source.

8. In the Data Source Configuration dialog box, do the following, as shown in Figure 7–19.
   - Under Coordinate System, expand the drop-down list and select **UT83-CF**.
   - In the *X* field, type **1535406.6239**.
   - In the *Y* field, type **7272355.4011**.
   - Under Scale, for both the *X* and *Y* fields, type **12**.
   - Click **Close & Refresh**.

*If **UT83-CF** is not in the drop-down list, click*

▊ *(Choose Coordinate System) and search for it.*

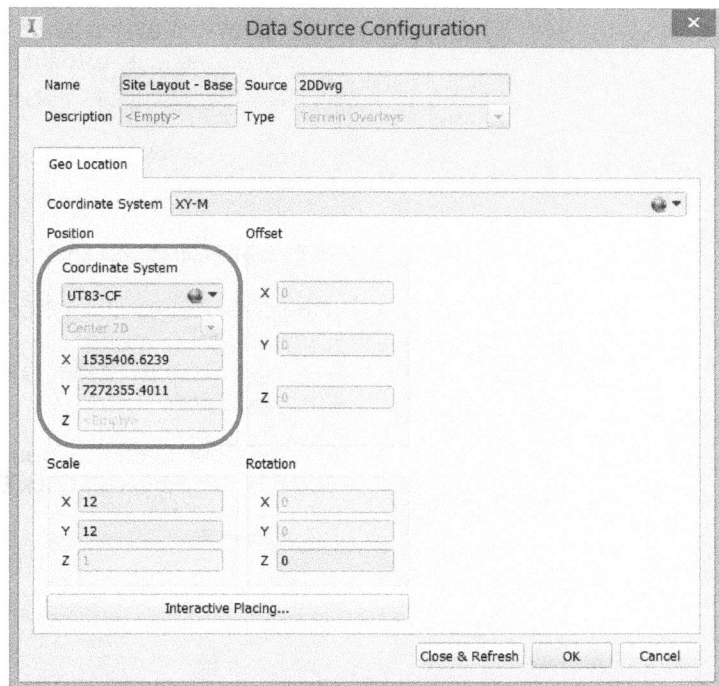

Figure 7–19

9. In the Utility Bar, click 🖽 (Control visibility, display, and selectability of features).

10. In the Model Explorer palette, under Overlays, to the right of

    Site Layout - Base, click 🔒 (Selectable/ Unselectable) to lock the new overlay.

Task 3 - Import AutoCAD Civil 3D Data.

In this task you will import the AutoCAD Civil 3D surfaces, pipes, and roads from the detailed design phase of the project.

1. Continue working in the same model as the last task. If you did not complete the last task, in the Quick Access Toolbar, expand *Switch Active Proposal* and select **A_Task3**.

2. In the Utility Bar, click 🖽 (Bookmark your current location) and select **School**.

---

3. In the Data Sources palette, expand ⬚ ▾ (Add file data source) and select **AutoCAD Civil 3D DWG**.

    *   If the Data Sources palette is not open, in the In Canvas tools, click 🔲 (Build, manage, and analyze your infrastructure model)>🔳 (Create and manage your model)>🗄 (Data Sources).

4. In the Select Files dialog box, browse to the *C:\InfraWorks Fundamentals Practice Files\ShareData\Civil Files\Source Drawings\Surfaces* folder, select **Site Layout-wPipes.dwg**, and click **Open**.

5. In the Choose Data Sources dialog box, select the objects shown in Figure 7–20. Click **OK**.

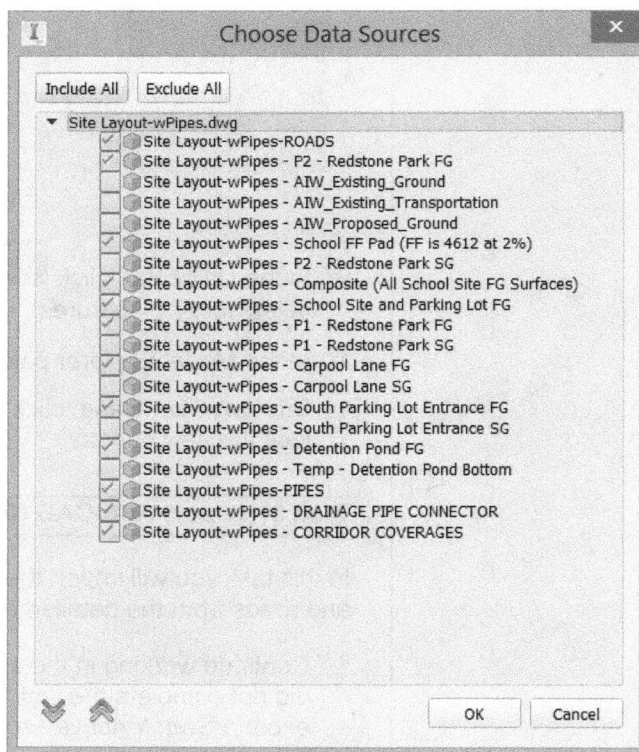

Figure 7–20

6. In the Data Sources palette, click 🔄 (Refresh).

7. Once the Status no longer displays *Processing*, in the Data Source palette, under *Roads*, double-click on the **Site Layout-wPipes-Roads** data source.

8. On the *Common* tab of the Data Source Configuration dialog box, next to Rule Style, click (Style chooser), as shown in Figure 7–21.

Figure 7–21

9. In the Select Style dialog box, select **Sidewalks with Lamps** and click **OK**.

10. In the Data Source Configuration dialog box, click **Close & Refresh**.

11. In the Utility Bar, click (Bookmark your current location) and select **Pond**.

Note the road going around the pond. This road is included in the model because alignments and corridors were used to create the pond grading in the AutoCAD Civil 3D software. You can select the road and try to delete it, but this does not always work.

Task 4 - Export an .IMX file.

In this task, you will export part of the model to send it to the AutoCAD Civil 3D software for the detailed design phase. To do so, you will use a bounding box to select the information surrounding the school so that another team member can create the detailed design for the school's grading plans.

1. Continue working in the same file as the last task. If you did not complete the last task, in the Quick Access Toolbar, expand *Switch Active Proposal* and select **A_Task4**.

2. In the Utility Bar, click ▣ (Bookmark your current location) and select **School**.

3. In the In Canvas tools, click ✖ (Setting and Utilities)> ▣ (Export IMX).

4. In the Export to IMX dialog box, expand the Define Interactively drop-down list and select **BBox**, as shown in Figure 7–22.

Figure 7–22

5. In the model, create the bounding box shown in Figure 7–23. Single-click the bottom left corner, and then double-click the top right corner.

Figure 7–23

6. Ensure that the *Target Coordinate System* is **UT83-CF**, and set *Target File* to **C:\InfraWorks Fundamentals Practice Files\ShareData\IM_Export.imx**.

7. Click **Export**.

7.2 Working with Autodesk Revit Models

Determining how a building is going to look in its surrounding environment is valuable for gaining stakeholder buy-in. Until recently, the best an architect could do was to approximate what the ground surface looked like using basic tools in the Autodesk Revit software. At the same time, civil professionals could only create basic 2D line work or a basic 3D model of the building in the AutoCAD Civil 3D software to simulate where the building was to be located. Using the Autodesk InfraWorks 360 software, architects, MEP engineers, and civil professionals can bring their models together into one model to better communicate how an entire project should look when construction is complete.

Figure 7–24 shows an Autodesk Revit MEP model of a building that has been imported into an Autodesk InfraWorks 360 model.

Figure 7–24

The tools used to import an Autodesk Revit model are the same as those used to import existing conditions data sources. The biggest difference in the importing process is that a coordinate system has not been assigned to most Autodesk Revit models. Therefore, you either have to know the exact coordinates of where to place the building, or you have to interactively place the building in the model. When importing an Autodesk Revit model, you can preview the model being imported and make any required corrections before placing it in the model. The Data Source Configuration dialog box is shown in Figure 7–25.

Models larger than 100 megabytes in size can negatively affect performance. It is recommended that you simplify large 3D models in their source applications before importing them. The import fails if the 3D model is larger than a gigabyte in size.

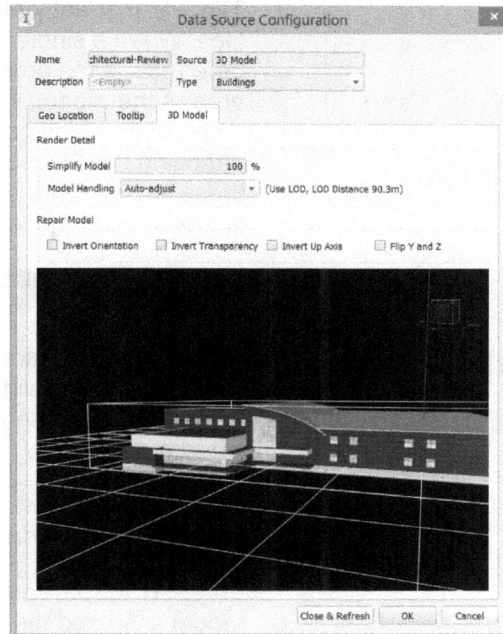

Figure 7–25

Render Detail

How the model renders in the Autodesk InfraWorks 360 model can be controlled using the Model Handling drop-down list in the *3D Model* tab of the Data Source Configuration dialog box. The options used to adjust the model are as follows.

- **Auto-adjust:** The Autodesk InfraWorks 360 software determines the settings for the 3D model. If the automatic setting applies a Level of Detail (LOD), you can change the *LOD Distance* setting by selecting the **Use LOD** option, and adjusting the *LOD Distance*.

- **Direct Display:** The **Repair Model** options and settings for Simplify Model are applied to the 3D model, but they do not adjust how the model is rendered. Use this setting if the model uses a small number of triangles to define its shape. For example, a house with little detail.

The LOD Distance setting is found in the Model Explorer. Higher level of detail settings enable you to see greater detail from a greater distance.

- **Use LOD:** Level of Detail settings generate a series of simplifications, assigning the best one based on viewing distance. If you select this option, ensure that you also set the *LOD Distance*.

- **Tile:** Permanently attaches the 3D model to multiple display tiles. When a single object spans multiple tiles, its display can be erratic. If the object is on the periphery of the displayed area of the model, it might not display at all, or might only display when you zoom in closer to the object. Permanently attaching the 3D model to multiple display tiles helps avoid these issues. This is especially helpful if the model is large or spans several model units (such as a bridge).

- **Use Dynamic LOD:** Sets the LOD dynamically.

Repair Model

When a model does not display as expected in the model, you might need to make slight adjustments to the model. The following five adjustment options can be used to repair the imported model.

- **Invert Orientation:** Inverts the direction of the *Face Normals* that form each surface of the model.

- **Invert Transparency:** Makes the transparent areas of the model solid and the solid areas transparent.

- **Invert Up Axis:** Flips the model upside-down.

- **Flip Y and Z:** Controls whether the *up* axis runs along the Y- or Z-axis since some applications use the Y-axis as the *up* direction, rather than the Z-axis.

How To: Import an Autodesk Revit Model

1. Sign in to the Autodesk InfraWorks 360 service.

2. In the In Canvas tools, click ⬛ (Build, manage, and analyze your industry model)> ▦ (Create and manage your model)> 🛢 (Data Sources).

3. In the Data Sources palette, click ⬛▾ (Add file data source) and select **Autodesk Revit**.

AUTODESK®
INFRAWORKS™ 360

To use this feature, access to the Internet, a Navisworks Manage license, and Autodesk® InfraWorks® 360 are required.

4. In the Select Files dialog box, browse to the required Autodesk Revit file and click **Open**.

- If the Data Import dialog box shown in Figure 7–26 opens, click **Send**.

Figure 7–26

- If the Transfer Navisworks Files message displays (as shown in Figure 7–27), click **Transfer**.

Figure 7–27

5. In the Data Sources palette, double-click on the Autodesk Revit model data source that you just imported.

6. In the common area, the **Type** can be set, as shown in Figure 7–28. By default, the *Type* is set to **Buildings**.

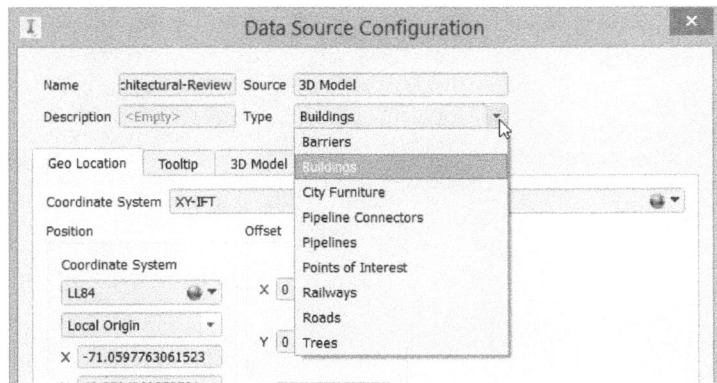

Figure 7–28

*This displays because you need a Navisworks Manage license to import Autodesk Revit files unless you clear the selection of the application option **Navisworks based Local Import** on the Data Import page.*

Only change the Type if the imported model is not a building.

7. In the *Geo Location* tab, set the X, Y, and Z values under *Position* or click **Interactive Placing**, as shown in Figure 7–29.

If provided, the Autodesk InfraWorks software can automatically read the location data from the Revit file.

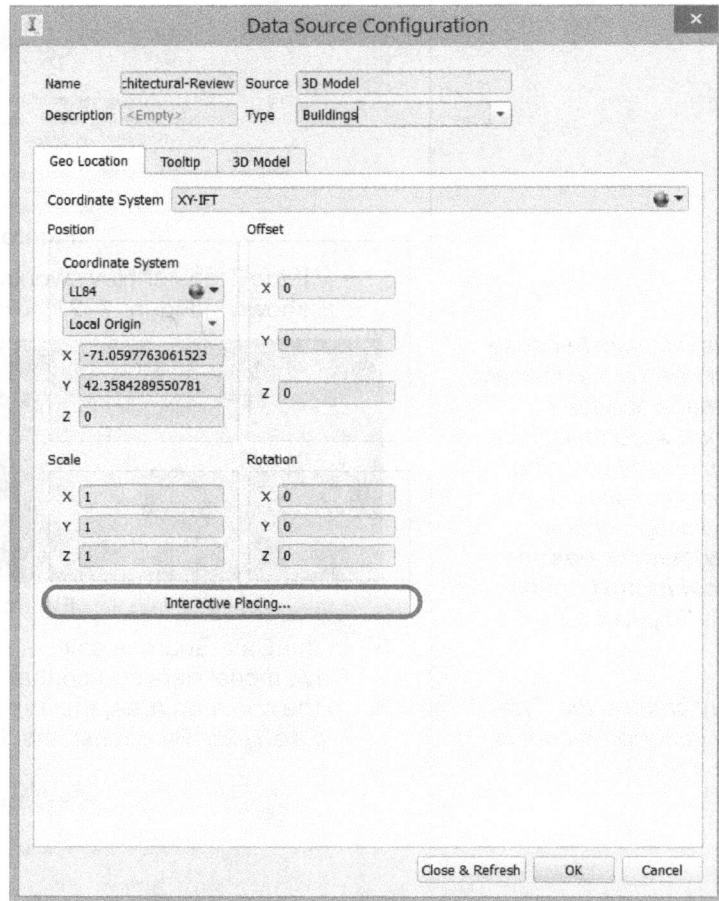

Figure 7–29

8. Preview the model in the *3D Model* tab, as shown in Figure 7–30.

   - Select an appropriate *Model Handling* option to set the Level of Detail (LOD).
   - Make any necessary adjustments to the model under the Model Repair area.

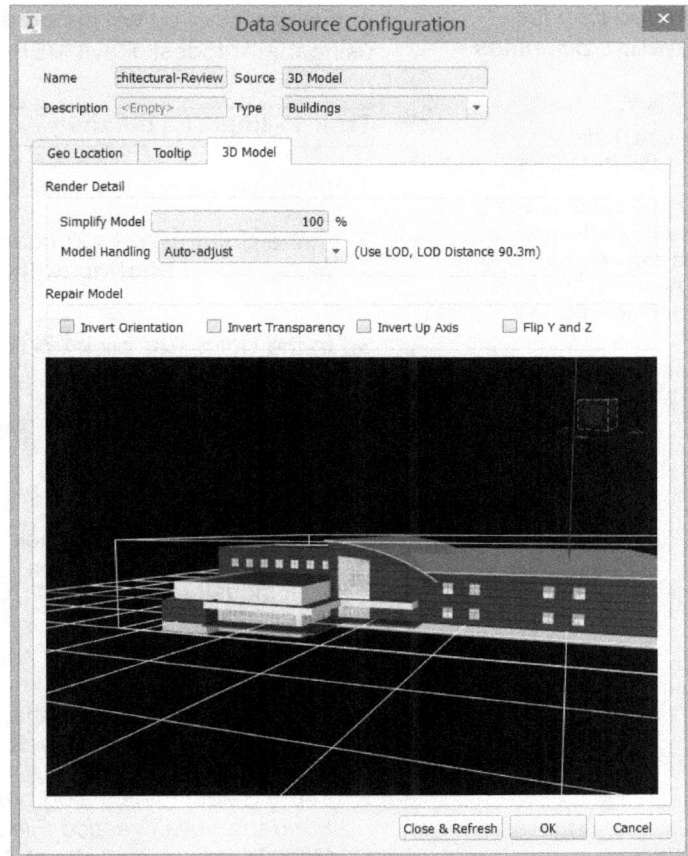

Figure 7–30

9. Click **Close & Refresh** to complete the import process and display it in the model.

Practice 7b

Import an Autodesk Revit File

Practice Objective

Estimated time for completion: 5 minutes

AUTODESK
INFRAWORKS 360

To complete this practice, access to the Internet, a Navisworks Manage license, and Autodesk® InfraWorks® 360 are required.

Import an Autodesk Revit File

Practice Objective

- Import an Autodesk Revit model and note how it fits with other design elements.

In this practice you will import a school model that was created using the Autodesk Revit MEP software.

Task 1 - Import a building.

1. In the Home Screen, click **Open**.

2. In the *C:\InfraWorks Fundamentals Practice Files\ShareData* folder, select **Sharing.sqlite** and click **Open**.

3. In the Utility Bar, click ▣ (Bookmark your current location) and select **School**.

4. In the Utility Bar, expand *Switch Active Proposal* and select **B_Task1**.

5. In the In Canvas tools, click ▣ (Build, manage, and analyze your industry model) > ▣ (Create and manage your model)> ▣ (Data Sources).

6. In the Data Sources palette, click ▣ (Add file data source) and select **Autodesk Revit**.

7. In the Select Files dialog box, browse to the *C:\InfraWorks Fundamentals Practice Files\ShareData* folder, select **MEP-Elementary-School-Architectural-Review.rvt** and click **Open**.

    - If the Data Import information dialog box displays (shown in Figure 7–31), click **Send**.

Figure 7–31

This dialog box prompts you that the custom textures that were part of the Autodesk Revit model will be ignored. Custom textures cannot be imported into the Autodesk InfraWorks 360 software.

- If the Data Import warning dialog box displays (as shown in Figure 7–32), click **OK**.

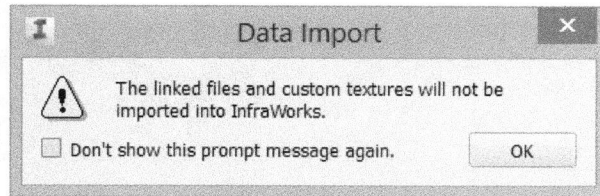

Figure 7–32

8. In the Data Sources palette, in the *Building* folder, double-click on the **MEP-Elementary-School-Architectural-Review** model data source that you just imported.

   Note: You might have to wait for the model to finish processing. You will know it is done when *In Progress* is replaced with *Imported* in the Status column, as shown in Figure 7–33.

Figure 7–33

9. In the Data Source Configuration dialog box, ensure that the *Type* is set to **Buildings**.

10. In the *Geo Location* tab, click **Interactive Placing**.

11. In the model, double-click to place the school model on the coverage, as shown in Figure 7–34.

Figure 7–34

12. In the Data Source configuration dialog box, click **Close & Refresh** to update the model. The Autodesk Revit model now displays in the Autodesk InfraWorks 360 model.

13. In the model, select the building. Then use the ⤒ (Move Gizmo) to reposition the model as required.

If changes are made to the original Autodesk Revit model, you will need to import the updated model.

7.3 Share Files Using the Autodesk InfraWorks 360 Service

Autodesk InfraWorks 360 is a cloud service that is only available to those that bought the Autodesk InfraWorks 360 software. It is used to store and share models over the Internet. Once you have signed into your Autodesk InfraWorks 360 account, you can share models, proposals, and scenarios.

The following is an example of how the Autodesk InfraWorks 360 service can be used to share and collaborate on files:

- A group is created by your team's administrator, and you and your team are invited to join the group.

- An architect publishes a model to the group.

- You download and make changes to the architect's Autodesk InfraWorks model.

- You synchronize your local changes with the online version.

- The architect synchronizes with the online model and notes how the changes affect the model.

- You and your team continue to make changes and synchronize your versions to the model in the cloud. Any conflicts are automatically resolved throughout the process.

Sign In

When you first start Autodesk InfraWorks 360, you should be asked to sign into your Autodesk Account. If you do not have an account, click **Need an Autodesk ID?** in the Autodesk Account Sign In screen to create a new account. Once signed in, your login information is saved for 14 days and determines what tools are available to you. You should not see the Autodesk Account Sign In screen for 14 days unless you manually sign out.

How To: Sign In to Autodesk InfraWorks 360

1. In the Autodesk Account Sign In screen, type your user name and password, as shown in Figure 7–35. Click **Sign In**.

Figure 7–35

Manage Group Memberships

Models are shared using groups to ensure that you can control who is able to access the model. To create groups and assign people to them, you must be a group administrator.

Users Roles

Anyone can create a free account and become an Autodesk InfraWorks 360 user. You do not need to own a copy of the software in order to create an account. Therefore, each person inside a firm and all of the firm's clients can create an account. The key is knowing the user rights level that each individual should be assigned. User rights fall into four roles, as listed below.

- **Admin:** Initially, only one administrator is assigned to an account. However, the admin can give Admin rights to any user's account. Admins have the ability to create groups, add users, and download/upload or synchronize models to the cloud.

- **Author:** Authors can only download and synchronize models that they have downloaded, to the cloud. They cannot upload new models to the cloud.

- **Publisher:** Publishers can upload/download, and synchronize models to the cloud. They can also upload scenarios to the cloud.

- **Reader:** Readers can only download and view models from the cloud. They cannot upload updates or new models to the cloud.

How To: Manage Group Memberships

If ⚇ is not displayed, click ⚇ (Manage groups and cloud models) to expand it.

1. In the Home Screen, click ⚇ (Manage group memberships).

2. In the Manage Group Memberships dialog box, *in the Administer Groups* tab, select the account the groups should be applied to, and then click ✛ (Add Group), as shown in Figure 7–36.

Figure 7–36

3. In the Add Group dialog box, type a name and description in the respective fields. Click **OK**.

4. Next to the new group, click **Users** to add users to the group.

   • This automatically switches to the *Add Users to Group* tab.

   • Alternatively, you can select the *Add Users to Group* tab manually.

The Administrator is automatically added to the group with an assigned role of Admin.

5. In the *Assign User to Groups* tab, select the group to work with at the top, and then click ✛ (Add User).

6. In the new row, type the email address that is connected to the user's Autodesk InfraWorks 360 account. Then assign them the role of Author, Publisher, or Reader, as applicable. Click **OK**.

How To: Assign Admin Rights

1. In the Home Screen, click ![icon] (Manage group memberships).
2. In the Manage Group Membership dialog box, select the *Set up Account Admins* tab.
3. Select the account that you want to add to the admin rights group in the Account drop-down list.

A list of users for the account displays.

4. In the Admin column, check the email address for the users that should obtain admin rights, as shown in Figure 7–37.

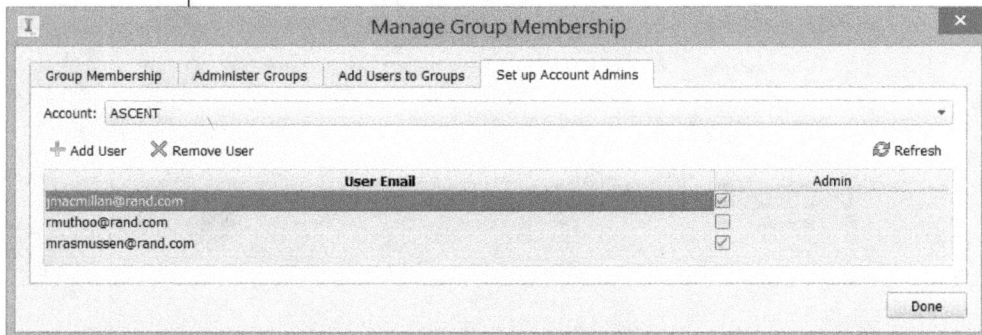

Figure 7–37

5. Click **OK**.

Working with Models

Publishing Models

When you publish a model, you make it available to others to see the selected proposals. By default, only the master proposal and common resources are published. Additional proposals can be published by selecting them in the Publish Model dialog box. You can also determine who has access to the model by selecting a group that has been created for you by a group administrator.

How To: To Publish a Model

1. Open the model you want to publish.

2. In the Utility Bar, click ![icon] (Publish this model to InfraWorks 360).

3. In the Publish Model dialog box, select the Group that you want to share the model with from the Group drop-down list.

4. Select the proposals you want to share in the *Select Resources* area, as shown in Figure 7–38. Type any Publishing Notes to describe what is included in this version of the model. Click **Publish**.

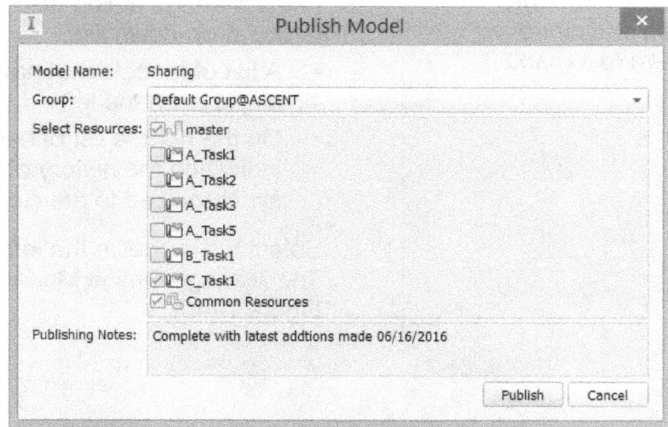

Figure 7–38

Accessing Online Models

Once a model has been shared, others that are invited can access it by selecting the model on the Home Screen, as shown in Figure 7–39. Click the appropriate thumbnail to download and open the model.

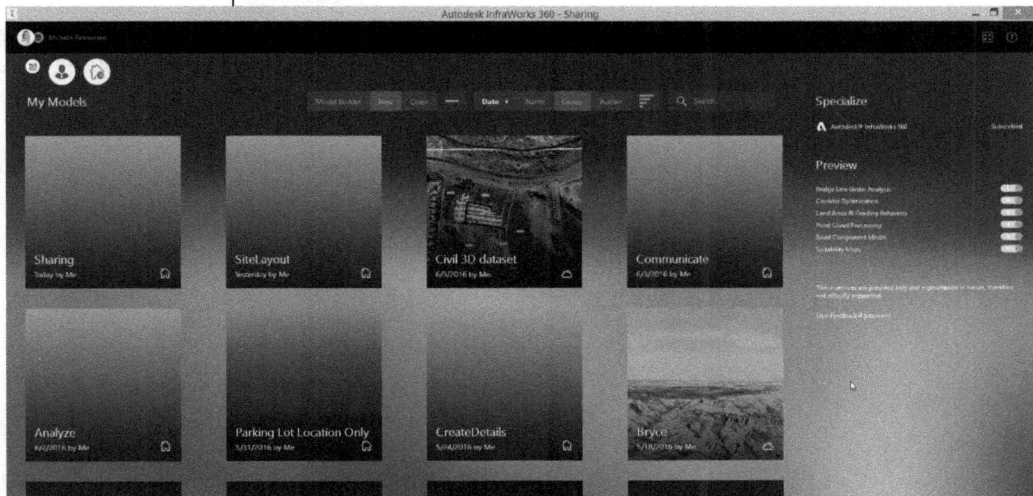

Figure 7–39

If the model does not display in the thumbnails on the Home screen, they can download it from the cloud.

How To: Download Models from InfraWorks 360

If ⚇ is not displayed,

click ⚇ (Manage groups and cloud models) to expand it.

1. On the Home screen, click ⚇ (Manage online models and scenarios).
2. In the Manage dialog box, select the model's group in the Group drop-down list.
   - A list of models that have been published to the cloud displays on the left.
   - On the right, a list of each model's history displays indicating the history of when the model was synchronized to the cloud.

3. Select the model in the left column and click ⬇ (Download). The Manage Online Models dialog box is shown in Figure 7–40.

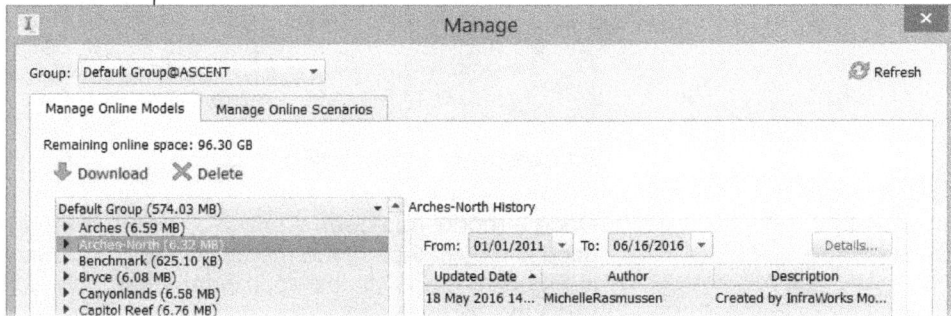

Figure 7–40

4. In the Download As dialog box, select the location in which the model is going to be saved on your computer, as shown in Figure 7–41.

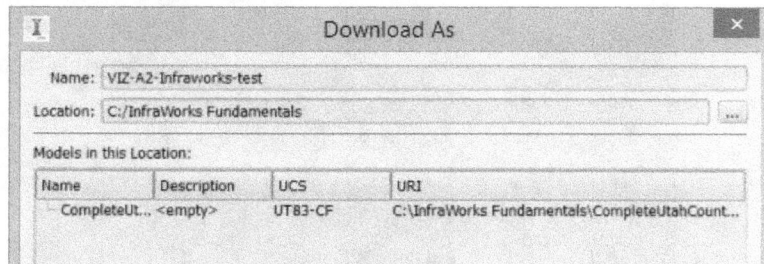

Figure 7–41

- If you no longer want to share a model, click ✖ (Delete) in the Manage dialog box to remove it from the group in the cloud.

Synchronizing Models

Synchronizing a model enables you to share your latest changes with others through the cloud, review changes others have made to the model, and resolve any conflicts between local and shared versions of the files. Conflicts are resolved automatically and you do not have any control over how they are resolved. The last local change usually takes precedence over a conflicting change from the online group, and deletions take precedence over updates.

It is extremely important that all members of a team use the same version of the Autodesk InfraWorks software. If one team member upgrades a model, the shared, cloud model also updates. Any changes that are not synced to the cloud before upgrading a model are lost. Communication is key to sharing models and upgrading them. It is best to sync changes frequently when working in a team environment.

If you do not have the required permissions to edit the model, Sync is grayed out in the Synchronize Model dialog box.

In the Synchronize Model dialog box, the *Local Last Changed* column indicates the last time you made changes to the model on your computer. The *Online Last Changed* column indicates when the model was last changed in the cloud. If ⚠ displays next to a file or proposal, the local file or proposal has not been shared with the cloud. Figure 7–42 shows the Synchronize Model dialog box.

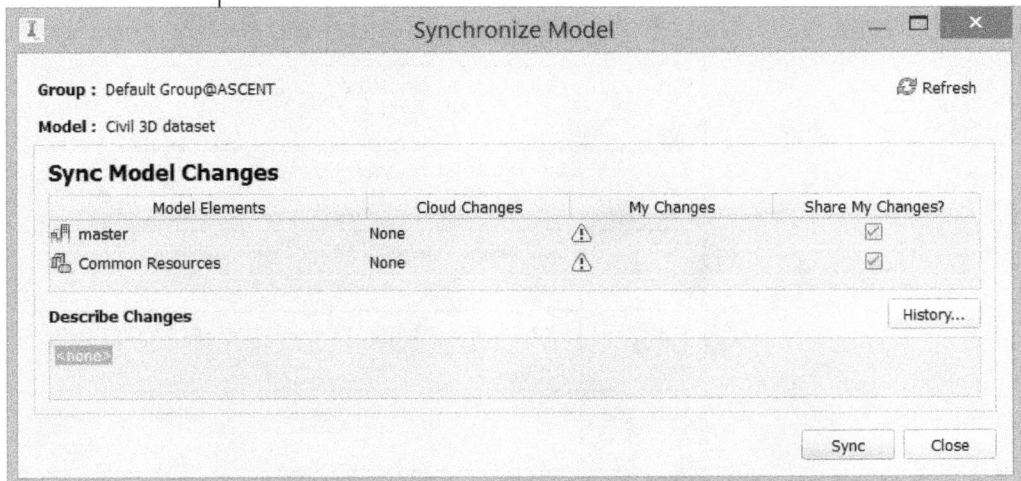

Figure 7–42

7.4 Working With Scenarios

Scenarios require the Autodesk InfraWorks 360 online service since they publish to the cloud when the model is synchronized.

Scenarios are packages that include all or part of a model for others to view on the Internet or on an Apple® device (e.g., an iPad® or iPhone®). Scenarios eliminate the need to have the Autodesk InfraWorks 360 software installed on a computer to review a project. Scenarios can be published to the Autodesk InfraWorks 360 service for sharing with the public or a project team. Figure 7–43 shows the Scenario palette.

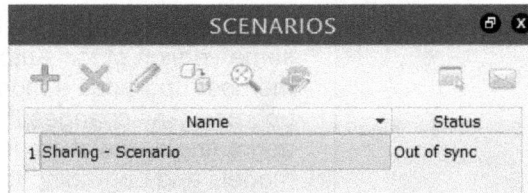

Figure 7–43

Scenario Palette

The Scenario palette provides tools to create, remove, modify, and share scenarios. The *Status* column communicates whether the scenarios is still generating, ready for viewing, or out of date. The tools found at the top the Scenario palette are as follows:

Icon	Description
	Add a new scenario.
	Remove the selected scenario(s).
	Edit the selected scenario.
	Duplicate the selected scenario.
	Zoom to the extents of the selected scenario(s).
	Edit the AOI (Area of Interest) of the selected scenario.
	Open in web browser.
	Email URL.

Scenario Asset Card

Name and Proposal

When creating a scenario, the *Name & Proposal* area describes the contents of the file. The *Name* and *Description* fields should never be left blank. This is where you select which proposal to share with others over the cloud.

Area of Interest

The *Area of Interest* area enables you to define the model extents, and to set the initial view that is displayed when the file is opened. Figure 7–44 shows the Scenario Editor asset card with the *Area of Interest* area expanded.

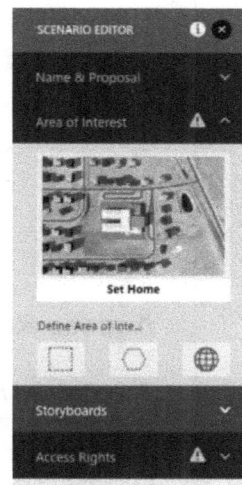

Figure 7–44

Define Area of Interest

The ⊕ **Entire Model** option shares everything that is modeled. If only a portion of the model is to be shared, select the ▢ (Bounding Box) or ⬡ (Polygon) option as required, and select the required area in the model.

Set Home Position

Setting the home position enables users to quickly navigate back to a set view. The view can be created by zooming the model to the location for the home view (this can be done while the Scenario Editor asset card is displayed). Then click **Set Home**, which saves the view as the home position.

Storyboards

Storyboards are saved presentations that help communicate the design to stakeholders. Including a storyboard in a scenario enables users to display the storyboard without installing the Autodesk InfraWorks 360 software. Figure 7–45 shows the Scenario Editor asset card with the *Storyboards* area expanded.

Figure 7–45

Access Rights

The *Access Rights* area displays which group has the ability to view the scenario. The group is set when publishing the model to the cloud. In addition to the group, you can toggle on the option to make the scenario available to the public, as shown in Figure 7–46.

Figure 7–46

How To: Create a Scenario

1. In the In Canvas tools, click [icon] (Create and conduct infrastructure design presentations)> [icon] (Scenario Browser).
2. In the Scenarios palette, click ✛ (Add a new scenario).
3. In the Create Scenario asset card, in *the Name & Proposal* area, type in the name and a description for the scenario. Then select which proposal to make available to others.
4. In the Scenario Editor asset card, in *the Define Area of Interest* area, select the type of boundary required, then define the extents boundary, if required.
5. In the model, navigate to the view you would like to set as the home view.
6. In the *Area of Interest* area, click **Set Home** to set the home view of the scenario to your current view of the model.
7. In the Scenario Editor asset card, in the *Storyboards* area, select the storyboards that you want to include.
8. In the *Access Rights* area, toggle Public Access on or off, as required.
9. In the Utility Bar, click, [icon] (Sync model changes to InfraWorks 360) to make the model available to others. Once the web views of the model are ready, an email is sent to you with a link.

You can continue working in the model even when an asset card is displayed.

Practice 7c

Share the Model Using a Scenario

Practice Objective

Estimated time for completion: 10 minutes

- Create a package that includes storyboards, points of interest, and watermarks to share on the Internet using scenarios.

In this practice you will create a scenario to be posted on the Internet.

Task 1 - Create a scenario.

1. In the Home Screen, click **Open**.

2. In the *C:\InfraWorks Fundamentals Practice Files\ShareData* folder, select **Sharing.sqlite** and click **Open**.

3. In the Utility Bar, expand *Switch Active Proposal* and select **C_Task1**.

4. In the Utility Bar, click ▨ (Bookmark your current location) and select **School**.

5. In the In Canvas tools, click ▣ (Create and conduct infrastructure design presentations)> ▭ (Scenario Browser).

6. In the Scenarios palette, click ✛ (Add a new scenario).

7. In the Scenario Editor asset card, note that the scenario name is automatically derived from the model name with **- Scenario** appended to the end (e.g., Sharing - Scenario). For the *Proposal to Publish*, select **C_Task1**.

8. In the *Area of Interest* area, click ▢ (Bounding Box) to define the scenario extents.

Remember to double-click on the last point to end the selection.

9. In the model, click points to set the scenario extents shown in Figure 7–47.

Figure 7–47

10. In the Utility Bar, click (Bookmark your current location) and select **SchoolEntrance** to orient the model view to that shown in Figure 7–48. In the Scenario Editor asset card, click **Set Home** to define the home view of the scenario.

Figure 7–48

11. In the Scenario Editor asset card, leave all of the other settings as their defaults

12. In the Utility Bar, click, (Publish model to InfraWorks 360) to make the model available to others.

Chapter Review Questions

1. Anyone can create groups and add members to them in the Autodesk InfraWorks 360 service.

   a. True

   b. False

2. When importing an Autodesk Revit model, which of the following is not one of the five adjustment options that can be used to repair the imported model?

   a. **Invert Orientation**

   b. **Flip Y and Z**

   c. **Flip X and Z**

   d. **Invert Up Axis**

3. Which type of file can be used to exchange design data between the Autodesk InfraWorks 360 software and the AutoCAD Civil 3D software or between two Autodesk InfraWorks models?

   a. .IMX

   b. .FBX

   c. .PNT

   d. .TIN

4. You can drag and drop .DWG files into an Autodesk InfraWorks model from Windows Explorer.

   a. True

   b. False

5. How do you share a model with someone who does not have InfraWorks?

   a. Create watermarks

   b. Duplicate the model

   c. Create saved views

   d. Create a scenario and publish the model

Command Summary

Button	Command	Location
	Data Sources	• **In Canvas Tools:** Build, manage, and analyze your infrastructure model> Create and manage your model
	Manage group memberships	• **Home Screen**
	Manage Online models and scenarios	• **Home Screen**
	Publish this model to InfraWorks 360	• **Utility Bar**
	Scenario Browser	• **In Canvas Tools:** Create and conduct infrastructure design presentations
N/A	**Sign In to InfraWorks 360**	• **Home Screen**
	Sync model changes to InfraWorks 360	• **Utility Bar**

Communicate the Design to Stakeholders

The most important part of any project is the approval process. Without buy-in from all of the stakeholders a project can be delayed, which can impact the project's timeline and budget. To ensure buy-in from all of the stakeholders, proper communication must take place. You need to ensure that everyone involved knows how the project is expected to look once it has been built. In this chapter you learn how to create high-end visualizations to help communicate the design intent. Images and storyboards are created to make this possible.

Learning Objectives in this Chapter

- Present a simple image of the model using a snapshot.
- Create a visual style for viewing the model in various ways.
- Present a slide-show of the design to stakeholders by creating storyboards.
- Publish scenarios of the model to the cloud for others to review.

8.1 Creating Images

The Autodesk InfraWorks 360 software enables you to create images of varying quality. You can create quick snapshots or realistic renderings of the model to communicate to stakeholders exactly how a project is expected to look when construction is finished.

Snapshots

A snapshot is a quick, low-resolution image of the current model view. Figure 8–1 shows an example of a snapshot. The image looks like the current view, and uses the current visual effects settings. Therefore, if shadows are turned off in the model, they do not display in the snapshot. The quality of the image can be adjusted using various settings, such as the level of detail (LOD), style, and snapshot resolution settings.

Figure 8–1

How To: Create a Snapshot

1. In the In Canvas tools, click ▣ (Create and conduct infrastructure design presentations)> ▣ (Create Snapshot).
2. In the Camera Snapshot dialog box, set the required resolution for the image, as shown in Figure 8–2. Click ⋯ (Browse) to set the path and filename for the image.

Figure 8–2

Snapshot images can be saved as .JPG, .PNG, or .TIFF images.

3. In the Select Image File dialog box, in the expanded Save As Type drop-down list, select the image type that you want to create, as shown in Figure 8–3. Enter the required filename and location and click **Save**.

Figure 8–3

4. In the Camera Snapshot dialog box, click **Save**.
5. To display the image, use Windows Explorer to open it from the saved location.

Visual Styles

When working with Snapshots, what you see in the model when you snap the image is how the image displays. This is controlled by the Visual Style. The Utility Bar enables you to change the current visual style. New visual styles can be created to highlight various aspects of the model, as shown in Figure 8–4.

Wireframe turned on in the View Settings, Visualization palette

Wireframe turned off in the View Settings, Visualization palette

Figure 8–4

New 💡

Different view settings can be assigned to each visual style. Visual styles and view configurations are saved locally, so that they are available in every model that you open. All of the view setting options can be found in one of two tabs in the View Settings panel.

Visualization Tab

The *Visualization* tab controls a range of lighting effects.

- Color
    - **Brightness**: Adjusts the amount of black in the model's colors.
    - **Contrast**: Adjusts the definition between areas of differing values to provide more image depth.
    - **Light Intensity**: Adjusts the overall brightness and intensity of colors uniformly.
    - **Sun Color**: Adds a tint to simulate sun position.
    - **Colorize**: Select between normal, gray scale, or sepia color schemes.
- Rendering
    - **High Visual Quality**: Toggles shadows for high or rough resolution model display.
    - **Wireframe**: When on, reduces features to 3D skeletons, displaying only lines and vertices.
    - **Animation**: Toggles water wave and cloud movement.
    - **Show Sky**: Toggles the display of the sky background.
    - **Surface Opacity**: Adjusts the transparency of the ground surface.
- Field of View
    - **Field of View**: Adjusts feature flatness, similar to a wide-angle lens on a camera.

Interaction Tab

The *Interaction* tab controls the visibility of certain tools and other interaction settings.

- Feedback
    - **Status Bar**: Toggles the cursor's coordinates on the bottom left of the model window.
    - **Tooltips**: Toggles the text, images, links, or model property values that display when you hover over a command or feature.
    - **Links**: Toggles the display of feature links to external data stores, tooltips, or maps.
    - **Edit mode**: Toggles the ability to make changes to model features.

- Navigation
  - **View Cube**: Toggles the display of the ViewCube.
  - **Proximity**: Toggles the display of tooltips when the proximity distance is reached.
  - **Automatic Zoom To Selection**: Toggles the automatic zoom on selected features.
  - **Highlight Sketched Features**: Toggles the linework that highlights sketched features when in drawing mode.
  - **Lock Mouse Above Ground**: Toggles the ability to view features below the surface.
  - **Show Statistics**: Toggles the display of feature statistics while in edit or draw mode.

How To: Create a New Visual Style

1. In the Utility Bar, expand the View Style drop-down and click **Add**.
2. In the Utility Bar, expand the View Style drop-down and click

   (Configure current view).
3. On the *Visualization* tab, make the required changes to adjust the model display, as shown in Figure 8–5.

Figure 8–5

4. In the View Settings panel, click ▣ (Change navigation and application feedback settings) to open the *Interaction* tab.
5. Set the required toggles to the right to turn them on or left to turn them off, as shown in Figure 8–6.

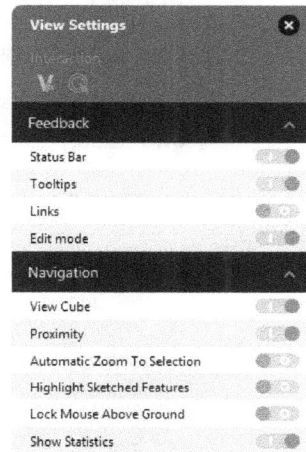

Figure 8–6

Practice 8a

Communicating the Design Using Images

Estimated time for completion: 10 minutes

Practice Objective

- Communicate the design intent to stakeholders using images.

In this practice you will create a snapshot using a bookmark orientation. You will also render an image of the same view.

Task 1 - Create a snapshot.

1. In the Home Screen, click **Open**.

2. In the *C:\InfraWorks Fundamentals Practice Files\ Communicate* folder, select **Communicate.sqlite** and click **Open**.

3. In the Utility Bar, click █ (Bookmark your current location) and select **StudentDropOff**. Ensure that **A_Task1** is the current proposal in the Utility Bar.

4. In the Utility Bar, for the Visual Style, select **Engineering View**. Then switch it back to the **Conceptual View** and note the differences.

5. In the In Canvas tools, click 🖥 (Create and conduct infrastructure design presentations) > 📷 (Create Snapshot).

6. In the Camera Snapshot dialog box, ensure that the resolution is set to the default, as shown in Figure 8–7. Click ⋯ (Browse) to set the path and filename for the image.

Figure 8–7

7. In the Select Image File dialog box, expand the Save as type drop-down list, and select **PNG Images**, as shown in Figure 8–8. Enter the required filename and location and click **Save**.

Figure 8–8

8. In the Camera Snapshot dialog box, click **Save**.

9. To display the image, use Windows Explorer to open it from the saved location.

Task 2 - Create a Visual Style.

1. In the Utility Bar, expand the View Style drop-down and click **Add**.

2. In the Utility Bar, expand the View Style drop-down and click ⚙ (Configure current view).

3. On the Visualization tab, make the following changes, as shown in Figure 8–9.
    - Set the *Brightness* and *Contrast* both to **50**.
    - Set the *Light Intensity* to **3**.
    - Toggle off **High Visual Quality**, **Animation**, and **Show Sky**.
    - Toggle on **Wireframe**.
    - Set the *Surface Opacity* to approximately **50**.

Figure 8–9

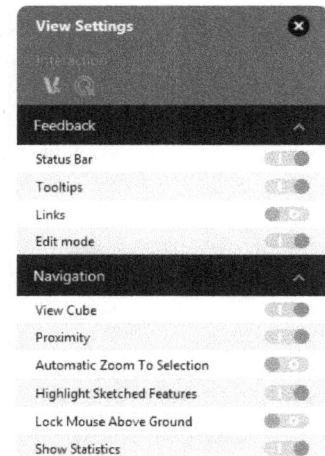

Figure 8–10

4. In the View Settings panel, click ▣ (Change navigation and application feedback settings) to open the *Interaction* tab.

5. Toggle on **Highlight Sketched Features**, as shown in Figure 8–10, above.

6. Close the View Settings panel.

8.2 Working with Storyboards

Storyboards are a collection of elements or keyframes that are combined together in a slide show to tell a compelling story about the design. The keyframes in a storyboard are generated from animations. These animations are either Path or Camera animations. Still images can also be incorporated using a Still Motion Camera animation.

Using storyboards, you can simulate driving through the model, get a birds-eye view of the model, or explore the model. Figure 8–11 shows the Storyboard palette.

Figure 8–11

- **Storyboard Name:** Displays the name of the current storyboard and enables you to edit the name as required.

- **Timeline:** Indicates when specific elements display and how long they remain in the view before changing to the next element.

- **Storyboard Tools:** Contains tools for creating elements and managing the storyboard.

- **Keyframe Settings:** Provides settings that can be specified for the active (selected) keyframe element.

Working with the Timeline

The Timeline identifies the sequence of the keyframes and details approximately how long each keyframe displays in the presentation. Keyframes can be an image, camera animation, or path animation.

Figure 8–12 shows a storyboard timeline and describes its contents. You can drag and drop keyframes to new locations in the timeline to change the order in which they display. You can also drag the right side of a keyframe to change its duration.

Figure 8–12

- **Play Head (blue square and line):** Indicates where play stops and resumes during playback. Double-click on the timeline to move the play head to a specific location.

- **Duration:** Lists the total time (i.e., start to finish) of the storyboard.

- **Playback Controls:** Starts and stops the presentation at the play head location. It also enables you to control whether the model view follows the storyboard position.

- **Captions and Titles:** Enables you to label specific views in the model to draw attention to points of interest.

- **Camera Paths and Animation Keyframes:** Thumbnails used to indicate what is presented at specific times along the timeline. You can drag and drop the thumbnails to change their order or duration.

- **Insertion Marker (red triangle and line):** Indicates where new elements display in the model when you add them. Click and drag the insertion marker to a location in the timeline to insert the next storyboard feature.

Playback Controls

The following playback controls can help you to view and navigate through the presentation.

Icon	Description
▶ / ⏸ (Play/ Pause)	Starts playing the storyboard from the location of the play head. Once in Play mode, the button displays as a pause button, which enables you to stop the animation without moving the play head from its current position in the timeline.
⏹ (Stop)	Stops playing the storyboard and causes the play head to return to its original position in the timeline.
(Follow Storyboard Position)	Causes the model view to change according to the current keyframe being played in the storyboard.

Adding Keyframes

The keyframes in a storyboard are generated from animations, which are either Path or Camera animations. In each animation category there are multiple animation types. All of the path and camera animation types are added from the Storyboard palette, as shown in Figure 8–13.

Path animations

Camera animations

Figure 8–13

Path Animations

Path animations can be used to automatically create a series of camera positions/angles along a path. There are three path animation options:

- **Add Camera Path Animation:** Creates a series of views starting at one view, which is manually set and ending at another view, which is also manually set.

- **Import a Camera Path:** Imports a saved path which is found in a point feature file (i.e., .DB, .SHP, .SDF, or .SQLITE files).

- **Create from Design Road:** Creates a path along the centerline of a design road.

*The **Create from Design Road** path animation type is only available when using the Roads and Highways Module of the Autodesk InfraWorks 360 software.*

Hint: Create from Design Road

When you create a path animation from a design road, you can set the horizontal and vertical offsets for both the camera and the target. You can also set the speed, direction of travel, and the keyframe density, as shown in Figure 8–14.

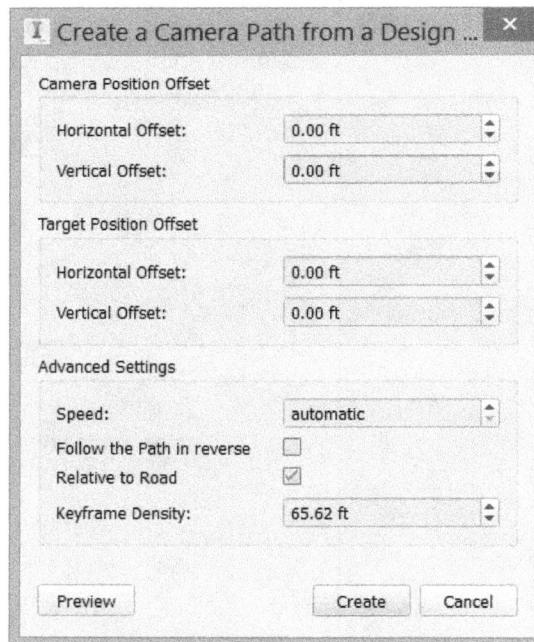

Figure 8–14

Camera Animations

Camera animations start the transition from a specific camera view, and end at another camera view, which is determined by the storyboard keyframe settings. There are eight camera animation options:

- **Crane Animation:** Moves the camera up and away from or down and towards the camera view.

- **Look Around Animation:** Rotates the view while the camera remains in a fixed position.

- **Orbit Animation:** The camera rotates around a fixed focal point in the shape of a sphere.

- **Pan and Zoom Animation:** The camera pans and zooms simultaneously. The effect is a zooming motion along a path that is determined by distance values and zoom percentages.

- **Recorded Walk:** The camera jumps directly to a shot and then plays a recording that you create. It highlights specific design elements from set angles, rather than by panning or zooming.

- **Still Motion:** Transitions the camera to a still motion shot. The camera does not move for the duration of this shot.

- **Track Animation:** Moves the camera to the left or right of the original camera view.

- **Zoom Animation:** The camera moves closer to or further away from the original focal point of the camera view.

Keyframe Settings

Each keyframe that you add to a storyboard has its own set of properties that can be set to control how the camera moves in the model. Figure 8–15 shows the settings for a Look Around Camera Animation keyframe.

Figure 8–15

The following are areas of the Keyframe settings that are used in multiple animation types.

- **Animation Type:** Lists the type of animation that was used to create the keyframe.

- **Transition Types:** Enables you to set the transition type when entering and exiting the keyframe. There are three transition types:
  - **Cut:** Moves directly to the current keyframe view.
  - **Fade from black:** After the previous keyframe, the view displays as black. It then fades into the current keyframe over a duration that you set using the setting to the right of the Transition drop-down list, as shown in Figure 8–16.

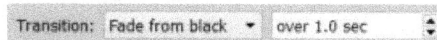

Figure 8–16

  - **Fade from white:** After the previous keyframe, the view displays as white. It then fades into the current keyframe over a duration that you set using the setting to the right of the Transition drop-down list, as shown in Figure 8–16.

- **Thumbnail Controls:** Enables you to change the model view or thumbnail view. The following options are available for all of the animation types.

  - ⊚ **(Go To Location):** Quickly sets the model view to be the location of the thumbnail.

  - ▣ **(Refresh):** Refreshes the thumbnail of the keyframe from the current scene content.

  - **Reset:** Changes the keyframe view to the current model view.

How To: Add a Path Animation

This procedure uses the Camera Path Animation as an example. The process is similar for the other Path animations.

1. In the Storyboard palette, move the Insertion Marker (red triangle and line) to the location on the timeline where you want to insert the new path animation.
2. Navigate to the view that you want to use as the starting point of the animation.
3. In the Storyboard palette, expand the Camera Animations

   drop-down list and click 🔀 (Add Camera Path Animation), as shown in Figure 8–17.

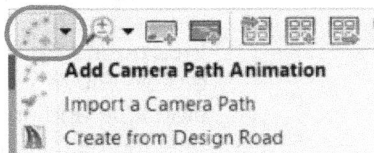

Figure 8–17

Note that the first keyframe displays as a thumbnail in the timeline, as shown in Figure 8–18.

Figure 8–18

4. In the *Storyboard Keyframe Settings* area, set the options in the Transition and Interpolate drop-down lists and the **Camera speed control** option, as shown in Figure 8–19. The settings displayed are applied to the currently selected keyframe.

Figure 8–19

Hint: Camera Path Settings

You can select one of three focal points for the camera view, set the camera speed, and determine the type of transition. The Camera Focal Point drop-down list contains options for setting the camera to **Look Along Path**, **Interpolate Direction**, or **Interpolate Focus Point**. The Camera Speed control options enable you to keep the camera speed as it is set by the current start time and duration, set a specific speed, or set the time until the next keyframe.

---

5. In the model, navigate to the required view to prepare the next keyframe in the camera path.
6. In the Storyboard timeline, click ⊞ (Add Keyframe) to the right of the first Keyframe's thumbnail.
7. Repeat Steps 4 to 6 to add additional camera positions to extend the path as required.

How To: Create a Camera Animation

This procedure uses the Pan and Zoom Animation as an example. The process is similar for the other camera animations.

1. In the Storyboard palette, move the Insertion Marker (red triangle and line) to the location on the timeline where you want to insert the new camera animation.
2. Navigate to the view that you want to use as the starting point of the animation.

3. In the Storyboard palette, expand the Camera Animations drop-down list and click ⌖ (Add Pan and Zoom Animation), as shown in Figure 8–20.

Add Crane Animation
Add Look Around Animation
Add Orbit Animation
Add Pan and Zoom Animation
Add Recorded Walk
Add Still Motion
Add Track Animation
Add Zoom Animation

Figure 8–20

4. In the *Storyboard Keyframe Settings* area, set the options in the Transition, Distance, and Zoom drop-down lists, as shown in Figure 8–21. The settings apply to the currently selected keyframe.

Figure 8–21

Add Captions and Titles

Captions and titles are located in the storyboard palette. These tools enable you to place labels, text, and images into multiple keyframes in the storyboard. An example of captions and titles is shown in Figure 8–22.

Figure 8–22

Captions

Captions are labels that overlay keyframes in the storyboard presentation. You can add multiple captions, which become stacked vertically, based on their assigned location. Click

(Add a new Caption) to create a caption in the model view. Use the caption settings to edit the caption's text, font, size, and transition settings.

Titles

Titles can include text and images to introduce the entire story, individual chapters of the story, or to display credits and

acknowledgments. Click (Add a new Title) to create a caption in the model view. Use the caption settings to edit the title's text, font, size, and transition settings.

Reusing Storyboards

If a storyboard is created in another model, you can reuse it by importing it into the current model. All of the camera positions and transitions from the previous model remain the same, but the current model's elements display in the keyframes.

- **(Export Current Storyboard):** Creates a .JSON file for sharing storyboards between Autodesk InfraWorks 360 models.

- **(Import Existing Storyboards):** Imports a .JSON file from another model.

Create & Share Storyboard Videos

Storyboards are most useful when you can share them with others. Unfortunately, most stakeholders do not have the Autodesk InfraWorks 360 software. Exporting a storyboard to a video enables anyone to display the presentation. Storyboards can be exported to a number of different encoders. The encoders that can be used when creating a video are as follows.

You can also use any DirectShow compatible encoders that are installed on your computer.

Format	Properties
Uncompressed Video	A generic .AVI format that does not have any properties that can be specified.

Windows Media® Video	Video compression format developed by Microsoft. You can select Windows Video Media 9 or Windows Video Media 9 Advanced Profile from Properties, and set the bitrate (kilobits per second).
DV Video Encoder	An .AVI format that encodes an uncompressed video stream into digital video (DV). You can set the video format, DV format, and resolution in the properties. Video formats include: • NTSC (National Television System Committee standard) • PAL (Phase Alternating Line)
MJPEG Compressor	An .AVI format that compresses an uncompressed video stream using motion JPEG compression. It does not have any properties that can be specified.

How To: Record a Video

1. To create a video from a storyboard, in the Storyboard Tools palette, click 📹 (Export Storyboard to Video).
2. In the Export Storyboard dialog box (shown in Figure 8–23), select the required encoder, filename, frame rate, and resolution.

Figure 8–23

3. Click **Record**.

Additional Storyboard Tools

Additional storyboard tools are used to create and manage storyboards and control the display of the timeline. The following tools are available.

Icon	Description
(Add New Storyboard)	Creates a new, empty storyboard.
(Zoom Out/In)	Zooms the timeline to display a longer or shorter presentation duration in the timeline viewing area.
2 sec ▼ (Zoom Resolution)	Sets the amount of time by which the timeline zooms in and out.
(Hide/Show Item Detail)	Displays or hides details connected to the currently selected item in the timeline viewing area.
(Show Storyboard Library)	Displays a list of storyboards associated with the current model and their duration.

Practice 8b

Estimated time for completion: 30 minutes

Communicating the Design Using a Storyboard

Practice Objective

- Communicate the design intent to stakeholders using a storyboard.

In this practice you will add path and camera animations to create a storyboard.

Task 1 - Create a storyboard.

In this task you will create a presentation to show how parents will use the carpool lane to pick up and drop off students. You will use a camera path animation to simulate driving up to the drop off location. You will then add camera path animations to get a bird's eye view of the school.

1. In the Home Screen click **Open**.

2. In the *C:\InfraWorks Fundamentals Practice Files\ Communication* folder, select **Communicate.sqlite** and click **Open**.

3. In the Utility Bar, select **Conceptual View** for the Visual Style.

4. In the In Canvas tools, click (Create and conduct infrastructure design presentations)> (Storyboard Creator).

5. If a blank storyboard is not available, in the Storyboard palette, click (Add New Storyboard).

6. In the Storyboard palette, rename the new storyboard as **Carpool**.

7. In the Utility Bar, click (Bookmark your current location) and select **1-Carpool**.

8. In the Storyboard palette, click ⚡ (Add Camera Path Animation). The first view displays as a thumbnail in the timeline, as shown in Figure 8–24. The default duration is 3 seconds.

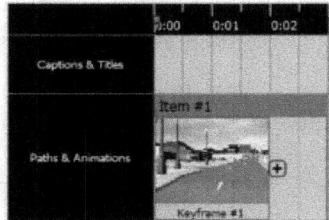

Figure 8–24

9. In the *Storyboard Keyframe Settings* area, do the following, as shown in Figure 8–25:

- Expand the *Transition* drop-down list and select **Cut**.
- Expand the *Interpolate* drop-down list and select **Interpolate Direction**.
- For *Time to next keyframe*, accept the default.

Figure 8–25

10. In the Utility Bar, click ▯ (Bookmark your current location) and select **2-Carpool**.

11. In the Storyboard timeline, click ⊞ (Add Keyframe), which displays to the right of the first Keyframe.

12. Repeat Steps 10 and 11 to add more camera positions and extend the path. Bookmarks have been created that will enable you to quickly move from one view to another along the path a car should follow to pick up students. Use the bookmarks in sequential order (3-Carpool, 4-Carpool, ..., 7-Carpool). When you have finished, the last keyframe view and the timeline should display as shown in Figure 8–26. The Camera Path Animation (Item#1) consists of these seven keyframes.

Figure 8–26

13. Move the Insertion Marker (red line) to the end of the storyboard.

14. In the Storyboard palette, expand the Camera Animations drop-down list and click ⬏ (Add Pan and Zoom Animation). The timeline displays as shown in Figure 8–27. This keyframe sets the camera to pan and zoom simultaneously as the driver looks for a student.

Figure 8–27

15. Ensure that the last keyframe is selected. In the keyframe settings, select **Distance Right**, type **15** for the distance measurement, and set the *Percentage Zoom-in* to **100%**, as shown in Figure 8–28.

Figure 8–28

16. In the Storyboard palette, click ⏵ (Play the current storyboard).

17. Move the Insertion Marker (red line) to the end of the storyboard.

18. In the Storyboard palette, expand the Camera Animations drop-down list and click ⬚ (Add Crane Animation). The timeline displays as shown in Figure 8–29.

Figure 8–29

19. In the keyframe settings, in the *Distance Up* field, enter **50**. In the *Distance Back* field, enter **50** again. Clear the **Lock camera on center-of-interest** option, as shown in Figure 8–30.

Figure 8–30

20. Move the Insertion Marker (red line) to the end of the storyboard.

21. In the Storyboard palette, expand the Camera Animations drop-down list and click ⊹ (Add Orbit Animation). The timeline displays as shown in Figure 8–31.

Figure 8–31

22. In the keyframe settings, in the *Angle left* field, type **90**, and in the *Angle up* field, type **45**, as shown in Figure 8–32.

Figure 8–32

23. In the Storyboard palette, click ▶ (Play the current storyboard).

Task 2 - Export the storyboard to video.

---

1. In the Storyboard palette, click 📹 (Export Storyboard to Video).

2. In the Export Storyboard dialog box, next to the *Filename* field, click ▭ (Browse).

3. In the Select Video File dialog box, enter the required filename and location and click **Save**.

4. In the Export Storyboard dialog box, click **Record**.

5. Using Windows® Media Player®, open and play the video you just created.

Task 3 - Create a storyboard from a design road.

If you have the Design Roads for InfraWorks module, you can create a storyboard much quicker than the process used in the first task. In this task you will create a new storyboard and use the car pool lane to create a path animation.

1. In the Utility Bar, click ▥ (Bookmark your current location) and select **StudentDropOff**.

2. In the Storyboard palette, click ▦ (Add New Storyboard).

3. In the Storyboard palette, rename the new storyboard as **Design Road**.

4. In the Storyboard palette, expand ⁘ (Add New Camera Path Animation) and select **Create from Design Road**.

5. In the model, select the car pool design road which was followed manually in Task 1.

6. In the Create a Camera Path from a Design Road dialog box, set the following, as shown in Figure 8–33.
   - *Camera Position Horizontal Offset*: **5**
   - *Camera Position Vertical Offset*: **5**
   - *Target Position Horizontal Offset*: **5**
   - Click **Create**

Figure 8–33

7. In the Storyboard palette, click ● (Play the current storyboard).

Chapter Review Questions

1. When creating a snapshot, in which file format(s) can the image be saved?

   a. JPG images (*.JPG)

   b. PNG images (*.PNG)

   c. TIFF images (*.TIF)

   d. All of the above.

2. When adding a title to a storyboard, which of the following can be included?

   a. Text only.

   b. Text and an image.

   c. An image only.

3. Which camera animation would you use to move the camera up and away from the current view?

   a. **Look Around Animation**

   b. **Still Motion**

   c. **Crane Animation**

   d. **Zoom Animation**

4. Which of the following is not a transition option?

   a. **Fade from Center**

   b. **Cut**

   c. **Fade to Black**

   d. **Fade to White**

5. Which of the following can be used as keyframes in a storyboard? (Select all that apply.)

   a. Snapshots

   b. Rendered images

   c. Path animations

   d. Camera animations

Command Summary

Button	Command	Location
	Create Snapshot	• **In Canvas Tools:** Create and conduct infrastructure design presentations
	Storyboard Creator	• **In Canvas Tools:** Create and conduct infrastructure design presentations
	Storyboard Player	• **In Canvas Tools:** Create and conduct infrastructure design presentations

Creating Design Roads Using the Roadway Design for InfraWorks 360 Module

The Autodesk Roadway Design for InfraWorks 360 module is a cloud-based add-on that enables you to add engineering parameters to road designs. The rule-based tool sets help you to quickly lay out a preliminary roadway design. During the creation process, you can instantly visualize the designed road in context with its surroundings. In this chapter, you learn how to set design speeds, adjust curve radii, and improve traffic flows through detailed interchanges and roundabouts.

Learning Objectives in this Chapter

- Create right of ways and easements for road corridors.
- Design an engineered road with precise design parameters (such as design speed, tangent length, and specific curve radii).
- Modify the horizontal layout of a design road.
- Modify the vertical layout of a design road.
- Design a road using component roads.
- Add superelevations to a component road.
- Modify how two design roads intersect using the Intersection asset card or stack.

New 💡

9.1 Parcels, Right of Ways, and Easements

Before a road can be built, it is important to ensure that the proper permissions are legally granted to anyone planning on using the road. This is done by will, by deed, or by contract. An easement grants the right to use property that is owned by another. Easements are most often used to deliver utilities (e.g., water, sewer, electrical, etc.) to parcels. Right of ways are easements that permit a person to travel or pass through a parcel of land that is not owned by the traveler. Easements on a deed generally remain with the land in perpetuity, while a right of way is often granted with an explicit expiration (25 years).

Information about existing right of ways, easements, and parcel boundaries can be obtained from the local recorders office or other government entities. Several government agencies provide electronic files representing parcel boundaries (in the form of Geographic Information data) either for free or for a small fee.

Importing Property Boundaries

Some right of ways have been put aside by government agencies for road development for years. In cases like this, it is necessary to import existing property boundaries to ensure that your road proposals stay within the designated corridors. Importing parcel, easement, and right of way data is no different than importing any other GIS data. Once imported and configured, parcels, easements, and right of ways are listed in the Model Explorer under Area of Interest.

How To: Import Existing Parcel Boundaries

1. In the In Canvas tools, click ■ (Build, manage, and analyze your infrastructure model)>▨ (Create and manage your model> ▤ (Data Sources).
2. In the Data Sources panel, expand ▣ (Add file data source) and select the type of file required, as shown in Figure 9–1.

Figure 9–1

3. Select the file containing the property boundary data. Click **Open**.
4. In the Data Sources explorer, double-click on the property boundary layer to open the Data Source Configuration dialog box.
5. Set the *Type* to **Parcels**, **Easements**, or **Right of Ways**, as shown in Figure 9–2, then check the following:

    *   On the *Geo Location* tab, confirm that the *Coordinate System* is set correctly.
    *   On the *Source* tab, set the *Draping Options* and set *Clip to model extent*, as required.
    *   On the *Table* tab, fill in as many table fields as you can.

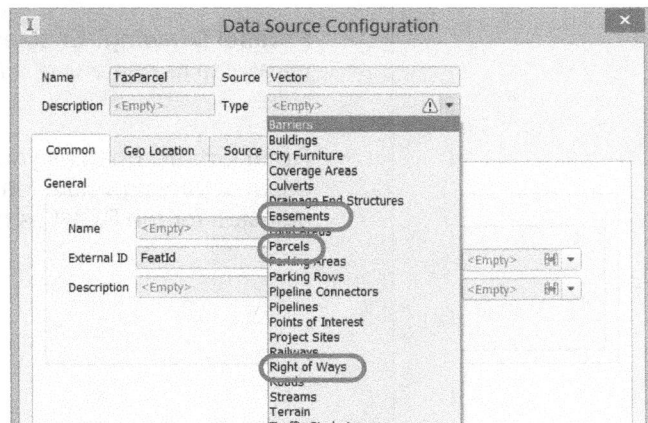

Figure 9–2

6. Click **Close & Refresh**.

Create Parcels and Easements

If electronic versions of the property boundaries are not available, you might need to manually create a parcel or easement. This can be done using the tools that are available in the Roadway Design for InfraWorks 360 module.

How To: Manually Create Parcels or Easements

1. In the In Canvas tools, expand ![icon] (Design, review and engineer roads)>![icon] (Design roadways), and click either ![icon] (Parcels) or ![icon] (Easements), as required.
2. In the model, click the first vertex for the starting point of the property boundary.
3. Move the cursor in the direction of the next vertex. If you know the required distance, type it and press <Enter> to lock in the distance. Click to set the vertex when the angle seems correct.
4. Repeat Step 3 for all but the last vertex.
5. Move the cursor in the direction for the last vertex. If you know the required distance, type it and press <Enter> to lock in the distance. Double-click to set the last vertex when the angle looks correct.

Create Right of Ways

You create Right of ways (ROW) slightly different than parcels and easements. When drawing a ROW, there are three options:

- **Free-Form Shape:** Enables you to create free-form polygons.

- **Parallel Drawing:** Enables you to offset an existing feature parallel to its centerline, with equal or varying values on each side.

- **Road Offset:** Enables you to select a road to offset with equal or varying values on each side. The length can also be adjusted for the ROW as required.

How To: Create a Right of Way From a Road

1. In the model, select the design road.
2. Right-click and select **Add Right of Way**.

How To: Manually Create a Right of Way

1. In the In Canvas tools, expand (Design, review and engineer roads)> (Design roadways), and click (Right of Ways).
2. In the model, click the starting point centerline for the ROW.
3. Move the cursor in the direction of the next centerline vertex. If you know the required distance, type it and press <Enter> to lock in the distance. Click to set the centerline vertex when the angle looks correct.
4. Repeat Step 3 for all but the last centerline vertex.
5. Move the cursor in the direction of the last centerline vertex. If you know the required distance, type it and press <Enter> to lock in the distance. Double-click to set the last vertex when the angle looks correct.

Practice 9a

Work With Parcels

Practice Objectives

- Import existing parcels lines from GIS data.
- Create right of ways for the new roads.

Estimated time for completion: 10 minutes

In this practice, you will import GIS data provided by the city and configure it as parcels. Then you will create new right of ways for proposed roads.

Task 1 - Import and configure existing parcel boundaries.

1. In the Home Screen, click **Open**.

2. In the *C:\InfraWorks Fundamentals Practice Files\ RoadwayDesign* folder, select **DesignRoad.sqlite** and click **Open**.

3. In the Utility Bar, click ▦ (Bookmark your current location) and select **ProjectArea**. Ensure that **A_Task1** is the current proposal.

4. In the In Canvas tools, click ▦ (Build, manage, and analyze your infrastructure model)>▦ (Create and manage your model>▦ (Data Sources).

5. In the Data Sources panel, expand ▦ (Add file data source) and select **SHP** for the type of file, as shown in Figure 9–3.

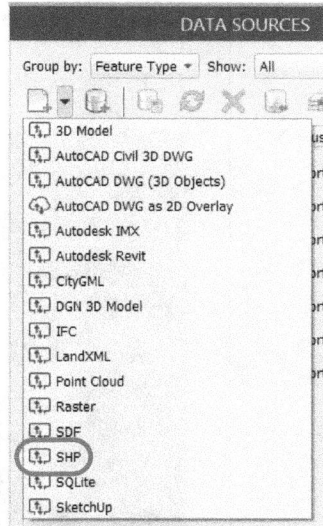

Figure 9–3

6. Browse to *C:\InfraWorks Fundamentals Practice Files\Shape Files*, select **TaxParcel.shp** and click **Open**.

7. In the Data Sources explorer, double-click on the **TaxParcel**[1] layer to open the Data Source Configuration dialog box. Set the following parameters, as shown in Figure 9–4:

    *   *Type:* **Parcels**
    *   *Geo Location* tab, *Coordinate System*: **UT83-CF**
    *   *Source* tab, *Draping Options*: **Drape**
    *   *Source* tab: **Clip to model extent**
    *   *Table* tab, *Name*: **PARCEL NO**
    *   *Table* tab, *Description*: **ACREAGE**
    *   *Table* tab, *Tag*: **OWNERNAME**
    *   *Table* tab, *User Data*: **MKT_CNTVAL**

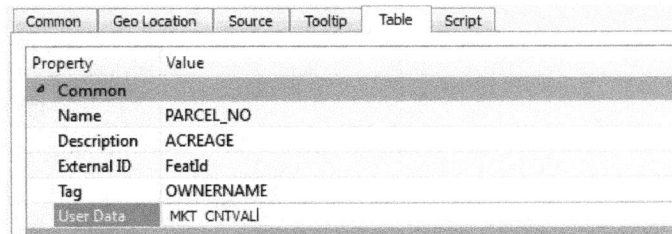

Figure 9–4

8. Click **Close & Refresh**.

1. (Department, GIS Division of the Utah County Information Systems, 2013)

Task 2 - Create a Right of Way from a road.

1. In the model, select the design road shown in Figure 9–5.

Figure 9–5

2. Right-click and select **Add Right of Way**.

3. Press <Esc> to release the selection.

9.2 Roadway Design

Design Roads

Design roads follow two sets of standards: Road Design Standards, which are preprogrammed into the software, and project design standards, which are manually input by you.

The Road Design Standards parameters are set when creating the model in the New Model dialog box, under the *Design Standards* section, as shown in Figure 9–6. The American Association of State Highway and Transportation Officials (AASHTO) design criteria is the most commonly used standard within the United States of America. In addition to setting the standards, you can set the driving direction for the road to be the left or right side of the road. Alternately, if the Design Standards were not set when creating the model, you can set them during the design process using the Model Properties dialog box, as shown in Figure 9–7. You can also set the driving direction for the road to be the left or right side of the road.

Figure 9–6

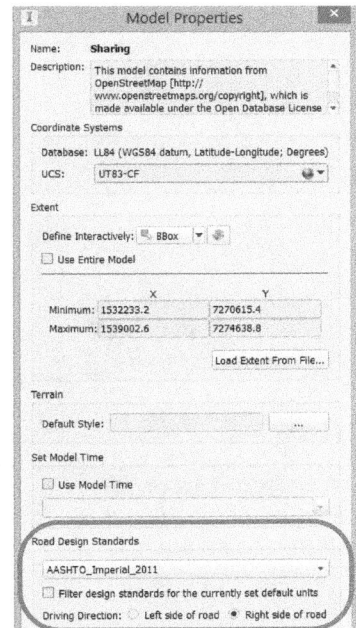

Figure 9–7

Convert Conceptual Roads

Conceptual roads can be turned into a design road quickly. While in edit mode, select the conceptual road, right-click and select **Convert to Design Road**, as shown in Figure 9–8.

Figure 9–8

Hint: Imported AutoCAD Civil 3D Roads

If you have the Roadway Design for InfraWorks 360 module installed, roads that you import from the AutoCAD Civil 3D software or from an .IMX file automatically become a design road.

Once the road has been converted to a design road, you can select the type of road that sets the correct design speed in the Design Road asset card (also referred to as a stack, due to the way it turns into other asset cards depending upon the Selected Mode chosen), as shown in Figure 9–9.

*Throughout this course, the Design Road asset card is referred to as "Road asset card" when the Selected Mode is set to **Geometry**. When the Selected Mode is set to anything else, it is referred to as the "(Selected Mode) stack".*

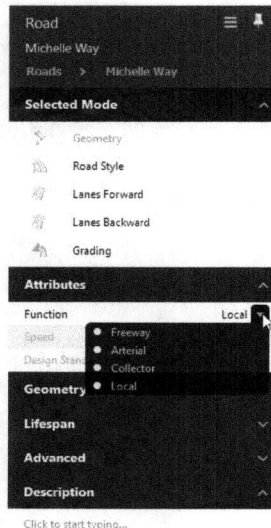

Figure 9–9

Road Types

Selecting the correct road type is a crucial part of setting the design parameters. There are multiple road types that are available in the Roadway Design for InfraWorks 360 Module, as shown in Figure 9–10. Four of these road types automatically set the default design speed to be used for the roadway design.

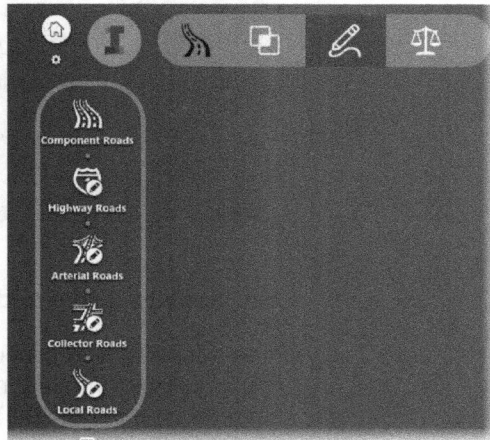

Figure 9–10

Road Types Which Set the Design Speed

The Design speed is the maximum speed that the road is designed for, and should not be confused with the legally permitted travel speed. The default design speed for a roadway depends upon the type of road being designed. A full list of the available options is shown in the table below.

Icon	Road Type	Maximum Design Speed
	Highway Roads	70 mph
	Arterial Roads	50 mph
	Collector Roads	40 mph
	Local Roads	30 mph

If a road's design speed changes, you can change it during the creation process by typing the new speed in the *Speed* field that displays next to the cursor, as shown in Figure 9–11.

Figure 9–11

Horizontal Curves and Spirals

The design speed property of a roadway sets the minimum and maximum permitted curve radius and spiral lengths for a given point of intersection (PI) along a roadway. When you use the Highway Roads command, the default curve type is set to *Spiral Curve Spiral*. For all other design road commands (i.e., arterial, collector, or local), the default curve type is set to *Curve*. To change the curve type used at a PI, right-click on the curve to display a fly-out menu, shown in Figure 9–12. As you set the PI's, tangent lines (which project all of the way to the actual point of intersection) display in yellow, curves display in blue, and spirals display in orange, as shown in Figure 9–12.

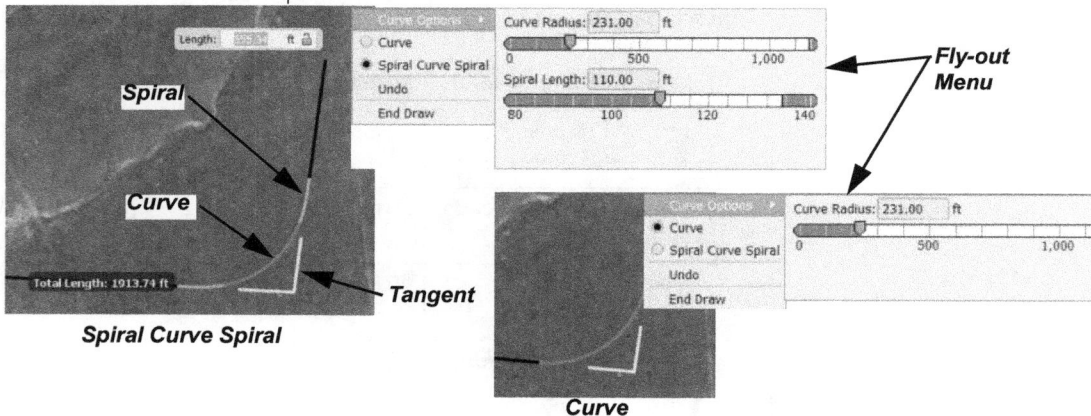

Figure 9–12

How To: Create Design Roads from Scratch

1. In the In Canvas tools, expand ![icon] (Design, review and engineer roads), and click ![icon] (Design roadways).
2. Select one of the four road types from the expanded tool group, shown in Figure 9–13.

Figure 9–13

3. In the Select Draw Style asset card, select an appropriate road style according to the type of road being designed, as shown in Figure 9–14.

Figure 9–14

4. In the model, click to set the starting point of the new roadway.
5. In the model, move the cursor in the direction toward the next PI. Type a design speed and distance in their respective fields, and then press <Enter> to set the values. Click to set the second PI when the angle looks correct.
6. In the model, move the cursor in the direction toward the next PI and then right-click to display the curve options.
7. Select **Curve** or **Spiral Curve Spiral** for the transition between tangents, according to the project requirements, as shown in Figure 9–15.

Figure 9–15

8. Use the slider to set the Curve or Spiral Curve Spiral parameters, or type the required values into the respective fields.
9. Type a design speed and distance in their respective fields and press <Enter> to set the values. Then click to set the next PI once the angle looks correct.
10. Repeat Steps 6 to 9 until all but the last horizontal PI' is set for the roadway design.
11. Double-click to set the last point or right-click and select End Draw, as shown in Figure 9–15, above.

Design Road Annotation

New 💡

When a design road is selected in the model and you are zoomed in close enough, station annotation displays at certain geometry points, as shown in Figure 9–16. This annotation is for informational purposes only and cannot be modified.

Horizontal Curve Annotation

Vertical Curve Annotation

Figure 9–16

Practice 9b

Create a Design Road

Practice Objectives

- Replace a sketched road with a design road in order to apply design parameters to it.
- Create a design road from scratch.

Estimated time for completion: 15 minutes

In this practice, you will create a new proposal. Then you will turn an existing sketched road into a design road in order to add engineering parameters. Finally, you will add a new design road to access the future parking lot for the white water park.

Task 1 - Convert a sketched road to a design road.

1. In the Home Screen, click **Open**.

2. In the *C:\InfraWorks Fundamentals Practice Files\ RoadwayDesign* folder, select **DesignRoad.sqlite** and click **Open**.

3. In the Utility Bar, click ▣ (Bookmark your current location) and select **ProjectArea**. Ensure that **B_Task1** is the current proposal.

4. In the Utility Bar, expand *Switch Active Proposal* and select **Add New**.

5. In the Add New Proposal dialog box, type **DesignRoad** for the name and click **OK**.

6. In the model, select the road shown in Figure 9–17.

Figure 9–17

7. Right-click on the road and select **Convert to Design Road**, as shown in Figure 9–18.

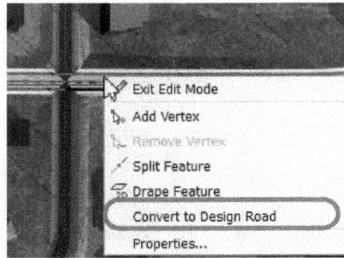

Figure 9–18

8. In the Road asset card that displays, expand the *Attributes* area and ensure that *Function* is set to **Local**, as shown in Figure 9–19.

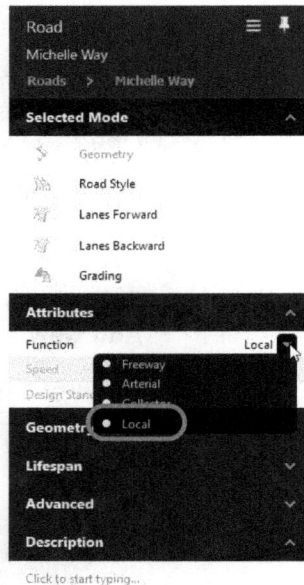

Figure 9–19

9. Press <Esc> to release the road selection.

10. In the Utility Bar, click (Bookmark your current location) and select **School**.

11. In the model, select the carpool lane north of the school that was imported from the AutoCAD Civil 3D software.

12. In the Road asset card, expand the *Attributes* area and set the *Function* to **Local**.

Note that when you are zoomed in at this level, and select a design road, annotations display.

13. Press <Esc> to clear the road selection.

14. In the Utility Bar, click ▣ (Bookmark your current location) and then select **River**.

15. In the model, select **Redwood Rd** (shown in Figure 9–20)

Figure 9–20

16. Right-click on the road and select **Convert to Design Road**.

17. In the Road asset card that displays, expand the *Attributes* area and set the *Function* to **Collector**, as shown in Figure 9–21.

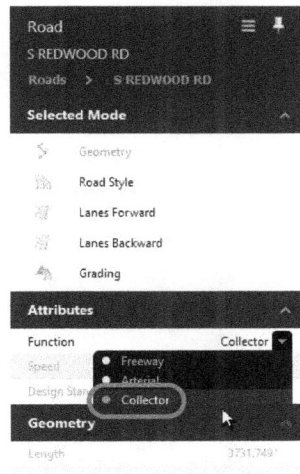

Figure 9–21

18. In the *Speed* field, type **45**.

19. Press <Esc> to clear the road selection.

Task 2 - Create a new design road.

In this task, you will create a new local design road. POI (Point of Interest) tacks have been placed to help you pick the points of intersection (PIs).

1. Continue working in the same model as the last task. If you did not complete the last task, in the Utility Bar, expand *Switch Active Proposal* and select **B_Task2** to make it current.

2. In the Utility Bar, click ▯ (Bookmark your current location) and select **River**.

3. In the In Canvas tools, click ⟐ (Design, review and engineer roads) > ✎ (Design roadways) > ⟐ (Local Roads).

4. In the Select Draw Style asset card, select **Street > Sidewalk with Lamps**, as shown in Figure 9–22.

Figure 9–22

5. In the model, click to set the starting point of the new roadway at the **Point 1** POI tack shown in Figure 9–23.

Figure 9–23

6. In the model, move the cursor to the east and click on the **Point 2** POI tack shown in Figure 9–23.

7. In the model, complete the following steps:
   - Move the cursor to the east near **Point 3**.
   - Right-click to display the curve options.
   - In the Curve Radius field, type **80** and press <Enter> to lock it in. (Note that the curve slider becomes red because 80' is below the minimum permitted radius, according to the road's set design speed.)
   - Click on the **Point 3** POI tack shown in Figure 9–23.
   - Keeping the same curve radius, double-click the **Point 4** POI tack shown in Figure 9–23 to complete the road.

9.3 Modifying Horizontal Layouts

You can change the horizontal layout of a design road using gizmos or the Road asset card.

Horizontal Gizmos

When the design road is selected and the Road asset card is set to the *Geometry* edit mode, gizmos display at various points along the road. Each gizmo is used to modify the roadway in specific ways, as described in the table below.

Gizmo	Location	Description
▪	Point of Intersection (PI)	Located at the endpoint of a road or at the horizontal point of an intersection. Changes the endpoint or PI location in the plan view, which changes the bearing and distance of the tangent.
▬	Midpoint	Located at the midpoint of a road tangents. Changes the location of the road tangent, without changing its bearing or distance.
●	Curve Radius (magenta)	Located at the midpoint of a curve. Changes the horizontal curve radius, affecting the curve's start/end points and length. Note that Spiral Curve Spiral curves do not contain this gizmo.
◗	Point of Tangency (cyan)	Located at the endpoint of a curve where it meets a tangent. Changes the horizontal curve radius, affecting the curve's start/end points and length. Note that Spiral Curve Spiral curves do not contain this gizmo.

When you right-click on different gizmos or segments of the road, different fly-out menus or fields display next to the cursor. Right-clicking on a Curve displays the menu shown in Figure 9–24. This menu enables you to change the curve into a spiral.

Figure 9–24

Design Road Asset Card

The Design Road asset card has multiple edit modes (stacks) found in the *Selected Mode* section. The current edit mode is highlighted in the color orange, as shown in Figure 9–25. Each edit mode provides options for editing different parts of the design road. For example, the asset card must be set to the Geometry edit mode for the horizontal or vertical gizmos to display in the model.

*Throughout this course, the Design Road asset card is referred to as "Road asset card" when the Selected Mode is set to **Geometry**. When the Selected Mode is set to anything else, it is referred to as the "(Selected Mode) stack".*

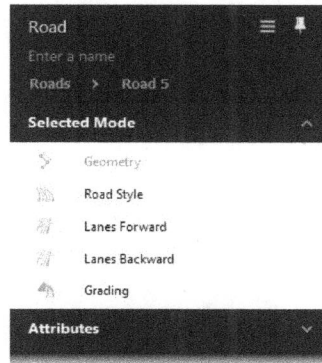

Figure 9–25

* The top of the Road asset card lists the road name, which can be modified. At the bottom of the asset card, a description of the road can be added.

Geometry Edit Mode (Road Asset Card)

The Geometry edit mode (shown in Figure 9–26) displays information about the road.

* The *Attributes* area displays the road type (Function), design speed, and design standards used. Only the **Function** can be changed in the *Attributes* area. Changing the **Function** should also change the design speed.

* The *Geometry* area displays the total length of the road, the range of elevations, and the range of grades along the road. Nothing in the *Geometry* area can be modified.

* The *Lifespan* area enables you to enter a **Creation Date** and **Termination Date** for the road.

* The *Advanced* area enables you to add **Tags**, **User Data**, **Tooltips**, and **Links**.

Road	≡	📌
River Dr.		
Roads > River Dr.		

Selected Mode	^
⚡ Geometry	
🛣 Road Style	
🛣 Lanes Forward	
🛣 Lanes Backward	
🛣 Grading	

Attributes	^
Function	Local ▾
Speed	30.0 mph
Design Standards	AASHTO_Imperial_...

Geometry	^
Length	1675.813'
Elevation Range	4502.64' - 4583.45'
Grade Range	4.82 % - 4.82 %

Lifespan	^
Creation Date	
Termination Date	

Advanced	^
Tag	
User Data	
Tooltip	
Link	

Description	^
Click to start typing...	

Figure 9–26

Road Style Mode (Road Style Stack)

The Road Style mode enables you to change the style of the road. You can change the style for the entire road using the stack, as shown in Figure 9–27. While in the Road Style mode, you can right-click on the road in the model to add, split, or delete zones, as shown in Figure 9–28. This enables you to change the style for a portion of the road.

Figure 9–27

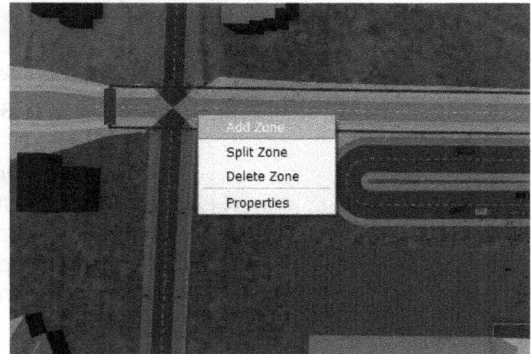

Figure 9–28

The available commands are described as follows:

Command	Description
Add Zone	Adds a new road style to the road in the defined area. Both a beginning and ending point are selected along the road.
Split Zone	Adds a new road style to the road from the point selected, to the ending station of the road. Only one point is selected along the road.
Delete Zone	Deletes the selected style zone, causing the selected zone to return to the original road style.

How To: Change the Road Style for Part of a Design Road

1. In the model, select the design road.
2. In the Road asset card, set the edit mode to **Road Style**.
3. In the model, right-click on the road and select **Add style** or **Split style**.
4. In the Select Style dialog box, select an appropriate road style. Click **OK**.
5. In the model, click a beginning (and, if you added a style zone, an ending point) for the style zone. The section of roadway between the beginning and ending points takes on the new road style.

Lanes Forward/Backward (Lanes Forward/Backward stack)

The *Lanes Forward* and *Lanes Backward* modes enable you to change the number of lanes that are used in each direction, as shown in Figure 9–29. Similar to the *Road Styles* mode, you can change the typical cross-section of the road by adding lanes to either the entire roadway, or one section of the road, as shown in Figure 9–30.

Figure 9–29

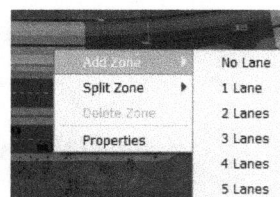

Figure 9–30

The available commands are as follows:

Command	Description
Add Zone	Adjusts the number of lanes for the road within the defined area. Both a beginning and ending point are selected along the road.
Split Zone	Adjusts the number of lanes for the road from the point selected to the ending station of the road. Only one point is selected along the road.
Delete Zone	Removes the selected zone to return to the original number of lanes defined in the road style.
	Note: This command is only available if lanes have been added to a road. To remove a lane from a standard road, enter the required number of lanes in the *Lanes* field.

Grading (Grading stack)

Enhanced

The *Grading* mode enables you to set the daylight slopes from the edge of the style template to the existing ground surface. You can chose between a fixed width or fixed slope grading method. When the *Fixed Width* option is selected, you can only set the **Grading Limit** parameter for the road, as shown in Figure 9–31. However, selecting the *Fixed Slope* option enables you to change the **Material**, **Cut Slope**, **Fill Slope**, and the **Grading Limit**, as shown in Figure 9–32.

Figure 9–31

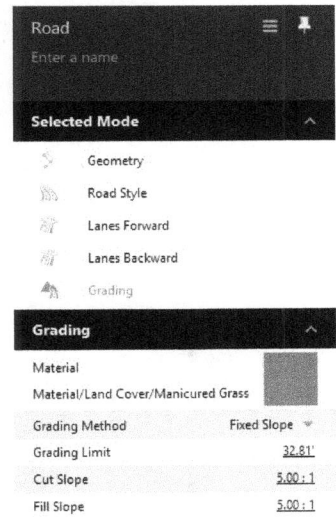

Figure 9–32

Altering the grading using the Road asset card applies the grading parameters for the entire road, as well as both sides of the road. Alternatively, in the Grading stack, you can select a specific grading on one side of the road and edit its parameters independent of the rest of the road, as shown in Figure 9–33.

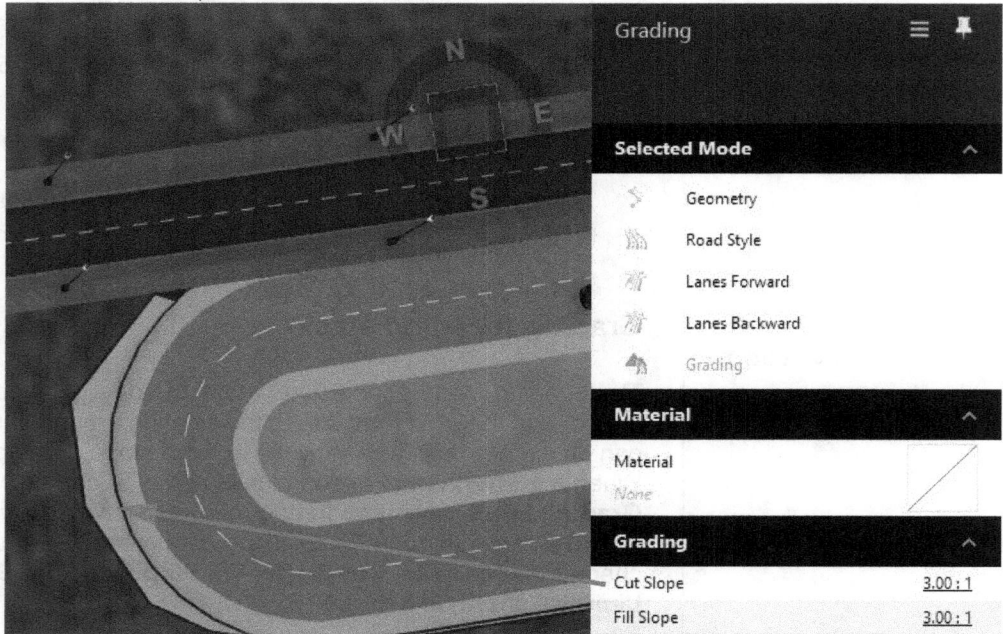

Figure 9–33

9.4 Modify Vertical Layouts

Vertical Gizmos

When the model view is rotated more than 45 degrees from plan view, a different set of gizmos display that enable you to change the vertical design of a design road. A full list of the available gizmos is shown in the table below.

Gizmos	Location	Description
⬡	**Point of Vertical Intersection (PVI)**	Located at the endpoint of roads or at the vertical point of intersection (PVI). Changes the PVI station or elevation, but not both at the same time.
●	**High/Low Point of Curve**	Located at the highest point of a crest curve, or the lowest point of a sag curve. Changes cannot be made with this gizmo: it is for reference only.
⬟	**Point of Vertical Tangency**	Located at the endpoint of a vertical curve where it meets the tangent. Changes the curve length, affecting the curve's start/end points and radius.
◀	**Maintain Tangent Grade**	Located at the point of vertical intersection when the PVI is selected. Changes the PVI location while keeping the grade of one tangent.

Additional tools display when you right-click. Depending on where you right-click, a different fly-out menu displays. Right-clicking on a tangent line displays the tools shown in

Figure 9–34. Right-clicking ⬡ (PVI Gizmo) displays the tools shown in Figure 9–35.

Note: The Add Bridge and Drainage options only display in the menu if you have the Autodesk Bridge Design and Autodesk Drainage Design for InfraWorks 360 modules.

Figure 9–34

Figure 9–35

How To: Add and Adjust Points of Vertical Intersection in the Model View

1. In the model, select the design road.
2. Rotate the view more than 45 degrees past plan view to display the vertical gizmos.
3. Right-click on the design road where you need to add a PVI. Select **Add PVI** from the fly-out menu.
4. In the model view, click ⬡ (PVI Gizmo). In the *Elevation* field, type a new elevation or type the station field to change its location, as shown in Figure 9–36. Alternatively, you can click and drag ⬡ (PVI Gizmo) up and down to change the elevation, or drag it left and right to change its station.

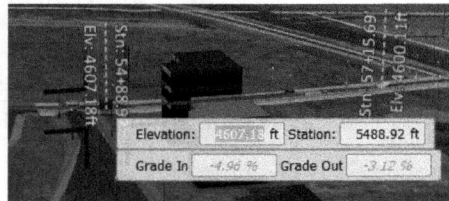

Figure 9–36

Profile View

When you right-click anywhere on any the design road, the *Show in Profile* option displays in the fly-out menu. This opens a panel that shows the stations and elevations at the road centerline, as shown in Figure 9–37.

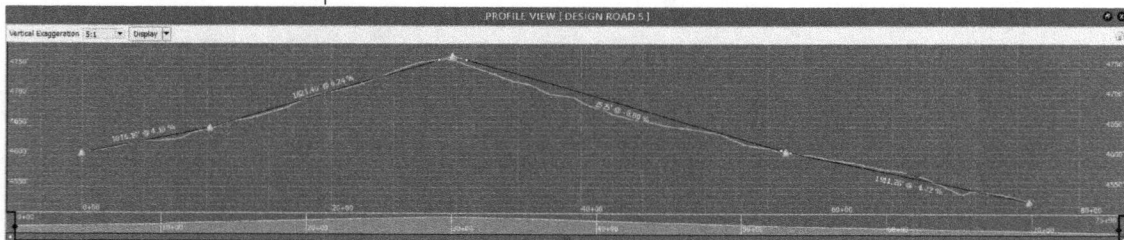

Figure 9–37

- You can control the vertical exaggeration and select which items display in the profile view in the top left corner of the panel. Items that can be displayed include:
  - Horizontal geometry
  - Existing ground
  - Culverts
  - Finished ground

- The mouse wheel can be used to zoom in/out of the profile view.

- Holding the left mouse button enables you to pan in the profile view.

- Only two gizmos display in the profile view, which are described as follows:

Gizmos	Location	Description
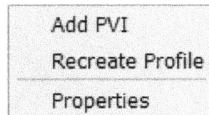	**Point of Vertical Intersection (PVI)**	Located at the endpoint of a road or at the vertical point of an intersection. Changes the endpoint or PVI station and elevation.
	Point of Vertical Tangency	Located at the endpoint of a vertical curve where it meets the tangent. This gizmo is for display purposes only and does not modify the profile.

Additional tools display when you right-click inside the profile view. Depending on where you right-click, a different fly-out menu displays. Right-clicking on a tangent line provides the tools shown in Figure 9–38. Right-clicking on either of the profile view gizmos provides the tools shown in Figure 9–39.

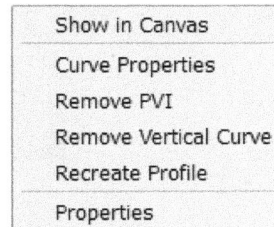

Add PVI
Recreate Profile
Properties

Figure 9–38

Show in Canvas
Curve Properties
Remove PVI
Remove Vertical Curve
Recreate Profile
Properties

Figure 9–39

How To: Adjust Points of Vertical Intersection (PVI) in the Profile View

1. In the model, select the design road.
2. Ensure that the Road asset card is set to **Geometry** mode.
3. Right-click anywhere on the design road and select **Show in Profile** from the fly-out menu.

4. In the Profile View, click ▲ (PVI Gizmo) and drag the PVI to its new station and elevation, as shown in Figure 9–40.
   - If the **Auto update model** option is checked in the Profile View palette, the change happens simultaneously in the model. If this option is not checked, the model updates as soon as you move the cursor into the model.

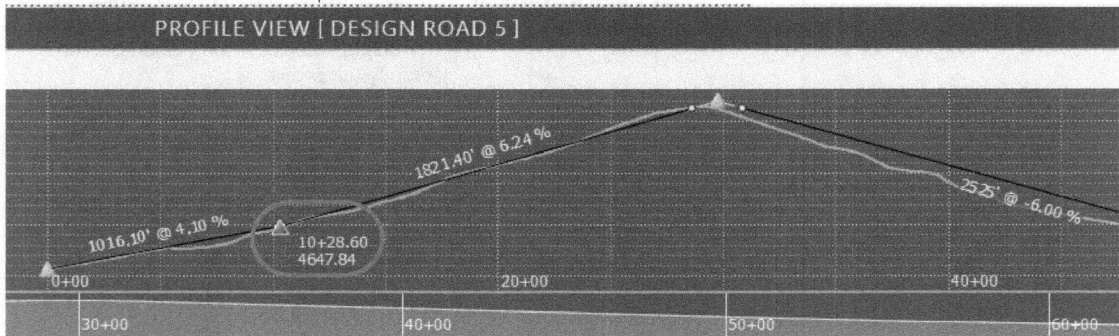

Figure 9–40

Practice 9c

Modify Design Roads

Practice Objective

- Modify the design road using the asset card and gizmos.

Estimated time for completion: 20 minutes

In this practice, you will modify the alignment by adjusting the horizontal curve radii and splitting the road into two different styles (typical cross-sections). Then you will set the daylight slopes for the road and adjust the vertical design by inserting PVI's and moving gizmos as required, as shown in Figure 9–41.

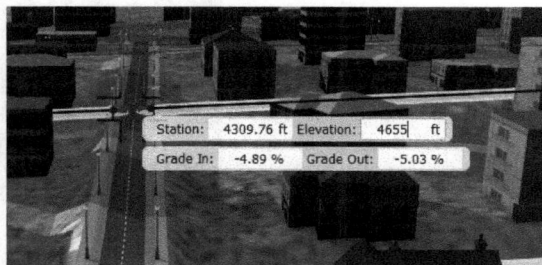

Figure 9–41

Task 1 - Modify the horizontal design.

In this task, you will modify the horizontal layout of the design road by modifying the curve radius, adding another style to a portion of the road, and adding daylight slopes.

1. Continue working in the same model as the last practice. If you did not complete the last practice, in the Utility Bar, expand *Switch Active Proposal* and select **C_Task1** to make it current.

2. In the Utility Bar, click ▥ (Bookmark your current location) and select **New Neighborhood**.

3. In the model, select the road that was converted to a design road in the last practice.

Gizmos display in the model on the design road.

4. In the Road asset card, ensure that the *Selected Mode* is set to **Geometry**.

5. Zoom in on the west end of the road (near the church), as shown in Figure 9–42.

Figure 9–42

6. In the model, click on ● (Curve Radius Gizmo) at station 23+83.96', as shown in Figure 9–42, above. In the *Radius* field, type **60**. Press <Enter> to accept the radius.

7. Repeat Step 7 for the curve at station 26+24.47'. Press <Enter> to release the curve radius gizmo.

8. In the Utility Bar, click 🔲 (Bookmark your current location) and select **Change Style**.

9. In the Road asset card, set the *Selected Mode* to **Road Style**.

10. In the Road Style stack, click in the *Style* field and select **More Styles**.

11. In the Select Style dialog box, select the **Sidewalk and Greenspace** road style, as shown in Figure 9–43. Click **OK**.

The entire road should change styles.

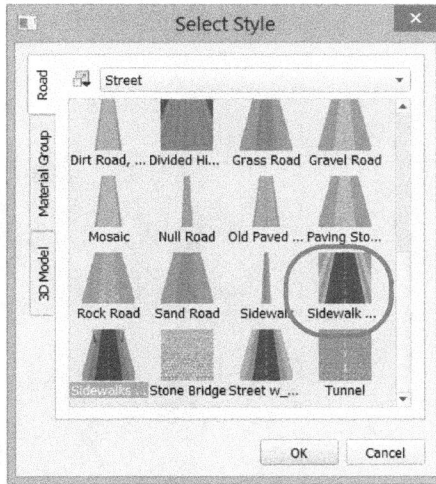

Figure 9–43

12. With the road still selected, right-click on the road and select **Split Zone**, as shown in Figure 9–44.

Figure 9–44

13. In the Select Style dialog box, select the **Sidewalk with Lamps** road style, as shown in Figure 9–45. Click **OK**.

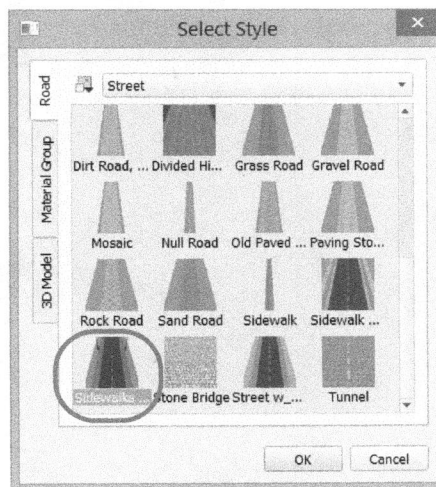

Figure 9–45

14. In the model, click a point near station **49+50** for the beginning of the style zone, as shown in Figure 9–46. Zoom in on the split point to see how the park strip area of the road transitions from a hard scape to grass.

The road narrows before reaching the school zone to help slow traffic down.

Figure 9–46

15. In the Road asset card, set the following options, as shown in Figure 9–47:
    - *Selected Mode*: **Grading**
    - *Grading Method*: **Fixed Slope**
    - *Material*: **Manicured Grass**
    - *Grading Limit*: **33'**
    - Ensure that *Cut Slope* and *Fill Slope* are set to **3.0:1**.

Figure 9–47

16. Press <Esc> to release the selected road.

Task 2 - Adjust the vertical profile of the design road.

1. Continue working in the same model as the last task. If you did not complete the last task, in the Utility Bar, expand *Switch Active Proposal* and select **C_Task2**.

2. Click 🔲 (Bookmark your current location), and then select **DesignElevations**.

   Notice that there are several locations where there is a lot of fill required along the new design road, as shown in Figure 9–48. This could cause flooding issues for the proposed homes. In this task, you will modify the vertical design of the new road to prevent flooding in the neighborhood.

Figure 9–48

3. In the model, select the design road. In the Road asset card, set the *Selected Mode* to **Geometry**.

Since the DesignElevations bookmark is rotated more than 45 degrees from a plan view, anything you do, effects the vertical design.

4. In the model, right-click on the intersection labeled **Point 1** in Figure 9–49. Select **Add PVI** from the fly-out menu. Do the same for **Point 2** in Figure 9–49.

Figure 9–49

5. In the model, right-click on the ⬢ (PVI Gizmo) for Point 1. Select **Show in Profile** from the fly-out menu.

Pan and zoom as required to see the PVI.

6. In the Profile View, click ▲ (PVI Gizmo) to move the PVI you just inserted closer to the Station **7+00** and elevation **4650**, as shown in Figure 9–50.

Note that all Profile View changes regenerate simultaneously in the model as soon as you move the cursor into the model window.

Figure 9–50

If the Point 2 PVI disappears, right-click and re-add it.

7. In the model view, left-click on ⬡ (PVI Gizmo) at Point 2. In the *Elevation* field, type **4655**, as shown in Figure 9–51. The sketch road becomes an overpass at the intersection.

Figure 9–51

8. Select the design road running north to south. Right-click at the point 2 intersection and select **Add PVI**.

9. Click the new ⬡ (PVI Gizmo). In the *Elevation* field, type **4655**, as shown in Figure 9–52.

Figure 9–52

9.5 Component Roads

Component Roads provide much more flexibility when designing roads. They enable you to add, delete, and modify each component of the road (lanes and curbs) separately, as shown in Figure 9–53. This means that you do not have to create a new road style for every minor change to the road cross-section. If design roads already exist in the model, you can convert them into a component road.

Figure 9–53

How To: Convert a Design Road to a Component Road

1. In the model, select a design road.
2. Right-click on the design road and select **Convert to Component Road**, as shown in Figure 9–54.

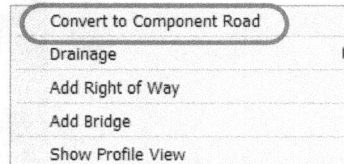

Figure 9–54

3. In the Convert Road asset card, do the following, as shown in Figure 9–55:

   - **Choose a Style:** Click the down arrow to select **All styles** to convert the entire road at once, or select one of the road styles currently applied to one or more style zones of the selected road.

   - **Choose a Matching Assembly:** Click the Assembly Style link to select a style from the Select Draw Style asset card.

   - **Convert Settings:** Toggle on or off the *Preview the matching assembly* option.

   - Click **Convert**.

Figure 9–55

How To: Create a Component Road

1. In the In Canvas tools, click (Design, review and engineer roads) > (Design roadways) > (Component Roads).

2. In the Select Assembly asset card, select the assembly closest to your needs, as shown in Figure 9–56.

Figure 9–56

3. In the model, click to set the starting point of the new roadway.

4. In the model, move the cursor toward the next PI. Type a design speed and distance in their respective fields, and then press <Enter> to set the values. Click to set the second PI when the angle looks correct.

5. In the model, move the cursor in the direction toward the next PI and then right-click to display the curve options.

6. According to the project requirements, select **Curve** or **Spiral Curve Spiral** for the transition between tangents, as shown in Figure 9–57.

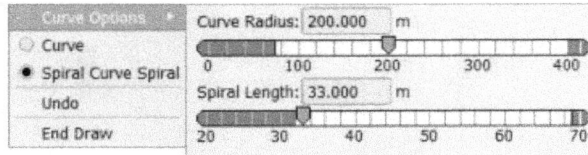

Figure 9–57

7. Use the slider to set the **Curve** or **Spiral Curve Spiral** parameters, or type the required values into the respective fields.

8. Type a design speed and distance in their respective fields and press <Enter> to set the values. Then click to set the next PI once the angle looks correct.

9. Repeat Steps 6 to 8 until all except the last horizontal PI is set for the roadway design.

10. Double-click to set the last point or right-click and select **End Draw**.

Add Detail to Component Roads

Not every road is created the same. Typical road cross sections vary according to their location and use. A freeway has a much different cross section than a local road. Even local road cross sections can vary as the road crosses into a new governing jurisdiction. Consider the following examples:

- One city might require a meandering sidewalk for pedestrians and bikes, while another have bike lanes that are adjacent to vehicular traffic.

- One city might require a curb and gutter, while another might not, as shown in Figure 9–58.

- One area of a city might require a specific type of street light, while another area might require something different, as shown in Figure 9–58.

- One soil type may allow for a 2:1 slope for the daylight lines, while other soil types might require a more gradual slope.

Figure 9–58

When working with component roads, you can add new components (sub-assemblies) and decorations as required along specific stations. In addition, you can easily change entire assemblies along component roads and the grading of the daylight lines as the road crosses different soil types.

How To: Add Components to a Component Road

1. In the model, select the component road.
2. In the Road asset card, ensure that the selected mode is set to **Geometry**.
3. Right-click on the component road and select **Insert Road Component**.
4. In the Select Component asset card, select the assembly you want to insert.
5. In the model, proceed as follows:

   - Place the cursor so that the orange line is located where the new component belongs, as shown in Figure 9–59.
   - Double-click to place the component and end the command.
   - Alternatively, you can click once to place the component, and then adjust the length using the component's gizmo, as shown in Figure 9–60. Once you have adjusted the component's length, press <Esc> to end the command.

Figure 9–59

Figure 9–60

6. Select the new component and make any necessary changes to its length using the component's gizmo. Also make any necessary changes to its properties using its stack, as shown in Figure 9–61.

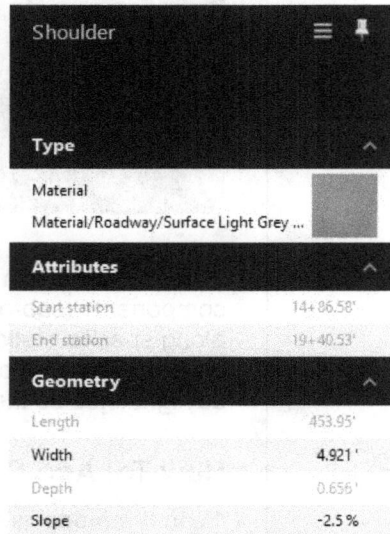

Figure 9–61

7. Press <Esc> to clear the selection of the component.

How To: Add Decorations to Component Roads

1. In the model, select the component road.
2. In the Road asset card, ensure that the selected mode is set to **Geometry**.
3. Right-click on the component road and select **Place Decorations**.
4. In the Select Decoration asset card, select the city furniture you wish to insert.
5. In the model, place the cursor so the orange line is located where the new decoration belongs and then double-click to place the component.
6. Select the new component and make any necessary changes to its length using the component's gizmo. Also make any necessary changes to its properties using its stack, as shown in Figure 9–62.

Hint: You can use the filter at the top to narrow your search for decorations.

Figure 9–62

7. Press <Esc> to clear the selection of the component.

How To: Replace Assemblies on Component Roads

1. In the model, select the component road.
2. In the Road asset card, ensure that the selected mode is set to **Geometry**.
3. Right-click on the component road and select **Replace Assembly**.
4. In the Select Draw Style asset card, select the required assembly.
5. In the model, either:

   - Hover over the component road and double-click to place the assembly over a selected section

   OR

   - Single-click to begin drawing the assembly at a specific station. Click again to indicate at which station the assembly should end.
6. Press <Esc> to clear the selection of the component.

Reuse Assemblies

The biggest benefit surrounding road styles is that you can create a style and reuse it for multiple roadways. Component roads use assemblies rather than styles. Fortunately, component road assemblies can also be saved for reuse.

How To: Save an Assembly for Reuse

1. In the model, select the component road you wish to reuse.
2. Right-click on the component road and select **Add to Library**.
3. In the model, click to select a cross section of the component road to add to the library.
4. In the Add To Library asset card, type a name and press <Enter>.

Roadside Grading

New 💡

Similar to other design roads, roadside grading for component roads can be controlled in the asset card. One difference is that you must toggle on roadside grading before you can set the material, slopes, or limit, as shown in Figure 9–63. Once on, you have more control over roadside grading on component roads than you do over other design roads.

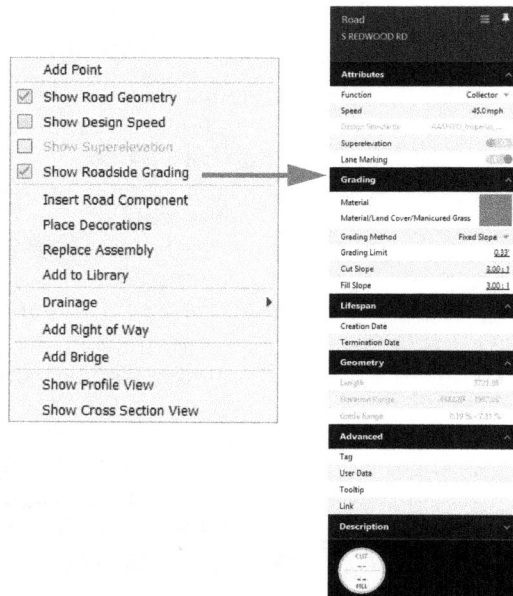

Figure 9–63

How To: Modify Roadside Grading Sections

1. In the model, select the component road.
2. Right-click and select **Show Roadside Grading**, as shown in Figure 9–64.

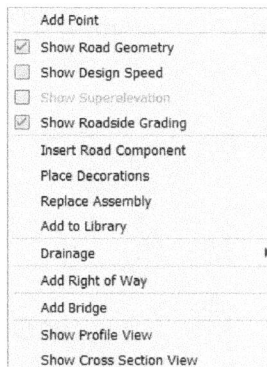

Add Point
☑ Show Road Geometry
☐ Show Design Speed
☐ Show Superelevation
☑ Show Roadside Grading
Insert Road Component
Place Decorations
Replace Assembly
Add to Library
Drainage ▸
Add Right of Way
Add Bridge
Show Profile View
Show Cross Section View

Figure 9–64

3. In the Road asset card, under Grading, set the required material, grading method, grading limit, and cut slope, as shown in Figure 9–65.

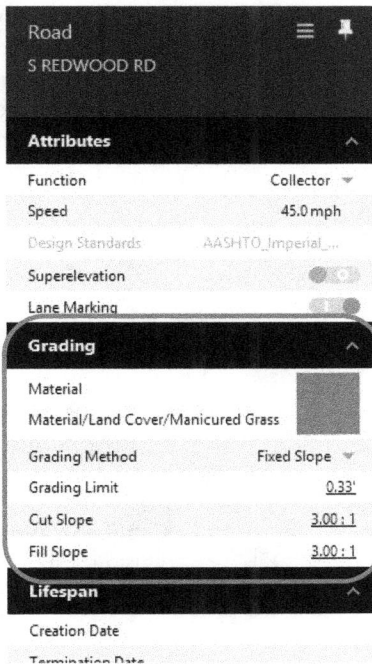

Road
S REDWOOD RD

Attributes ⌃

Function	Collector ▾
Speed	45.0 mph
Design Standards	AASHTO_Imperial_...
Superelevation	⬤◯
Lane Marking	◯⬤

Grading ⌃

Material	
Material/Land Cover/Manicured Grass	
Grading Method	Fixed Slope ▾
Grading Limit	0.33'
Cut Slope	3.00 : 1
Fill Slope	3.00 : 1

Lifespan ⌃

Creation Date
Termination Date

Figure 9–65

New 💡

Calculate Quantities

When a component road is selected, the Road asset card displays a cut and fill option at the bottom of the asset card. By clicking on this option, additional tools are available, as shown in Figure 9–66.

Figure 9–66

How To: Compute Quantities

1. In the model, select the component road.

2. In the component road asset card, click ⬤ (Earthwork quantities).

3. In the component road asset card, click ⚙ (Specify settings).

4. In the Earthwork Setting panel, set the *Station Increment* value, and toggle on which geometry you want to sample, as shown in Figure 9–67. Close the Earthwork Setting panel.

Earthwork Setting	✕
Station Increment	66ft
Sample at Key Station	⬤
Include Intersection & Roundabout	⬤
Include Bridge	⬤

Figure 9–67

5. In the component road asset card, click ⬤ (Compute earthwork quantities). Wait for it to process.

6. To see the results, in the component road asset card, click 🏗 (View detail values). The Earthwork Quantities panel displays, as shown in Figure 9–68.

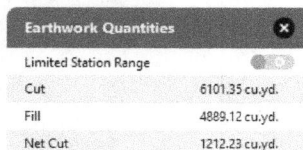

Earthwork Quantities	✕
Limited Station Range	⬤
Cut	6101.35 cu.yd.
Fill	4889.12 cu.yd.
Net Cut	1212.23 cu.yd.

Figure 9–68

7. To create a report, in the component road asset card, click
   .
8. In the Save Quantities dialog box, type a file name, browse to the folder where you want to save the file, and then click **Save**.
9. When the file is done saving, Windows Explorer automatically opens the location where you saved the file. Double-click on the file to open it in Microsoft Excel, or right-click on it and select **Open with...** to open it in a different program.
10. When opened in Microsoft Excel, the report displays similar to that shown in Figure 9–69.

	A	B	C	D	E	F	G	H	I	J
1	Station (ft)	Cut (cu.yd.	Cut area (a	Fill (cu.yd.	Fill area (a	Cumulativ	Cumulativ	Cumulativ	Note	
2	0	0	0.002	0	0	0	0	0		
3	66	185.7	0.002	27.31	0	185.7	27.31	158.39		
4	109.05	124.58	0.002	16.55	0	310.27	43.86	266.41		
5	132	62.01	0.002	9.43	0	372.28	53.3	318.98		
6	174.67	109.22	0.002	22.77	0	481.5	76.06	405.43		
7	198	57.15	0.001	16.48	0	538.65	92.55	446.1		
8	240.28	102.66	0.002	37.54	0.001	641.31	130.08	511.23		
9	264	59.9	0.002	24.76	0.001	701.21	154.84	546.37		
10	310.11	129.79	0.002	73.86	0.001	831	228.7	602.3		
11	330	59.03	0.002	42.95	0.001	890.03	271.65	618.38		
12	371.52	123.33	0.002	88.21	0.001	1013.36	359.86	653.5		
13	396	73.74	0.002	49.54	0.001	1087.1	409.4	677.7		
14	462	198.48	0.002	130.84	0.001	1285.59	540.24	745.35		
15	518.92	175.08	0.002	106.44	0.001	1460.67	646.68	813.98		
16	528	28.76	0.002	16.13	0.001	1489.43	662.82	826.62		
17	584.34	174.92	0.002	83.86	0.001	1664.35	746.67	917.68		
18	594	29.34	0.002	11.05	0.001	1693.69	757.73	935.97		
19	650.15	177.71	0.002	47.2	0	1871.41	804.92	1066.48		
20	660	32.46	0.002	5.65	0	1903.87	810.58	1093.29		
21	715.77	195.65	0.002	26.36	0	2099.52	836.94	1262.59		
22	726	37.45	0.002	4.02	0	2136.97	840.96	1296.01		
23	781.38	179.64	0.002	17.32	0	2316.6	858.29	1458.32		
24	792	29.88	0.002	2.54	0	2346.49	860.83	1485.66		
25	858	178.2	0.002	16.26	0	2524.69	877.09	1647.6		
26	924	170.77	0.002	19.44	0	2695.45	896.53	1798.93		
27	990	151.17	0.001	21.51	0	2846.62	918.03	1928.59		
28	1056	169.09	0.002	13.36	0	3015.71	931.4	2084.32		
29	1122	160.41	0.001	17	0	3176.13	948.39	2227.73		
30	1188	155.78	0.002	47.45	0.001	3331.91	995.85	2336.06		
31	1235.57	168.4	0.003	40.37	0	3500.31	1036.22	2464.09		
32	1243.51	32.18	0.002	5.25	0	3532.49	1041.47	2491.02		
33	1246.28	10.82	0.002	1.76	0	3543.3	1043.23	2500.08	Start - intersection	
34	1397.67	286.32	0.001	119.14	0.001	3829.63	1162.36	2667.26	End - intersection	
35	1400	4.37	0.001	1.56	0	3834	1163.92	2670.07		

Figure 9–69

Practice 9d

Estimated time for completion: 25 minutes

Work With Component Roads

Practice Objectives

- Convert a design road to a component road.
- Add new details to the component road.

In this practice, you will convert a design road into a component road. Then you will add new components and decorations to the road, as shown in Figure 9–70.

Figure 9–70

Task 1 - Convert a design road into a component road.

1. Continue working in the same model as the last practice. If you did not complete the last practice, in the Utility Bar, expand *Switch Active Proposal* and select **D_Task1** to make it current.

2. In the Utility Bar, click ▣ (Bookmark your current location) and select **3-WayIntersection**.

3. In the model, select Redwood Rd, as shown in Figure 9–71.

Figure 9–71

4. In the Road asset card, ensure that the selected mode is set to **Geometry**.

5. In the model, right-click on *Redwood Rd* and select **Convert to Component Road**, as shown in Figure 9–72.

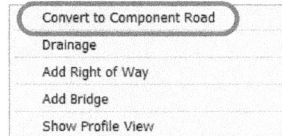

Convert to Component Road
Drainage ▶
Add Right of Way
Add Bridge
Show Profile View

Figure 9–72

6. In the Convert Road asset card, do the following, as shown in Figure 9–73:

   • *Choose a Style*: Select **All styles**.

   • *Choose a Matching Assembly*: Click the **Assembly Style** link. Then, in the Select Draw Style asset card, select the **Two Lanes** style.

   • *Convert Settings*: Toggle on the **Preview the matching assembly** option.

   • Click **Convert**.

Convert Road ✖

1. Choose a Style

Street Style   All styles ▼

2. Choose a Matching Assembly

Assembly Style   Two Lanes

3. Convert Settings

Preview the matching assembly

Convert   Cancel

Figure 9–73

7. Press <Esc> to clear the selection of the road.

Task 2 - Add detail to a component road.

In this task, you will add components and decorations to Redwood Rd.

1. Continue working in the same model as the last task. If you did not complete the last task, in the Utility Bar, expand *Switch Active Proposal* and select **D_Task2** to make it current.

2. In the Utility Bar, click ▦ (Bookmark your current location) and select **3-WayIntersection**.

3. In the model, select **Redwood Rd**.

4. Right-click on Redwood Rd. and select **Insert Components**.

5. In the Select Component asset card, select the **Lane** assembly.

6. In the model, do the following:
   - Place the cursor so the orange line is located at the center of the two lanes, as shown in Figure 9–74.
   - Click once to place the component, and then adjust the length using the length gizmos, as shown in Figure 9–75. Apply the lane assembly from station **0** to station **3110**.

Figure 9–74

Figure 9–75

Hint: In between adding each component, you might need to press <Esc> to deselect the component and select the road.

7. Repeat Steps 5 to 7 to add the following components, as shown in Figure 9–76.
   - Add another lane assembly to the west side of the road.
   - Add the **Curb & Gutter** assembly to both edges of the road.
   - Add the **Sloped Grass Median** to both sides of the road from station **0** to station **1450 with a 50' transition**.
   - Add the **Sidewalk** assembly to both sides of the road from station **0** to station **1400 with a 0' transition**.

Figure 9–76

- Note: When working with a sidewalk or median that can have transitions, select the interior gizmo. Then use the *Station* and *Transition Length* fields to help you set them correctly, as shown in Figure 9–77.

Figure 9–77

8. Right-click on Redwood Rd. and select **Place Decorations**.

9. In the Select Decoration asset card, type **Light** in the search, and then select **Street Light w_3 Bulbs**.

Note that the lights only go to station 1400 since both components surrounding it only extend that far. To add lights to the end of the road, you would have to add another decoration.

10. In the model, place the cursor so that the insertion line follows the edge of the sidewalk and grass median on the east side of the road, as shown in Figure 9–78. Click to place the decoration.

Figure 9–78

The client wants to see what a less expensive light looks like. On the west side of the road, you add a different style of light to show them how it looks in contrast with the first light. Once they decide which light they like best, you can simply change the assembly on one side of the road.

11. Right-click on Redwood Rd. and select **Place Decorations**.

12. In the Select Decoration asset card, type **Light** in the search, then select **Lightpole**.

13. In the model, place the cursor so the insertion line follows the edge of the sidewalk and grass median on the west side of the road, as shown in Figure 9–79. Orbit the model so that you can see the results.

Figure 9–79

14. In the Decoration stack, for the Rotation, type **180** and then press <Enter>, as shown in Figure 9–80.

Figure 9–80

15. Press <Esc> to clear the selection of the decoration. Examine the model.

The client has decided that they prefer the more expensive three-bulb street light. Rather than remove the single light pole, you can simply change the decoration.

16. In the model, click on the light decoration on the west side of the road slowly twice to display the Decoration stack.

17. In the Decoration stack, click on the style and select **More Styles**.

18. In the Select 3D Model Style dialog box, select **3D Model/City Furniture/Street Light w_3 Bulbs**, as shown in Figure 9–81. Click **OK**.

To get to the City Furniture folder, double-click on Parent, and then double-click on City Furniture.

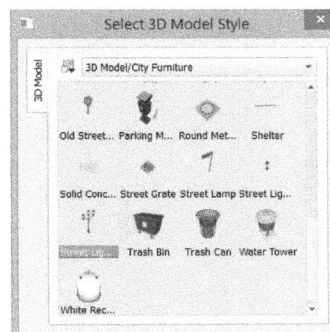

Figure 9–81

19. Press <Esc> twice to clear the selection of the decoration and component road.

Task 3 - Save a new assembly.

1. If you did not complete the last task, in the Utility Bar, expand *Switch Active Proposal* and select **D_Task3** to make it current.

2. In the model, select Redwood Rd.

3. Right-click on Redwood Rd. and select **Add to Library**.

4. In the model, click to select a cross section of Redwood Rd, as shown in Figure 9–82.

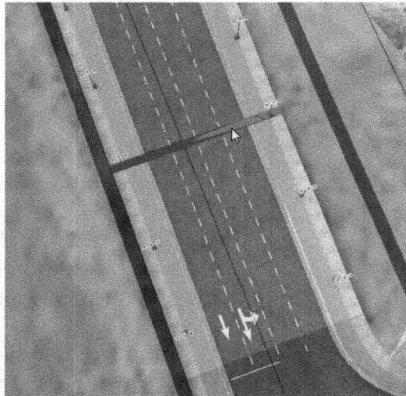

Figure 9–82

5. In the Add To Library asset card, type **Collector** for the name and press <Enter>.

Task 4 - Set roadside grading.

1. If you did not complete the last task, in the Utility Bar, expand *Switch Active Proposal* and select **D_Task4** to make it current.

2. In the model, select Redwood Rd.

3. Right-click and select **Show Roadside Grading**, as shown in Figure 9–83.

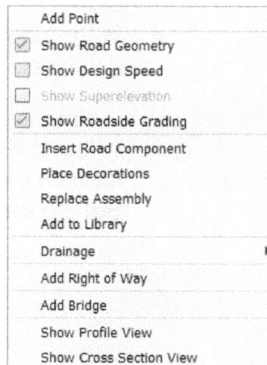

Figure 9–83

4. In the Road asset card, under Grading, set the *Grading Method* to **Fixed Slope** and the *Material* to **Manicured Grass**, as shown in Figure 9–84

Note that you might not notice a difference in the side slopes because Redwood Rd follows the existing ground so closely.

Figure 9–84

Task 5 - Calculate Quantities.

1. If you did not complete the last task, in the Utility Bar, expand *Switch Active Proposal* and select **D_Task5** to make it current.

2. In the model, select Redwood Rd.

3. In the component road asset card, click (Earthwork quantities).

4. In the component road asset card, click ⚙ (Specify settings).

5. In the Earthwork Setting panel, set the *Station Increment* value to **66**, and toggle on all of the geometry options to sample them, as shown in Figure 9–85. Close the Earthwork Setting panel.

Figure 9–85

6. In the component road asset card, click ▶ (Compute earthwork quantities). Wait for it to process.

7. To display the results, in the component road asset card, click ⛏ (View detail values). The Earthwork Quantities panel displays, as shown in Figure 9–86.

Figure 9–86

8. To create a report, in the component road asset card, click 🔲 (Generate report).

9. In the Save Quantities dialog box, type a file name, browse to where the file should be saved, and click **Save**.

10. When the file is done saving, Windows Explorer automatically opens to the location where you saved the file. Double-click on the file to open it in Microsoft Excel. The report displays similar to that shown in Figure 9–87.

	A	B	C	D	E	F	G	H	I	J
1	Station (ft)	Cut (cu.yd.	Cut area (a	Fill (cu.yd.	Fill area (a	Cumulativ	Cumulativ	Cumulativ	Note	
2	0	0	0.002	0	0	0	0	0		
3	66	185.7	0.002	27.31	0	185.7	27.31	158.39		
4	109.05	124.58	0.002	16.55	0	310.27	43.86	266.41		
5	132	62.01	0.002	9.43	0	372.28	53.3	318.98		
6	174.67	109.22	0.002	22.77	0	481.5	76.06	405.43		
7	198	57.15	0.001	16.48	0	538.65	92.55	446.1		
8	240.28	102.66	0.002	37.54	0.001	641.31	130.08	511.23		
9	264	59.9	0.002	24.76	0.001	701.21	154.84	546.37		
10	310.11	129.79	0.002	73.86	0.001	831	228.7	602.3		
11	330	59.03	0.002	42.95	0.001	890.03	271.65	618.38		
12	371.52	123.33	0.002	88.21	0.001	1013.36	359.86	653.5		
13	396	73.74	0.002	49.54	0.001	1087.1	409.4	677.7		
14	462	198.48	0.002	130.84	0.001	1285.59	540.24	745.35		
15	518.92	175.08	0.002	106.44	0.001	1460.67	646.68	813.98		
16	528	28.76	0.002	16.13	0.001	1489.43	662.82	826.62		
17	584.34	174.92	0.002	83.86	0.001	1664.35	746.67	917.68		
18	594	29.34	0.002	11.05	0.001	1693.69	757.73	935.97		
19	650.15	177.71	0.002	47.2	0	1871.41	804.92	1066.48		
20	660	32.46	0.002	5.65	0	1903.87	810.58	1093.29		
21	715.77	195.65	0.002	26.36	0	2099.52	836.94	1262.59		
22	726	37.45	0.002	4.02	0	2136.97	840.96	1296.01		
23	781.38	179.64	0.002	17.32	0	2316.6	858.29	1458.32		
24	792	29.88	0.002	2.54	0	2346.49	860.83	1485.66		
25	858	178.2	0.002	16.26	0	2524.69	877.09	1647.6		
26	924	170.77	0.002	19.44	0	2695.45	896.53	1798.93		
27	990	151.17	0.001	21.51	0	2846.62	918.03	1928.59		
28	1056	169.09	0.002	13.36	0	3015.71	931.4	2084.32		
29	1122	160.41	0.001	17	0	3176.13	948.39	2227.73		
30	1188	155.78	0.002	47.45	0.001	3331.91	995.85	2336.06		
31	1235.57	168.4	0.003	40.37	0	3500.31	1036.22	2464.09		
32	1243.51	32.18	0.002	5.25	0	3532.49	1041.47	2491.02		
33	1246.28	10.82	0.002	1.76	0	3543.3	1043.23	2500.08	Start - intersection	
34	1397.67	286.32	0.001	119.14	0.001	3829.63	1162.36	2667.26	End - intersection	
35	1400	4.37	0.001	1.56	0	3834	1163.92	2670.07		

Figure 9–87

New 💡

9.6 Design Road Superelevation

You can apply superelevations to component roads. Once applied, you can inspect cross sections through critical stations of the road. Superelevation critical station gizmos display as blue slices along the road, as shown in Figure 9–88. In addition, yellow and red tracks display beside the roadway, representing runoff and runout areas, which are also shown in Figure 9–88.

Figure 9–88

How To: Apply Superelevations to Component Roads

1. In the model, select a component road.
2. In the Road asset card, under *Attributes*, toggle on the **Superelevation** option, as shown in Figure 9–89.
3. Adjust the *Superelevation Input* values, as shown in Figure 9–89.

Figure 9–89

4. Press <Esc> to clear the selection of the road.

How To: View Road Cross Section Attributes in the Cross Section Viewer

1. Once superelevations are applied to a road, select the road in the model.
2. Click on a superelevation critical station gizmo. The Cross Section Viewer should display, as shown in Figure 9–90.

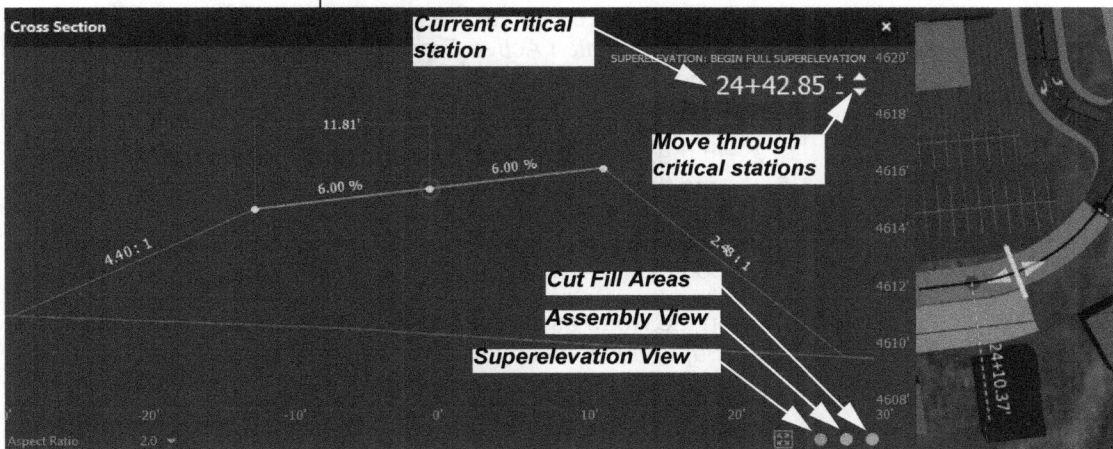

Figure 9–90

3. Click ▲/▼ (Next/Previous Critical Section) in the viewer to view other critical stations.

Practice 9e

Review Superelevations

Practice Objectives

Estimated time for completion: 5 minutes

- Turn on superelevations for review.

In this practice, you will display the superelevation data for a component road, and then review the superelevation critical stations, as shown in Figure 9–91.

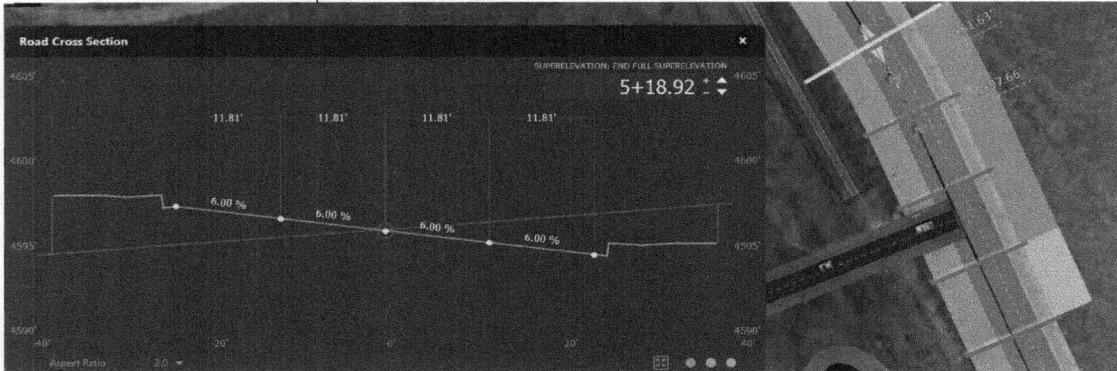

Figure 9–91

Task 1 - Display the superelevations for review.

1. Continue working in the same model as the last practice. If you did not complete the last practice, in the Utility Bar, expand *Switch Active Proposal* and select **E_Task1** to make it current.

2. In the Utility Bar, click ▥ (Bookmark your current location), and then select **RoundAbout**.

3. In the model, select Redwood Rd (road running north to south).

4. In the Road asset card, under *Attributes,* toggle on the *Superelevation* option, and then adjust the *Superelevation Input* values, as shown in Figure 9–92.

Figure 9–92

5. Click on a superelevation critical station gizmo, as shown in Figure 9–93. Review the superelevation data in the Cross Section Viewer.

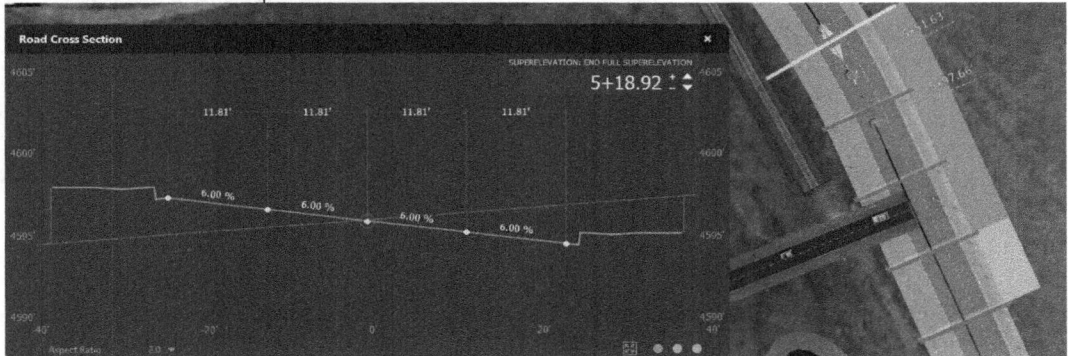

Figure 9–93

6. Click ![icon](Next Critical Section) in the viewer to view other critical stations in the current view.

7. Press <Esc> twice to clear the selection of the road.

9.7 Working With Intersections

When two design roads intersect each other, an intersection object is automatically created. Selecting an intersection in the model causes an Intersection asset card to display, as shown in Figure 9–94.

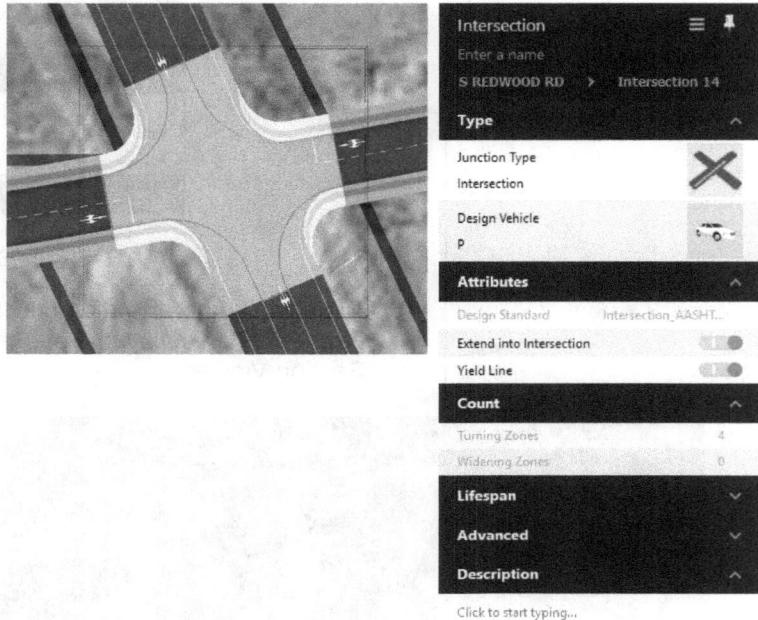

Figure 9–94

Similar to design roads, there are multiple Edit Modes for Intersections. The edit modes that are available depends on what you have selected in the model. Clicking once on the intersection enables you to set the Junction Type and other settings in the Intersection stack. Clicking twice on the intersection enables you to edit specific parts of the intersection. Depending on where you click the second time, you can edit the Lane Markings or Turning Zones, as shown in Figure 9–95.

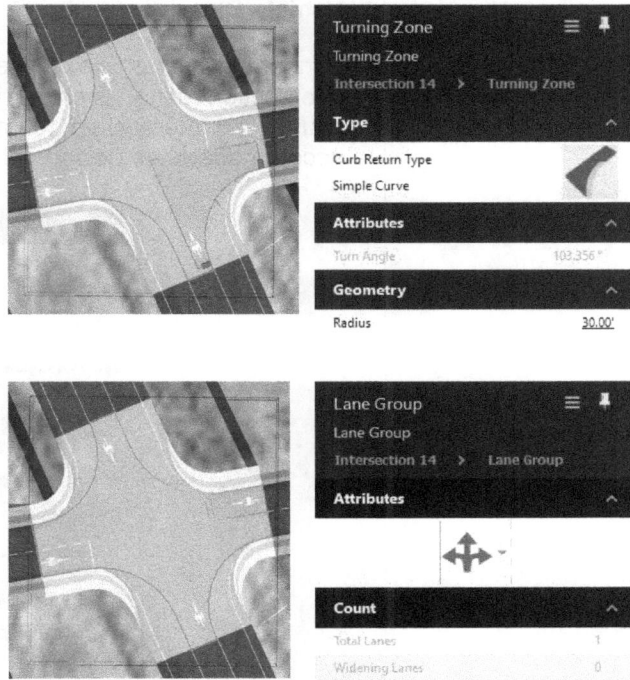

Figure 9–95

Junction Type

When an intersection is selected, the Type area displays in the Intersection asset card. Two Junction Types are currently available, as shown in Figure 9–96.

Figure 9–96

Standard Intersection

The standard intersection junction type is for three-way and four-way intersections. When a standard intersection junction type is selected, you can modify the vehicle class and turning zones. You can also create a traffic simulation.

Vehicle Class

Various design vehicle classes are available to set for the intersection rating, as shown in Figure 9–97. Changing the rating causes the intersection geometry to adjust in order to accommodate the design vehicle class.

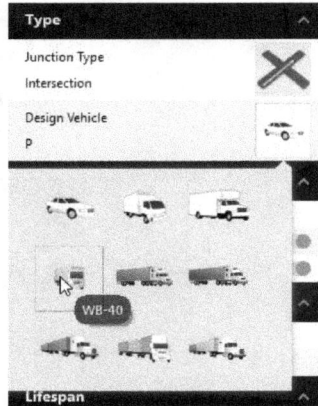

Figure 9–97

Turning Zone

Once an intersection is selected, you can select any of the turning zones within the intersection. This causes the Turning Zone stack to display, as shown in Figure 9–98. The curve type and curve radius for the curb return can be modified using the Turning Zone stack. If the **Simple Curve with Taper** option is selected, the radius, offset and taper parameters can all be set, as shown on the far right in Figure 9–98

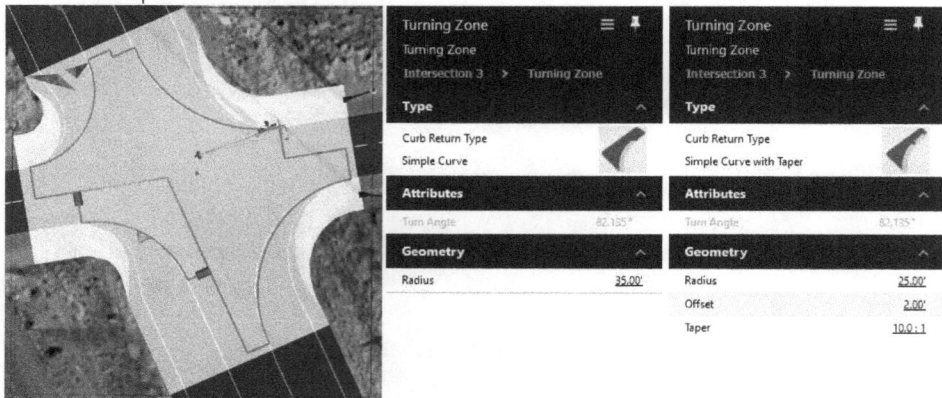

Figure 9–98

Lane Markings

In the Intersection stack, under *Attributes,* you can modify how lanes are painted through the intersection. Lane markings can extend into intersections and create a yield line, as shown in Figure 9–99.

Figure 9–99

In order to set the directional arrows that indicate which way traffic can flow, you must select the Lane Group in the model. In the Lane Group stack, you can set the turn arrows under *Attributes*, as shown in Figure 9–100

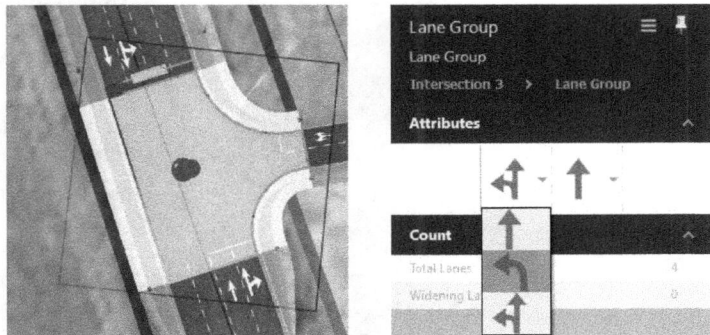

Figure 9–100

9.8 Roundabouts

The Roundabout junction type replaces the intersection geometry with a circular intersection for almost continuous traffic flow in one direction around a central island. There are several roundabout options to select from, as shown in Figure 9–101

Figure 9–101

Once a roundabout is placed, you can use gizmos to modify it in both the horizontal and vertical directions, as shown in Figure 9–102. To see the vertical gizmos, the model must be orbited more than 45 degrees from a plan view.

Figure 9–102

Practice 9f

Modify Intersections

Estimated time for completion: 20 minutes

Practice Objectives

- Modify a standard intersection.
- Create a roundabout where two design roads intersect.

In this practice, you will modify a standard intersection to increase the curb radius. Then you will turn another standard intersection into a roundabout to create a more continuous traffic flow.

Task 1 - Modify a standard intersection.

1. Continue working in the same model as the previous practice. If you did not complete the previous practice, in the Utility Bar, expand *Switch Active Proposal* and select **F_Task1** to make it current.

2. In the Utility Bar, click ▣ (Bookmark your current location) and select **RoundAbout**.

3. Select the design road that goes to the west.

4. Use the ▣ (PI gizmo) to extend the road at least to the center of Redwood Rd, as shown in Figure 9–103. This creates an intersection feature.

Figure 9–103

5. In the Utility Bar, click ▣ (Bookmark your current location) and select **Lake Rd Intersection**.

6. Select the intersection. In the Intersection stack, in the *Design Vehicle* area, select **WB-40**, as shown in Figure 9–104.

Figure 9–104

7. In the model, select the northeast turning zone of the intersection.

8. In the Turning Zone stack, change *Taper* to **20:1**, as shown in Figure 9–105.

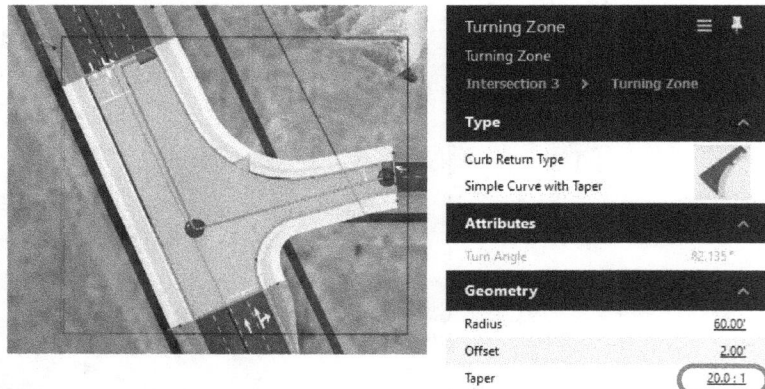

Figure 9–105

9. In the model, select the north lane group of the intersection. In the Lane Group stack, change the center lane to a left only, as shown in Figure 9–106.

Figure 9–106

10. Press <Esc> to clear the selection of the intersection.

Task 2 - Turn a standard intersection into a roundabout.

1. Continue working in the same model as the previous task. If you did not complete the previous task, in the Utility Bar, expand *Switch Active Proposal* and select **F_Task2** to make it current.

2. In the Utility Bar, click ☐ (Bookmark your current location) and select **RoundAbout**.

3. Select the intersection shown in Figure 9–107.

Figure 9–107

4. In the Intersection asset card, in the *Type* area, for the Junction Type, select **Roundabout**.

5. In the Roundabout drop-down list, select **FHWA 2000-Urban Compact Roundabout**, as shown in Figure 9–108.

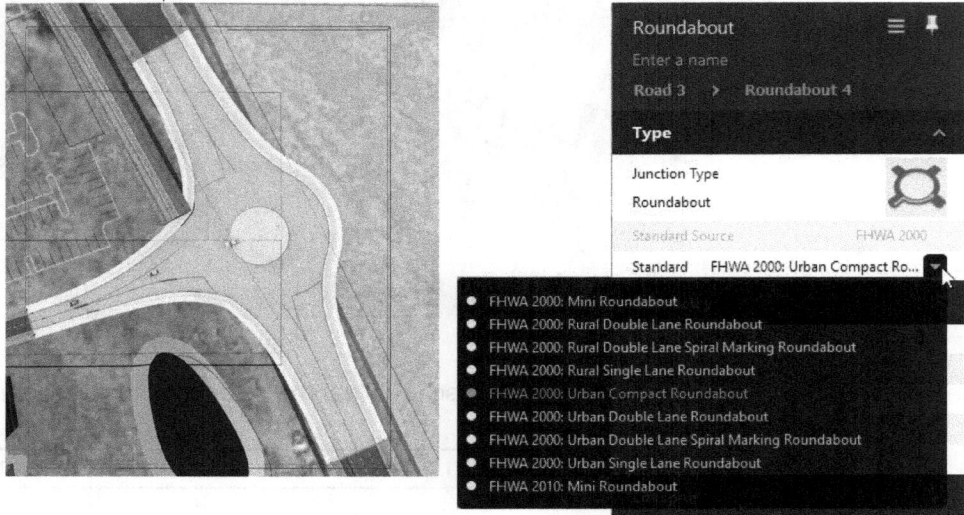

Figure 9–108

6. In the model, select the center island of the roundabout. Click

    (Offset roundabout center position gizmo) and move the center close **25** feet to the east and **22** feet to the south, as shown in Figure 9–109.

Figure 9–109

7. Orbit the model more than 45 degrees from plan view. Click

   (Adjust roundabout tilted plane slope gizmo) and move it up **4**%, as shown in Figure 9–110.

Figure 9–110

8. Press <Esc> to clear the selection of the roundabout.

Chapter Review Questions

1. How does a Right of Way differ from a Parcel or Easement?

   a. There is no difference.

   b. A Right of Way enables you to offset an existing feature parallel to its centerline, while Parcels or Easements must have each segment drawn in.

   c. Parcels or Easements enable you to offset an existing feature parallel to its centerline, while a Right of Way must have each segment drawn in.

2. Which of the following road types would be used to set a maximum design speed of 50 mph?

   a. Highway

   b. Arterial

   c. Collector

   d. Local

3. Which of the following dialog boxes can be used to set the design road standards? (Select all that apply.)

   a. New Model

   b. Application Options

   c. Model Properties

   d. Model Explorer

4. You can modify design road annotations that display in the model window when the road is selected.

   a. True

   b. False

5. Which *Edit Mode* does the Road asset card need to be set to in order to make gizmos display along the design road?

   a. Grading

   b. Lanes Forward

   c. Lanes Backward

   d. Style

   e. Geometry

6. You can click on a specific grading on one side of the road to edit its parameters independent of the rest of the road.

    a. True

    b. False

7. Intersection Objects are created automatically when two design roads cross each other.

    a. True

    b. False

8. Intersections can be any of the following. (Select all that apply).

    a. Single Point Urban Interchange (SPUI)

    b. 3-way Intersection

    c. 4-way Intersection

    d. Roundabout

Command Summary

Button	Command	Location
	Artillery Roads	• **In Canvas Tools:** Design, review, and engineer roads>Design roads
	Collector Roads	• **In Canvas Tools:** Design, review, and engineer road>Design roads
	Highway Roads	• **In Canvas Tools:** Design, review, and engineer roads>Design roads
	Local Roads	• **In Canvas Tools:** Design, review, and engineer roads>Design roads
	Profile View	• **In Canvas Tools:** Design, review, and engineer roads>Review and modify roadway designs

Analyzing Design Roads Using the Roadway Design for InfraWorks 360 Module

Once you have created a design road, it is important to analyze it to ensure that it meets the design criteria. In this chapter, you learn how to analyze sight distances and improve traffic flows through detailed interchanges. Then you learn how to balance cut and fill quantities for the vertical design using cloud-based optimization tools. Finally, you generate plan and profile sheets in order to communicate the design to contractors.

Learning Objectives in this Chapter

- Add traffic movement to your project by running a traffic simulation.
- Identify the best horizontal location for a new roadway by running a corridor optimization.
- Balance a design road's cut and fill values by running a vertical optimization.
- Analyze a roadway and intersection for sight distance obstructions.
- Generate a plan and profile sheet set for a design road.

10.1 Traffic Simulation

The Traffic Simulation module provides a way to run a traffic study of the project using a cloud-based traffic engine. Since it is cloud based, the model must be published to the cloud before a simulation can be run.

Once a model is published, the Traffic Simulation module can generate an animation file based on traffic demand. Traffic can include all modes of transportation, not just private vehicles. During the traffic study, the following can be defined:

- Demand matrices

- Profiles

- Vehicle types

- Driver types

The animation files that are created can be played in the model, adding traffic movement to your project. Additionally, traffic analysis results can be displayed as info-graphics in the model, as shown in Figure 10–1. Color coded queue lengths which are based on demand, display in the traffic study area for each design road intersection.

AUTODESK INFRAWORKS 360

To use this feature, access to the Internet and Autodesk® InfraWorks® 360 are required.

Red queues indicate delays that exceed a threshold

A selection polyline indicates the study area

Colored queues represent the delay time

Figure 10–1

General Steps

The modeling process:

1. Define the traffic study area.
2. Add zones for traffic origin/destination/parking.
3. Define traffic demand.
4. Generate trips from demand.
5. Run simulation, collecting the results.
6. Analyze the results.

How To: Define a Traffic Study Area

1. In the In Canvas tools, expand ![icon] (Design, review and engineer roads) > ![icon] (Perform analysis in preparation for road design), and click ![icon] (Traffic Simulation).
2. In the model, define a polyline to indicate the Traffic Study Area boundary.
3. If sketch roads are included in the boundary, a message displays indicating that you have the option to turn them into design roads so that they can be analyzed during the traffic simulation, as shown in Figure 10–2. Click **Yes** or **No**, as required.

The Design Roads are highlighted to indicate which roads can be analyzed using a traffic study

Figure 10–2

4. In the Traffic Study Area asset card, select the *Result Volumes* that suite your needs, as shown in Figure 10–3.

Figure 10–3

5. In the Simulation drop-down list, select the simulation length you wish to run, as shown in Figure 10–4.

- **Quick Simulation:** Runs for 10 minutes.
- The other simulations require more time to process.

Figure 10–4

Note: Running a simulation costs cloud credits.

6. Click **Run Simulation**.

Traffic Analyst Panel

The Traffic Analyst Panel is where advanced parameters and multiple simulation variants are added to the traffic analysis. Figure 10–5 shows the Traffic Analyst Panel with the Intersection control panel open. Changing parameters and variables helps you to better predict traffic flow. For the best results, run the simulation a few times and analyze the distribution of results.

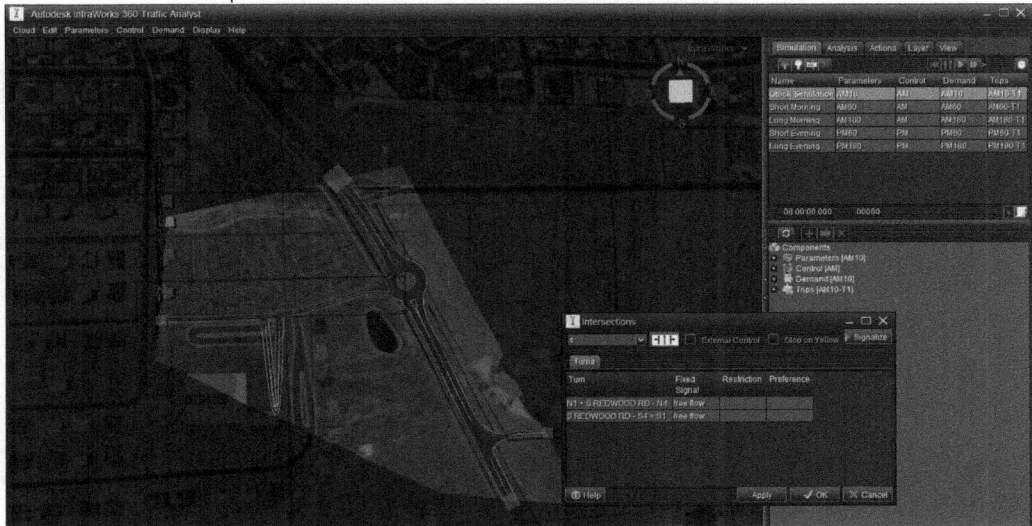

Figure 10–5

Parameters

Several parameters can be set during a traffic analysis, including:

- **Terms**: Windows of time during the day, specified as HH:MM. An unlimited number of terms can be defined for a network. Terms can overlap or be sequential, and can also specify the day of the week (weekday or weekend or a specific day).

- **Behaviors and Mobs**: Behaviors are assigned to either person types or vehicle types. They control decisions made by each person. A group of behaviors is a MOB (Mix of Behaviors).

- **Restrictions and Speed Controls**: Restrictions are applied to surfaces to control the types of people or vehicles that can move on the surface.

- **Vehicle Types**: Controls the size, movement, and display of a vehicle in the model. A group of vehicle types is called a fleet.

You can access the MOBs window by using a button at the bottom of the Behaviors window.

A MOB must be created before restrictions can be added.

Behaviors are applied to vehicle types.

Controllers

The Intersection Controller enables you to control conflicts between different streams of traffic. Each lane of an intersection can have a different control signal or no signal at all. When a lane is selected in the controller, an arrow displays in the Traffic Analyst Panel indicating the direction of traffic, as shown in Figure 10–6.

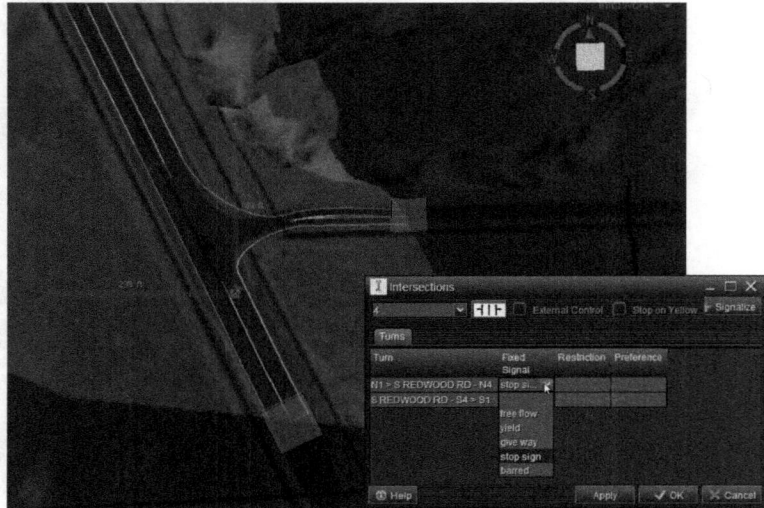

Figure 10–6

The Fixed Signal options below are listed in order of increasing priority:

* **Barred:** The turn is closed to all traffic.

* **Stop Sign:** The approaching traffic has a stop sign and must stop before proceeding through the intersection.

* **Give Way:** Approaching traffic has a Give Way sign and slows down accordingly.

* **Yield:** Approaching traffic is on the main road, but must cross an opposing stream, and must slow down on approach.

* **Free Flow:** Approaching traffic is on the main road, has priority, and does not need to check for conflicting traffic.

Demand

The Demand Editor enables you to modify the traffic counts for various times of day and origin points. Three tabs exist in the Demand Editor:

- **Directed Demand:** Uses origin-destination matrices where demand between all origin-destination pairs is known. When an origin point is selected in the Demand Editor, arrows display in the Traffic Analyst Panel indicating the destination of traffic, as shown in Figure 10–7.

Figure 10–7

- **Undirected Demand:** Uses traffic volumes from an origin zone along with turning counts.

- **Transport Demand:** Lists all public transport services, departure times, and associated vehicle types.

How To: Control Traffic Flow per Intersection

1. Create a Traffic Simulation.
2. In the model, select the Traffic Study area boundary.
3. Right-click and select **Traffic Analyst Panel**.
4. Click **OK** in the two Traffic Simulation dialog boxes that display.
5. In the **Control** menu, select **Intersections**.
6. In the Intersections panel, select the intersection or roundabout to work with from the Intersection drop-down list.

7. Select a control in the *Fixed Signal* column for each turn, as shown in Figure 10–8.

Select Intersection or Roundabout to work with

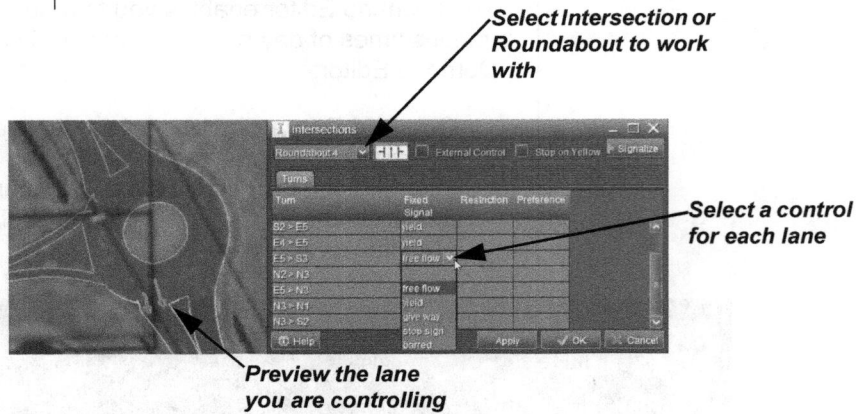

Select a control for each lane

Preview the lane you are controlling

Figure 10–8

8. Click **OK**,
9. In the **Demand** menu, select **Demand**.
10. In the Demand Editor, select the appropriate tab for the type of matrices required for the project:
    - Directed Demand
    - Undirected Demand
    - Transport Demand

11. Click ▣ (Add) to add an additional matrix, origin, or destination.
12. Input the traffic count for each profile.
13. Click **OK**.

Practice 10a

Estimated time for completion: 20 minutes

I | AUTODESK®
INFRAWORKS™ 360

To complete this practice, access to the Internet and Autodesk® InfraWorks® 360 are required.

If you receive a message indicating that you do not have rights to upload the model to the cloud, duplicate the model and try again.

Run a Traffic Study

Practice Objective

- Generate an animation file based on the default traffic demand.

In this practice, you will create a traffic study to analyze traffic flow along the design roads using default traffic counts. You will also set control signals for each lane at the signalized intersection.

Task 1 - Run a traffic study.

1. In the Home Screen, click **Open**.

2. In the *C:\InfraWorks Fundamentals Practice Files\ RoadwayDesign* folder, select **AnalyzeDesignRoads.sqlite** and click **Open**.

3. In the Utility Bar, expand *Switch Active Proposal* and select **A_Task1** to make it current.

4. In the Utility Bar, click ▣ (Bookmark your current location) and select **ProjectArea**.

5. In the In Canvas tools, expand 🖉 (Design, review and engineer roads) > ▣ (Perform analysis in preparation for road design), and click 🚗 (Traffic Simulation).

6. A message should display noting that the model must be published. In the message's dialog box, click **Publish Model**.

7. In the Publish Model dialog box, select the resource **A_Task1**. Click **Publish**, and then click **OK**.

8. In the Publish Model message, click **Close**.

9. After publishing the model, the view reverts back to the Home view. In the Utility Bar, click ▣ (Bookmark your current location) and select **ProjectArea**.

10. In the In Canvas tools, expand ![icon] (Design, review and engineer roads) > ![icon] (Perform analysis in preparation for road design), and click ![icon] (Traffic Simulation). The Design Roads are highlighted to indicate which roads can be analyzed using a traffic study.

11. In the model, define a polyline to indicate the Traffic Study Area boundary, as shown in Figure 10–9. Ensure that you double-click on the last point to finish the boundary.

Figure 10–9

12. In the message box that displays, click **Yes**, as shown in Figure 10–10.

Figure 10–10

13. In the Traffic Study Area asset card, set the following options, as shown in Figure 10–11:
    - *Results Volume*: **Per Lane**.
    - *Simulations*: **Quick Simulation**.

Figure 10–11

Running this simulation costs 1 cloud credit.

14. Click **Run Simulation**.

15. Click **OK** in the Traffic Simulation dialog box that displays.

16. With the Traffic Study area boundary still selected, right-click and select **Traffic Analyst Panel**.

17. Click **OK** in the two Traffic Simulation dialog boxes that display.

18. In the **Control** menu, select **Intersections**.

19. In the Intersections panel:
    - In the Intersection drop-down list, select **Intersection 5**.
    - Select the *Fixed Signals* for each lane, matching those shown in Figure 10–12. Click **Apply**.

Figure 10–12

20. In the Intersections panel:
    - In the Intersection drop-down list, select **Roundabout 11**.
    - Select *Fixed Signals* for each lane, matching those shown in Figure 10–13.

Figure 10–13

21. Click **OK**,

22. In the **Demand** menu, select **Demands**.

23. In the Demand Editor, set the Directed Demand matrix for the project so that they match those shown in Figure 10–14.

Figure 10–14

24. Click **OK**.

25. In the Traffic Analyst Panel, *Simulation* tab, click [▶] (Play). Note how the cars bunch up at the intersections and roundabout, as shown in Figure 10–15.

Figure 10–15

26. In the Traffic Analyst Panel, *Simulation* tab, click

    ▯▯ (Pause).

27. In the **Control** menu, select **Intersections**.

28. In the Intersections panel:

    • In the Intersection drop-down list, select **Roundabout 11**.

    • Click ⊣⊺⊦ (Edit Turn Lanes).

    • Three lanes have conflicts. Fix them automatically by clicking **Repair**, as shown in Figure 10–16. Click **Close**.

    • Click **OK**.

Figure 10–16

29. In the Traffic Analyst Panel, *Simulation* tab, click ▶ (Play). Note how the cars now flow better at the roundabout.

30. In the Traffic Analyst Panel, *Simulation* tab, click

    ▯▯ (Pause).

31. Close the Traffic Analyst Panel.

Running this simulation costs 1 cloud credit.

32. In the Traffic Study Area asset card, click **Run Simulation**.

33. Click **OK** in the Traffic Simulation message that displays.

You must give the simulation time to complete before you can play the animation.

34. In the Animation Player asset card, click ▶ (Play). Note that there are Red queues, which indicate delays that exceed a threshold, as shown in Figure 10–17.

Figure 10–17

35. In the In Canvas tools, expand 🔖 (Design, review and engineer roads) > ▣ (Perform analysis in preparation for road design), and click 🚗 (Traffic Simulation) to toggle off the traffic simulation boundary.

10.2 Corridor Optimization

The Corridor Optimization module provides advanced optimization algorithms for finding an optimal horizontal roadway alignment. This cloud service uses the model terrain and other GIS information in the model to create cost effective and environmentally friendly solutions. The best available path is calculated by setting the start and end points for the road. The optimal time for performing a corridor optimization is when you are first considering where to layout the roadway.

AUTODESK
INFRAWORKS 360

To use this feature, access to the Internet and Autodesk® InfraWorks® 360 are required.

Advanced Settings

When the Advanced Settings are expanded in the Corridor Optimization palette, additional constraints can be added to the corridor.

Cost Zones & Suitability Map

Avoidance zones can be specified to ensure that the new road corridor does not pass through environmentally sensitive or other high cost areas. These zones can be drawn in manually by selecting the **Draw avoidance zones** link. Alternatively, they can be activated by opening a suitability map by selecting **Open suitability map** then selecting the option to **Include the current suitability map**, as shown in Figure 10–18.

Figure 10–18

Construction Rules

Setting construction rules provides a method of ensuring bridges are placed and tunnels are cut where cut/fill heights exceed a maximum height. Additionally, roadside grading values can be set, as shown in Figure 10–19.

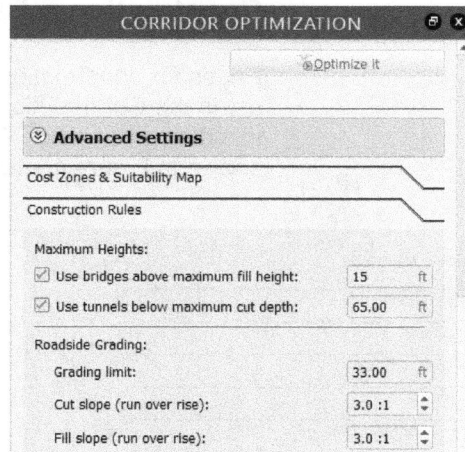

Figure 10–19

Alignment Constraints

Minimum radius can be set under the Alignment Constraints, as shown in Figure 10–20.

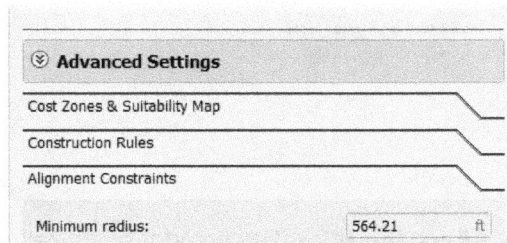

Figure 10–20

Profile Constraints

Maximum grade can be set under the Profile Constraints, as shown in Figure 10–21.

Figure 10–21

Construction & Earthwork Cost

Prices for construction and earthwork cost items can be set using the Construction & Earthwork Cost dialog box. To access this dialog box, click **Construction & Earthwork Cost**, as shown in Figure 10–22.

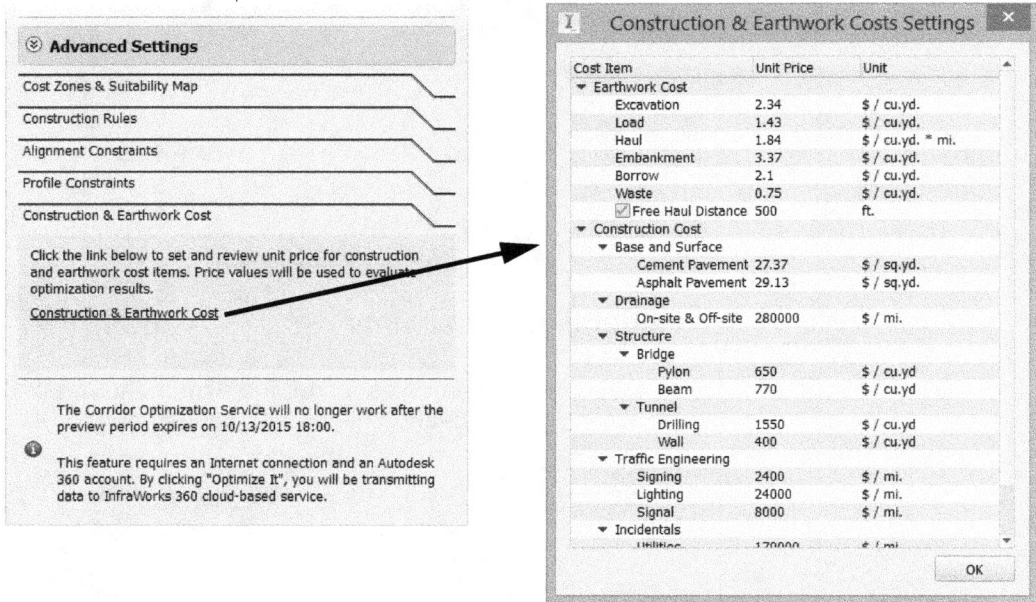

Figure 10–22

Job Monitor

The corridor optimization results are communicated through the Job Monitor panel, which displays automatically once you run an optimization. The status of all optimizations that have run are displayed, as shown in Figure 10–23.

Figure 10–23

Status

The *Status* column displays the current status of your optimization. There are three status icons, which are as follows:

Icon	Status	Description
	Queued	Indicates that the profile has been sent to the cloud for computing, but has not started yet.
	In Progress	Indicates that the profile is currently being optimized in the cloud.
	Completed	Indicates that the optimization calculations are complete.

Viewing Results

The results of the optimization can be viewed by:

- Downloading a report.

- Importing the data into a new proposal in the model.

Report

In the Job Monitor panel, in the *Report* column, clicking

(Click to download an optimization report) opens a file and displays the results of the calculations. This report displays items including alignment information, profile information, construction information, etc.

Figure 10–24 shows a sample report with the suggested horizontal and profile view for the design road.

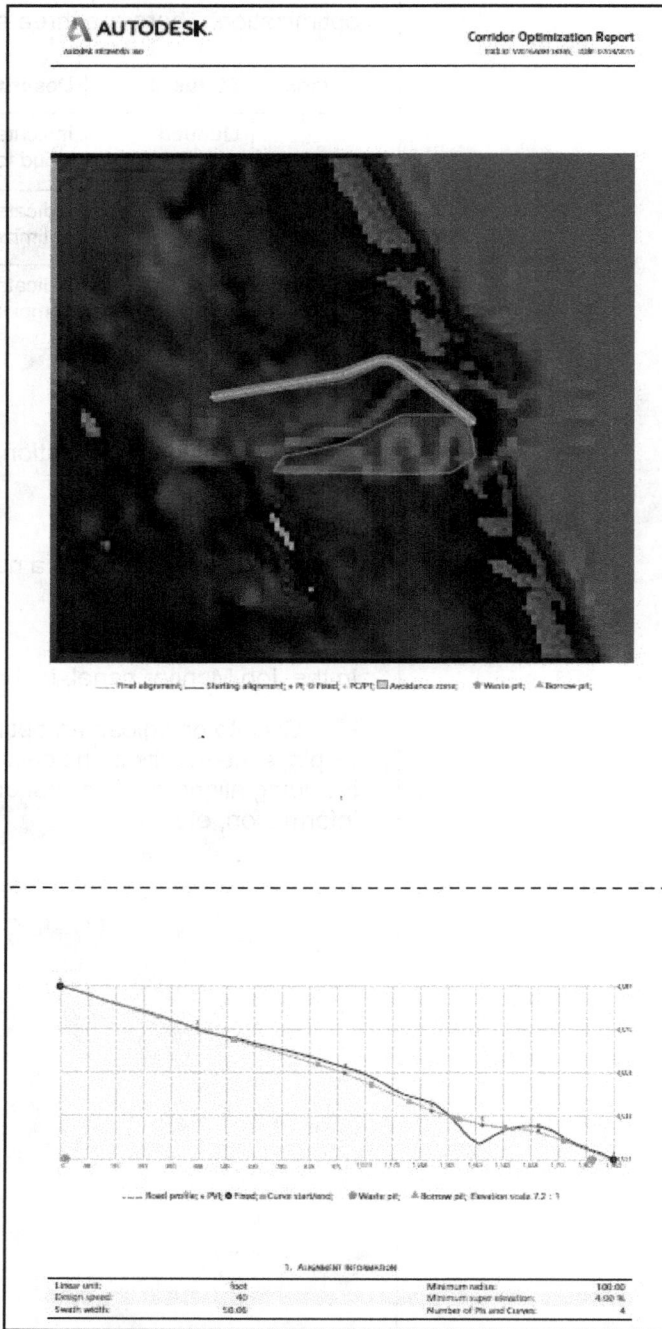

Figure 10–24

Create a Proposal from Results

In addition to downloading the results in a file, you can also view the results by importing the roadway into a new proposal in the model. To do this, in the Job Monitor panel, in the *Results* column, click 🗔 (Create a proposal to view the results in the model).

How To: Run a Corridor Optimization

1. In the In Canvas tools, expand 🐾 (Design, review and engineer roads) > 🔲 (Perform analysis in preparation for road design), and click 🏔 (Corridor Optimization).
2. In the Corridor Optimization palette, set the following options, as shown in Figure 10–25.
   - Select an appropriate *Design speed* for the project
   - Select the *Structure styles* for the Road, Bridge, and Tunnel.
   - For the *Path*, click ✛ (Define PIs).

Figure 10–25

3. In the model, click to set the start PI and the end PI.
4. In the Corridor Optimization palette, expand the *Advanced Settings* area.

If the Job Monitor panel does not open, in the In Canvas tools, click

(Design, review, and engineer roads)>

(Review and modify roadway designs)>

(Job Monitor).

5. Under the Cost Zones & Suitability Map, click **Draw avoidance zones**.

6. In the Cost Zones asset card, click (Draw avoidance zones). In the model, create polylines to define areas to avoid.

7. Under the Cost Zones & Suitability Map, click **Open suitability map**.

8. In the Suitability Maps asset card, expand the Select a Map drop-down list and select the appropriate map for your needs.

9. In the Corridor Optimization palette, select the **Include the current suitability map** option.

10. In the *Construction Rules* area, set the maximum cut/fill heights and the roadside grading parameters as required.

11. In the *Alignment Constraints* area, set the minimum radius.

12. In the *Profile Constraints* area, set the maximum grade.

13. In the *Construction & Earthwork Cost* area, click **Construction & Earthwork Cost** to open the dialog box and set costing values.

14. In the Corridor Optimization palette, ensure that the correct path is selected, and then click **Optimize it**.

15. In the Job Monitor palette, under the *Report* column, click

(Click to download an optimization report) to review the results in a report format.

16. In the Job Monitor palette, under the Results column, click

(Create a proposal to view the result in the model).

17. Click **Yes** in the Information dialog box.

18. Type a name and click **OK** to create the proposal.

Practice 10b

Identify the Best Location for a New Roadway

Practice Objective

- Locate the best location for a roadway based on a suitability map.

Estimated time for completion: 15 minutes

After seeing the plan, the approving agency would like another option for the roadway that accesses the white water park parking lot. In this practice, you will use a suitability map in the corridor optimization to find the best location for a new roadway.

AUTODESK
INFRAWORKS™ 360

To complete this practice, access to the Internet and Autodesk® InfraWorks® 360 are required.

Task 1 - Run a corridor optimization.

1. Continue working in the same model as the previous practice. If you did not complete the previous practice, in the Utility Bar, expand *Switch Active Proposal* and select **B_Task1** to make it current.

2. In the Utility Bar, click ▣ (Bookmark your current location) and select **River**.

3. In the In Canvas tools, expand 🐾 (Design, review and engineer roads) > ▣ (Perform analysis in preparation for road design), and click ▲ (Corridor Optimization).

4. In the Corridor Optimization palette, set the following options, as shown in Figure 10–26:
   - *Design speed*: **40 mph**
   - *Road Structure style:* **Two Lanes**

   - For the *Path*, click ✛ (Define PIs).

Figure 10–26

5. In the model, click to set the start PI at the roundabout and the end PI on the north-west corner of the proposed parking lot, as shown in Figure 10–27.

Figure 10–27

6. In the Corridor Optimization palette, expand the *Advanced Settings* area.

7. In the *Cost Zones & Suitability Map* area, click **Draw avoidance zones**.

8. In the Cost Zones asset card, click (Draw avoidance zones). In the model, create the area shown in Figure 10–28. Ensure that you double-click to finish the boundary.

Figure 10–28

9. In the *Cost Zones & Suitability Map* area, click **Open suitability map**. In the Suitability Maps asset card, expand the Select a Map drop-down list and select **Water Features**.

10. In the Corridor Optimization palette, select the **Include the current suitability map** option.

11. In the *Alignment Constraints* area, set the minimum radius to **100**.

This could take as much as 25 minutes, depending on the current load in the cloud.

12. In the Corridor Optimization palette, ensure that **Path - (1)** is selected. Leave all other constraints as they are and click **Optimize it**.

13. If the Job Monitor panel does not open, in the In Canvas tools, click ![icon] (Design, review, and engineer roads)> ![icon] (Review and modify roadway designs)> ![icon] (Job Monitor).

14. In the Job Monitor palette, under the Report column, click ![icon] (Click to download an optimization report) to review the results in a report.

15. In the Job Monitor palette, under the Results column, click ![icon] (Create a proposal to view the result in the model). Click **Yes** in the Information dialog box.

16. Type **NewCorridor** for the name and click **OK** to create the proposal.

Since the optimal results (shown in Figure 10–29) indicate that the best route crosses the pier road, you decide to just create a road from the beginning of the pier to the parking lot rather than on the south side of the river. For time's sake, this is done for you in preparation for the next exercise.

Figure 10–29

10.3 Balance Cut and Fill Along the Roadway

Profile Optimization

Multiple vertical design options can be calculated quickly using profile optimization tools. Running a profile optimization enables you to enter specific cost information for the project area. This information is used to reduce haul charges, thus decreasing the cost of the project. During the analysis process, certain parameters can be set to ensure that project constraints are met.

Profile Constraints

A number of profile constraints can be set under the *Advanced Settings* of the Profile Optimization panel, including:

- Maximum grade

- Minimum PVI spacing

- Required drainage grade

- PVI frequency

- Anchored PVIs

Anchored PVIs are necessary when the design road must match existing or proposed conditions, such as when the road crosses another road, or requires a specific clearance. The *Profile Constraints* area of the Profile Optimization panel is shown in Figure 10–30.

Figure 10–30

Quantities Options

Borrow and waste pits can be added to the model at specific stations to reduce mass haul charges. The capacity of each pit and the access distance from the road can both be set in the *Quantities Options* area, as shown in Figure 10–31.

Type	Station (ft.)	Access distance (ft	Capacity (cu.yd.)
Borrow P ▾	1202.24	2.98	100000
Waste Pit ▾	3938.35	12.77	150000

Quantities Options

Borrow/waste pits:

Figure 10–31

Construction Rules

Construction rules can be set to determine what to do when a cut or fill becomes too deep. If a fill height is above the specified value, a bridge is used rather than fill material. Alternatively, if a cut depth is beyond the specified value, a tunnel is used to reduce the environmental impact. This is set in the *Construction Rules* area of the Profile Optimization panel, as shown in Figure 10–32.

Construction Rules

Maximum Heights:

☑ Use bridges above maximum fill height: 10 ft

☑ Use tunnels below maximum cut depth: 45 ft

Figure 10–32

Construction and Earthwork Cost

The cost of the project can be estimated by entering construction and earthwork costs for the area where the project is located. These are defined in the Construction & Earthwork Costs Settings dialog box, as shown in Figure 10–33.

Cost Item	Unit Price	Unit
⊟ Earthwork Cost		
Excavation	2.34	$ / cu.yd.
Load	1.43	$ / cu.yd.
Haul	1.84	$ / cu.yd. " mi.
Embankment	3.37	$ / cu.yd.
Borrow	2.1	$ / cu.yd.
Waste	0.75	$ / cu.yd.
☑ Free Haul Distance	500	ft.
⊟ Construction Cost		
⊟ Base and Surface		
Cement Pavement	27.37	$ / sq.yd.
Asphalt Pavement	29.13	$ / sq.yd.
⊟ Drainage		
On-site & Off-site	280000	$ / mi.
⊟ Structure		
⊟ Bridge		
Pylon	650	$ / cu.yd
Beam	770	$ / cu.yd
⊟ Tunnel		
Drilling	1550	$ / cu.yd
Wall	400	$ / cu.yd
⊟ Traffic Engineering		
Signing	2400	$ / mi.
Lighting	24000	$ / mi.
Signal	8000	$ / mi.
⊟ Incidentals		

Figure 10–33

Cloud Credits

When you click **Optimize It** within the Profile Optimization panel, your design is transmitted to the Autodesk InfraWorks 360 cloud-based service. The cloud-based service runs the calculations enabling you to continue working on the design. Since this command uses the cloud, cloud credits are required to optimize the profile. The number of credits that are required varies according to the length of the road, and the amount of vertical change that is happening in the project. The exact amount of credits can be calculated by clicking **Click here to check** in the Profile Optimization panel, below the *Construction and Earthwork Cost* area, as shown in Figure 10–34.

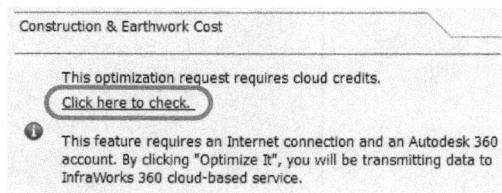

Construction & Earthwork Cost

This optimization request requires cloud credits.
Click here to check.

ⓘ This feature requires an Internet connection and an Autodesk 360 account. By clicking "Optimize It", you will be transmitting data to InfraWorks 360 cloud-based service.

Figure 10–34

Optimize It

Once you have entered all of the information, you can send the roadway to the cloud for calculating. Do this by clicking **Optimize It** in the Profile Optimization panel, as shown in Figure 10–35.

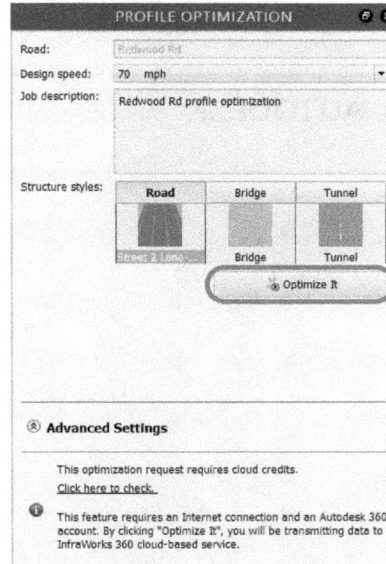

Figure 10–35

Job Monitor

Viewing Results

Similar to a Corridor Optimization, the results of the profile optimization can be viewed in two different ways:

• Downloading a * report.

• Importing the data into a new proposal in the model.

Report

In the Job Monitor panel, in the *Report* column, clicking

(Click to download an optimization report) opens Adobe Reader or PDF Reader and displays the results of the calculations. This report displays things like: the total project cost, total construction cost, a haul diagram, cut and fill quantities along the roadway, as well as additional information. Figure 10–36 shows a sample report with the suggested profile view for the design road.

Create a Proposal from Results

In addition to downloading the results in a file, you can also view the results by importing the corrected profile into a new proposal in the model. To do this, in the Job Monitor panel, in the *Results* column, click 🖼 (Create a proposal to view the results in the model).

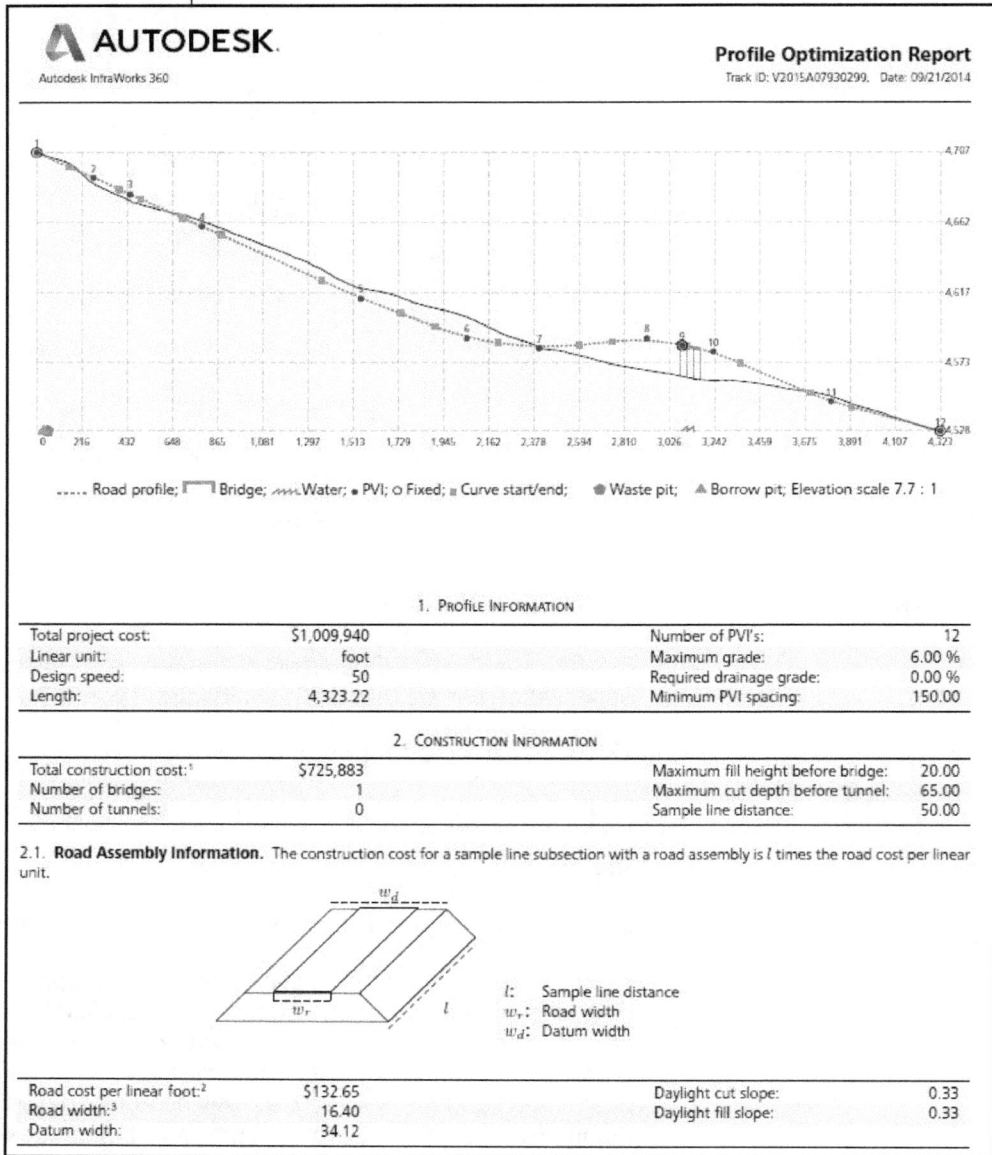

Figure 10–36

Practice 10c

Perform a Vertical Optimization

Practice Objective

- Balance the cut and fill quantities for a design roadway

In this practice, you will run a vertical optimization for the parking lot access road. You will then import the new proposal to view the results, shown in Figure 10–37.

Figure 10–37

Estimated time for completion: 10 minutes

**AUTODESK
INFRAWORKS 360**

To complete this practice, access to the Internet and Autodesk® InfraWorks® 360 are required.

Task 1 - Run a vertical optimization.

1. Continue working in the same model as the last practice. In the Utility Bar, expand *Switch Active Proposal* and select **C_Task1** to make it current.

In order to save time, a new road was added as indicated at the end of the last exercise.

2. In the Utility Bar, click ▥ (Bookmark your current location) and select **River**.

3. In the model, select the parking lot access road shown in Figure 10–38.

Figure 10–38

4. In the In Canvas tools, click ![icon] (Design, review, and engineer roads)> ![icon] (Review and modify roadway designs)> ![icon] (Profile Optimization).

5. In the Profile Optimization panel, set the *Design speed to* **40 mph** and the *Structure styles* to **Road**, as shown in Figure 10–39. Then expand the *Advanced Settings* area.

Figure 10–39

6. In the Profile Optimization panel, under *Advanced Settings*, expand Profile Constraints and set the *Maximum grade* to **6**. In the *Anchored PVIs* area, uncheck PVI **2**, as shown in Figure 10–40. Leave all other settings as the default.

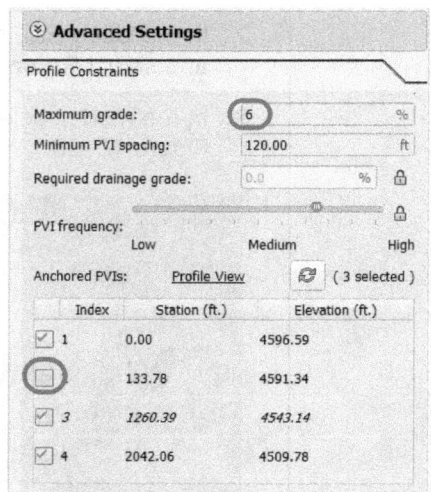

Figure 10–40

*This costs 100 cloud credits. If you want to save your credits, a copy of the report is available in the class files and a proposal with the results is available called **Profile OptimizationResults.***

7. In the Profile Optimization panel, leave all other settings as is, scroll to the top, and click **Optimize It**.

8. If the Job Monitor panel does not open, in the In Canvas tools, click (Design, review, and engineer roads)> (Review and modify roadway designs)> (Job Monitor).

9. In the Job Monitor palette, under the Report column, click (Click to download an optimization report) to review the results in a report format.

10. In the Job Monitor palette, under the Results column, click (Create a proposal to view the result in the model). Click **Yes** in the Information dialog box.

11. Type **NewProfile** for the name and click **OK** to create the proposal.
    - Note: You might have to return to Steps 7-9 once the cloud finishes processing of the profile.

10.4 Sight Distance Analysis

Roadway Sight Distance Analysis

A sight distance analysis is run on design roads to identify blind spots and sight failure zones, where a driver's line of sight is compromised by obstructions. There are six visual options for roadway analysis:

- **Sight Zones:** Displays colors on the analyzed lane to indicate safe and compromised sight zones.

- **Accident Zones:** Darkens portions of the analyzed lane to indicate where sight problems make accidents likely.

- **Sight Envelopes:** Displays colors on a range of desired sight distances beyond the road boundary, and shows the effect of obstructions.

- **Sight Regions:** Displays sight regions relative to manually placed sight pins. Darkened areas indicate where the sight line is compromised by obstructions.

- **Sight Lines:** Displays the sight line from the eye point to the target point at the required sight distance. If any obstructions within sight regions negatively affect visibility at the eye point where the sight pin is placed, the first and last blocked sight lines are also shown.

- **Distance Line:** Displays a line from the eye height of manually placed sight pins, to the required sight distance.

Intersection Sight Distance Analysis

Running a sight distance analysis on intersections provides visual cues for sight triangles, as shown in Figure 10–41. Both visible areas and obstructions are displayed in the model using a set color coding system.

Figure 10–41

The table below lists the color codes used for sight distance analysis for both roadways and intersections.

Color	Description
Light blue	Indicates zones with clear visibility.
Yellow	Indicates sight failure zones.
Red	Indicates obstructions.

How To: Conduct a Sight Distance Analysis on a Roadway

1. In the model, select the design road.

2. In the In Canvas tools, click ![icon] (Design, review, and engineer roads)> ![icon] (Review and modify roadway designs)> ![icon] (Sight Distance).

3. Set the following settings in the Sight Distance panel (shown in Figure 10–42):

   - *Method:* Select either **Stopping Sight Distance**, or **Passing Sight Distance**.
   - *Direction:* The direction of travel (**Forward** or **Backward**).
   - *Lane:* Select which lane to analyze. Note: **Lane (1)** is the lane that is closest to the centerline.
   - *Obstruction Types:* Select or clear the **Road Decorations** option.
   - Select the obstruction types you want to include in the analysis. The options available in the Obstruction Types area vary depending on the road type used, and includes trees, barriers, lamps, and other common road elements.

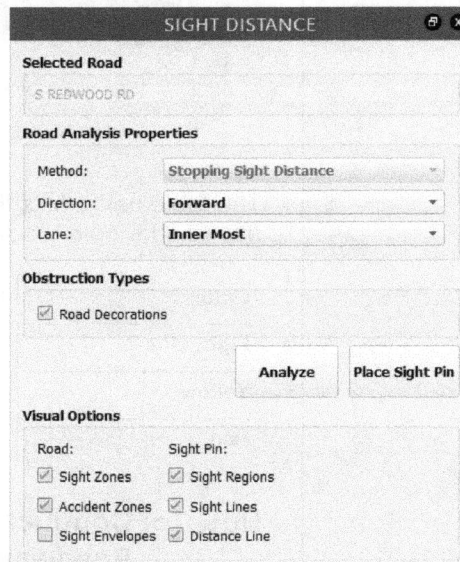

Figure 10–42

4. Click **Analyze**.
5. Select or clear the items in the *Visual Options* area that you want to include in the analysis. The items are toggled on/off in the model. You do not need to rerun the analysis if you change the items that are displayed in the model.
6. Click **Place Sight Pin** to place any required sight pins in the model.
7. Close the Sight Distance panel to clear the sight analysis.

How To: Conduct a Sight Distance Analysis on an Intersection Object

1. In the model, select the intersection object.

2. In the In Canvas tools, click ![icon] (Design, review, and engineer roads)> ![icon] (Review and modify roadway designs)> ![icon] (Sight Distance).

3. Set the following settings in the Sight Distance panel (shown in Figure 10–43):

   - *Approach:* Select the approach road
   - *Traffic control:* **Stop**, **Yield**, or **No control**
   - *Maneuver:* Select a maneuver pattern from those available.
   - *Obstruction Types:* Select or clear the **Road Decorations** option.
   - Select which obstruction types to include in the analysis.
   - Click **Analyze**.
   - Select or clear the *Visual Options* you want to include in the analysis.

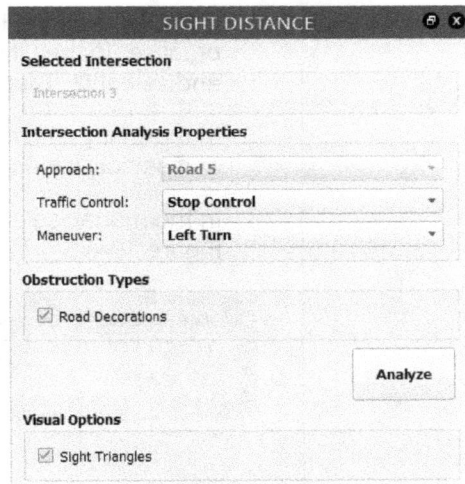

Figure 10–43

4. Close the Sight Distance panel to clear the sight analysis.

Practice 10d

Analyze Sight Distance

Practice Objective

- Analyze the roadway and the intersection for sight distance obstructions.

Estimated time for completion: 10 minutes

In this practice you will complete a sight distance analysis for the design roadway and the intersection of the new road with Redwood Rd, shown in Figure 10–44.

Figure 10–44

Task 1 - Analyze the roadway.

1. Continue working in the same model as the previous practice. In the Utility Bar, expand *Switch Active Proposal* and select **D_Task1** to make it current.

2. In the Utility Bar, click ⬛ (Bookmark your current location) and select **ProjectArea**.

3. In the model, select the new design road shown in Figure 10–45.

Figure 10–45

4. In the In Canvas tools, click 🚶 (Design, review, and engineer roads)> ⚖ (Review and modify roadway designs)> 🏃 (Sight Distance).

5. In the Sight Distance panel, set the following options:
   - **Method:** Stopping Sight Distance
   - **Direction:** Forward
   - **Lane:** Lane (1)
   - **Obstruction Types:** Select **Road Decorations**

6. Click **Analyze**.

7. Select the Visual Options shown in Figure 10–46.

If the driving side of the road is set in the Road Design Standards in the Model Properties dialog box, you might not see the option to set the driving side in the Sight Distance dialog box.

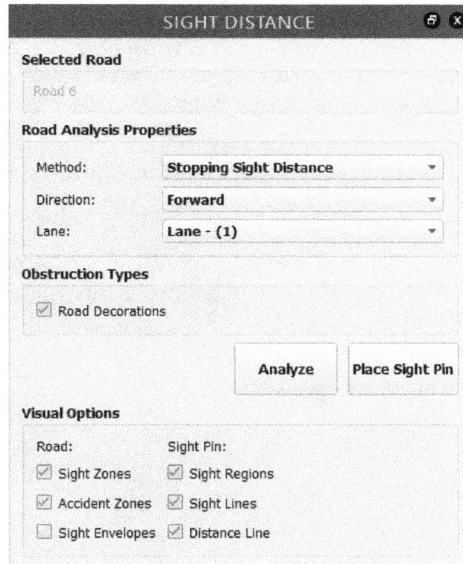

Figure 10–46

8. Close the Sight Distance panel to clear the sight analysis.

9. In the Sight Distance asset card, click **Place Sight Pin**.

10. Click various points in the model to place sight pins and display the results.

Chapter Review Questions

1. When running a traffic simulation, where do you control the traffic per intersection?

   a. Traffic Simulation asset card

   b. Traffic Analyst panel

2. When is the optimal time to perform a corridor optimization?

   a. When you are first considering where to layout the roadway.

   b. After you have laid out a few alternatives, and are ready to compare them.

   c. Right before creating the profile view.

   d. After you have cut plan and profile sheets.

3. Cut and Fill quantities can be balanced automatically using which of the following tool(s)?

   a.

   b.

   c.

   d.

4. Which of the following visual options can be selected when running a sight distance analysis on an intersection?

   a. Sight Zones

   b. Accident Zones

   c. Sight Regions

   d. Sight Triangles

Command Summary

Button	Command	Location
	Corridor Optimization	• **In Canvas Tools:** Design, review, and engineer roads>Perform Analysis in preparation for road designs
	Job Monitor	• **In Canvas Tools:** Design, review, and engineer roads>Review and modify roadway designs
	Profile Optimization	• **In Canvas Tools:** Design, review, and engineer roads>Review and modify roadway designs
	Sight Distance	• **In Canvas Tools:** Design, review, and engineer roads>Review and modify roadway designs
	Traffic Simulation	• **In Canvas Tools:** Design, review, and engineer roads>Perform Analysis in preparation for road designs

Introduction to the Bridge Design for InfraWorks 360 Module

The Autodesk Bridge Design for InfraWorks 360 module is a cloud-based add-on that enables you to add bridges to design roads. The rule-based tool sets enable you to quickly lay out bridges. During the creation process, you can instantly visualize the designed bridge in context with its surroundings.

Learning Objectives in this Chapter

- Describe many of the bridge components that are inserted when a bridge is added to a design road.
- Add bridges to a design road over waterways, railways, or other roadways.
- Edit bridges using gizmos and bridge asset cards.
- Analyze the Bridge Line Girders for Structural Strength.
- Send design bridges to other software for the detailed design phase.

Enhanced 🔍

11.1 Bridge Components

The Autodesk Bridge Design for InfraWorks 360 module enables you to add bridge structures to any design road. Bridges can be used where overpasses are required, where the road crosses a river or ravine, or where the road intersects a railway that you do not want interfering with traffic. Bridges are very complex structures that contain multiple sub-components. Figure 11–1 illustrates many of these components. In addition to the components listed below, parametric bridge components can also be added in the style palette.

Figure 11–1

The bridge deck is used to select the bridge in order to make changes to it. All other components are controlled using the bridge style, or specific component gizmos. Before you can add a bridge to the model, you must have a design road.

Hint: Automatic Bridge Creation

If you have a license for the Bridge Design for InfraWorks 360 module, before you start creating design roadways, bridges are created automatically if the design road crosses a water feature.

How To: Add a Bridge to a Design Road

1. In the model, draw a design road.

2. In the In Canvas tools, click ![icon] (Design, review and engineer bridges)>![icon] (Design bridges).

3. In the expanded tool group, click the ![icon] (Precast | Girder Bridge) or ![icon] (Steel Plate Girder Bridge) for the type of bridge you want to create, as shown in Figure 11–2.

Figure 11–2

4. In the model, click on the design road at the station where you want to start the bridge. Alternatively, you can type the starting station and press <Enter>.

5. In the model, click on the design road at the station where you want the bridge to end. Alternatively, you can press <Tab> and type the bridge length, or you can press <Tab> twice to type the ending station, then press <Enter>, as shown in Figure 11–3.

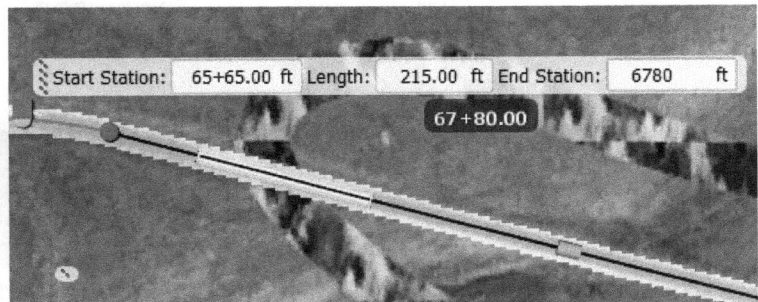

Figure 11–3

11.2 Modify Bridges

Once a bridge has been created, it can be modified using the Bridge asset card, gizmos, properties, and the Style palette.

Bridge Asset Card

The Bridge asset card is referred to as "Bridge asset card" when the bridge deck is selected. When the anything else on the bridge is selected, it is referred to as the "(Selected Component) stack".

The Bridge asset card enables you to change the type of bridge being modeled, the number of piers used to support the bridge, the clearance below the bridge, or the deck and bearing attributes, as shown in Figure 11–4.

Figure 11–4

Bridge Clearance

To ensure that the bridge has the correct clearance for traffic below it, the clearance envelope can be displayed in the model. The clearance envelope is a purple box that indicates the clearance height required for the bridge. The **Show clearance envelope** option is found in the Bridge asset card, as shown in Figure 11–5.

Figure 11–5

Once the **Show clearance envelope** option is turned on, all of the values within the *Clearance* area can be modified. Changing the *Height* value changes the height of the clearance envelope only. To change the height of the bridge, you must right-click on the bridge deck in the model and select **Update Vertical Profile**, as shown in Figure 11–6. This causes the profile of the road to adjust to accommodate the clearance envelope.

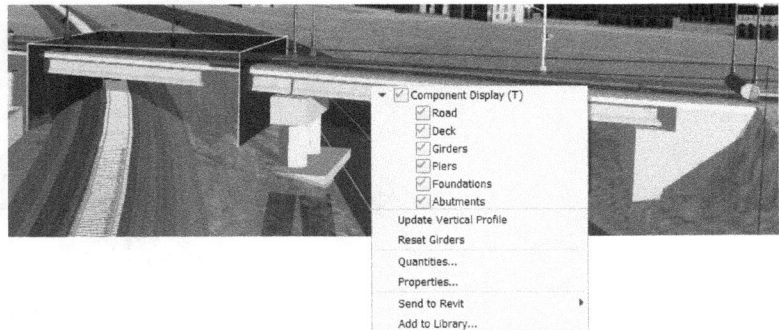

Figure 11–6

Bridge Gizmos

When the bridge deck is selected, gizmos display at the beginning and ending stations of the bridge. Selecting either gizmo enables you to change the station for that specific gizmo, as shown in Figure 11–7.

Figure 11–7

If both the beginning and ending stations require changing, the space between the two gizmos can be selected. This enables you to change both stations at the same time, as shown in Figure 11–8.

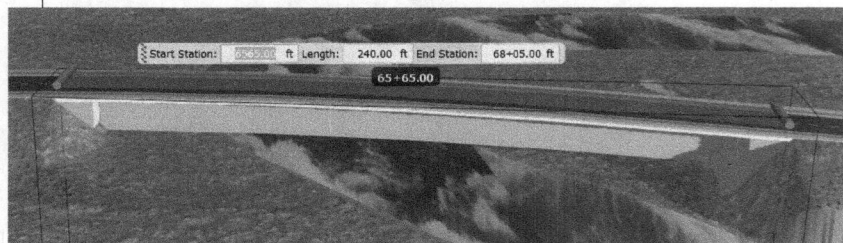

Figure 11–8

Selecting a pier causes a control gizmo to display. Clicking ▪ (Control Gizmo) for the pier enables you to change the location of the pier. Additionally, you can rotate each pier with the ◠ (Rotate Gizmo), as shown in Figure 11–9.

Figure 11–9

Bridge Properties

Properties for each component of a bridge can be modified using the component stack (asset card). Select the bridge component that needs to be modified to display its stack. Different properties are available depending upon which component of the bridge is selected in the model, as shown in Figure 11–10.

Bridge		
Bridge 1		
Road 6 > Bridge 1		
Type		^
Road style		
Bridge type		Precast I ▼
Select assembly...		
Attributes		^
Design standard		AASHTO LRFD ▼
Number of piers		0
Bearings		^
Left offset		0.0'
Right offset		0.0'
Spacing		0.0'
Round bearings		
Height		0.33'
Width		1.31'
Depth		1.31'
Sole plate height		0.13'
Sole plate width		1.64'
Sole plate depth 1		0.82'
Sole plate depth 2		0.82'
Masonry plate height		0.13'
Masonry plate width		1.64'
Masonry plate depth 1		0.82'
Masonry plate depth 2		0.82'
Clearance Envelope		^

Bridge Deck stack

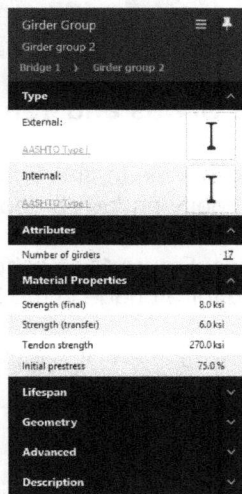

Girder Group		
Girder group 2		
Bridge 1 > Girder group 2		
Type		^
External:		
AASHTO Type I		
Internal:		
AASHTO Type I		
Attributes		^
Number of girders		17
Material Properties		^
Strength (final)		8.0 ksi
Strength (transfer)		6.0 ksi
Tendon strength		270.0 ksi
Initial prestress		75.0 %
Lifespan		∨
Geometry		∨
Advanced		∨
Description		∨

Girder Group stack

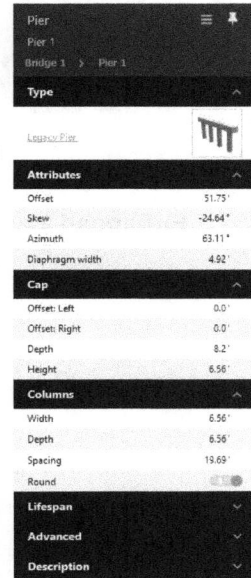

Pier		
Pier 1		
Bridge 1 > Pier 1		
Type		^
Legacy Pier		
Attributes		^
Offset		51.75'
Skew		-24.64°
Azimuth		63.11°
Diaphragm width		4.92'
Cap		^
Offset: Left		0.0'
Offset: Right		0.0'
Depth		8.2'
Height		6.56'
Columns		^
Width		6.56'
Depth		6.56'
Spacing		19.69'
Round		
Lifespan		∨
Advanced		∨
Description		∨

Pier stack

Figure 11–10

Style Palette

As with any other Autodesk InfraWorks 360 object, the style of a bridge can be modified by dragging a different style onto the object from the Style palette>*Road* tab>Bridge Deck catalog, as shown in Figure 11–11.

Figure 11–11

Enhanced

Bridge Styles and Templates

In the Style Palette, the *Bridge* and *Bridge Template* tabs enable you to modify bridge components. The *Bridge Template* tab houses different parametric parts for bridges that follow specific standards. Figure 11–12 shows some of the settings that can be modified for a bridge in the Bridge Style dialog box.

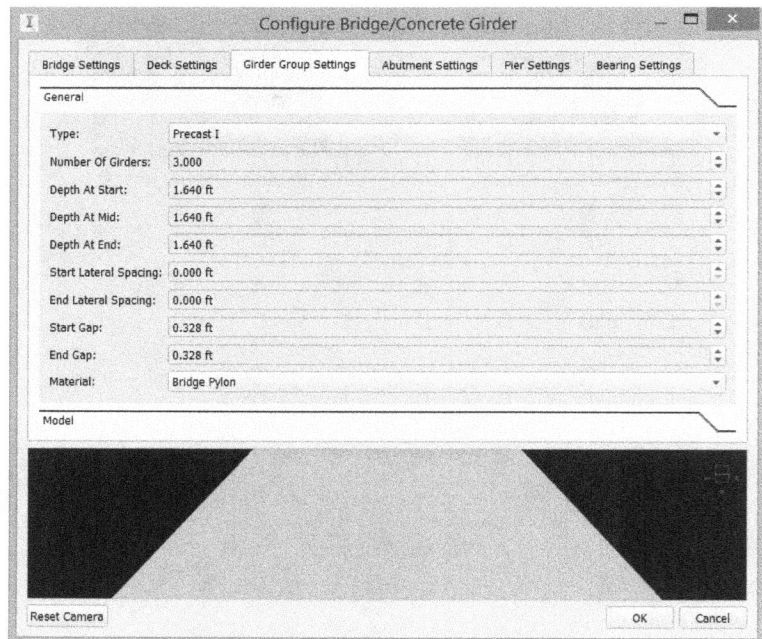

Figure 11–12

In addition to the bridge styles, it might be necessary to modify the road style. The road style determines the lane striping, road decorations, and number of lanes for the bridge. There are several road styles that are specific to bridge applications, as shown in Figure 11–13.

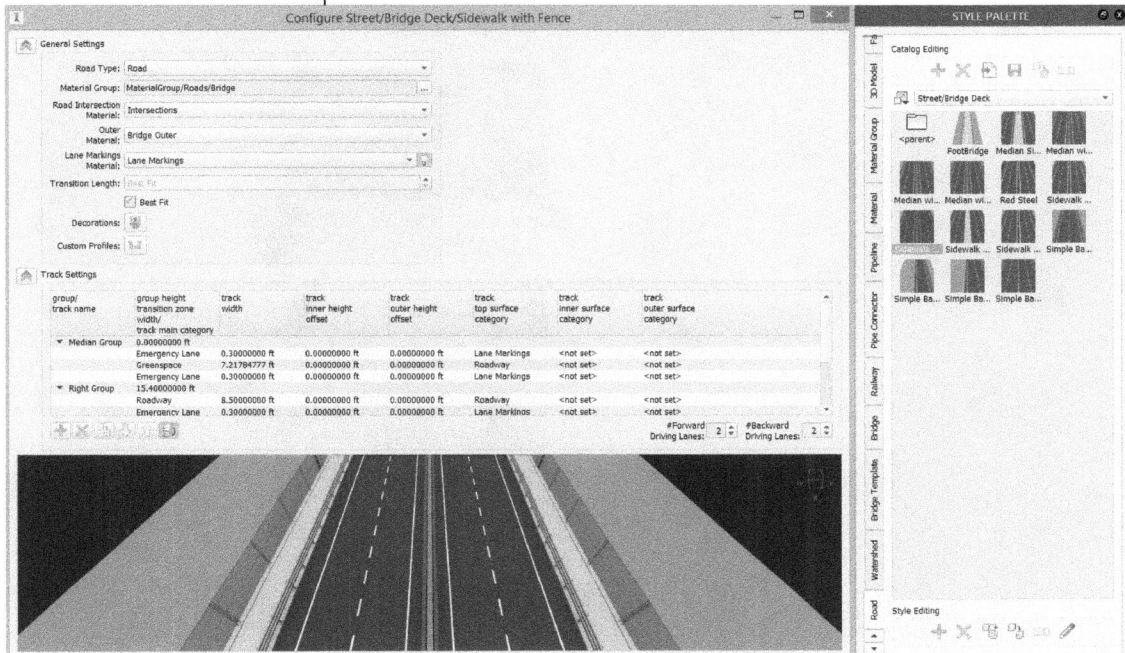

Figure 11–13

How To: Modify the Number of Bridge Piers Using the Bridge Asset Card

1. In the model, select the design bridge deck. The Bridge asset card displays.
2. In the Bridge asset card, change *Number of piers*, as shown in Figure 11–14.

Figure 11–14

3. Press <Esc> to clear the bridge selection.

How To: Modify the Bridge Using Gizmos

1. In the model, select the design bridge deck, and then click on the bridge beginning or ending station gizmo.
2. Drag the bridge gizmo to a new location to change the length of the bridge. Alternatively, you can type a new station value for the beginning or ending station and press <Enter>, as shown in Figure 11–15.

Figure 11–15

3. Press <Esc> to clear the bridge selection.

Practice 11a

Work with Bridges

Practice Objectives

Estimated time for completion: 10 minutes

- Add a bridge to the design road to provide passage over the river.
- Modify the design bridge to change the starting and ending stations and number of piers.

In this practice, you will add a bridge to the design road where the road crosses the white water river as shown in Figure 11–16. This river is part of the development, and the road provides access for rafters and kayakers to the future parking area near the take out point.

Figure 11–16

Task 1 - Create a design bridge.

1. In the Home Screen, click ▦ (Open).

2. In the *C:\InfraWorks Fundamentals Practice Files\Bridges* folder, select **DesignBridges.sqlite** and click **Open**.

3. In the Utility Bar, click ▥ (Bookmark your current location) and select **DesignBridge**. Also ensure that **A_Task1** is the current proposal.

4. In the In Canvas tools, click ▦ (Design, review and engineer bridges)> ✎ (Design bridges)> ▨ (Precast Girder Bridge).

5. In the model, click on the design road that crosses the white water river and connects to the pedestrian fishing pier (Road 6).

6. In the *Start Station* field, type **1420**. Press <Tab> twice, and in the *Length* field, type **210**, as shown in Figure 11–17. Press <Enter>

Figure 11–17

7. In the Select Road Style dialog box, click **Sidewalk with fence**, as shown in Figure 11–18. Click **OK**.

If the Select Road Style dialog box does not display, in the Bridge asset card, click the Road style under the Type area.

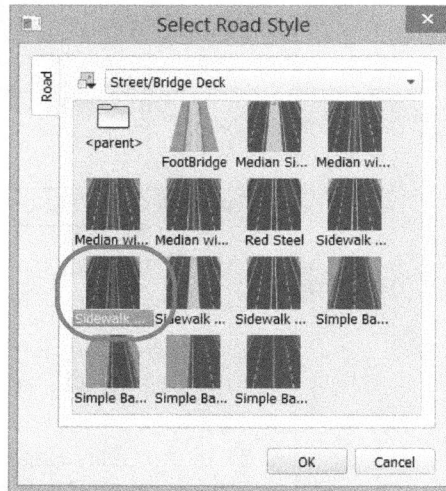

Figure 11–18

8. Press <Esc> to clear the selection of the bridge.

Note that it is unlikely that a 2 lane road would become a 4 lane road just over a bridge. In a real workflow, you would go into the bridge style and modify the number of lanes. If you have time, and want a challenge exercise, make the necessary changes in the bridge style.

Task 2 - Modify the bridge to remove the pier.

In this task, you will modify the bridge using the Bridge asset card to remove the pier.

The first time you click on the bridge, the road asset card displays.

1. Continue working in the same model as the last task. If you did not complete the last task, in the Utility Bar, expand *Switch Active Proposal* and select **A_Task2** to make it current.

2. In the Utility Bar, click ▢ (Bookmark your current location) and select **DesignBridge**.

3. In the model, click slowly twice on the design bridge deck to display the Bridge asset card.

4. In the Bridge asset card, change the *Number of piers* to **0**, as shown in Figure 11–19.

Figure 11–19

5. Press <Esc> to release the bridge selection.

11.3 Bridge Line Girder Analysis

Girders

Girders can be edited individually or in groups (interior and exterior). Autodesk InfraWorks 360 contains multiple precast girder styles. You can assign different girder styles to each girder in a bridge, or assign styles to a group of girders.

- Clicking on a bridge once selects the road and displays the Design Road asset card.

- Clicking on a bridge twice selects the bridge and displays the Bridge asset card.

- Clicking on a bridge a third time selects a bridge girder group and displays the Girder Group stack.

- Clicking on a specific girder displays the Girder stack.

The Girder Group stack and the Girder stack are shown in Figure 11–20.

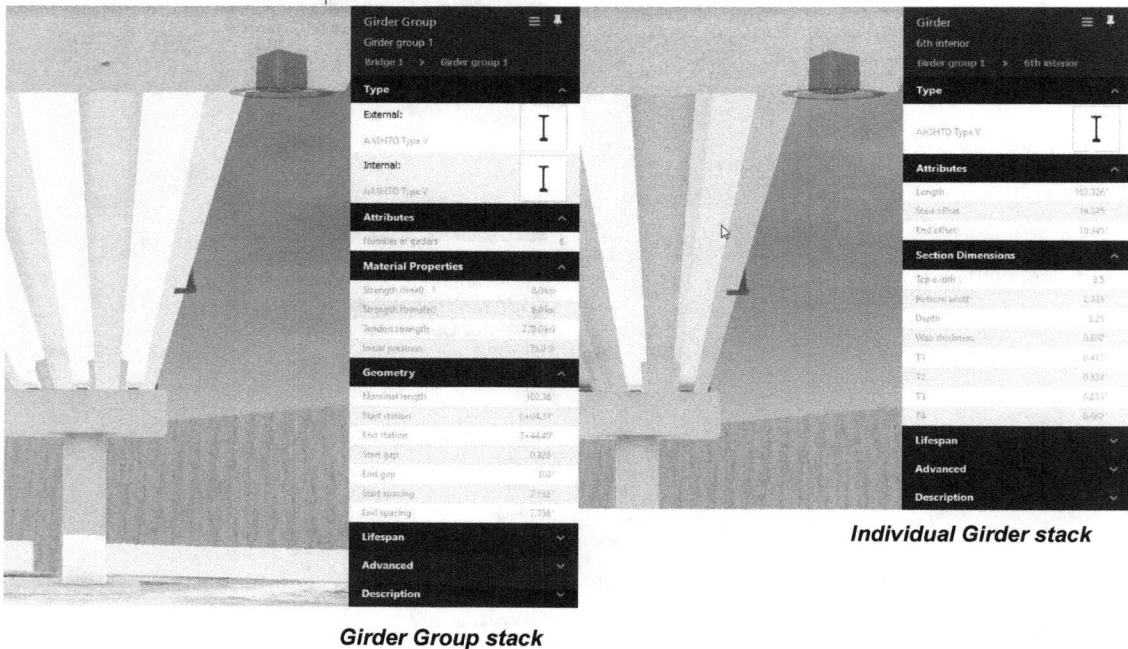

Girder Group stack

Individual Girder stack

Figure 11–20

In the Girder stack, in the *Type* area, when you click inside the girder image, a girder schematic palette displays, as shown in Figure 11–21.

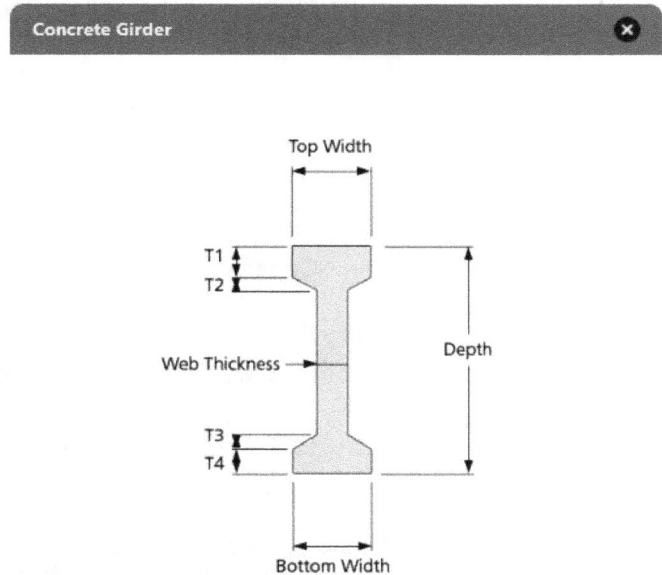

Figure 11–21

Girder Analysis

AUTODESK
INFRAWORKS 360

To use this feature, access to the Internet and Autodesk® InfraWorks® 360 are required.

The structural strength of pre-stressed concrete bridge girders can be verified using the Autodesk InfraWorks 360 cloud service. Initial results can be viewed in the model. A full girder design document can be purchased using cloud credits. The design optimization is computed using the Autodesk Structural Bridge Design.

Project Information

Information provided during the analysis displays in the final *.PDF report. By completing as much information as possible, others reading the report can identify the project it belongs to and the company that created the report. The following information can be added to the report, as shown in Figure 11–22:

- Job name

- Job number

- Project name

- Company name

- Address

- Logo file

- User name

- User initials

Figure 11–22

Once an analysis is complete, selecting any girder displays the results of the analysis in the Line Girder Analysis stack, as shown in Figure 11–23.

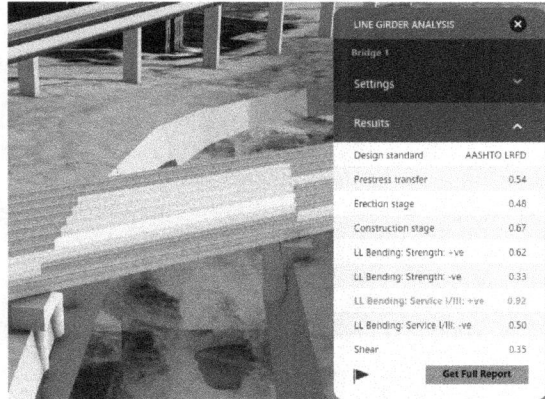

Figure 11–23

Additional analysis information can be viewed by clicking **Get Full Report**. A sample report is shown in Figure 11–24.

Figure 11–24

AUTODESK
INFRAWORKS 360

To use this feature, access to the Internet and Autodesk® InfraWorks® 360 are required.

How To: Run a Bridge Line Girder Analysis

1. In the model, select the bridge you want to analyze.

2. In the in Canvas Tools, click ▦ (Design, review and engineer bridges) > ▦ (Perform analysis on your bridge design) > ▦ (Line Girder Analysis).

3. In the Line Girder Analysis stack, enter the *Job name* and *Job number*.

4. In the Line Girder Analysis stack, click **Project Information**.

5. In the Project Information asset card, enter all of the available project information. Close the card.

6. In the Line Girder Analysis stack, enter a *Permissible Factor*. This factor is applied to the permissible values during the tendon design.

7. Check or clear **Reverse bending plot**.

   - This affects the graphic representations that are received in the detailed girder documentation (full report). It changes the direction of bending moments but not the direction of torsion moments.

8. Check or clear **Consider harped tendons**. This sets whether harping is considered in the tendon design.

9. Click **Start Analysis.**

10. Once complete, select a girder to view the results in the Line Girder Analysis stack.

11. Click **Get Full Report** to view the full PDF report.

Cloud credits might be charged when you get the full report.

Practice 11b

Estimated time for completion: 10 minutes

AUTODESK
INFRAWORKS™ 360

To complete this practice, access to the Internet and Autodesk® InfraWorks® 360 are required.

Run a Girder Analysis

Practice Objective

- Analyze the bridge girders for structural strength.

In this practice, you will analyze the bridge girders for structural strength.

Task 1 - Analyze a design bridge.

1. Continue working in the same model as the previous practice. If you did not complete the previous practice, in the Utility Bar, expand *Switch Active Proposal* and select **B_Task1** to make it current.

2. In the Utility Bar, click 🔲 (Bookmark your current location) and select **DesignBridge**.

3. In the model, select the design bridge. Right-click and expand *Component Display (T)*. Clear the selection of **Road** and **Deck** (as shown in Figure 11–25) to make it easier to see the girders.

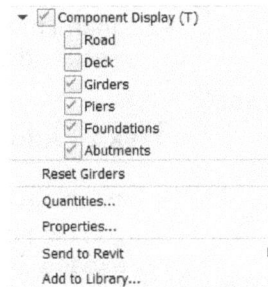

Figure 11–25

4. In the In Canvas tools, click ⬚ (Design, review and engineer bridges) > 🔲 (Perform analysis on your bridge design) > 🔲 (Line Girder Analysis).

5. In the Line Girder Analysis stack, set the following:
   - *Job name*: **Utah County Development**
   - *Job number*: **2015720**

6. In the Line Girder Analysis stack, click **Project Information**.

If this information is already filled in, it is because the last person to use your computer already filled it in. The information remains on the system for convenience.

Once you start the analysis, it will take some time to process.

7. Enter the following information in the Project Information asset card:
   - *Project name*: **White Water Park**
   - *Company name*: **ASCENT**
   - *Address*: **630 Peter Jefferson Parkway, Suite 175, Charlottesville, VA 22911**
   - *User name*: Enter your name
   - *User initials*: Enter your initials
   - Close the Project Information asset card

8. In the Line Girder Analysis stack, leave all other settings as they are and click **Start Analysis**.

When the analysis is complete, it should return **4 Girders analyzed, 0 Girders satisfy design requirements**.

9. Press <Esc> to clear the selection of the bridge.

Hint: Analysis Time Requirements

If the analysis is taking too long, you can open the next proposal to see the results.

1. In the Utility Bar, expand *Switch Active Proposal* and select **B_Task2** to make it current.

2. In the model, click on the bridge twice to select it. The results display in the Line Girder Analysis stack.

Task 2 - Add a pier and rerun the girder analysis.

1. Continue working in the same model as the previous task. If you did not complete the previous practice, in the Utility Bar, expand *Switch Active Proposal* and select **B_Task2** to make it current.

2. In the Utility Bar, click 🔲 (Bookmark your current location) and select **DesignBridge**.

3. In the model, click twice on the bridge to select it.

4. In the model, click the start and end gizmos and change the starting station to **1450** and the ending station to **1600**.

5. In the Bridge asset card, set the number of piers to **2**.

6. In the model, select each pier and rotate it so that it is parallel to the river banks. Then move them as required to place them at the water's edge, as shown in Figure 11–26.

Figure 11–26

7. With the bridge still selected, in the in Canvas Tools, click

   ⊥ (Design, review and engineer bridges) > ▣ (Perform

   analysis on your bridge design) > ▤ (Line Girder Analysis).

8. In the Line Girder Analysis stack, leave all the settings as they are and click **Start Analysis**.

   When the analysis is complete, it should return **51 Girders analyzed, 45 Girders satisfy design requirements**.

Processing the full report can take as long as 10-15 minutes for this specific project. Other projects might take more or less time depending on complexity and cloud service processing load.

*If you click **Get Full Report**, you might be charged cloud credits. As of the release of this student guide, it listed the charge as **Free**.*

9. In the model, select one of the center girders to display the results in the Line Girder Analysis stack, as shown in Figure 11–27.

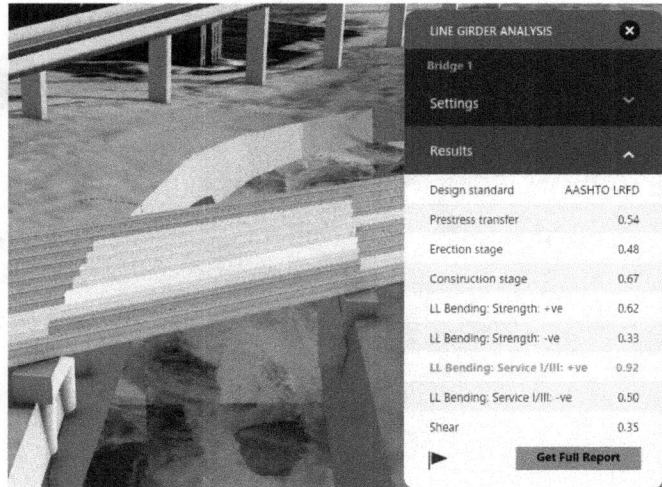

Figure 11–27

Hint: Analysis Time Requirements

If the analysis is taking too long, you can open the next proposal to see the results.

1. In the Utility Bar, expand *Switch Active Proposal* and select **C_Task1** to make it current.

2. In the model, click on the bridge twice to select it. The results display in the Line Girder Analysis stack.

11.4 Detail Design for Bridges

A key benefit to designing the bridge in the InfraWorks 360 software is the ability to view the bridge in the context of its surroundings without losing any time on the design. When you are ready to move the bridge into the detailed design phase, you can move the design quickly into the Autodesk Revit or Autodesk NavisWorks software.

Send a Bridge to Autodesk Revit

The Autodesk Revit software provides many more tools for designing bridges than the Autodesk InfraWorks 360 software. Fortunately, you can send the bridge from InfraWorks to Revit with a simple right-click command. When doing so, you have two options on how they are included in the Autodesk Revit software:

- As Revit Families

- As Direct Shape

How To: Send a Bridge to Autodesk Revit

1. In the model, click once to select a design road.
2. Click to select the bridge deck.
3. Right-click on the bridge and select **Send to Revit**, as shown in Figure 11–28.

You must have the Autodesk Revit software installed on the machine to complete this.

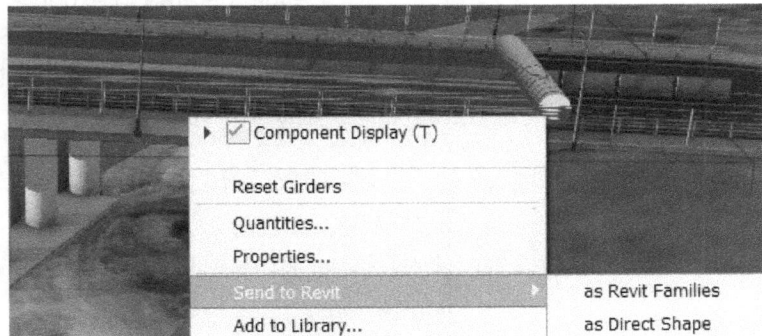

▶ ☑ Component Display (T)	
Reset Girders	
Quantities...	
Properties...	
Send to Revit ▶	as Revit Families
Add to Library...	as Direct Shape

Figure 11–28

When the command is complete, the Autodesk Revit software should open the new *.RVT file.

Open a Bridge in Autodesk NavisWorks

The design can be opened directly in the NavisWorks software to uncover design problems and constructibility issues more effectively and plan the construction sequencing. There are two options when porting an Autodesk InfraWorks model to Autodesk NavisWorks.

- **Option 1:** First, open the bridge in AutoCAD Civil 3D. Then open the DWG file in Navisworks.

- **Option 2:** From Autodesk InfraWorks, export a 3D Model which you can append to the Autodesk NavisWorks file.

If a 3D model is used to move a design into Autodesk NavisWorks, you can export the model as a single file or multiple files. The benefit of using multiple files is that you can select which features in the model to export.

How To: Export an Autodesk InfraWorks Model to Autodesk NavisWorks

1. In the In Canvas Tools, click ![icon] (Settings and Utilities)> ![icon] (Export 3D Model).
2. In the Export to 3D Model File dialog box, do the following, as shown in Figure 11–29:
   - Define the area to export.
   - Set the Target Coordinate System.
   - Determine if you want a single or multiple files.
   - Click Export.

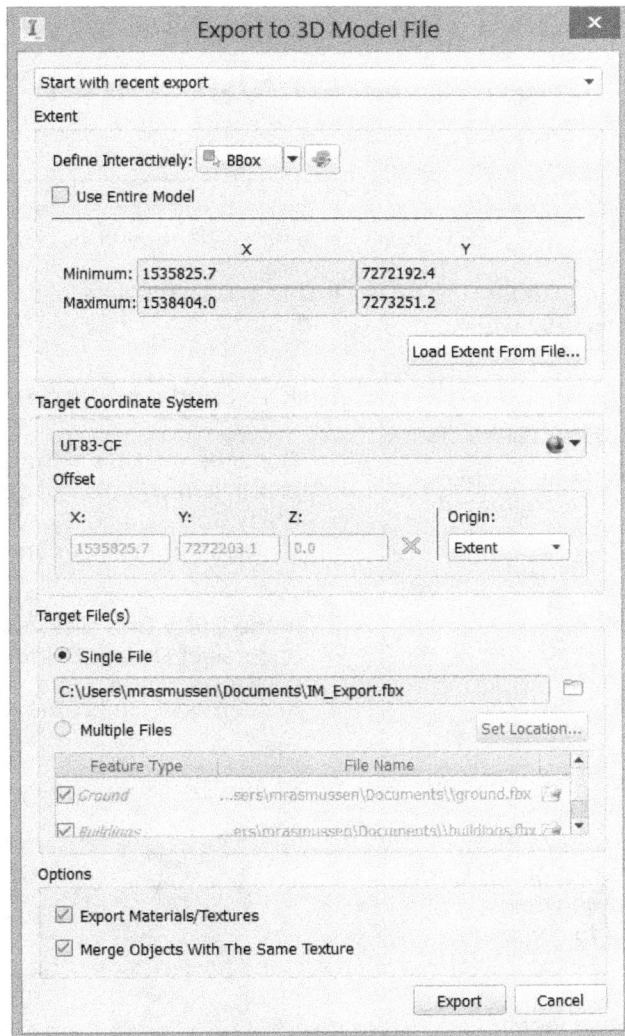

Figure 11–29

Practice 11c

Send the Bridge to the Detailed Design Phase

Practice Objectives

- Send a bridge to the Autodesk Revit software for the detailed design.
- Create a 3D model of the bridge for the Autodesk NavisWorks software.

In this practice, you will analyze the bridge girders for structural strength.

Estimated time for completion: 5 minutes

AUTODESK® INFRAWORKS™ 360

To complete this practice, access to the Internet and Autodesk® Revit® software are required.

Task 1 - Send a bridge to Autodesk Revit.

1. Continue working in the same model as the previous practice. If you did not complete the previous practice, in the Utility Bar, expand *Switch Active Proposal* and select **C_Task1** to make it current.

2. In the Utility Bar, click 🔲 (Bookmark your current location) and select **DesignBridge**.

3. In the model, select the design bridge.

4. Right-click on the bridge and select **Send to Revit>As Direct Shape**, as shown in Figure 11–30.

You must have the Autodesk Revit software installed on your machine to complete this step.

Note: Even though the deck was toggled off, the deck is included in the export.

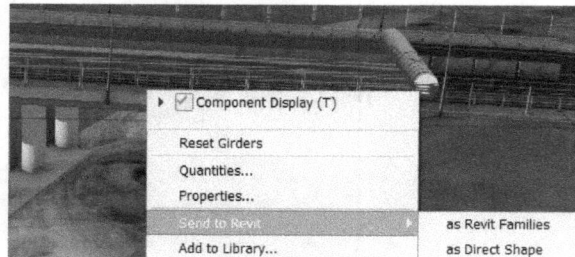

Figure 11–30

Task 2 - Send a Bridge to Autodesk NavisWorks.

1. In the In Canvas Tools, click ⚒ (Settings and Utilities)> 🖼 (Export 3D Model).

2. Next to *Define Interactively*, select **BBox**. Define the bounding box as shown in Figure 11–31.

Figure 11–31

3. Ensure that the Target Coordinate System is set to **UT83-CF,** as shown in Figure 11–32:

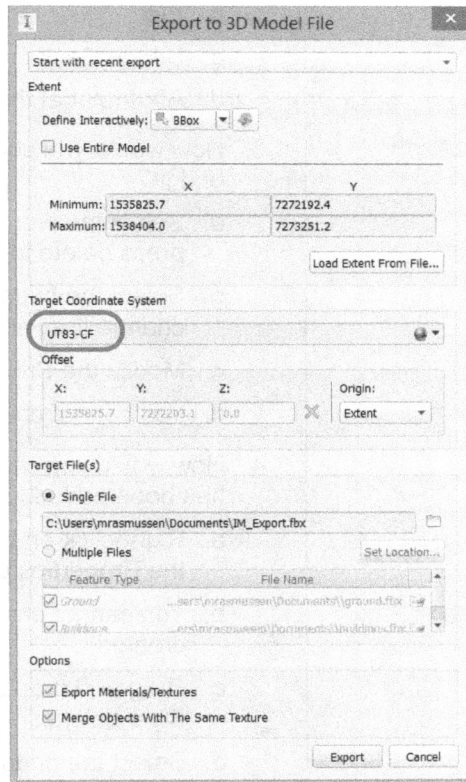

Figure 11–32

4. Ensure that *Target Files* is set to **Single**. Set the file path to *C:\InfraWorks Fundamentals Practice Files\Bridges\.*

5. Now the file can be imported into the Autodesk Navisworks or the Autodesk 3ds Max software. Click **Export**.

Chapter Review Questions

1. What key component do you need in the model before you can create a bridge?

   a. Design Roadway

   b. River

   c. Railway

   d. None of the above

2. What bridge component do you select in the model in order to change to the bridge beginning station?

   a. Girder

   b. Pier

   c. Bridge Deck

   d. Abutment at the beginning of the bridge

3. How would you change the number of piers that support the bridge?

   a. Select the pier and make copies to add more piers or press delete to remove piers

   b. Select the bridge deck and in the Bridge asset card, change the value in the Number of piers field.

   c. Modify the Bridge style in the Styles palette.

   d. You cannot change the number of piers.

4. How would you change the type of bridge in the model once it has been added to a design road? (Select all that apply.)

   a. Right-click on the bridge deck and select Properties. In the Properties palette, change the manual style.

   b. You cannot change the bridge type once it has been created.

   c. Drag and drop a different style from the *Bridge* tab of the Style palette.

   d. Select the bridge deck. In the Bridge asset card, change the value in the *Bridge Type* field.

5. What type of bridge girders can you run a Line Girder Analysis on?

   a. Concrete

   b. Steel

6. When you run a Line Girder Analysis, it costs cloud credits every time you make an adjustment and preview the results in the model.

   a. True

   b. False

Command Summary

Button	Command	Location
	Export 3D Model	• **In Canvas Tools: Settings and Utilities**
	Line Girder Analysis	• **In Canvas Tools: Design, review and engineer bridges > Perform analysis on your bridge design**
	Precast | Girder Bridge	• **In Canvas Tools:** Design, review, and engineer bridges > Design bridges
	Steel Plate Girder Bridge	• **In Canvas Tools:** Design, review, and engineer bridges > Design bridges

Introduction to the Drainage Design for InfraWorks 360 Module

The Drainage Design for InfraWorks 360 module is a cloud-based add-on that enables you to add drainage features to design roads. The rule-based tool sets enable you to quickly lay out a drainage network. The four step process enables you to identify and analyze watersheds and their stream flows, create and modify culverts, create pavement drainage networks, and review the quantities of materials for culverts or pavement drainage networks by road, type, and number. Although it does not require the Roadway Design for InfraWorks 360 module, using the two add-on products together provide you with a seamless work flow.

Learning Objectives in this Chapter

- Determine the extents of a watershed area.
- Create and Modify Culverts.
- Design pavement drainage along a design road.
- Calculate quantities for a drainage network.

12.1 Watershed Analysis

Determining the discharge of a stream is important for designing culverts and other structures used to protect transportation systems from being washed away. If you have the Drainage Design for InfraWorks 360 module, you can add drainage networks to the model. Before creating the drainage network, it is important to run a watershed analysis to determine the extents of a watershed area. By running a watershed analysis, the watershed extents and stream locations display in the model. Additionally, pins are placed where the streams cross a design road to indicate that either a culvert or bridge is required.

The analysis identifies the existing drainage patterns prior to road placement and design. Therefore, it uses the original terrain surface that was in the model before any design roads were created. A single analysis can identify multiple watersheds, each of which is a selectable feature. During the analysis process, square grids of terrain are sampled. The grid spacing and stream threshold can each be adjusted in the Create Watershed asset card, as shown in Figure 12–1. Lowering the values finds smaller streams, but also requires more analysis. Raising the value finds larger streams and reduces the analysis.

- **Grid Spacing:** Controls the size of the square grids sampled for the terrain.

- **Stream Threshold:** Sets the number of grid cells used to define streams. For example, a stream threshold of 50 indicates that a stream is created once there are a minimum of 50 upstream grid squares flowing into a stream's starting point.

Running a watershed analysis requires cloud credits because the calculations are done in the cloud.

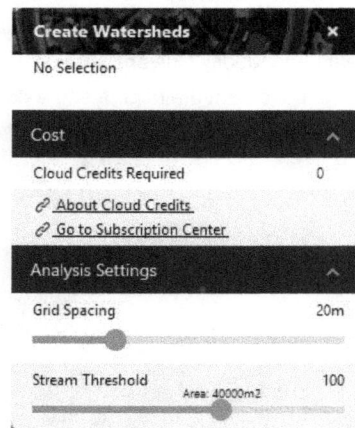

Figure 12–1

Modify Peak Flows

Once a watershed is created, selecting it opens the Watershed asset card. Within the Watershed asset card, the peak flows can only be modified if *Hydrology Method* is set to **User Defined**. However, two other methods are available which cause the *Peak Flows fields to calculate automatically*, as shown in Figure 12–2:

- **Regression** analysis is available for select areas. It enables you to set the state and region.

- **Rational** analysis enables you to enter a *Runoff Coefficient* and a *Rainfall Intensity* for 100 year storms.

Figure 12–2

How To: Run a Watershed Analysis to a Design Road

1. In the In Canvas tools, click ⬤ (Design, review and engineer drainage)> ✎ (Design drainage).

2. In the expanded tool group, click ⬔ (Create Watersheds). In the model, all of the design roads are highlighted, as shown in Figure 12–3.

Select a design road

Figure 12–3

3. Select how you want to calculate the watershed:

To calculate a watershed...	Start the analysis by...
Upstream from a point	Double-clicking on a point in a valley or low-lying area.
Along a design road	Select a design road and press <Enter>. The watershed is calculated upstream from the selected road.
Along a region of a design road	Selecting a design road, clicking to select the start and end points of the region, and then pressing <Enter>. The watershed is calculated upstream from the selected road.

4. In the Create Watershed asset card, set the *Grid Spacing* and the *Stream Threshold* sliders according to the terrain being analyzed, as shown in Figure 12–4.

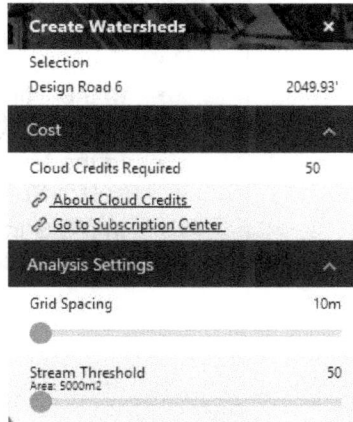

Figure 12–4

5. Once the analysis is complete, the watershed boundary and stream network display in the model. Additionally, a pin should display in the model at the point that a stream crosses the road, as shown in Figure 12–5.

Figure 12–5

6. In the model, select the watershed area.

7. In the Watershed asset card, do the following:
   - Set the *Hydrology Method*.
   - Set additional field values according to the Hydrology Method selected.

8. Press <Esc> to clear the selection of the watershed area.

9. To control the watershed area display, do the following, as shown in Figure 12–6:

- In the Utility Bar, click ▣(Control, display, and selectability of features).
- In the Model Explorer, right-click on *Surface Layers* and select **Surface Layers**.
- In the Surface Layers palette, click ♀/♀.(Show/Hide data source contents).

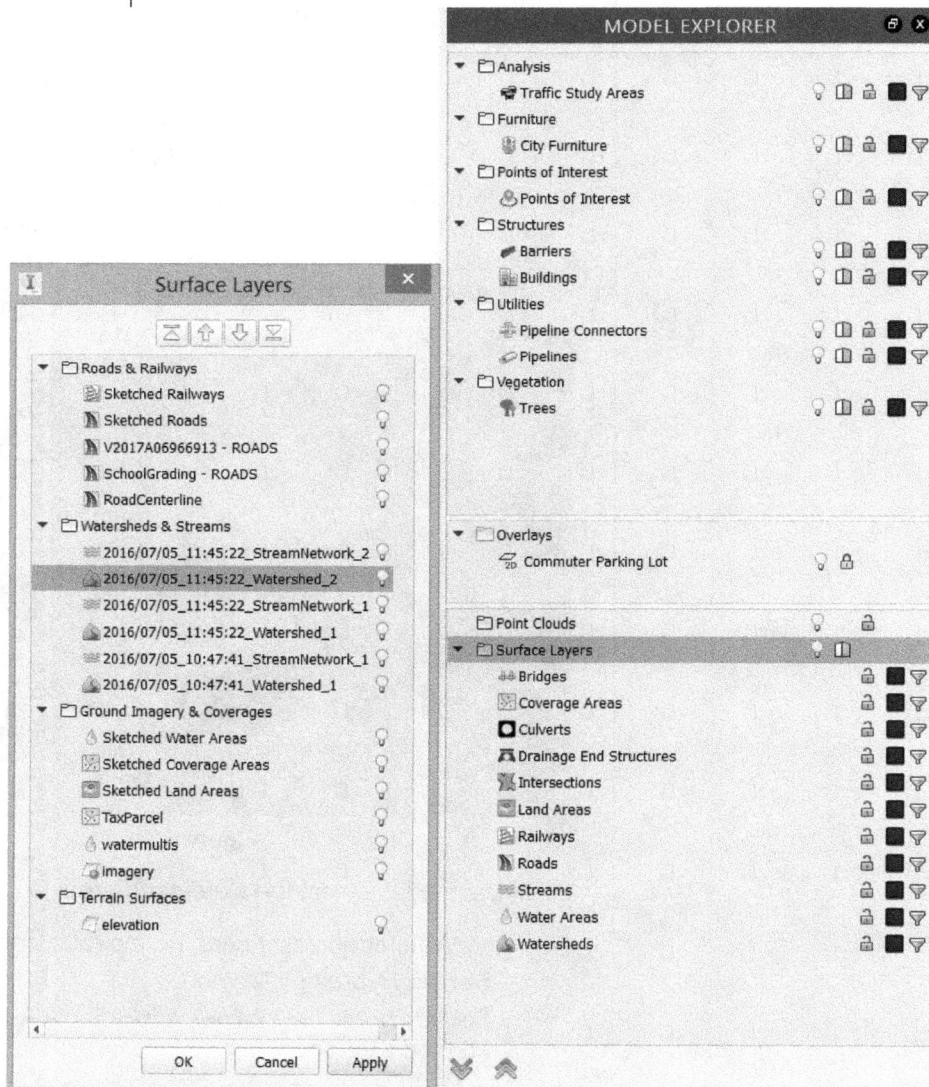

Figure 12–6

Practice 12a

Create a Watershed

Estimated time for completion: 5 minutes

AUTODESK® INFRAWORKS™ 360

To use this feature, access to the Internet and Autodesk® InfraWorks® 360 and cloud credits are required.

Practice Objective

- Create a watershed upstream from a design road.

In this practice, you will create a watershed, as shown in Figure 12–7.

Figure 12–7

Task 1 - Create a watershed for a design road.

1. In the Home Screen, click **Open**.

2. In the *C:\InfraWorks Fundamentals Practice Files\DrainageDesign* folder, select **DrainageDesign.sqlite** and click **Open**.

3. In the Utility Bar, click ⬚ (Bookmark your current location) and select **River**. Ensure that **A_Task1** is the current proposal.

4. In the In Canvas tools, click ◉ (Design, review and engineer drainage)> ✏ (Design drainage)> ⬔ (Create Watersheds).

5. In the message that displays, click **OK**.

6. The design roads are highlighted in the model.Select the design road with a bridge (Road 6). Then select the section shown in Figure 12–8.

Figure 12–8

7. In the Create Watershed asset card, set the *Grid Spacing* to **10** and the *Stream Threshold* to **50**, as shown in Figure 12–9.

Figure 12–9

The analysis costs 50 cloud credits.

8. Press <Enter> to analyze the bridge section of road.

9. In the message that displays, click **OK**.

10. In the model, select the watershed area.

11. In the Watershed asset card, set the following options, as shown in Figure 12–10:
- *Hydrology Method*: **Regression**
- *State*: **Utah**
- *Region:* **Region 3**

Figure 12–10

12. Press <Esc> to clear the selection of the watershed area.

12.2 Create and Modify Culverts

Add Culverts Automatically

Once a watershed analysis has been run, one or more culverts can be added to the model anywhere that streams cross the design road. Once added, the culvert information displays in the model in the form of tooltips, as well as in the Culvert asset card, as shown in Figure 12–11.

Figure 12–11

How To: Add Culverts at Stream Crossings Automatically

1. In the model, run a watershed analysis using the ![icon] (Create Watersheds) tool.
2. In the model, select the design road.
3. Right-click on the design road and select **Drainage>Add Culverts**, as shown in Figure 12–12.

The options that display in the shortcut menu change depending on whether the road is a component road or not.

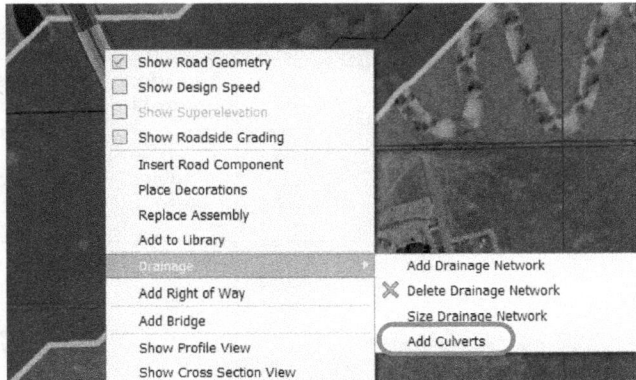

Figure 12–12

4. Culverts display in the model at each of the stream crossing pins that were placed during the watershed analysis. To clear the culvert selection, press <Esc>.

Create Culverts Manually

Culverts can be added automatically or manually. The benefit of adding a culvert manually is that it can be added to more then just design roads.

How To: Create a Culvert Manually

1. In the In Canvas tools, click ![icon] (Design, review and engineer drainage)>![icon] (Design drainage)>![icon] (Culverts).

2. Click two points in the model to place the beginning and ending points for the culvert.

3. Press <Esc> to clear the culvert selection.

Modify a Culvert

Culverts can be modified by gizmos or the Culvert asset card. If the culverts were created automatically using the **Add Culverts** command, then they can be updated automatically as well. If the road style or number of lanes are changed for a design road, the culvert length, slope, and invert elevations change to match the new design.

The gizmos available for editing culverts manually are described in the table below.

Gizmos	Transformation	Description
	Elevation/ Control Point	Stretches culverts horizontally and vertically, changing the elevation or beginning/ending point location.
	Headwall Height	Stretches the headwall height without changing its length or width.
	Move	Moves a culvert without changing its size or shape.
	Rotate	Rotates a culvert around its Z-axis.
	Size	Changes the size of the barrel.

The following features and options of a culvert can be modified using the Culvert asset card, shown in Figure 12–13:

- **Number of Barrels:** 1 or 2
- **Shape:** Box or Circular
- **Material:** Concrete or Corrugate Metal
- **Manning's n**
- **End Treatment:** Headwall Height and Flare Angle
- **Show Analysis results**
- **Tailwater Condition:** (dc+D)/2, Crown, Critical, Normal, or User Defined

Figure 12–13

Practice 12b

Create a Culvert

Estimated time for completion: 5 minutes

Practice Objective

- Create a culvert to a design road.

In this practice, you will create a culvert, as shown in Figure 12–14.

Figure 12–14

Task 1 - Add a culvert to a design road.

1. In the Home Screen, click **Open**.

2. In the *C:\InfraWorks Fundamentals Practice Files\DrainageDesign* folder, select **DrainageDesign.sqlite** and click **Open**.

3. In the Utility Bar, click ▣ (Bookmark your current location) and select **Bridge**. Ensure that **B_Task1** is the current proposal.

4. In the model, select Redwood Rd. Right-click and select **Drainage>Add Culverts**, as shown in Figure 12–15.

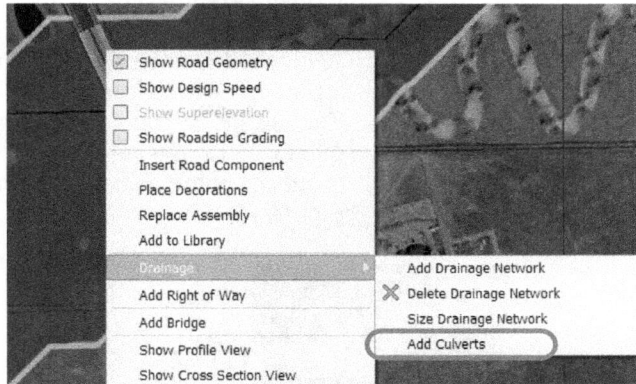

Figure 12–15

5. In the model, select the culvert (you can find it by zooming in on where the black watershed stream crosses Redwood Rd).

6. In the Culvert asset card, set *Barrels* to **2**.

7. In the model, click ⬦ (Control gizmo) to extend the end of the culvert past the sidewalk on each side of the road, as shown in Figure 12–16.

Figure 12–16

8. In the model, click ⤬ (Move in the Z axis gizmo) to move the culvert in the Z direction down 4 feet.

9. To clear the culvert selection, press <Esc>.

12.3 Pavement Drainage

In this course, structure refers to either an inlet or a manhole which is at the end of a pipe in the drainage network.

Industry standard rules and calculations inside the Autodesk Drainage Design module for InfraWorks 360 software provides analysis-driven design for pavement drainage networks. By inputting various coefficients and varying the AEP (Annual Exceedance Probability) setting, you can examine pipe runs in different storm level conditions. The data is displayed in the model or in the drainage structure's asset card, as shown in Figure 12–17.

Visual Inspection of Inlet Performance

Hydraulic Performance of a Pipe

Figure 12–17

General Workflow

The order in which commands are used for setting up the pavement drainage network is important. Certain commands do not work if specific steps are not completed first. For example, you cannot analyze the surface drainage unless you have already sized the pavement drainage. The following steps should be completed in the following order.

1. Create the conceptual design by adding pavement drainage to a design road.
2. Modify the design by moving, adding, and removing pipes and structures, as required.
3. Fine-tune the changes that have been made by sizing pavement drainage.
4. Analyze the surface drainage between inlets to verify performance of pipe runs.

Input Rainfall Quantities

A rainfall editor enables you to customize the rainfall content for a model.

How To: Customize Rainfall Content

1. In the In Canvas tools, click ⬤ (Design, review and engineer drainage)> ▣ (Analyze your model)> 🖾 (Rainfall Content).
2. In the Rainfall Content palette, double-click on any of the existing tables to open it for editing.

    - Alternatively, click ➕ (Add a new empty rainfall content of the current rainfall type) to create a new table.

3. In the Rainfall Editor panel, click in any of the fields that require editing and type in the new values, as shown in Figure 12–18.

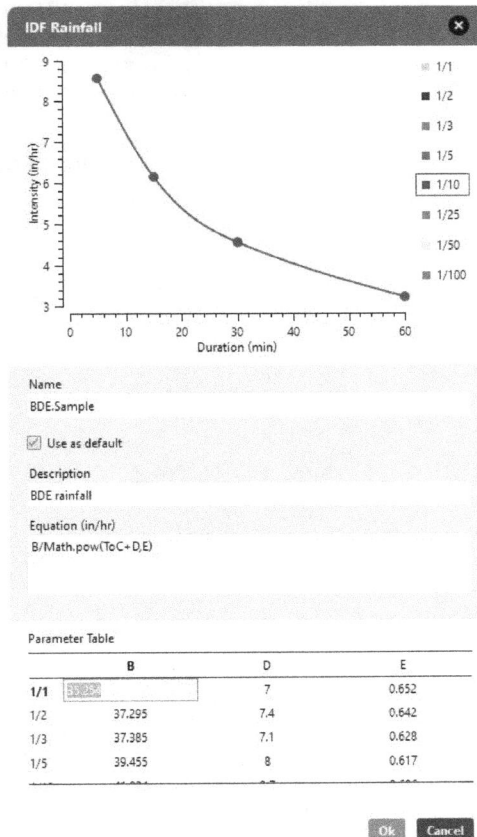

Figure 12–18

Create a Network

A design road must exist before a pavement drainage network can be added to the model. To add a network, simply edit the design road.

How To: Create a Pavement Drainage Network

1. In the model, select a design road.
2. Right-click on the design road and select **Drainage>Add Drainage Network**, as shown in Figure 12–19.

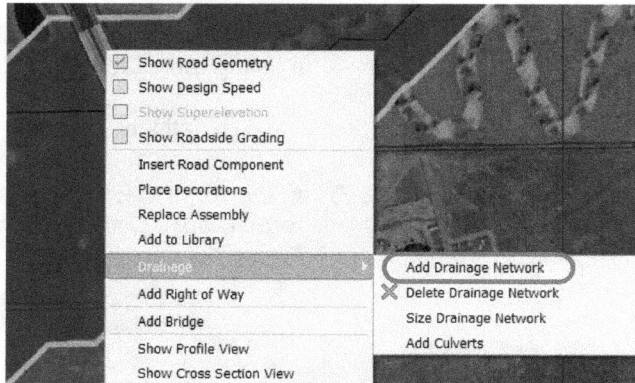

Figure 12–19

3. Press <Enter> to accept the selection and create the drainage.

Modify Drainage Networks

Similar to the other features in the Autodesk InfraWorks 360 software, drainage networks can be modified using gizmos.

Gizmo	Transformation	Description
	Elevation/ Control Point	Displays at each point of intersection along a pipe or at the center of each structure. In a 3D View, it can stretch features horizontally or vertically by changing the elevation of the vertex. In plan view, it becomes a Control Point.
	Rotate	Rotates a feature around the Z-axis.
	Control Point	Displays at each point of intersection of pipes, or center of structure. Stretches pipes by moving the selected vertex of the pipe. Moves the location of structures. Note: Additional control points can be added by holding <Alt> and selecting the new control point location.
	Move	Moves the selected feature or vertex.

When a pipe is selected in the model, the Pipe asset card displays. This asset card enables you to change the material of the pipe, size, and invert elevations, as shown in Figure 12–20. The length and slope are calculated values.

Figure 12–20

When a structure is selected in the model, the appropriate asset card displays, enabling you to change the type and the size of structure, as shown in Figure 12–21. If the *Type* field is selected, the Select Component asset card displays, which enables you to select from a number of predefined structure types.

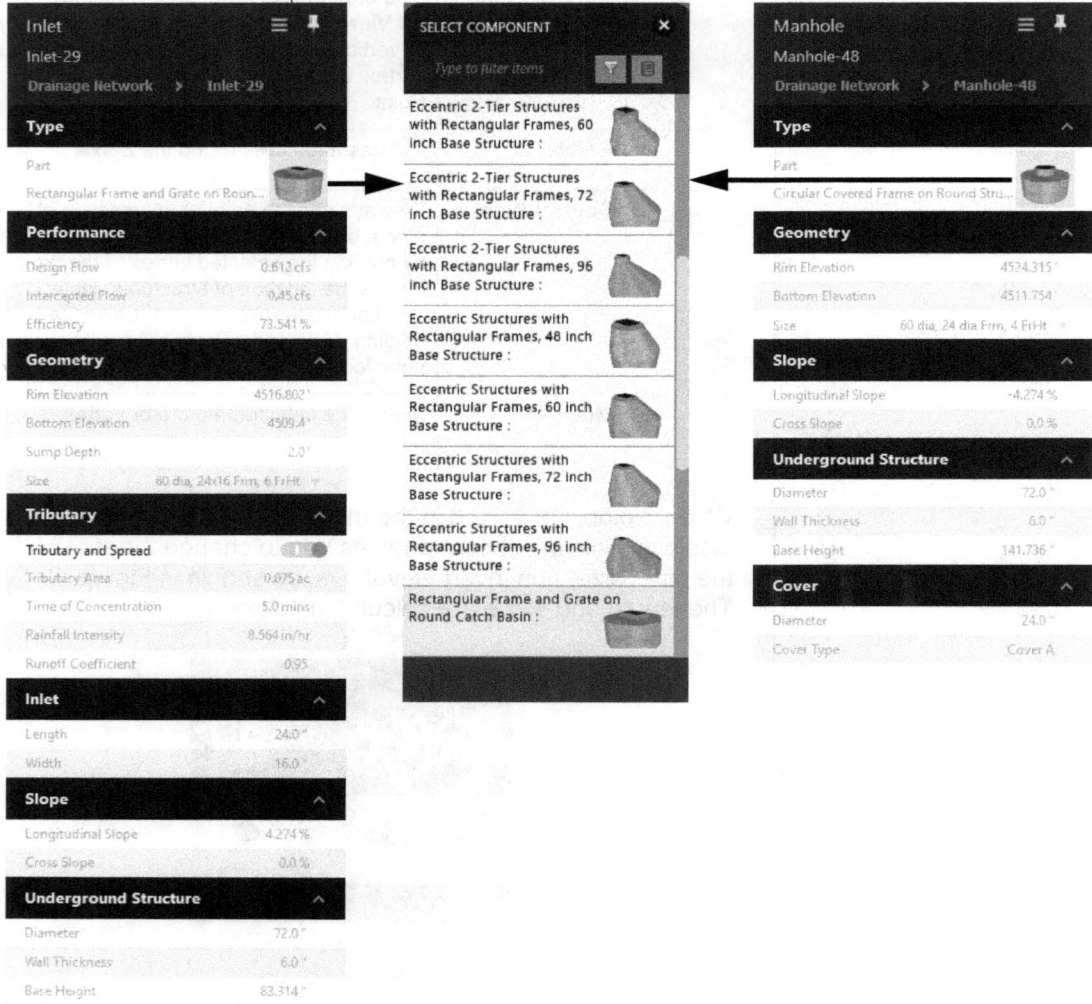

Figure 12–21

Hint: Design Road Changes

If you want to change a design road that already has pavement drainage added to it, do not modify the drainage network. It is best to delete the drainage network and add a new drainage network to any revised design roads.

How To: Add Drainage Features to an Existing Network

1. In the In Canvas tools, click ⬤ (Design, review and engineer drainage)> ✎ (Design drainage)> 🗺 (Drainage Networks).

2. In the Sketch Drainage Network asset card, set the appropriate inlet, manhole, and pipe types, sizes, and other parameters, as shown in Figure 12–22.

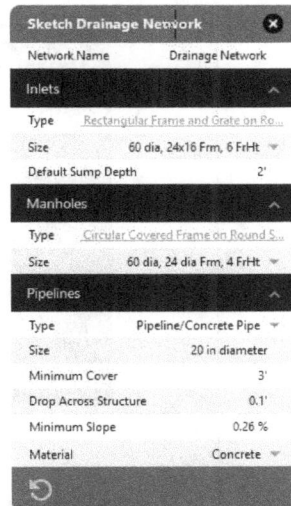

Sketch Drainage Network	✖
Network Name	Drainage Network
Inlets	⌃
Type	Rectangular Frame and Grate on Ro...
Size	60 dia, 24x16 Frm, 6 FrHt ▾
Default Sump Depth	2'
Manholes	⌃
Type	Circular Covered Frame on Round S...
Size	60 dia, 24 dia Frm, 4 FrHt ▾
Pipelines	⌃
Type	Pipeline/Concrete Pipe ▾
Size	20 in diameter
Minimum Cover	3'
Drop Across Structure	0.1'
Minimum Slope	0.26 %
Material	Concrete ▾

Figure 12–22

3. In the model, click to place the features. Right-click to change the feature(s) being placed or to enable the **Show high and low points** option, as shown in Figure 12–23.

Figure 12–23

4. Double-click to place the last feature or right-click and select **End Run**.

Size Pavement Drainage

After moving structures or adding your own structures to a design, it is necessary to fine-tune the placement and sizing of the structures. You can do this by running the **Size Pavement Drainage** command. This recalculates the pipe diameters, adjusts pipe slopes, and resizes connectors as required to accommodate any changes.

How To: Size Pavement Drainage

1. In the model, select the design road.
2. Right-click and select **Drainage>Size Drainage Network**, as shown in Figure 12–24.

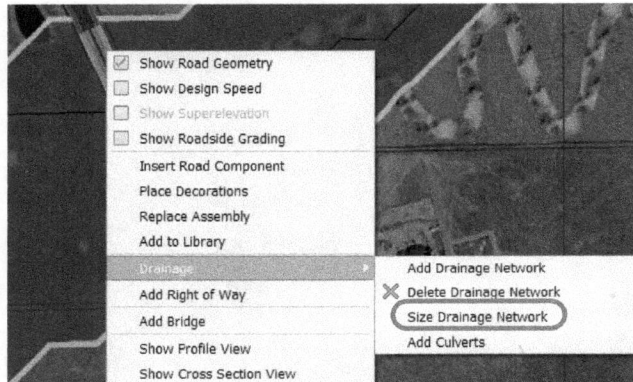

Figure 12–24

Analyze Pavement Drainage

Visual Inspection of Inlet Performance

Inlets are analyzed in real-time by the Autodesk InfraWorks 360 software. By selecting an inlet, you can visually inspect it to ensure that its performance meets the design parameters. When selected, the Inlet asset card displays along with the water capture, spread, and bypass, as shown in Figure 12–25.

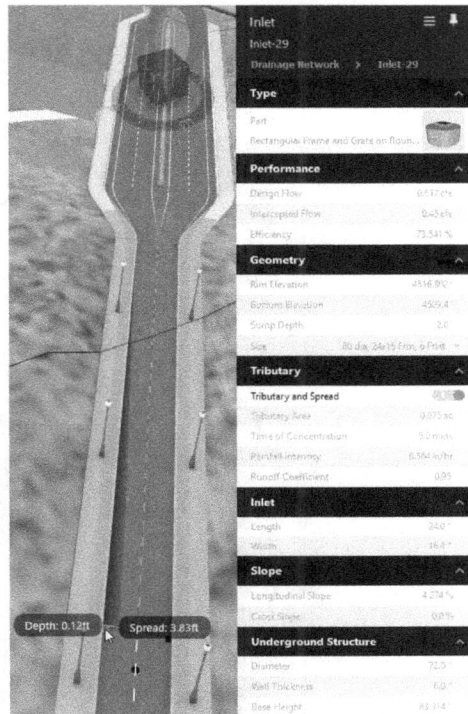

Figure 12–25

Hydraulic Performance of a Pipe

Flooded manholes and surcharged pipes can be identified visually in the model. After running an analysis, the EGL, HGL, and the Obvert of pipe elevations can be viewed by moving the cursor over the hatched area over the analyzed pipes.

How To: Analyze Pavement Drainage

1. Navigate the view below the terrain surface so that underground pipes and structures are displayed and selectable.
   - Alternatively, you can change the opacity of the surface to see below the ground.

2. In the In Canvas tools, click ⬤ (Design, review, and engineer drainage) > ▣ (Analyze your model) > ⬚ (Inspect Performance).

3. Adjust the AEP and Tailwater Condition values as required in the Analysis Settings asset card.
4. In the model, select one of the pipe connectors that are connected to the pipe you want to analyze. Then select the pipe connector on the opposite side of the pipe.
5. Press <Enter> to analyze the pipe.
6. Move the cursor over the vertical bar along the hatched bounding box to view analysis result, as shown in Figure 12–26.

Figure 12–26

- The blue bar indicates the hydraulic gradeline (water depth in the pipe).
- The green line represents the obvert (inside) of the pipe.
- The yellow line represents the energy gradeline.

Calculate Quantities

The cost of a project and staying within budget is very important. In order to better quantify the cost, you can quickly calculate the quantities required to build the drainage network.

How To: Calculate Drainage Network Quantities

1. In the In Canvas tools, click ⊖ (Design, review, and engineer drainage) > ▣ (Analyze your model) > ▦ (Quantities).
2. In the model, select the design road with the bridge and press <Enter>.
   - The results display, as shown in Figure 12–27.

QUANTITIES		
	Count	Length (ft)
Culverts	0	0.00
		Count
Inlets ▲		27
Rectangular Frame ...		27
- 60 dia, 24x16 Frm,...		27
		Count
Manholes ▲		15
Circular Covered Fra...		15
- 48 dia, 24 dia Frm,...		2
- 60 dia, 24 dia Frm,...		13
		Length (ft)
Pipelines ▲		1905
Circular		1905
- 18 in		1875
- 21 in		31
		Count
Outfalls		0

Figure 12–27

Practice 12c

Create a Pavement Drainage Network

Practice Objectives

- Add a pavement drainage network to a design road.
- Add inlets, pipes, and manholes to a drainage network.
- Size a pavement drainage network.
- Analyze a pavement drainage network.
- Calculate quantities for a drainage network.

Estimated time for completion: 20 minutes

In this practice, you will create a pavement drainage network. Then you will analyze it for performance, as shown in Figure 12–28.

Figure 12–28

Task 1 - Add a pavement drainage network to a design road.

1. In the Home Screen, click **Open**.

2. In the *C:\InfraWorks Fundamentals Practice Files\DrainageDesign* folder, select **DrainageDesign.sqlite** and click **Open**.

3. In the Utility Bar, click ▢ (Bookmark your current location) and select **Bridge**. Ensure that **C_Task1** is the current proposal.

4. In the model, select the design road that crosses the river, right-click and select **Drainage>Add Drainage Network**, as shown in Figure 12–29.

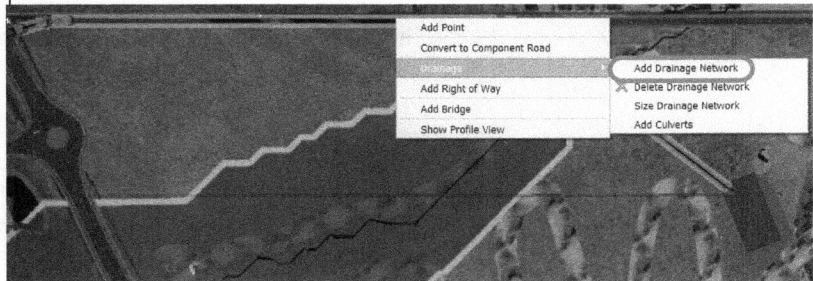

Figure 12–29

5. Accept all the defaults in the Add Drainage Network asset card and press <Enter> to add pavement drainage.

Task 2 - Modify pavement drainage.

1. Continue working in the same model as the previous task. If you did not complete the previous task, set **C_Task2** as the current proposal.

2. In the Utility Bar, expand the View Style drop-down and click

    ![icon] (Configure current view). In the View Settings asset card,

    click ![icon] (Change navigation and application feedback settings) to open the *Interaction* stack.

3. Under *Navigation*, toggle off the **Lock Mouse Above Ground** slider, as shown in Figure 12–30.

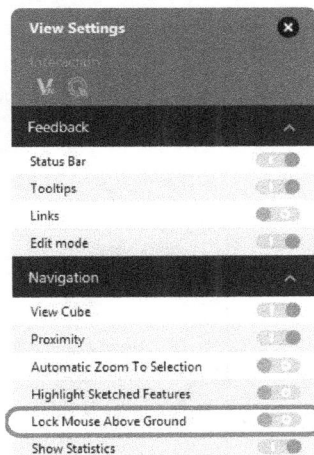

Figure 12–30

4. Close the View Settings asset card.

5. In the Utility Bar, click [icon] (Bookmark your current location) and select **AddDrainage**.

6. In the In Canvas tools, click [icon] (Design, review and engineer drainage)> [icon] (Design drainage)> [icon] (Drainage Network).

7. In the Sketch Drainage Network asset card, accept the default inlet, manhole, and pipe types, sizes, and other parameters.

8. In the model, click to place the first inlet on the north-east side of the road, as shown in Figure 12–31. Right-click and select **Manholes and Pipelines**.

Figure 12–31

9. In the model, click the inlet you placed in the previous step to connect the pipe to it. Move the cursor south-east and click to place the manhole on the centerline. Double-click on the manhole created in the last task, as shown in Figure 12–32.

When placing inlets, ensure that you select a point on the pavement and not the curb.

Figure 12–32

10. Right-click and select **Inlets and Pipelines**. Click to place an inlet across from the other one you created. Double-click on the manhole you created to end the pipe, as shown in Figure 12–33.

Figure 12–33

11. Press <Esc> twice to exit the command.

Task 3 - Size pavement drainage.

1. Continue working in the same model as the previous task. If you did not complete the previous task, set **C_Task3** as the current proposal.

2. In the model, select the design road with the bridge.

3. Right-click and select **Drainage>Size Drainage Network**, as shown in Figure 12–34.

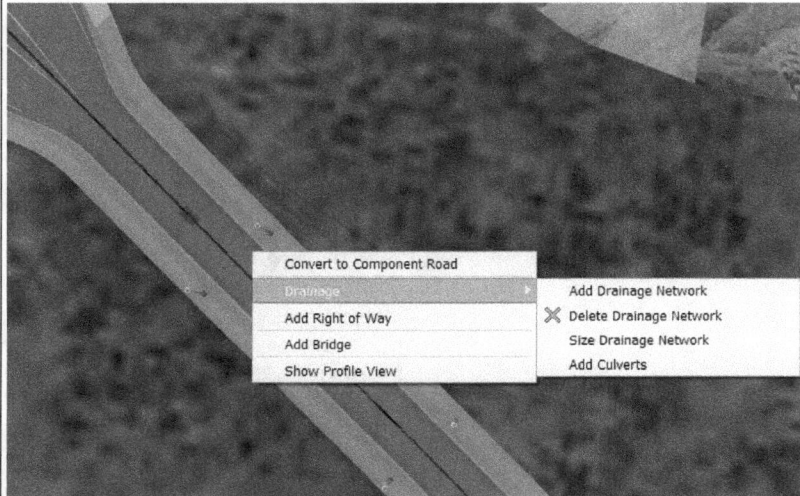

Figure 12–34

4. Press <Enter> to accept the default values in the Size Drainage Network asset card.

Task 4 - Analyze pavement drainage.

1. Continue working in the same model as the previous task. If you did not complete the previous task, set **C_Task4** as the current proposal.

2. Select one of the inlet structures to view its asset card and the water capture, spread, and bypass measurements.

3. In the Utility Bar, click ▉ (Bookmark your current location) and select **AnalyzeDrainage**.

4. In the In Canvas tools, click ⬤ (Design, review, and engineer drainage) > ⬚ (Analyze your model) > 🗂 (Inspect Performance).

5. In the Analysis Settings asset card, change *AEP* to **1/5**.

6. In the model, select the manhole you created earlier. Then select the manhole on the opposite side of the pipe, as shown in Figure 12–35.

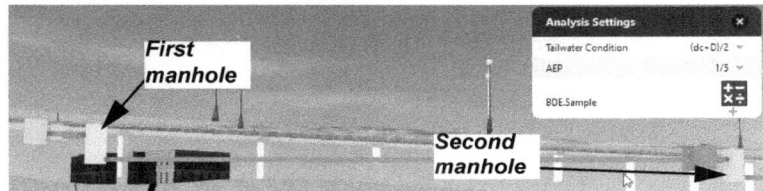

Figure 12–35

7. Press <Enter> to analyze the pipe.

8. Move the cursor over the vertical bar along the hatched bounding box to view analysis result, as shown in Figure 12–36.

Figure 12–36

9. Press <Esc> when done.

Task 5 - Calculate quantities.

---

1. Continue working in the same model as the previous task. If you did not complete the previous task, set **C_Task5** as the current proposal.

2. In the Utility Bar, click ▦ (Bookmark your current location) and select **AddDrainage**.

---

3. In the In Canvas tools, click ⬤ (Design, review, and engineer drainage) > ▣ (Analyze your model)> ▤ (Quantities).

4. In the model, select the design road with the bridge. The results display, as shown in Figure 12–37.

QUANTITIES		
	Count	Length (ft)
Culverts	0	0.00
	Count	
Inlets ▲	27	
Rectangular Frame ...	27	
- 60 dia, 24x16 Frm,...	27	
	Count	
Manholes ▲	15	
Circular Covered Fra...	15	
- 48 dia, 24 dia Frm,...	2	
- 60 dia, 24 dia Frm,...	13	
	Length (ft)	
Pipelines ▲	1905	
Circular	1905	
- 18 in	1875	
- 21 in	31	
	Count	
Outfalls	0	

Figure 12–37

Chapter Review Questions

1. Watershed areas can be calculated for the following. (Select all that apply)

   a. A single-low lying point

   b. A single-high point

   c. An entire design road

   d. A select station range of a design road

2. Culverts can be added to design roads automatically.

   a. True

   b. False

3. Which of the following must you do before you can analyze the surface drainage between inlets to verify the performance of pipe runs?

   a. Create the conceptual design by adding pavement drainage to a design road.

   b. Modify the design by moving, adding, and removing, pipes and structures as necessary.

   c. Run the (Create Watersheds) command.

   d. Fine-tune the changes that have been made by sizing pavement drainage.

4. How do you find the overt value of a pipe?

   a. Run the (Create Watersheds) command.

   b. Run the (Drainage Network) command.

   c. Run the (Inspect Performance) command.

   d. Select the pipe to open the Pipe asset card.

5. How do you size pavement drainage?

   a. Select the design road and right-click.

   b. Select a network feature and right-click.

   c. Run the (Drainage Network) command.

   d. Run the (Inspect Performance) command.

Command Summary

Button	Command	Location
	Create Watersheds	• **In Canvas Tools:** Design, review, and engineer drainage >Design drainage • **In Canvas Tools:** Design, review, and engineer drainage >Analyze your model
	Culverts	• **In Canvas Tools:** Design, review, and engineer drainage >Design drainage
	Drainage Network	• **In Canvas Tools:** Design, review, and engineer drainage >Design drainage
	Inspect Performance	• **In Canvas Tools:** Design, review, and engineer drainage >Analyze your model
	Quantities	• **In Canvas Tools:** Design, review, and engineer drainage >Analyze your model
	Rainfall Content	• **In Canvas Tools:** Design, review, and engineer drainage >Analyze your model

Example of a GIS Data Source

This appendix is an example of a Geographic Information System (GIS) data source, showing the GIS layers of Utah County[1]. This GIS was obtained from the GIS Division of the Utah County Information Systems department.

---

1. (Department, GIS Division of the Utah County Information Systems, 2013)

Utah County GIS Layers – Presented by the GIS Division of the Utah County Information Systems Department

For more information go to www.utahcountyonline.org

Road Centerlines

Tags

Roads, Transportation, Spillman

Summary

Road segments representing centerlines of all roadways or carriageways in the vicinity of Utah County. Data schema reflects ESRI's Local Government Data Model with additional fields pertinent for local Utah County processes and applications.

Description

Road segments representing centerlines of all roadways or carriageways in the vicinity of Utah County. Typically, this information is compiled from orthoimagery or other aerial photography sources. This representation of the road centerlines support address geocoding and mapping. It also serves as a source for public works and other agencies that are responsible for the active management of the road network. Data schema reflects ESRI's Local Government Data Model with additional fields pertinent for local Utah County processes and applications.

Credits

The GIS Division of Utah County's Information Systems Department.

Use limitations

While there are no constraints or warranties with regard to the use of this dataset, users are encouraged to attribute content to the GIS Division of Utah County Information Systems Department.

Extent

West -112.313967   East   -110.850577
North 40.681317   South 39.679831

Scale Range

Maximum (zoomed in)   1:5,000
Minimum (zoomed out) 1:500,000

Spatial Reference

NAD 1983 StatePlane, Utah Central Zone, FIPS 4302, US Survey Feet

Utah County GIS Layers – Presented by the GIS Division of the Utah County Information Systems Department

For more information go to www.utahcountyonline.org

Field	DataType	Length	AliasName	Description
OBJECTID	Object ID		ObjectID	Sequential unique whole numbers that are automatically generated.
GLOBALID	Global ID		GlobalID	Global Identification number (Needed for replication)
CENTERLINEID	Text	20	Centerline ID	A unique id for the road centerline segment
FROMLEFT	Long		Left From Address	Lowest address range on left side of the road
TOLEFT	Long		Left To Address	Highest address range on left side of the road
FROMRIGHT	Long		Right From Address	Lowest address range on right side of the road
TORIGHT	Long		Right To Address	Highest address range on right side of the road
ROADPREDIR	Text	2	Road Prefix	The directional prefix of the address
ROADNAME	Text	50	Road Name	Primary street name. If a numbered street (i.e. 200 WEST) also has another well known name like "FREEDOM" BLVD. "FREEDOM" would generally be designated the primary name and "200 WEST" the alternate name
ROADTYPE	Text	4	Road Type	The type of road (Street, Road, Avenue, etc...)
ROADPOSTDIR	Text	2	Post Direction	Suffix Direction
FULLNAME	Text	125	Full Road Name	The full primary name of the road including any prefix and/or suffix and street type
ALTROADNAME	Text	30	Alternate Road Name	The secondary or alternative name of the road. A numbered street name, such as 200 WEST, would generally be listed as the alternate name while "FREEDOM" in FREEDOM BLVD would be the road's primary name.
ALTROADTYPE	Text	4	Alternate Road Type	Alternate street type (Street, Road, Avenue, etc...)
ALTROADNAME2	Text	30	Alt Road Name2	Second alternate street name
ALTROADTYPE2	Text	4	Alt Road Type2	Second alternate street type
MUNILEFT	Text	30	Municipality on Left	The municipality on the left side of the road. "Unicorporated" if in Utah County but not within a municipality.
MUNIRIGHT	Text	30	Municipality on Right	The municipality on the right side of the road. "Unicorporated" if in Utah County but not within a municipality.
ZIPLEFT	Text	5	Zip on Left	Zip code on left side of the road
ZIPRIGHT	Text	5	Zip on Right	Zip code on right side of the road
FEDROUTE	Text	10	Federal Route	The federal route name. Used to populate the number within the highway marker shield
FEDRTETYPE	Text	20	Federal Route Type	A functional classification of route that can be used to symbolize the route if detail beyond what is provided in ROADCLASS is needed
AFEDROUTE	Text	10	Alternate Federal Route	The alternate federal route name. Used to populate the number within the highway marker shield
AFEDRTETYPE	Text	20	Alternate Federal Route Type	A functional classification of route that can be used to symbolize the route if detail beyond what is provided in ROADCLASS is needed
STROUTE	Text	10	State Route	The state route name. Used to populate the number in the state highway marker shields
STRTETYPE	Text	20	State Route Type	A functional classification of route that can be used to symbolize the route if detail beyond what is provided in ROADCLASS is needed
ASTRTE	Text	10	Alternate State Route	An alternate state route name. Used to populate the number in the state highway marker shields
ASTRTETYPE	Text	20	Alternate State Route Type	A functional classification of route that can be used to symbolize the route if detail beyond what is provided in ROADCLASS is needed
CTYROUTE	Text	10	County Route	County route name. Currently Utah County does not designate county route numbers, therefore, this field is not used
FAEROUTE	Text	10	FEA Route Number	Federal and eligible route number (a null value indicates not federal aid eligible road)
PROJECTID	Long		UC Project ID	Internal Utah County Project ID for B road segments
SURFACE	Text	20	Surface	Road Surface Type
CONDITION	Text	20	Condition	Condition of the road
ROW_WIDTH	Short		ROW Width	Right-of-way width in feet
ROADCLASS	Text	20	Road Class	Functional classification of roads based on type of service
RDCLASS_UHJCA	Text	5	UHJCA Class	Road classification based on Utah's Highway Jurisdiction & Classification Act (A = State, B = County, C = Municipalities, D = Public thoroughfares.
CFCCCODE	Text	3	CFCC Code	CFCC Code (Census Feature Classification Code)
OWNEDBY	Short	2	Owned By	Indicates which organization owns the asset
MAINTBY	Short	2	Maintained By	Indicates which organization maintains the asset
DCLASSID	Text	4	D Road ID	Internal Utah County ID number for D Class road segments
RS2477	Text	3	RS2477	Indicates whether the road segment is designated a RS2477 road
COUNTYNAME	Text	20	County Name	The county name the road segment is located in
CULDESAC	Text	5	Cul de sac	A flag that indicates whether the road segment depicts a cul-de-sac circle
ONEWAYDIR	Text	10	One Way Indicator	A code that indicates whether the traffic flows with, or against, the direction of the vertices
ROADLEVEL	Long		Above or Below Grade	A code that indicates whether the traveled roadway is above or below grade
INWATER	Text	5	In Water	A flag that indicates whether the segment of the road is crossing water
SOURCEFEATUREID	Text	20	Source Feature ID	ID of the segment that may be related to another source database
DATASOURCENAME	Text	100	Data Source	Name of the source of this data
LASTUPDATE	Date		Last Update Date	Last date the road segment was edited
LASTEDITOR	Text	100	Last Editor	Last person's username that edited the road segment
ISVISIBLE	Text	5	Is Visible	Flag indicating if the segment should be visible on a map
EDITCOMMENTS	Text	250	Edit Comments	Comment Field

Index
